DATE DUE

Imagining India

Imagining India

RONALD INDEN

Basil Blackwell

Copyright © Ronald Inden 1990

First published 1990

Basil Blackwell Ltd
108 Cowley Road, Oxford, OX4 1JF, UK

Basil Blackwell, Inc.
3 Cambridge Center
Cambridge, Massachusetts 02142, USA

British Library Cataloguing in Publication Data

A CIP catalogue record for this book is available
from the British Library.

Library of Congress Cataloging in Publication Data

Inden, Ronald B.
   Imagining India/Ronald Inden.
      p.   cm.
   Bibliography: p.
   Includes index.
   ISBN 0–631–16923–7
   1. India—Study and teaching—Europe. 2. India—Study and
   teaching—United States. I. Title.
   DS435.8.147   1990   89–36150
   954′.0072—dc20   CIP

Typeset in 10 on 11pt Ehrhardt
by Footnote Graphics, Warminster, Wiltshire
Printed in Great Britain by TJ Press Ltd, Padstow

Contents

Acknowledgements

Many people have contributed to this book. To begin, I must offer a special thanks to Paul Greenough and Sheldon Pollock, who first invited me to talk on the topic of orientalism and India in 1983 at the University of Iowa. Several people have been patient enough to make comments and suggestions on earlier drafts or in some other way made a major intellectual contribution to this book. Among these are John Comaroff, Richard Davis, Nick Dirks, Shelly Errington, Judy Farquhar, Jim Fitzgerald, Jean-Claude Galey, Ranajit Guha, Jim Hevia, John Kelly, Frank Perlin, Carl Pletsch, A. K. Ramanujan, Bill Sewell, Brian Smith, Burton Stein, Piers Vitebsky, and David Washbrook. I am especially grateful for the close reading and criticisms made by Mark Hobart. Finally, I am so deeply indebted to my colleague and friend Barney Cohn that mere words of gratitude seem insufficient repayment.

I am grateful to the University of Chicago Press and Weidenfeld and Nicolson for permission to publish extracts from Louis Dumont's *Homo Hierarchicus* English translation © 1970 by George Weidenfeld and Nicolson Ltd. and by The University of Chicago (original French edition, *Homo Hierarchicus: Le système des castes et ses implications*, © 1966 by Editions Gallimard); to Souvenir Press for permission to publish extracts from Joseph Campbell's *Oriental Mythology*; to Methuen and Co. for permission to publish extracts from A. M. Hocart's *Caste: A Comparative Study*; and to the curator of the Musée Gustave Moreau, Geneviève Calambre, for her kind assistance. Thanks are also due to the Committee for Southern Asian Studies at the University of Chicago; to Jonathan Walters, and to Sean Magee and the staff at Basil Blackwell for their assistances in the preparation of this book.

Introduction

This book is about 'human agency', about the capacity of people to order their world. In it I criticize the knowledge of 'Others' that Europeans and Americans have created during the periods of their world ascendancy. The specific object of my critique is the Indological branch of 'orientalist discourse' and the accounts of India that it has produced since the Enlightenment, but it also takes on the other disciplines that have had a major part in making these constructs of India – the history of religions, anthropology, economics, and political philosophy.

My perspective is that of a historian who would like to open up the closed unitary world that academic discourses have helped to manufacture with their Eurocentric world histories. I wish to make possible studies of 'ancient' India that would restore the agency that those histories have stripped from its people and institutions. Scholars did this by imagining an India kept eternally ancient by various Essences attributed to it, most notably that of caste. I attempt here to reflect back and analyse the assumptions consciously made and the presuppositions tacitly held in these knowledges. Without going through this process, without historicizing the knowledge that constitutes Indology, without placing it in its relationships to other knowledges, its practitioners will continue to reproduce unwittingly the depictions of the past.

To some extent, I focus on a critique of Indological depictions of India's early history, for those who love essences also dote on their origins, the moments of their first manifestation. I devote more space, however, to the representation of a 'Hindu' India, and especially of its 'medieval' history, because this was the time when the ancient institution of caste is supposed to have become most fully manifest.

The reader will find that the discourses I analyse are populated by a number of curious metaphors. Among these are the metaphors of India as a female (see 3.1), Indian thought as a dream (see 1.3.2, 3.2.2), caste society as a centrifuge (see 2.2.3), and of Hinduism as a jungle or even a sponge (see 3.1). Such metaphors are to a large extent constitutive of the phenomena they describe, and not merely figures of speech or imperfect shorthands that can and should ultimately be dispensed with. Each of them is, furthermore, loaded with implications for action (or inaction). That is, they are also models of how people ought to or must act. The importance of such metaphors in social scientific language has, of course, long been commented upon (e.g. Pratt, 1978: 3–9). What is not usually noted, however, is the invidious way in which writers have used their metaphors to constitute the European world's Others. Whether explicitly stated or not, Indological discourses tend to compare these denigrating metaphors with metaphors that elevate the Self. One of the metaphors that recurs in social scientific discourses, that of man or society as a machine, is always peering over the shoulder of the Indologist when he likens Hinduism to a sponge or caste to a centrifuge. I shall be pointing to these metaphors and their invidious uses throughout this book.

One of the major purposes of Indological discourses has been to give the impression that the world was ordered in a natural, stable way. Scholarly writing achieved this by building 'essences' into its metaphors. As I define it, essentialism is the idea that humans and human institutions, for example, the 'individual' and the 'nation-state', are governed by determinate natures that inhere in them in the same way that they are supposed to inhere in the entities of the natural world. The long-standing quest to write a science of the human world as a machine or self-regulating system, exemplified by the West, has held such essences as fundamental. Without them, prediction and the control of nature could not be achieved. Indians and their institutions, too, had their essences, but scholars have presumed these to be the wildness, extremity, and disorder of the jungle metaphors they use. A major concern will be to criticize the essentialism in Indological texts.

I propose as an alternative to the essentialism that flows from determinist scientific approaches (and from Romantic responses to them), a theory of human agency. I argue that far from embodying simple, unchanging essences, all agents are relatively complex and shifting. They make and remake one another through a dialectic process in changing situations. The general rubric under which I deploy this notion of human agency in order to rework previous depictions of India (and of the West, too) is that of an 'imperial formation'. By this I mean a complex polity consisting of overlapping and contending agents related to one another in a 'world' whose spokesmen claim universality for it. Here, too, metaphor is implied – alas, the superior realm of a pure language of observation has failed to materialize – but the metaphors I try to elaborate in a discursive manner under this rubric are those, such as dialogue or battle of the social world itself. Most important, I try to use them in an anti-essentialist manner, one that enables people to make their history at least as much as history makes them.

My intellectual stance in this project draws primarily on the work of the post-Hegelian philosopher, R. G. Collingwood (1889–1943), but also on the ideas of Foucault and Gramsci. Interestingly, their positions converge more with those of the Indian discourses I am trying to open up than with the dominant European ideologies of the past two hundred years. Ancient Indians would have found the utopian notion of a society in which science and a perfect market or classless community would obviate the need for politics very strange indeed.

If we shift the major presuppositions and assumptions of Indological discourse, it is possible, I argue, to construct a picture of Hindu India that differs greatly from the ones we have inherited. Such a shift of presuppositions need not, cannot, be confined to the study of India by South Asia specialists. The theory of human agency I am trying to articulate in this book also extends to the study of other regions of the world – Islam, Africa, China and Japan, pre-Columbian and Latin America, and Eastern Europe – for, although the content of each of these varies, the principles used to construct them have been similar. Furthermore, as I show, these regions have not been constituted in isolation; they have been defined the one in relation to the other. Hence, the change in the study of one region necessarily implies changes in the studies of other regions.

But there is an equally important point to make here. It follows from the anti-essentialist approach I take. I will argue that Euro-American Selves and Indian Others have not simply interacted as entities that remain fundamentally the same. They have dialectically constituted one another. Once one realizes the truth of this, he or she will begin to see that India has played a part in the making of nineteenth- and twentieth-century Europe (and America) much greater than the 'we' of scholarship, journalism, and officialdom would normally wish to allow. The subcontinent was not simply a source of colonial riches or a stage-setting in which Western hunters could stalk tigers, the sons of British merchants and aristocrats could make a financial killing, or the spiritualist find his or her innermost soul (or its Buddhist absence). More than that, India was (and to some extent still is) the object of thoughts and acts with which this 'we' has constituted *itself*. European discourses appear to separate their Self from the Indian Other – the essence of Western thought is practical reason,[1] that of India a dreamy imagination,[2] or the essence of Western society is the free (but selfish) individual, that of India an imprisoning (but all-providing) caste system. But is this really so? To be sure, these discourses create a strange, lop-sided complementarity between the Western Self and its Indian Other. Yet the consequence of this process has been to redefine ourselves. We have externalized exaggerated parts of ourselves so that the equally exaggerated parts we retain can act out the triumph of the one over the other in the Indian subcontinent. We will be unhampered by an otherworldly imagination and unhindered by a traditional, rural social structure because we have magically translated them to India.

Because of the mutually constituting relations of Western Selves and their Others, it also follows that it is not possible to change our intellectual practices directed at Others without changing those practices as applied to the Self as well.[3] So this book is about more than the study of India. It is also about more

---

[1] Utilitarianism, behaviourism, rational choice theory, and game theory are examples of hyper-rationalist discourses.

[2] Theosophy, Jungian psychology, and symbolic anthropology are instances of discourses that privilege the imagination.

[3] See, for example, Bernal's critique (1987) of classical scholarship on ancient Greece and the sustained effort to make the ancient Greeks the perfect expression of Aryanness by suppressing the multiple origins of Greek culture.

than anthropology and history and 'area studies', the disciplines with warrants to study Others. It is about the intellectual practices of the core social sciences as well – psychology, economics, sociology – those which constitute the Self as object and study it.

PLAN OF THE BOOK

Chapter 1 reveals the 'foundations' of the constructs scholars have made of India. I then turn to the ways in which 'orientalist' discourse has been constituted as an 'imperial knowledge' based on the universally valid methods of natural science. I argue that certain texts, among them the history of the empiricist and Utilitarian, James Mill, and the world history of the idealist and rationalist, G. W. F. Hegel, have been 'hegemonic' within Indology.

Chapter 2 reviews the idea of caste, the feature that distinguishes India in these discourses from the rest of the world. That feature can be understood, however, only by looking at the features held to mark the 'West' off from India and to distinguish India from the other regions of Asia, for these features constituted an interacting whole in orientalist discourse. The essence given to each 'civilization' defined and confirmed that of the others. So I look at caste here from the standpoint of India's place in this global scheme. Caste may have been, and – however much we soften our language in the post-Independence period – still is the main 'pillar' of Indological constructs. It was, however, not the only one. I have identified three others. The next three chapters are accounts of these other pillars.

Chapter 3 deals with the religion called Hinduism. Historians of religion and Indologists have not only taken their Hinduism to be the essential religion of India; they have viewed it as the exemplification of the mind of India, the mentality that accompanies caste. The essence of that mind was its 'feminine' imagination, source of the dream-like world-view of the Indians. She was an inferior substitute for the West's masculine, world-ordering rationality. So, in the end, Indians were seen as concerned more with the renunciatory quest of the individual for mystic absorption into an absolute than even with the ordering of their caste society. The effect of these wild fabrications of the nineteenth-century European imagination was to give pre-eminence to caste, the type of society epitomizing at once both constraint and excess, as opposed to the freedom and moderation of Western civil society, and to the lone renouncer rather than the individual-in-society. The result was not, as scholars often claimed, to depict India 'as it was'.

Indologists' desires to elevate their West by denigrating this Indian Other were not, however, fulfilled simply by turning it into the land of Hindu castes and fakirs. Theirs was an imperial project that entailed the wholesale intellectual deconstitution of Indian economic and political institutions, accomplished with the third and fourth pillars of their construct.

Chapter 4 focuses on India's strange, essentially rural 'political economy'. Scholars have depicted the Indian village as the archetypal peasant community, the product primarily of revenue collectors and secondarily of Marx's idea of the Asiatic mode of production and Henry Sumner Maine's sociology. The essence they attributed to this village was antiquity or traditionality – an organic social solidarity composed of collective actors and a specialized, but closed, economy of subsistence exchanges.

Chapter 5 takes up the versions of oriental despotism given to India. Scholars construed the Hindu state of both past and present as a 'divine Kingship', but they did not agree on what that was. Some saw it as a form of absolutism and the instrument for perpetuating a divisive caste society. Others argued that the essentially Hindu state was a form of clan monarchy inherently weak because of feuding. The divinity of the first justified its tyranny, the second signified its irrationality and ineffectuality. In so far as this kingship was able to enforce a political unity, it was due to the presence in India of the West's world-ordering rationality, carried there by conquerors. The history of this state is one of failure in orientalist narratives. Overcome by the centrifugal forces of caste because the Western presence had diminished, the Hindu state collapses and ends with the thirteenth-century conquest of north India by Muslim Turks.

Chapter 6 suggests how my idea of 'imperial formation' might act as a replacement for the construct of Hindu civilization that I criticize in the previous chapters. I focus on some connected examples from the so-called early medieval period, the one in which most of my own research of the past fifteen years has concentrated. Looking at evidence on the complex agents of the Indian town and countryside, I first show how 'caste' may be rethought as a form of citizenship. I then turn to the question of Hindu states. Far from being a cover for despotism or a symptom of irrationality, divine kingship was a set of practices that enabled kings and courts to establish political societies of kings – imperial formations – which were dialectically ordered rather than administratively united or feudally divided. These polities presupposed a changing reality and ongoing political action rather than the transcendent, depoliticized utopian polities that have been the stuff of so many social theories in the West. Unity in an imperial formation was, therefore, considered an achievement of action, not a prerequisite for it. Once we accept these differences, it is possible to show that Indian states constituted a succession of imperial formations in each of which a single dynasty exercised hegemony that was continually contested. My major example, the Rashtrakuta imperial formation of the medieval period, can be seen as a polity that was as unified and as well-endowed as the administrative empires scholars have projected on to ancient India.

My main argument, then, is that the agency of Indians, the capacity of Indians to make their world, has been displaced in those knowledges on to other agents. The makers of these knowledges have, in the first instance, displaced the agency of the Indians on to one or more 'essences', and in the second instance on to themselves. The essences that they have imagined have been caste, the Indian mind, divine kingship, and the like. Although several generations of scholars have characterized and valued these essences in a variety of ways, they have for the most part considered them as somehow inferior, at least in the sense of explaining why India 'lost out' to the West. Since the civilization of India has been governed, they assume, by these dubious essences from the moment of its origin, that civilization's place in the world has been, so to speak, predetermined from the beginning. Lacking the essences taken to be characteristic of the West – the individual, political freedom, and science – Indians did not even have the capacity on their own to *know* these essences. They did not, so one would have to conclude, have the capacity to *act* in the world with rationality. The European scholars and their doubles, the colonial administrators and traders, assumed for themselves the power to know these hidden essences of the Other and to act upon them. They would act both for themselves and for the Indians. Lest we think these practices affected only India, we should consider that the West's image of itself as the epitome of the modern has depended, for two hundred years, on these changing portrayals of India as the embodiment of the ancient.

1
Knowledge of India and Human Agency

1.1 ESSENCES

Now it is the interest of Spirit that *external* conditions should become *internal* ones; that the natural and the spiritual world should be recognized in the subjective aspect belonging to intelligence; by which process the unity of subjectivity and (positive) Being generally – or the Idealism of Existence – is established. This Idealism, then, is found in India, but only as an Idealism of imagination, without distinct conceptions; – one which does indeed free existence from Beginning and Matter (liberates it from temporal limitations and gross materiality), but changes everything into the merely Imaginative; for although the latter appears interwoven with definite conceptions and Thought presents itself as an occasional concomitant, this happens only through accidental combination. Since, however, it is the abstract and absolute Thought itself that enters into these dreams as their material, we may say that Absolute Being is presented here as in the ecstatic state of a dreaming condition. (Hegel, 1956: 139)

1.1.1 Science's Imperial Metaphor – Society as a Mechanical Body

The historian and Indologist Vincent Smith (1848–1920) published what he himself referred to as the first 'connected relation' of India's history before the Muslim conquests of the twelfth century.[1] He believed that the civilization of India, which orientalists call by the name of Hindu, had reached its peak under the benevolent despots Chandragupta and Asoka Maurya (in the third and fourth centuries BC), the Gupta emperors (fourth to fifth centuries AD) and the last great imperial ruler, Harsha (seventh century). After that Indian civilization declined. Although Smith himself assumed that political chronology provided the 'framework' for the history of a civilization, he thought that India

[1] A. L. Basham says of this not altogether original scholar, who served in the Indian Civil Service in the Northwest Provinces and Oudh 1871–1900, that 'his activities and strength lay chiefly in collating the results supplied by other scholars in their various departments' (1961b: 266–74).

was peculiar in this regard. Compared with the other civilizations of Europe, China, and the Near East, India appeared to be singularly lacking in political unity and, therefore, in history. Writing seventy years earlier, Hegel, whose world history was the global narrative of which orientalism was a part, provided the reason for this. I have reproduced it at the head of this chapter: India was a land dominated by imagination rather than reason. Still earlier, commentators like James Mill had argued that in India an exotic institution, caste, prevented political unity (see 5.2).

Smith did not, therefore, claim to be revealing any secret when, prior to his account of India's 'medieval' kingdoms, he made this representation to his readers: 'Harsha's death loosened the bonds which restrained the disruptive forces always ready to operate in India, and allowed them to produce their natural result, a medley of petty states, with ever-varying boundaries, and engaged in unceasing internecine war.' India's 'natural' disunity permitted him to conclude that centralized authoritarian rule imposed from outside is the only way to unity. Note how the historian himself takes the standpoint of the imperial bureaucrat and how he invidiously compares India's political condition with that of his atomistic 'body politic': 'Such was India when first disclosed to European observation in the fourth century BC, and such it always has been, except during the comparatively brief periods in which a vigorous central government has compelled the mutually repellent molecules of the body politic to check their gyrations and submit to the grasp of a superior controlling force.' Smith continued his commentary on India's political condition:

In political institutions no evolution took place. No sovereign arose endowed with commanding abilities and capable of welding together the jarring members of the body politic, as Chandragupta Maurya, Asoka, and in a lesser degree the Gupta kings and Harsha of Kanauj had done. The nearest approach to the position of universal lord of Northern India was made by Mihira Bhoja of Kanauj (*c.* AD 840–90), but unluckily we know next to nothing about his character or administration. Even the heavy pressure of Muslim invasion failed to produce effective cohesion of the numberless Hindu States, which, one by one, fell an easy prey to fierce hordes of Arabs, Turks, and Afghans, bound together by stern fanaticism. (1924: 371)

The decline which Smith retailed was not confined to the state. Literature, he told us, 'sank below the level of Kalidasa', dramatist of the Gupta period (India's Shakespeare); in the sciences 'no advance was made'; and even in religion, a 'grave loss' was sustained with the 'gradual extinction' of Buddhism. Smith admitted that the 'aesthetic value of abundant mediaeval sculpture is the subject of keen controversy', but that whatever one might think, 'the art of coinage certainly decayed so decisively that not even one mediaeval coin deserves notice for its aesthetic merits.' He also conceded that 'architecture was practised on a magnificent scale', and that the Hindu architects deserved praise for this, even though their penchant for detail invited 'hostile criticism by its excess of cloying ornament'.

Smith concluded, in the passage which makes the transition to his account of the 'medieval' kingdoms, on this ominous note:

The three following chapters, which attempt to give an outline of the salient features in the bewildering annals of Indian petty states when left to their own devices for several centuries, may perhaps serve to give the reader a notion of what India always has been when released from the control of a supreme authority, and what she would be again, if the hand of the benevolent power which now safeguards her boundaries should be withdrawn. (1924: 372)[2]

Not many today would defend Smith's openly imperial stance. Yet we cannot so easily walk away from Smith's discourse, the language practices he used to formulate propositions about the world. Embedded in it are certain assumptions that were not his alone. Nor were they confined to the upholders of the British Raj. Smith's Indology belonged to a much larger movement of world dominance, one that has changed a great deal since his time but is still very much with us. We can see this wider world in the major metaphor he uses, that of a 'body politic' or society as an atomistic cosmos or machine. The notion that a polity is or ought to be fashioned in the image of the mechanical and atomistic cosmos of Galileo can be traced back to Hobbes.[3] It marks off the imperial knowledges of the British, French, and Germans in the nineteenth and twentieth centuries from the theology-based knowledges of their imperial predecessors in Europe, the Spanish and Portuguese. At once simple to apprehend and yet rife with problems, this metaphor of a body politic or society as a machine has been one of the most often used metaphors in the social sciences, but it is not the only metaphor we shall encounter in this study.

[2] For more on Smith, see 5.4. I cannot agree with the late A. L. Basham, intellectual descendant of Smith in Britain's post-imperial phase, when he tries to explain away Smith's aloof and insensitive stance toward India with a psychological hypothesis – his xenophobia might be due to something that happened to Smith, an Englishman living in Ireland, during his youth (Basham, 1961b: 266–74).

[3] Here, from his Introduction of 1651, is Hobbes's metaphor:

Nature, the art whereby God hath made and governs the world, is by the *art* of man, as in many other things, so in this also imitated, that it can make an artificial animal. For seeing life is but a motion of limbs, the beginning whereof is in some principal part within; why may we not say, that all *automata* (engines that move themselves by springs and wheels as doth a watch) have an artificial life? For what is the *heart*, but a *spring*; and the *nerves*, but so many *strings*; and the joints, but so many *wheels*, giving motion to the whole body, such as was intended by the artificer? *Art* goes yet further, imitating that rational and most excellent work of nature, *man*. For by art is created that great LEVIATHAN called a COMMONWEALTH, or STATE, in Latin CIVITAS, which is but an artificial man; though of greater stature and strength than the natural, for whose protection and defence it was intended; and in which the *sovereignty* is an artificial *soul*, as giving life and motion to the whole body; the *magistrates*, and other *officers* of judicature and execution, artificial joints; *reward* and *punishment*, by which fastened to the seat of the sovereignty every joint and member is moved to perform his duty, are the *nerves*, that do the same in the body natural; the *wealth* and *riches* of all the particular members, are the *strength*; *salus populi*, the *people's safety*, its business; *counsellors*, by whom all things needful for it to know are suggested unto it, are the *memory*; *equity*, and *laws*, an artificial *reason* and *will*; *concord, health*; *sedition, sickness*; and *civil war, death*. Lastly, the *pacts* and *covenants*, by which the parts of this body politic were at first made, set together, and united, resemble that *fiat*, or the *let us make man*, pronounced by God in the creation (1946: 5).

Indeed, as I have already indicated, metaphorical usage has been vital in the construction of India as the West's Other. Because of the importance of metaphor, it is worth pausing for a moment to consider how we shall approach it.

What is the status of this complex figure of speech in Smith (and in the other Indologists' works to be examined)? Or to frame the question more broadly, how are we to understand metaphorical usages in social scientific discourses?[4] Certainly one of the problems posed by the metaphorical aspects of language is their ambiguity. Is the tenor (body politic) of a metaphor only to be *compared* with its vehicle (machine) for purposes of clarifying or extending our knowledge? That is, is it to be taken as an open representation (to ourselves or our readers) of those aspects or parts of the tenor on which we wish to elaborate for some stated reason? Or is the vehicle to be *equated* with it, to be taken as a closed representation of the tenor as it really is, a representation that ends or even precludes discussion? I will say more about representation below. For now let me say that the difference between these two interpretive strategies is great. I take the former of these positions, but I would not wish to impose this view on Smith and other students of things Indian. Many Indologists and other human scientists may have consciously assumed that their metaphors were representations of reality or unconsciously presupposed it. Whatever the case, this ambiguity, in turn, causes another problem for us.

If it is not possible to determine precisely what Smith intended by the use of this metaphor (assuming he had any such conscious intent), what am I to say about it? The answer I would propose is to shift the question from the author's intentions to the readers' interpretations. It is possible to argue that this metaphor has certain metaphysical contents and that readers (and most likely the author, too) understood this metaphor with those contents in mind. Before I do this, however, I had better say something about metaphysics to calm the nerves of those readers who feel a migraine coming on at the mere mention of the word.

The term metaphysics has been used in many ways in different discourses. Most of the scholars who will pass in review here have been vaguely empiricist or positivist, that is, counting only that knowledge of the observable world (including texts in the sense of physical objects) which is perceptible, to wit, positive to the senses, as genuine knowledge. They would view metaphysics as knowledge of the unobservable and consider it a discredited mode of philosophy to be found in Europe (rather than in Anglo-America) and associated with Hegel and his followers. I mostly take up the distinction Collingwood makes between descriptive (or historical) and speculative metaphysics (1972: 17–77). I shall engage in the former in attempting to reconstruct the major asumptions that European scholars of South Asia in the nineteenth and twentieth centuries

---

[4] I do not wish to enter here into the debate over whether metaphors are essentially decorative and dispensable figures of speech or, contrarily, constitutive of entire discourses or world-views. See Andrew Ortony's useful introduction to the issues (1979: 1–16), the classic of I. A. Richards (1936), and the widely read work of Max Black (1962). Along with Hesse (1983), I prefer to see metaphor as an aspect of language usage rather than as a type of language or figure of speech which can be isolated so that an essence of it can be located.

have made (more or less consciously) about reality (ontology) and about knowledge of it (epistemology). More narrowly, I shall be concerned to bring out the presuppositions that silently inhabit their words and thoughts and the consequences that attend them.[5] I should say at once that I consider the metaphysics of scholarship as continuous with the presuppositions that are embedded in the practices of everyday life. Which is to say that the analysis of metaphysics here overlaps considerably with the the work many of my readers have been doing all along when they engage in anthropologists' cultural or semiotic analyses or historians' studies of popular mentalities. Like Collingwood and some others since, I take the position that to disclaim the metaphysical entailments of one's thought can have the unfortunate consequence of making one a prisoner of them. Finally, one can more fully appreciate one's own views of the world through a process of the historical reconstruction and criticism of the metaphysics hidden in texts than one can from a supposedly literal scanning of them.

What, then, does Smith's metaphor presuppose and what are its consequences? The metaphor of a polity as a single body (which I read as a metonym for person) is plausible as an open-ended metaphor. It postulates the possibility that the multiple agents making up a polity could be organized and act as though a single agent, that is, with a singleness of purpose and will. Which is to say that the idea of a body politic would seem to require the presence of a mind. On first inspection, we seem, thus, to be dealing with a metaphor that focuses on the organic and ideal aspects of a polity in its comparison. There is good reason for theorizing states as complex agents capable of unified action and for talking about them as polities rather than societies. Collingwood does just this in his *New Leviathan*, consciously picking up this strand of Hobbes, and he does so in such a way as to make the mental aspects of polities continuous with their physical aspects. This, however, is not the effect of Hobbes's own metaphor of a body politic.

This metaphor of numerous, differently constituted agents as forming a single body or person does not go in the direction Collingwood and I will take it below (1.2.2) because it is almost inseparable from another metaphorical usage, that of the body (politic) as a machine, a usage found in Hobbes's formulation.[6]

---

[5] I distinguish consequences here as a historical problem from entailments in a formal, logical sense.

[6] The status of this metaphor in Hobbes's work is itself a matter of debate. According to Michael Oakeshott in the Introduction to his edition of the *Leviathan* (1946: xix–xxi), Hobbes did not believe the natural world *is* a machine, but only that it is *like* it – for him philosophy was concerned with reason, which he took to be the determining of immediate causes and effects, as in a machine. Some philosophers of science today would say he was using it as a model of nature to focus on those features in which he was interested and not as a representation of nature as it is. The difficulty with this view and with Oakeshott's is that it does not *dispose* of the metaphysics of the metaphor; all it does is to *displace* it from the knowable, the material world, on to the knower, the natural philosopher. Incidentally, Oakeshott attributes the misinterpretation of Hobbes to the false use of an architectural metaphor which finds coherence in making Hobbes's civil philosophy, ancestor of today's social science, as the top storey of a philosophical house or system rather than as part of a system united by the 'thread' of his idea of philosophy.

The message received with this metaphor is, then, not only that a number of differently composed agents can and should be made over into a single body, but that the composition and actions of that body are analogous with those of a mechanical cosmos. We are, thus, talking not only about a unified order through this metaphor but about one in which political reality may or perhaps does conform to the reality of 'nature'. Here, I am afraid, is where Smith's metaphor seizes up and turns nasty. Whereas Hobbes elaborated discursively on this metaphor, arguing for a naturalist conception of man and of the state, Smith does not. His use of the metaphor allows his reader (whether intentionally or not) to take it as given that political order is like the classical idea of natural order. His is, I would contend, a closed rather than open representation.[7] Far from being a dead metaphor, however, his use of it is all the more deadly because of the silence it imposes on the subject.[8] Let us now prise open this man-eating clam. Let us ask ourselves what is entailed, from the standpoint of agency, in comparing a body politic with a machine, as Smith's trope of a body politic does.

1.1.2   Indology as Natural Science

The major effect of the comparison of a polity with a machine is to transfer the physical scientists' notion of 'system' from mechanics to a body politic. According to that perspective, a system consists of hierarchically arranged levels of discrete, interdependent parts.[9] So a state with its ministries and provinces and districts, cities and villages, and individual subjects or citizens is arranged like the solar system: heavenly bodies consist of solid masses which in turn consist of molecules, which consist of atoms.

How does this system claim to order itself? It supposedly does so by a principle of *binary opposition* among its levels and not simply one of distinction. Like the sun, which is the source of heat and light – power – and not the planets, so the state and not its provinces possesses absolute sovereignty. A natural system is also characterized by *mutual exclusion* among its parts. Just as different objects do not occupy the same space, so different states and provinces have different territories; they do not overlap.

As we have all to some degree been trained into textbook versions of classical natural scientific thinking, we are prone to impute certain characteristics to the human world that is supposed to be ordered on the model of an exemplary natural world in Smith's metaphor. What are these? Let me enumerate nine which cause difficulty for the idea of human agency that I wish to construct.

[7] He commits what Meszaros (1986: 238) calls the metaphorical fallacy, the main function of which 'is to *exempt* the advocated attitudes from a *rational scrutiny*'.

[8] As Meszaros notes of such 'self-referential' metaphors as this, it 'is eminently suitable to produce mystifications' (1986: 249).

[9] Hobbes started up a major industry; there is a vast literature on the different but closely related notions of system introduced into the social from the natural sciences. Three classic statements from this century are Parsons (1951: 536–55), Radcliffe-Brown (1957: 19–45), and, on 'open' systems, Ludwig von Bertalanffy (1968: 139–54).

1   It is *objective*. It exists as it is apart from any knowledge of it and does not differ with the interests or perspectives of those who know about it.
2   It is necessarily *unified*. All its parts operate together toward the same goal or in accord with the same design.
3   It is *bounded*, in that it is isolable from any other systems and can be known apart from them.
4   It is *atomist* and consists ultimately of fundamental units that are the smallest, irreducible entities in it, to wit atoms in physics, individuals in the social world.
5   It is *complete*; any diminution of its parts would impair its working; any addition would be redundant.
6   It is *self-centred*, that is, it has a directing centre and a directed periphery.
7   It is *self-regulating*; it operates automatically, apart from the original and perhaps occasional intervention of a Prime Mover, equatable with the guiding mind of this giant body (see below).
8   It is *determinist*. Its parts follow universal laws; events in it are discrete, each cause having a definite effect, which is to say that the future is determined by the past.
9   It is *essentialist*. The phenomena that make up the world are manifestations of 'essences', objective determinate entities that underlie their 'surface' features or appearances, e.g., 'sovereignty is the essence of the state'.

We should not think here that Indology was marginal to the project of making the human sciences in the image of the natural sciences and assume that Smith has had recourse to his machine metaphor merely as a stylistic device or to make what he had to say sound vaguely more scientific. Indology as a branch of comparative philology was right at the centre of the action in the middle of the nineteenth century: the philologists themselves were making strong claims to have their discipline treated as a natural science. One of the most important of these claimants was the Indologist Friedrich Max Müller (1823–1900), hailed as one of the foremost orientalists of the nineteenth century.[10] He argued in a lecture whose title, 'The Science of Language One of the Physical Sciences' (1864: I, 1–28), succinctly reveals his purpose, for the importance of comparative philology. All our scientific knowledge rests on language, yet we have, until now, no science of language itself. He is also careful to distinguish the new science of which he is midwife from language-learning and antiquarianism. Comparative philology, according to Müller, studies language as the sole object of enquiry and not as a means. It should, hence, be classed as a *physical* rather than a *historical* science (1864: I, 24), those being, for him, the two branches of science.

Simply declaring philology a natural science was, of course, not enough to make it so. It had to adopt a scientific method in approaching its object. Müller

[10] He was Professor of Comparative Philology at Oxford and editor of the voluminous *Sacred Books of the East*.

provides this. There are, he asserts, three stages in the history of a science.[11] The first of these is empirical and is engaged in by all peoples at all stages of development. The second stage is classificatory and that is where real science begins: 'An empirical acquaintance with facts rises to a scientific knowledge of facts as soon as the mind discovers beneath the multiplicity of single productions the unity of an organic system. This discovery is made by means of comparison and classification' (1864: I, 15). As we can already see, even in this brief quotation, Müller assumes that nature is ordered according to a unitary principle and that the order 'out there' is discovered by the investigator and not constructed. Indeed, he speaks at one point of 'discovering ... nature's plan' (I, 16). The third stage in the history of science was theoretical or metaphysical and was concerned with the discovery of the laws of nature (I, 8). Philology was mostly concerned with the second stage. We can best see how important classification was to Müller and how much his idea of it presupposes by looking at his own language:

And when the whole kingdom of plants has thus been surveyed, and a simple tissue of names been thrown over the garden of nature; when we can lift it up, as it were, and view it in our mind, as a whole, as a system well defined and complete, we then speak of the science of plants, or botany. We have entered into altogether a new sphere of knowledge where the individual is subject to the general, fact to law; we discover thought, order, and purpose pervading the whole realm of nature, and we perceive the dark chaos of matter lighted up by the reflections of a divine mind. (1864: I, 16)

As may already be apparent, Müller was not a straightforward empiricist. He combined his empiricism with a rather strong dose of religious idealism. So for him the essences uncovered by scientists are parts of the divine plan itself. That does not mean, however, that he was any less deterministic. According to him, the work of classification teaches that 'nothing exists in nature by accident ... there are laws which underlie the apparent freedom and variety of all created things' (I, 18). Since those laws indicate the 'presence of a purpose in the mind of the Creator' (I, 18), we are apparently either not supposed to feel constrained or supposed to realize that attempts at resistance would be futile.

Now, a natural system is an idea of order, as Max Müller so eagerly insists. Let us immediately remind ourselves, however, that it is one possible form of order even though the authority behind (above?) this particular notion of order might advance the imperial claim that it was the only true one. The very hint that entities might overlap and change their composition; that events might constitute a continuous process and that future events might be underdetermined by past events would not be seen by those who try to cover the social sciences with the purple mantle of the natural sciences as providing the principles of another kind of order. They would speak of such characteristics as the symptoms of disorder or breakdown.

The metaphor of a body politic as a machine, as the material cosmos, presupposes the presence of a maker and user of the machine, one who designs,

[11] Müller apparently derived this from William Whewell (1794–1866), *History of the Inductive Sciences, From the Earliest to the Present Time*, first pub. 1837.

creates, and sets the machine in motion. That agent consists, by definition, of non-matter, that is, spirit, will, or mind. One activity of this mind is taken as its essential attribute. I refer to this, in Weberian manner, as the principle of world-ordering rationality, that practical reason which, translated into force, makes the machine possible and keeps it going.[12] Some describe it as scientific, instrumental or economic rationality, or just rationality. Most also treat it as the essence of the mind. Though the complement of the body, such consciousness stands not inside the machine, but outside it. We have here, then, a dichotomy between the knower and known. The knowing subject transcends its object; it is not part of it. If there is a 'ghost' in the machine, it is the principle of world-ordering rationality placed there by its maker.[13]

The epistemology entailed in Smith's metaphor, that which constitutes Indology as a natural science, assumes that true knowledge merely represents or mirrors – another metaphor – the separate reality which the knower transcends. That is, the knower represents the world as it is in a mind as free of preconception as possible. What the philosopher Rorty says in a discussion of one replacement for the representational theory of knowledge is apropos:

> The difficulty stems from a notion shared by Platonists, Kantians, and positivists: that man has an essence – namely, to discover essences. The notion that our chief task is to mirror accurately, in our own Glassy Essence, the universe around us is the complement of the notion, common to Democritus and Descartes, that the universe is made up of very simple, clearly and distinctly knowable things, knowledge of whose essences provides the master-vocabulary which permits commensuration of all discourses. (1979: 357)

The knowledge of this theory tends to have the same characteristics I listed for the world it supposedly mirrors precisely because it thinks it mirrors its object. It pretends to objectivity, asserting that it is 'value-free' or 'neutral' (all the while claiming to be able to predict and control events). Its specialized fields are tightly bounded, reflecting the discreteness of phenomena out there. It is atomist, believing that knowledge comes in the form of discrete sense data or facts and is increased by enquiring into small areas (new studies 'fill gaps', add new blocks to an edifice). It assumes completeness (the 'exhaustive' or 'definitive' study). It dreams of a unified body of knowledge in that specialists in one discipline follow the same methods as those in the others (sociology should be as 'rigorous' as the 'hard' sciences, only its phenomena are more complex). It is also self-centred in thinking that its position is the Olympian one from which the truth is to be gained. And it is self-regulating; only practitioners of science can determine the truth. It claims certainty, being grounded in reason (rationalism) or observation (empiricism). Finally, its knowledge consists of essences, as Rorty so nicely states it.

Adherence to this position is loaded with implications for agency. Since his knowledge is natural and objective the human scientist has been able to claim that it is not contestable (that is, not a matter for 'political' discussion), even though it claims predictability and control over human affairs (Fay, 1975: 49–69).

---

[12] For a discussion of the essentialism in Weber, see Hindess (1987: 137–53).
[13] The soul of the body politic for Hobbes was his idea of sovereignty.

This epistemology has also tended to produce a hierarchic relationship between knower and known, which privileges the intellectual essences of the scientists and other experts and leaders who act on their expertise, while belittling the knowledges and capacities to act of the peoples who comprise the objects of their studies and actions.[14]

Smith himself invoked this theory of knowledge when he talked about the relationship a historian should have to his material. Arguing that even eyewitness accounts 'cannot be accepted without criticism' because their bad intentions are 'clouds which obscure the absolute truth', he then turned to the knowing subject himself: 'Nor is it possible for the writer of a history, however great may be his respect for the objective fact, to eliminate altogether his own personality.' Firmly committed to the representational theory of knowledge, he stated as a truism that 'Every kind of evidence, even the most direct, must reach the reader, when presented in narrative form, as a reflection from the mirror of the writer's mind, with the liability to unconscious distortion.' Smith has, however, 'endeavoured to exclude the subjective element so far as possible . . .' (1924: 4). Smith, who was unwilling to admit his and his colleagues' interests as part of this discourse, then went on to serve them in the guise of an objective history.

Classification, Max Müller informed us, is where true science begins. The principle of classification used by those who have adhered to the representational theory of knowledge is more often than not taxonomic, placing phenomena into hierarchically ordered, mutually exclusive classes, each of which had its defining attributes or essences. The reason for this, of course, is that taxonomies 'mirrored' the systems of objects supposed to exist 'out there'. Again and again, scholars and officials have used taxonomies for the classifying of Others. They have decorated their world with 'types' of society (and of family, economy, political system, etc.) – the primitive and civilized, peasant and urban, agricultural and industrial, traditional and legal-bureaucratic, ancient and modern, feudal and capitalist, mechanical and organic. Some scholars have preferred to distribute these types in space, while others have been inclined to turn them into 'stages' and string them out in 'time'. Either way, whether inadvertently or intentionally, the effect of this has been to reduce different agents to inferior positions within the museum of one mankind they have constructed. Inevitably the analyst has represented (*sic!*) the highest type or most advanced stage, thus providing himself with justification for his position of hegemony.

The notion that is probably the most important of the presuppositions to be found in these naturalist ideas of system and their metaphorical representations is that of essence. From the standpoint of human agency, we might even wish to declare essence as the absolute presupposition of this metaphysics. Social science discourses that have emulated the classical discourses of the natural sciences can barely proceed without talking about the natures, essential, intrinsic, or inherent properties, the defining features, or the fundamental characteristics of the objects they have isolated for systematic study.

[14] Mark Hobart (1985: 183–4) speculates on the advantages of an essentialist view of things for rulers and a nominalist view on the part of those in revolt.

We can see the importance of essence to Smith's world in the advice he offered to constitutional reformers. He argued that benevolent despotism, a combination of paternalism and centralized bureaucracy necessitated by India's inherent divisiveness, had always been the key to government in India. That was an integral part of the Indian tradition, an essence which he revealed as a potentially dangerous monster over which he, as historian, stood guard:

Reformers are apt to forget the immeasurable antiquity of Indian tradition. The ancient scriptures are neither obsolete nor dead. They still express the inmost thoughts of the voiceless myriads of to-day as truly as they record the sentiments of their ancestors in the distant past. No passing wind of doctrine can shake the rock of Indian tradition. The shadows flee away, the wall remains. The fly on the rim buzzes for a moment, the wheel of life rolls on. Truly, 'it is neither safe nor easy to meddle with traditional ideas in India'. (Smith, 1919: 22–3)

Apart from caste itself, perhaps the most important attribute in Smith's representation of India as a deficient body politic was world-ordering rationality. The metaphor of society as a machine presupposed the notion of a unitary reason with the will or capability of knowing and maintaining the system that Smith saw as synonymous with order itself. He alleged that Indian civilization had not ever possessed the political order that flows from rationality, leaving his readers to infer that she must have lacked that essential attribute itself. Indians, who in this discourse are not the rational individuals of Western political economy and civil society, but the accidents of castes and races, devoid of practical reason, had been incapable of taking themselves out of Hobbes's state of nature.[15] India, therefore, had to succumb to and rely upon the importation of a masculine European hero in order to create order out of her mutually repellent molecules of conflicting castes and races. Just as the man of practical reason was the rational master and maker of the machine and just as God was the one cause of the universe, so the British would become the bearers of rationality in relation to an India that they would make over into a machine of a body politic.[16]

The consequences for agency of this essentialism have been immense. Smith and his colleagues have assumed essences such as caste and rationality to be fixed premises for action and not the result of acts in changing circumstances. Placing them before history rather than at its shifting frontier, they have transformed those essences – 'God', 'reason', 'liberty', 'modernity', the 'free

[15] By a process of circular reasoning which seems hard to escape in discourses constituting the European self and its others, we might note that Hobbes adduces as evidence for this state of nature, to which no one had direct access in most of the world, reports of conditions of 'savage people' in America. There, 'except for the government of small families, the concord whereof dependeth on natural lust, have no government at all; and live in that brutish manner, as I said before' (1946: 83).
[16] The assumptions made by the students of Indian civilization about essences, while doubtless derived from the metaphysics of textbook science, are vague. They are far from the differing notions of essence deployed by philosophers and theologians over the course of a complex history, never mind the hyper-refined arguments that have gone on in analytic philosophy, for example Brody (1980: 84–155).

market', or, on the left, 'equality', 'democracy', the 'welfare state', or the 'revolution' – into agents. They have treated one or the other of them as the true subject of history, who used the people and institutions of some nation-state or the other as instruments. So history has not been a tale of the contingent. It has been teleological: a hypostatized agent has been made to move a community towards its natural and spiritual destiny. This notion of agency is what Collingwood has referred to as the doctrine of substantialism. According to this doctrine (which overlaps with the idea of essence), the agent of history is taken to be an ideal or material something that underlies, but is not itself affected by, historical acts. As Collingwood puts it, 'the agent from which they flow, being a substance, is eternal and unchanging and consequently stands outside of history' (1956: 43). Those who assume or presuppose essences consistently take what we might call an *expressivist* view of actions. The actions of historical figures are seen as expressions of the substantialized agents or essences that stand behind history.

Collingwood, in his critique of this metaphysics, called it 'scientific' thinking of the sort that was exemplified in older textbooks on logic, and distinguished it from philosophical thinking (1933: 26–31). One critic, Roy Bhaskar, has referred to it as the position of 'empirical realism' (1979: 25), others as 'positivism' in one of its many guises (Bryant, 1985: 1–10). The reader, however, should not emerge from this discussion with the impression that the intellectual practices to which Smith's metaphor speaks have been as uniform as their authors might pretend. The very idea of a system constituted of opposed but interdependent parts itself permitted a continuous debate about which of the opposing principles or which of the levels of constituents is more fundamental. That is, the construction of a system around dualisms or dichotomies has been seen to raise the question of which term in a pair was the more important. This question has had to be asked and answered because of the desire to maintain unity. If the universe is one and knowledge of it is one, then the principle by which it is ordered or the constituent of which it is made has also, ultimately, to be one.

There have, thus, been many debates. Is the fundamental unit of study the smallest entity in a system (the 'individual' as atom, as most neoclassical economists, behavioural psychologists, and positivist political historians, like V. A. Smith, favouring the dominant mechanical character of the metaphor, would insist)? Or is it the system as a whole (as many functionalist sociologists, anthropologists, and left-of-centre social historians have argued, picking up the submerged organic element in the metaphor in order to emphasize the whole's transcendence of its parts)?[17]

Is the ultimate ground of social reality to be found in a base/society (materialism) or superstructure/culture (idealism)? Are we to find the essence

---

[17] The differences between these two positions are many, yet there has been a persistent tendency for the organic to be displaced by the mechanical: for example, the notion of the homeostatic organism in biology. It is this organism that we mostly find in evolutionism and functionalism, which talk about social systems as fulfilling 'needs'. On the incompatibility of evolutionism with history, see Nisbet (1969). For the anti-democratic implications of evolutionism, see Hirst (1976). For a critique of functionalism see Giddens (1977: 96–129).

of the human world inside the individual in the form of a 'human nature' (man as economic animal in liberalism, Reaganism and Thatcherism) or are we to discover it in a social formation in the form of a 'social structure' (the social forces and relations of production in Marxism or unconscious mental oppositions in structuralism)? Other differences also abound. Some, for example, have been more reductive of the cultural or social to the environmental, social, or psychological, while others have opted for the relative autonomy of these phenomena and the disciplines that study them (see 2.2.1, 3.3). Accordingly, some have been more imperialist in their claims than others. Finally, it should be noted that many human scientists have, happily, violated the canons of classical science and used naïve notions of agency in many of their descriptions.

It is also worth pointing out that the ideas of what constitutes a system and how the social world ought to match up have also changed as thinkers have changed their minds about the machines they consider exemplary. Hobbes had before him an automaton or clock. Later scholars have probably given primacy to steam engines, aeroplanes, telegraphs, radios, televisions, and, most recently, the computer, where the machine (having shed almost all its moving parts) is equated with the mind itself.

Certain thinkers have, furthermore, demurred to a greater or lesser extent. And they have done so, off and on, from the very time that the ideology of natural science gained hegemony in Europe.[18] These humanist dissenters, mostly descendants of Kant and the Romantic idealists, have justifiably claimed that the subjectivities of others have to be taken into account. In recent decades those who object to the excesses of naturalism have taken positions variously labelled relativist, hermeneutical, phenomenological, or interpretive. I shall review their work on India below (2.3). Let me just say here that their discussions of the importance of language in constructing reality and of seeing meanings in 'context' have provided an excellent corrective to the more sweeping claims that have been made by the advocates of natural scientific methods. Yet their challenge has been less formidable than it might first seem. Most have taken a position that supplements or complements the absolutist position of the naturalists rather than displacing it. Max Müller's views on science, for example, clearly fall into this category. Far from criticizing their essentialism, these idealists have tended to replace their clearly knowable material essences with a set of their own ineffable mental or spiritual essences, and have pitched notions of free will against the determinism of the empirical realists. Max Weber and some of his followers, who have argued that the essences their colleagues have discussed do not exist in an external social reality, but only in language or thought as 'ideal types' or 'heuristic devices', would even claim to have synthesized the two positions.[19] Theorists in the

---

[18] One such was G. Vico (1668–1744), whose work was ignored until recently. Collingwood's comments on his views and their reception are pertinent (1956: 63–71).

[19] These approaches have a complicated history and diverse branches, but see Weber (1959) and Schutz (1967). Hindess (1977: 1–77) lays bare some of the highly problematic presuppositions of the students of meaning from a post-scientific materialist angle. One of the more sophisticated recent contributions to this effort is that of the philosopher Charles Taylor (1985: 1–114). The essay of Peter Winch (1958), which draws on Collingwood in certain

human sciences have thus not agreed, on either side of the dualist divides, on what the essences are, on which are more fundamental, or where they are to be found. Nearly all these discourses have, however, presupposed their existence in some fashion. We are justified, with Foucault (1974: 31–9), in seeing these interrelating discourses, now converging, now diverging, as making up what he calls a 'discursive formation', a construct that bears a close resemblance to Collingwood's 'scale of forms', introduced below (1.2.1).[20]

Orientalists also face their object with these dualist dilemmas on their minds. One of them, Denis Sinor, agrees with the relativist criticism that 'Asia' is not a 'historical' entity, but only 'geographical', because the term is 'imposed from outside and unknown to the inhabitants of that great continent'. This should not, however, stop the scientific scholar's quest for essences organized in taxonomic form: 'While this may be so, it in no way impairs the validity of the term. The bat, the elephant, and the whale, different as they are, are all mammals, even though they are unaware of the facts.' To be fair, Sinor does not think, *pace* Max Müller, that he himself can proceed as a biologist. He wants us also to supplement objective science with its opposite, a bit of subjectivity: 'The historian must remember that the notions and activities of any individual are meaningful only if set against their own background' (1970: xiv–xv). The point though is that the addition of inner meaning does not challenge the metaphysics of a natural science, for the pursuers of both meanings and mechanisms are looking for essences.

The postulation of a split-level world, one consisting of diverse, manifest actions (on the one hand) and a uniform, underlying human nature or social structure (on the other) repeatedly diverts our attention from the actions of agents to hidden essences, the substantialized agents that proliferate in the discourses of the human sciences. Because scholars, trained into the pre-suppositions of these sciences, have assumed that the transitory and shifting agents of the Indian subcontinent are merely the accidents of an underlying essence, the caste type of society, they have drawn us away from the analysis of those complex actions that are, or were, said to be responsible for the making and remaking of the agents and inter-relationships that have constituted Indian worlds. We repeatedly look past the intricacies of agency that are involved in the meetings of caste or village or district councils, and in the holding of a royal court. We look through the detailed activities that were entailed in a royal progress, a 'conquest of the quarters', the performances of the annual round of activities that reproduced and altered South Asian countrysides, and perennially defer analysis of the efforts and procedures involved in the building and dedication of a temple, monastery, or a mosque and the performance of their

---

limited respects, is more closely tied to the empiricist tradition. The debate in the social sciences is taken up in earnest in Wilson (1977) and again in Hollis and Lukes (1982) and yet again in Overing (1985). See also, for one of the most interesting contributions, Hirst and Woolley (1982: 211–73).

[20] I have purposely dropped here Foucault's earlier notion of episteme because, despite his efforts to move away from it, the idea still retains some of the characteristics of structuralism that are identical with the metaphysics of classical science – unity, determinism, boundedness, mutual exclusion, etc.

rites. The purpose of this book is to turn the study of India away from the search for essences to the exploration of these activities in their own right.

1.1.3 Metaphysical Malaise at Science's Summit

The metaphor of a body politic as a machine that Smith seems to have mobilized so confidently is now in danger of being overthrown, not so much by those it has colonized but by its own elite within the natural sciences themselves. Physicists have sabotaged the metaphysics of classical scientific discourse with their uncertainty principles and subatomic particles (Powers, 1982: 124–72), while guerrillas from the philosophy and history of science have subjected ever more refined and defensive varieties of empiricism or positivism to barrages of criticism (Hacking, 1983: 1–17, 65–74). As a result, 'verification-ism' has given way to 'falsificationism', itself giving way to relativism or instrumentalism (Chalmers, 1976: 35–72, 113–34), the latter of which gives up the claim that positivism is the only method to be used for any study, urging believers instead to study only those things that fit the positivist method. One might even go so far now as to ask if scientific practices have ever conformed to textbook prescriptions. The answer that braver commentators such as Feyer-abend (1978) would give is 'Mostly not' when it comes to the major innovations in science, as distinct from what Thomas Kuhn calls 'normal science' (1970: 23–42). Whence the sense that there is a 'crisis', or, better, a malaise, in the social scientific disciplines.

Some scholars, taking advantage of the disarray that has resulted from the destabilization of the metaphysics of natural science, have made serious efforts to criticize and transcend the dualities that have constituted the naturalism and humanism of the social sciences. The most notable and long-standing critics have been the members of the Frankfurt school of critical sociology, especially Habermas (1971). The intellectual stance I take, both in the criticisms I have already made and in those to follow, as well as in my attempt to construct an alternative metaphysics, runs parallel to these in some respects.[21] My major point of departure from them has to do with the question of where we go for an alternative metaphysics.[22]

It is here that the attempt to open up a discussion about 'complex agency' suggested by R. G. Collingwood will, I hope, make a contribution. Following

---

[21] Among the most important for me is the post-structuralist commentator on the human sciences, Michel Foucault (1973, 1976, 1977). I have also made use of Nelson Goodman, constructionist philosopher of mind (1984: 29–53), and, indirectly, Jacques Derrida's deconstructionism. Nearly as helpful has been my reading of Roy Bhaskar on 'transcendental realism' in the philosophy of science (1979) and, with severe reservations, of Anthony Giddens, in critical sociology, on human agency (1984).

[22] Giddens (1977: 112–17) criticizes certain uses of system and attempts to overcome the deficiencies of both the naturalist and humanist positions with his theory of 'structuration'. The major difficulty this theory faces, however, is that it continues to presuppose the metaphysics of the 'naturalist' social sciences when it is used to analyse collective agents such as the 'nation-state' (Giddens, 1981–85). Bhaskar (1979) tries to retain a notion of structure for the social sciences by introducing the idea of an 'open system' into it, for which he has been rightly criticized (Carchedi, 1983: 27–30).

him, I introduce the metaphysics of 'overlapping classes' and 'scale of forms' as possible replacements for the metaphysics of system and essence that linger in the human sciences. I also argue, again following Collingwood, that we should displace certain notions of society with an idea of 'polity'. Collingwood's perspective was that of a post-Hegelian, a systematic philosopher and historian whose thought straddled both the British empiricist and realist and the European-based idealist traditions.[23] It is no accident that I also make considerable use of the ideas of the Marxist Italian intellectual and politician, Antonio Gramsci (1891–1937) (1971), especially his notion of 'hegemony', for he was indirectly linked to Collingwood through their common critical reading of the Italian idealist, Benedetto Croce (1866–1952). As important as my reading of these earlier European thinkers has been my interaction with certain Indian texts. My struggle to understand them, as much as anything else, has led me to develop the ideas in this book.[24]

Giddens observes that 'it is important to stress that social science stands in a relation of tension to its 'subject-matter' – as a potential instrument of the expansion of *rational autonomy* of action, but equally as a potential *instrument of domination*' (1976: 159). My argument is that the social sciences have figured more as the latter than the former, especially when they have turned their attention to the polities that stood outside the golden circle of the 'West'. The purpose of their sciences more often than not has been to constitute those others as agents who can be managed, that is, whose behaviour can be 'predicted' and 'controlled'. The very attempt to create a science of the social in accord with the canons I have outlined here was and still is imperializing because it claims that a privileged, unitary knowledge can displace the disputable knowledges of the agents about which it knows and that some kind of administrative expertise, based on that superior knowledge and wielded on behalf of market forces or a welfare state, can replace political action or greatly reduce its sphere. I am committed to building on and extending the aspects of the social sciences and history that have been liberating for people and helping them to act as fuller, more knowledgeable agents.

Let me now turn to a brief discussion of the alternative metaphysics of agency that would supplant the metaphysics of essences and advance this project.

1.2   AGENTS: SYSTEMS OF OVERLAPPING CLASSES

1.2.1   Agents Simple and Complex

Indology and the other social sciences have constituted their object of study in accord with what I have called the metaphysics of classical textbook science or one of its modifications. The effect of this has been to displace agency on to

[23] On Collingwood, see, besides the works cited below, his *Autobiography* (1939) and Krausz (1972).

[24] Most valuable among these has been the *Vishṇudharmottara Purāṇa* (1912), a narrative of the 'past' (*purāṇa*), probably composed at and for an imperial court in Kashmir in the eighth century.

essences and to make the actions of agents into expressions of (or departures from) those essences. Let me now ask whether it is possible to formulate an idea of human agency and especially one that is capable of talking about combined agents, such as the state or society, Hobbes's body politic, without displacing agency on to essences or substantialized agents. Can we theorize agents without resorting to the metaphysics of a natural system (or its woolly, subjectivist opposite)? The answer I give here, with the help of Collingwood, is 'yes'. It is possible to pick up the strand that Hobbes and his naturalist successors have chosen to ignore in the metaphor of a body politic and elaborate on it.

I begin with a discussion of the problem of how agents are constituted. I argue that agents are constituted neither as systems in the classical mechanical sense nor outside of natural systems in the opposite, idealist sense. They are constituted as systems, but the systems here are themselves constructed along different lines. They consist of overlapping entities which agents themselves are making and remaking and relating to one another through a dialectical process into 'scales of forms'. Continuing, I argue that because our notion of 'society' as the main category of analysis itself entails the displacement of agency on to essence, we should replace the notion of society with the idea of a polity. I then go on to discuss the idea of 'imperial formation' which I see as replacing the notions of 'empire', 'civilization' or 'world system' that scholars have used to construct the relations among polities. I conclude with a review of how knowledge from this alternative perspective relates to its object.

When I use the expression 'human agency', I mean the realized capacity of people to act effectively upon their world and not only to know about or give personal or intersubjective significance to it. That capacity is the power of people to act purposively and reflectively, in more or less complex inter-relationships with one another, to reiterate and remake the world in which they live, in circumstances where they may consider different courses of action possible and desirable, though not necessarily from the same point of view.

People do not act only as agents. They also have the capacity to act as 'instruments' of other agents, and to be 'patients', to be the recipients of the acts of others. The importance of these aspects of agency, though often ignored in general treatments of agency, can hardly be exaggerated in the study of orientalist discourse (and in the imperial practices of which it was constitutive and by which it was constituted). From the standpoint of agency, we could say that colonialism consisted quite precisely of the attempt to make previously autonomous (or more autonomous) agents into instruments (colonialism in South Asia spawns innumerable words for these 'agents' – *dalal, maqaddam, dobhashi, munshi*, etc.) through which the colonizers could fulfil their desires and into patients, those who had to be variously pacified or punished, saved, reformed, or developed. Yet we should not think of persons or institutions when they act as instruments or patients as mere adjuncts or even chattels of some superior owner. A person, or institution, acting as an instrument or patient may be, from his, her, or its point of view, a more or less willing one. Indeed, the idea that instruments and patients are both complicit and resistant is implied in the notion of hegemony to which I turn below (see 1.3.1).

When I said above that agency is the capacity to act in inter-relationship with other agents, I did so in order to avoid, at the very outset of this bit of theorizing, the fallacy of opposing a construct of the 'individual' to one of 'society'.[25] Nor should we assume that the purposes or intentions of agents consist of master plans which actions implement or even that agents are always conscious of or clear about their purposes.[26]

The privileging of intentionality is not the only assumption to be avoided. If we are to produce a viable theory of human agency we should also take care not to lapse into individualism. One of the major problems that derives from the use of the metaphor of a body politic as a machine is that it takes the 'individual', like the atom of classical physics, as the fundamental unit of analysis. Once we understand the essence of this unit, no further analysis need be undertaken because all are everywhere the same. We must reject this assumption of homogeneity. There is, in my view, no abstract and simple agent built into every situation. That is, I do not conceive of agents as isolates equatable with (or reducible to) an abstract, biologically grounded notion of the 'person' or his or her intentions, as they often are in philosophical discussions (Ayer, 1968: 116–28). Certain agents may deem other agents in a variety of situations to be simples or individuals, but such denominations should not be confused with an absolute, irreducible simplicity or with the idea that there is a fixed human nature causing a person to act in determinate ways.[27] Persons looked at close up are themselves constituted in ways that are often complicated, disparate, and contentious (for example, higher and lower souls, disproportionate humours, conflicting desires). The mind Freud postulates, comprised of an id (its animal nature), its super-ego (internalized parents and emperors and moral codes), and an ego (a rational self supposed to command the other two, but often dominated by them), and the 'creative genius' of an artist or scientist are but two well-known examples.

Another way of putting this is to say that persons as agents are themselves

---

[25] An excellent critique of this dichotomy from within psychology can be read in Henriques, Hollway, Urwin, Venn, and Walkerdine (1984: 11–25).

[26] Collingwood's comments on Greco-Roman rationalism are apposite here:

> Now the idea that every agent is wholly and directly responsible for everything he does is a naïve idea which takes no account of certain important regions in moral experience. On the one hand, there is no getting away from the fact that men's characters are formed by their actions and experiences: the man himself undergoes change as his activities develop. On the other hand, there is the fact that to a very great extent people do not know what they are doing until they have done it, if then. The extent to which people act with a clear idea of their ends, knowing what effects they are aiming at, is easily exaggerated. Most human action is tentative, experimental, directed not by a knowledge of what it will lead to but rather by a desire to know what will come of it. Looking back over our actions, or over any stretch of past history, we see that something has taken shape as the actions went on which certainly was not present to our minds, or to the mind of any one, when the actions which brought it into existence began. (1956: 41–2)

[27] Nature in humans provides possibilities and sets limits, but even these are not always fixed (as medicine continues to show in a positive and ecology in a negative sense).

composed of entities that *overlap*.[28] If I may return to my Freudian example, the super-ego is different in *kind* from the ego in that it is concerned with social and moral goods, while the ego is personal and concerned with the person's survival. Yet they are also different in *degree* in that both are concerned with rationality, the one with giving good reasons for conducting oneself as it says, the other with making rational choices between alternatives from the standpoint of their use to the self. They are related as *opposites* – the super-ego may push a person to destroy himself, the opposite of what the ego is trying to do, but then again they may also be related as *distincts* – the two may, through analysis, be brought into a complementary relationship or one in which their goals converge.

At this point it is clear that the constituents of the mind do not form a system (in Freud) that classical scientism would recognize. They are not separate, bounded and determinate entities that function at discrete levels as interdependent parts of a unitary, machine-like whole. Not only do the parts overlap, but the relationships among them seem to undergo a process of continual change or reproduction, but not in ways that are uniform from one mind to another. Finally, it is difficult here to separate subject from object. The parts of the mind are themselves agents and instruments and patients, too, in their own remaking. What have we here? Is this simply a confused example of non-system? Or is it a system that is too complex, one with too many variables? Collingwood says 'no' on both accounts. He argues that we do have here an example of a system. It is not a system, however, that differs only in degree from a more typical natural system. It also differs in kind.

The name Collingwood gives to the sort of system which such overlapping entities compose is 'scale of forms'. The relationships among these entities are not simply those of physical force, as in a mechanical system. They are what Collingwood calls dialectical. Though in part a Hegelian, Collingwood uses a notion of dialectic that differs from both Hegel and Marxian notions, and especially from the caricatures of their ideas that abound. Although he sometimes uses this term alone, in his discussion of polities (see below) he paired a dialectical process with another which he dubbed, after Plato, eristical. By the former term, he means a relationship in which the two parties move from a position of non-agreement to one of agreement. By the latter, he refers to a situation in which the two interacting parties start from a position of disagreement and attempt to gain triumph over one another.[29] Through this double process of interaction, agents, or even parts of agents, attempt to retain or alter their positions in a system or systems. But it is very important to keep in mind here that as agents or their constituents raise or lower their positions, converge or diverge, or even extrude a rival, they also alter their content. So, when the

[28] Collingwood introduces the notion of overlapping classes in his account of the differences between classification schemes made according to scientific principles and those made in accord with philosophical ones (1933). Later (1971) he uses it in his discussion of communities and polities.

[29] For Collingwood the dialectic that obtains between agents in a scale of forms is neither inherently destructive, as Marxists have tended to see it, or cumulative, as idealists have construed it.

ego takes command of the super-ego and id of a person, making them into its instruments, it is not the case that the entities are simply shifted about in their relations like so many blocks. Their very content as agents, instruments, and patients is also transformed. The energy of the id is sublimated; the super-ego is criticized and loses some of its overbearing edge, and the ego constitutes itself as confident and 'normal', now ready to act rather than be acted upon.

This same argument can be extended to talk about the relationship of persons as agents to compound agents, those consisting of two or more persons – families, castes, clubs, business firms, schools, churches, and governments. To say that these differ from persons in *kind* will not shock most social scientists. Hobbes and Smith notwithstanding, a state is not a giant person. Yet this assumption does great damage, for the notion that there are two sorts of entities here tends to combine with the assumption that they are mutually opposed to one another. If the one is the fundamental unit of study, the other must not be. Whence the endless arguments made by those who would either reduce the social to the individual or subsume the individual in society. Whence also the almost universal tendency to see agency as a property of persons and structure as a property of institutions (Giddens, 1979: 1–8, 49–95). If, however, we were prepared to accept the possibility that persons and institutions also differ in *degree* – persons do act together as though one person – and so to see them as overlapping entities, we would allow ourselves to avoid assuming at the outset of a study that either individuals or societies are to be given ontological priority over one another.

Agents compounded of more than one person are no more to be seen as inherently unified than are persons themselves. Certainly I wish to avoid the notion that complex agents are enlarged persons, as in legal discourses, a leviathan of a mechanical man, as in Hobbes, or homeostatic organisms, as in evolutionism and functionalism. My second assumption is, therefore, that complex agents may be more or less dispersed, that is, less or more unified, in their constitution and practices. The Jewish or Palestinian nations are obvious examples of dispersed agents. Others, such as today's multinational business corporations or yesterday's East India Company, are less obvious examples because, like most complex agents that *claim* to be inherently unified, these are, or were, in fact united only on certain occasions or in certain circumstances. Think, for example, of the unity displayed by people of most political parties when the British Queen opens Parliament after a general election and compare it with what happens there on ordinary working days.

The problems of producing unity of purpose or action are, in this theory, even greater for relatively more complex agents than they are for relatively simple agents such as persons, especially if we do not think of the complex agent as a bounded 'system' with objective, fixed needs that such hypostatized entities might be fulfilling. This is why daily routines, initiations, courses of study or apprenticeship, meetings, assemblies, courts, parades, processions, and the like are so important. Actions here *make* what order there is in the human world, shaping and altering both the simpler and more complex agents and not merely 'expressing' or 'symbolizing' it. Finally, it follows from the processual character of a scale of forms that agents are never inherently complete. They or others may declare themselves complete (to wit, happy, successful, cured, saved) at certain moments, but that completeness is always provisional and perspectival. This ceaseless dialectical (or eristical) movement among compound agents, through which degrees and kinds of agency, instrumency, and patiency are changed or even reconstituted, is the very process by which one party or ideology, according to Gramsci, attains hegemony (see 1.3.4).

Some of the complex agents on which I concentrate in this book are villages and unions of villages, councils of citizens, royal courts, castes and caste councils, religious orders or sects, armies, trading companies, universities, and professional associations. But I will also be dealing with some agents, to wit, the gods Vishnu and Siva (3.4.1), whom some might wish to dismiss as agents. I am going to assume, however, that such agents, whose very existence may be contested, may in a sense be real. The persons and institutions of a community may indeed attribute a great deal of or even a determining power to a god or gods, ancestors, ghosts, to the state, to reason, to law, to the market, to society, to the party, to the crown, to the people. We may take such agents to be real to the extent that complexes of discursive and nondiscursive practices constitute and perpetuate them, even if some would deny their reality. Indeed, some of the most important quarrels in history have been about such larger-than-life agents.

1.2.2 From 'Society' to Polities

The most important of the complex agents with which I deal, however, are those I will refer to as polities. Social scientists (and journalists, not to mention the 'average citizen') have relied heavily on the term 'society', to talk about the human world. It has become the term used in social scientific discourse to talk about virtually any complex agent – tribe, village, clan, nation-state, linguistic or ethnic group that occupies, or is seen wishing to occupy, its own territory. These are the entities likened to the machine or organism of the physical and biological sciences. This usage masks the empirical complexity of these agents by treating them (or ideal types of them) as if they were unitary, determinate objects, the manifestations of some underlying essence or the product of some substantialized agent, a pure class of persons who share some permanent something despite their actual (dis)organization at any one time. Another voluntarist usage of the term 'society', evoked in the same breath as this mechanistic one, gives the almost opposite impression – that these compound agents are purely purposive organizations, all of whose members have consciously and freely joined their wills to its. Both are also implicit in the metaphor of the body politic as a machine.

Why does this dual usage persist? The reason has to do with the very nature of the project which the social sciences and their partners, government and business, have set for themselves: the construction of a human world knowable and controllable as is the natural world, but yet retaining the notion of the individual as a free subject. We are all fundamentally agents; no one is in any major respect an instrument or patient of other agents.

I prefer, following Collingwood, to set aside this concept of a society in favour of an idea of 'polity' (1971: 131–223). I do this because it recognizes rather than suppresses the 'mixed' nature of the entities which the social sciences refer to as societies. It focuses attention on the relationship of ruler and ruled and on the disagreement and conflict that are integral to the ongoing making of a 'society' as an empirical entity. It also points to the respects in which persons and institutions are related as instruments and patients and not simply as agents. At the same time, I will, again following Collingwood, use the term 'society' to designate complex agents that people *do* in some sense join, for example a trade union or the Royal Asiatic Society. In particular, I will use the term 'ruling society' to designate those compound agents that are rulers not only of themselves but of others. Examples of these in ancient India were village councils, assemblies of the rural and urban citizenries, and royal courts. Temples and religious orders, whose higher devotees ruled over varying aspects their own lives and of those of lower grades, are other examples of societies with more limited writs.

Since persons may be accorded capacities that differ in both kind and degree, I will assume that joining a society often entails the creation and perpetuation of inequalities among its members. I do not, in other words, assume that all who join inherently possess the same degree of 'free will'. One example Collingwood gives is of marriage, into which the wife does not everywhere enter on an equal footing with her husband (1971: 168–9).

I will distinguish a society in this sense from what Collingwood defines as a 'non-social community', those persons who share something (as in the first social scientific usage above), but who do not constitute a ruling society. Such persons – children, slaves, conscripts, war captives, immigrants – are almost invariably in the relationship of ruled to a society or societies of rulers, their instruments and patients. Many non-social communities (I am thinking of trade unions here, persons who shared a trade) have made themselves into societies and constituted themselves as agents. What this distinction recognizes is that agency as a realized capacity is not a given. Persons constituted by others as a non-social community may, through a process of interaction among themselves and with those who claim to rule them, make themselves into a ruling society. On the other hand, ruling societies may also force other societies to disperse or disband (at least officially). A polity, then, is neither a society or a non-social community. It is both, a non-social community with a ruling society, which itself may, as Collingwood puts it, 'be subdivided into a multiplicity of graded subclasses demanding as their qualification for membership strength of will in different degrees' (1971: 187). At every turn, these claim to speak and act for themselves and others while those others concede or deny such claims. The point, then, is that polities are mixed. They always consist both of societies of limited scope that differ from one another and of relatively non-social communities.

Like other agents, a polity can be thought of as a scale of forms. Collingwood, it will be recalled, argues that the constituent parts of a polity may be related both dialectically and eristically. Let us look at political parties from this angle. They can be viewed as compound agents attempting, both dialectically (by discursive argument aimed at agreement) and eristically (by threats, punishments, and mystifications aimed at victory) to gain ascendancy over each other and to win over the majority of the citizens and produce out of the state a single scale of forms in which the constitution of the polity itself is shaped, to a greater or lesser degree, in accord with its programme, in which its ideology becomes, as a Gramscian analysis would put it, the 'hegemonic' ideology, reducing other parties to a lower position in the scale of forms (see 1.3.4). So far as ancient India is concerned, we could take its system of four 'castes' (*varṇas*) or, as I prefer to call them, estates, the lordships and masteries out of which Indian polities were constructed, and its differing religious orders as instances of scales of forms rather than as Smith's jarring molecules.

As a scale of forms, as a system in that sense, a polity is also characterized by its provisionality. Its ruling agent – council, state, sovereign – is a permanent society, 'because its work is never done' (Collingwood, 1971: 184). Within even the simplest imaginable polity, three problems have, according to Collingwood, continually to be solved. These are: the work of imposing order on the 'nursery' which is ever being replenished with persons – children – who do not have the capacity as such to join the ruling society of the polity in which they are born; the work of ordering the ruling agent; and the work of ordering the relationship between the two. Together these make up the minimum content of what he calls the 'constitutional' problem of a body politic (185–6). Because it is continually changing its composition and because its members differ in their interests and purposes, the 'constitution' of a polity is, thus, not a settled thing. It is something that its members continually alter and renew, decentring and recentring it. Though Gramsci would have differed from Collingwood on some points, he would probably have agreed with Collingwood when he stated that, 'A body politic is a non-social community which, by a dialectical process also present in the family, changes into a society' and that it was 'a process never completed' (Collingwood, 1971: 177, 184).

1.2.3 Imperial Formations

I use the term 'imperial formation' to extend the idea of polity outlined above. I employ it to refer to a complex agent consisting of overlapping and contending polities that more or less successfully relate themselves to each other in what they consider, or at least concede as constituting, a single way of life, one that its more active proponents seek to represent as potentially universal in extent. The polity claiming to speak and act for an entire imperial formation has, however, to contend with a wide variety of polities and societies which themselves pursue different strategies in their relations with the hegemonic polity. Following a universalizing strategy, it may claim to involve local and relatively isolated communities within 'its' imperial formation, while they themselves, opting for what I refer to as peripheralizing or localizing strategies, may attempt to deny or resist inclusion. Just as it is not possible to understand the regional without taking into account the global, so, I would maintain, it is not possible to understand the would-be rulers of an imperial formation without understanding the activities of those over whom they would exercise paramount rule.

My idea of imperial formation is not altogether new. Indeed, it is partly inspired by the ancient Indian idea of the 'circle of kings', which I shall take up later (6.2.1). It also bears a certain resemblance to the ideas of 'social formation' and 'world system' used by Marxists and to the ideas of 'empire' and 'civilization' used by liberal or conservative historians and sociologists.

Certain Marxists have come to use the expression 'social formation' as their substitute for the idea of 'society', but without freeing themselves of the latter's deficiencies from the standpoint of agency. The term offloads the agency of polities on to the ensemble of social classes and institutions that accompany a 'mode of production'. Although I do not wish to specify in advance what the social and economic institutions or practices of an imperial formation are or are not, I do not want to give up the concern with the social division of labour and reproduction and their relationship to economic forms. Rather I wish to incorporate those concerns, shorn of some of their more worrisome essentialisms and reductionisms, into my own idea. Hence I use the term imperial formation, which replaces the idea of social formation in much the same way that polity would replace society.

One critical variant on the idea of a social formation, Immanuel Wallerstein's idea of a 'world system' goes some way toward focusing on the global interrelations of economies and polities to one another and has gained a certain ascendancy. Wallerstein distinguishes two varieties of world system, the 'world empire' and 'world economy', each built around a distinct 'mode of production'. The earlier of these two is the 'world empire' (which arises out of the 'mini-system', the oldest and simplest 'social system', in which families large or small are the units of production and relations are reciprocal, that is, surpluses are evenly distributed). The world empire's mode of production, a conflation of Marx's ancient, feudal and Asiatic modes, is 'redistributive'. Its economy, though larger, remains relatively closed and static. Surpluses in a world empire, however strong or weak its centre, are exacted by state officials in the form of a 'tribute' and distributed among themselves, at the expense of primary producers who remain perennially at the subsistence level. This type of world system has given way, in the course of the sixteenth to nineteenth centuries, to that of the present, the capitalist system, which is a world economy rather than a world empire. It is distinguished from its predecessors by a principle of capital accumulation, and consequently of ceaseless change and growth (Wallerstein, 1974).[30]

The holism of Wallerstein has much to commend it as a corrective to the atomism of many classical or liberal economists and modernization theorists, who have looked on 'nations' or 'societies' as enlarged versions of the 'individual' agents – recall the leviathan itself – presupposed in their theories, each competing with the other on an even footing. This view has been partly responsible, as will be seen (5.2), for the depiction of India, and especially of 'medieval' India, as a congeries of self-contained warring states. None the less, I prefer to distinguish my idea of an imperial formation from his concept of a

[30] For a more theoretical discussion, see Wallerstein (1979: 132–64), and for criticism, see Dale (1984: 183–207).

world system. I do so for at least three reasons. First, I do not see an imperial formation as a closed, determinate system, one that is operating relentlessly according to a single specifiable principle (e.g., the principle of accumulation in the present-day world economy). Second, the concept of a world system is typological. When all is said and done, the world empire of the past remains a negative or incipient form of the world economy of the present. Finally, and most importantly, there is the question of agency in Wallerstein's theory. Despite his attempts to avoid the cruder forms of economism, his work continues to presuppose the existence of a substantialized agent for each of his world systems, this being its mode of production. He also remains committed to the materialist teleology that provides history with a purposive agent and requires that a system persist until exhausted by its inner contradictions. It is not just, as we shall see, that there are problems with the concept of a mode of production. More difficult is the fact that the reification of a mode of production undermines the capacity of agents to make their history (both in the past and in the present). At best, people can, with correct knowledge, become the willing instruments of the true agent of their history – its mode of production – or step aside and stoically watch it pass by.

Why not then stay with the more conventional terms 'empire' or 'civilization'? The difficulty with the term empire derives from the long-standing tendency in national and political histories to equate polities with the idea of the unitary, administered dynastic or national state of the last few centuries of European history. By extension, the notion of empire has come, as in Vincent Smith, to be used to refer to a polity consisting of one state and the conquered or acquired territories over which it claims exclusive administrative competence. The very terms of this discursive apprehension of a complex polity thus preclude the possibility that we could describe polities organized according to different principles (except, of course, as antecedents of the modern state). The difficulty with the ideas of 'civilization' and 'culture' that human scientists have used revolve around two alternate views (Williams, 1976: 57–60, 87–93). The one sees civilization as a material, technological, and instrumental arrangement, in which sense it is opposed to culture. The other considers civilization the spiritual, artistic, and inherently valuable moral achievement of a people, a view that equates civilization with 'culture'. The former is undesirable because it presupposes an opposition between ideas and institutions that I wish to deny. The second is wanting because it privileges an elite and generally idealist notion of what is valuable and subsumes the economic and political.

Finally, people have tended to use both the terms 'civilization' and 'culture', like the term 'nation', to describe complex political agents as the expression of some underlying essence – freedom, democracy, humanity, Englishness, the American character, reason – rather than as the products of ongoing, dialectic-ally constituted and necessarily transient human agents. Quests for essences have been accompanied by a tendency to deny the existence of that which does not express it, that which is excluded from the category of nation-state, empire, or civilization. Smith did just that twice over; first, when he denied that India on her own could ever be the expression of that essence of the West, practical reason; second, when he made the British empire appear as the sole expression of it in Europe, ignoring the counterclaims to ownership of the French, never mind the Germans. I prefer to use 'imperial formation' to theorize and describe the complex entities with which I am concerned, because it is precisely this essentialism that I criticize, and because I argue that the denied, subsumed, or excluded is necessarily a partner in constituting the included. Without the dark rock of Indian tradition under its feet, European rationality would not have seemed so bright and light.

Later in this book I shall be concerned with imperial formations centred on Indian practices, but I also use the idea of an imperial formation to organize my thoughts about the complex polities of Europe and orientalist discourses. The discourses I will designate as orientalist belong to two imperial formations. These are the Anglo-French, which lasted from the time of the Napoleonic Wars down to the Second World War, and its successor, the imperial formation of the present, that of the US and USSR. Although these discourses have many antecedents in another, prior imperial formation, that of the Spanish and Portuguese (sixteenth to eighteenth centuries), I take care to distinguish them. The intellectual practices of the Spanish and Portuguese remained largely centred on Christian theology, while those of their British, French, German, and American successors have centred predominantly on the idea of a natural philosophy or science, the major target of my criticisms. An analysis of Hispano-Portuguese discourses on Asia constitutes another project, one that others will have to undertake.

Let me conclude this introduction to imperial formations with a brief account of the one we live in at present. The United States of America presently claims primacy in an imperial formation of global dimensions. Its unity is constituted by a 'free market economy' of sovereign and equal nations and individuals and not by the political and administrative 'empires' of its Anglo-French predecessor. Yet these are not the mutually exclusive entities they appear to be in the metaphor of a polity as a machine, for they are also related in a single scale of forms, that of the 'three worlds'. As can be seen in Pletsch's analysis (1981: 565–90) of this 'cosmology', this is a crude but excellent example of a scale of forms, for it consists of three overlapping groupings of polities – a free world, headed by the US; a communist world, headed by the 'arch-enemy' of the US, the USSR; and a third world of 'underdeveloped' spectators. While much is made of the opposition of the US and USSR to each other, in the name of a 'cold war', the rhetoric that issues forth from each assumes that the other is also distinct (Russian literature is highly prized in the US and American 'popular culture' in the USSR) and that they are related by differences in degree (standards of living, military strength, GNP) as well as in kind (capitalism and socialism). Otherwise how could each claim that it will eventually come to include the other in its world not as a province in an empire, but in the sense that the opponent will convert to its own way of thinking or be buried in an avalanche of consumer goods or missiles? At the same time, both of the 'superpowers' hope ultimately to win over the nations of the third world to their point of view, and a great deal of dialectical and eristical activity goes on in agencies such as the UN and the World Bank, not to mention the CIA and the KGB, with that purpose in mind. Since it is primarily their culture or religion that keeps the countries of the third world, of which India is the flagship, from developing into 'advanced' nations (see 5.6), the implication once again is that even this benighted world overlaps with the first two. If even those who have tried to constitute themselves in accord with the metaphysics of a classical science order their world (however tacitly) with the notions of overlapping classes and a scale of forms, we can, I think, begin to grasp how powerful the idea of an imperial formation might be in talking about those complexes of polities that were more inclined to think openly about these principles of classification and order.

1.2.4 Knowledge as a Scale of Forms

The shift from system in the classical scientific sense to system as a scale of forms has several important implications for the theory of knowledge that human scientists in general and Indologists in particular have used. The representational theory of knowledge rests on the assumption either that the order it sees in the world is unitary, objective, determinate, and complete or, when it is not so bold, that the means for making observations of the world do or can have those same characteristics. Taxonomic or typological knowledge, it claims in its braver moments, simply mirrors what exists out there.[31] The perspective of a scale of forms converges with that of those who reject this assumption. With Goodman (1976: 7–8), it holds that the knowledge of the knower is not a disinterested mental representation of an external, natural reality. It is a construct that is always situated in a world apprehended through specific knowledges and motivated by practices in it. What is more, the process of knowing actively participates in producing and transforming the world that it constructs intellectually.

We can develop this point (that knowledge in part constructs reality) further by taking the lead from Quine (1964: 73–9), who argues, from within the homeland of logical positivism, that translations are underdetermined, the effect of which is to undermine the very possibility of a neutral, observation language. Knowledge is, if we accept this argument, always underdetermined by its very situatedness. There are always different knowledges that can be constructed in a particular situation. Different arrangements from the standpoint of different agents with different purposes are always possible (Collingwood, 1933: 49–51). Just think of the abortion or 'right to life' issue with its irreconcilable Roman Catholic and secular, liberal perspectives. There are, by virtue of this same relative indeterminacy, always bound to be differences among the persons of a polity over how that polity itself should be constituted as well as differences over how people and resources should be distributed. There is, therefore, no plane outside the lived world from which a unitary, objective knowledge of reality can be had. No utopian science of human desires (liberal economics) or needs (Marxist economics) ever has or is ever likely to eliminate

[31] This is the position realists might take. Idealists and, in another way, certain rationalists, for example structuralists, would displace order on to an underlying mental structure (previously known under the label of transcendent ideas, mind, or even God). A genuine empiricist would prefer to locate order in the mental processes of the classifier.

politics either in the more superficial distributive sense or in the more important constitutive sense. Knowledge, in other words, always has had and will continue to have a political aspect (just as politics always has an epistemological aspect).

From this argument about situatedness, it is appropriate to draw two conclusions. First, I agree with Bhaskar (1979: 1–28) that Kant's position ought to be reversed. The knower does not transcend the world that he or she takes as object; on the contrary, the reality in which the knower is situated transcends him or her. Yet I do not want to leave the impression, with this reversal, that knower and known remain fundamentally separated from one another. Agents and their worlds are in a dialectical relationship with one another, transforming, or as Goodman would say, constructing one another in a continual process. Whence my second conclusion, that knower and known are not fundamentally different from one another but, in principle, continuous the one with the other. They overlap, differing not just in kind from one another but also in degree; and they are related not only as opposites, as in the dualist theory which contrasts mind with matter, but also as distincts.[32]

Two additional points are worth making here, both of which I extend from Collingwood. First, if knowledge of all phenomena is underdetermined and of the social world even more so, then the surest knowledge of them must be retrospective, both for the agents themselves and for the more removed scholars. We can, from a situated perspective, have definite knowledge of why a scale of forms took the shape it did and we can use that as a rough guide for future action, but we cannot (as the proponents of textbook science would have claimed) predict what shape a scale of forms will take. Second, the completeness of knowledge as a scale of forms is also, for the same reason, always provisional. As circumstances change, agents revise it (Collingwood, 1972: 191–2). Again, consider the way in which we are beginning to rethink what acts constitute murder or euthanasia as medical technology changes, or of the efforts political parties to adapt to or bring about changes in class consciousness. Another way to state the matter is to say that the makers of a scale of forms tend to decentre themselves and their knowledge. The very success of Japan in the eyes of the first world is also an embarrassment for the West's own economic theory because, as US economists themselves point out, the Japanese do not have the individuals who are supposed to be the fundamental units of a market economy. There are also those ideas set aside or left out of a particular revision. For example, the appropriately labelled 'externalities' of free-market economics, the social costs of an expanding economy (Hirsch, 1977: 102–14) may be the very things that make people insist on more state regulation. Such inconsistencies (themselves due to the underdetermination principle) provide the impetus for further reworkings of a scale of forms.

---

[32] Quite often what social scientists do when they talk about related pairs such as culture and nature, base and superstructure, or status and power is to theorize them as opposites, while treating them as both opposites and distincts (for example, the notion that culture is a denial or suppression of nature and also a transformation or refinement of it). Which is to say that the phenomena they wish to study as opposites may better be taken as opposed in some respects but continuous in others.

To summarize, the metaphysics of typology asks us to explain actions in its own *a priori* terms as the product of a single, determinate human nature or social structure, and displaces the metaphysics of the people whose actions are to be explained on to these essences. One consequence of such displacements is, quite understandably, a continual postponement of the study of the metaphysics of the Other on the grounds that it is, like all metaphysics, not verifiable and that science has a proven theory applicable to all. The metaphysics of a scale of forms, by contrast, requires a study of different metaphysical systems, for it assumes that the agents and actions of those systems' makers will themselves have been constructed, within limits, in accord with their own metaphysics.

At this point, let me declare a relativism alert. The idea that different cultures, like Kuhn's paradigms in science, may be 'incommensurable' itself presupposes that there be sufficient overlap, enough similarity between them, that the knower can see the differences. That is, it presupposes that the knower is already positioning the unknown culture within a scale of forms, however unwitting, crude, and tentative his or her process of doing so may be. Like Collingwood, I reject the assumption that civilizations, cultures, or periods in history are to be thought of as self-contained entities, for to do so makes the mistake of thinking of them as things in nature (1956: 159–65, 181–3). Ironically, this assumption that cultures can be assimilated to stones is a holdover from positivism, the very method which relativism is alleged to correct. Thinking explicitly with a scale of forms assumes overlap and permits us to place differing metaphysical systems in relation to one another at various places in a scale of forms without forcing us either to override other metaphysics with our own or pretending we must abandon the metaphysics of our world in order to understand the Other's. At the same time it also asks us to enquire into the dialectical and eristical processes by which agents place others in a scale of forms, which is to say it foregrounds the intellectual and political activities by which different polities attempt to hegemonize one another within imperial formations.

The attempt by Europeans in recent centuries to know the human world through a 'scientific', taxonomic metaphysics has, of course (disclaimers notwithstanding), also been an effort to order that world in accord with the canons of that metaphysics, to bring about the hegemony of a liberal world-view within and among various Euro-American polities. Max Müller revealed more than he intended about the effects of that all-important activity of classification on its object when he said: 'Let us take the old saying, *Divide et impera*, and translate it somewhat freely by "Classify and understand" ' (1882: 68). It would, therefore, be unwise to pretend that phenomena in the world that Euro-American discursive practices have produced – among these one would include the notions of 'private property', the 'abstract individual', the 'nation-state', and 'culture' or 'society' – can automatically be better accounted for by a scale of forms. Yet, it would be downright foolish, if Collingwood is right about the prevalence of overlapping classes in philosophical and everyday thought (and perhaps also in much of recent scientific thought as well!), to assume that a scale of forms has been expunged from contemporary discourses about the 'social'. Indeed, we have already seen in the example of the 'three worlds' that these two ways of apprehending and ordering the world themselves overlap in present-day practices.

1.3   ORIENTALIST DISCOURSE

1.3.1   Bias, Power, and Knowledge

Integral to the idea of 'imperial formation' is a notion of 'imperial knowledges'. These are the universalizing discourses, the world-constituting cosmologies, ontologies, and epistemologies, produced in those complex polities at their upper reaches by those persons and institutions who claim to speak with authority. We should not make the mistake of seeing these knowledges as unitary and imposed by force by a ruler sharply opposed to a completely passive population of the ruled. Following Gramsci (1971: 55–60, 210–76), I will refer to the deployers of this knowledge as 'hegemonic' agents.[33] They are the writers and institutions (for instance, a John Maynard Keynes or Milton Friedman, the World Bank or International Monetary Fund in economic debates) that have dominated the public discussions about others, not simply in a constraining or coercive sense, but also in the sense that they have been accorded positions of leadership. They appear successfully to speak not only for their own or some special interest, but for the interests of wholes, of others as well as of selves. They are the agents that have what Foucault referred to as the 'enunciative function' (1976: 86–106). The others involved in the process of shaping and reiterating hegemony – workers, the masses, middle America, the taxpayer, consumers – are themselves complicit in the process (as largely willing patients), tending to accept the premises of the discourse in which they participate as 'natural' or as 'common sense'.[34] Whether in nineteenth-century Europe or now in the USA, these leading persons and institutions have, as hegemonic agents, almost invariably offered up some metaphor-plated essence – rationality, the individual, the free market, the welfare state – and announced that is realized in its most 'developed' or 'advanced' form in the 'West'. Those discourses on science that I have just reviewed are important examples of imperial knowledges. Indeed, their hegemony in the Anglo-French imperial formation and in its successor, the US–Soviet imperial formation, the one in which we now live, distinguishes those formations from the earlier one, that of the Spanish and Portuguese, in which theological discourses held sway. The 'orientalist' discourses I now discuss presuppose these scientific discourses. In that respect they are distinct from their Iberian ancestors even though the discourses on Asia of all three of these formations can be taken as examples of imperial knowledges in their own right.

The term 'orientalism' (generally replaced nowadays by the expression 'Asian studies') has been used to designate this discursive practice in its widest sense.

---

[33] On Gramsci, see Femia (1987) and Laclau and Mouffe (1985).
[34] For a range of examples pertinent to this study, see Mackenzie (1986).

There is, of course, no discipline that takes as its object the study of the whole of Asia. The 'disciplines'[35] which constituted the core of orientalist discourse in the nineteenth century are the various branches of philology and textual study known by various names such as Sinology, Indology, and Arabic or Islamic studies. Often enough institutions have, since the Second World War, called them 'language and area studies'. Interestingly enough these are grouped in two major clusters that correspond rather closely to the two Orients their practitioners represent in their discourses (2.1). The one consists of the study of the Arabic, Persian, and Turkish languages and has Islam as its unifying subject. This is the orientalism about which we have heard so much since the publication of Edward Said's book of that name.

The other cluster of disciplines consists of the study of 'classical' Chinese (and of Japanese and other central and east Asian languages) and of Sanskrit, India's 'classical' language, along with other 'regional' languages of the subcontinent. It is unified only very loosely by the religion of Buddhism. The first of these clusters has as its professional organ in the United States, the Middle Eastern Studies Association. Scholars of the second cluster congregate annually under the rubric of the Association for Asian Studies. The name of this organization implies what the corresponding construct of the Orient says – that it represents the 'real' Asia, the truly other East.

Each of these linguistic disciplines and its area is also closely connected with the disciplines in the human sciences – anthropology, history of religions, philosophy, history, sociology, political science, economics, and psychology.[36] Despite this seeming diversity, however, it is possible to speak of a distinctly orientalist discourse and to single it out from among other overlapping discourses. First, it is about the 'civilized' rather than about the 'primitive'. This distinguishes it from anthropology which concerns itself with the latter more than the former. Second, it speaks of Asian Others in ways that contrast rather sharply with the way in which it speaks of itself. Third, it continually distinguishes the parts of Asia by reference to the same differentiating essences.

The discourse of orientalists, according to Edward Said (1978), presents itself as a form of knowledge that is both different from, and superior to, the knowledges that the Orientals have of themselves.[37] Backed by government funds, disseminated by universities, supported by the ACLS[38] and the SSRC,[39] endowed by the Ford Foundation, and given space in the *New York Review of Books*, the knowledge of the orientalist, known nowadays as an 'area studies' specialist, appears as rational, logical, scientific, realistic, and objective.

---

[35] The very choice of this word gives the impression that determinate knowledge will be forthcoming.

[36] It is a mistake to *equate* these disciplines with philology. They are much more than that. Either they have developed their own substantive views of the world or – and this has been the case in recent decades – they have taken them from the social sciences.

[37] An earlier version of this part of the chapter appeared separately (Inden, 1986b).

[38] American Council of Learned Societies; in Britain there is the University Grants Committee.

[39] American Social Sciences Research Council; its British counterpart is the Economic and Social Science Research Council.

The knowledge of the Orientals, by contrast, often seems irrational, illogical, unscientific, unrealistic, and subjective.

The knowledge of the orientalist is, therefore, privileged in relation to that of the Orientals, and it invariably places itself in a relationship of intellectual dominance over that of the Easterners. It has appropriated the power to represent the Oriental, to translate and explain his (and her) thoughts and acts not only to Europeans and Americans but also to the Orientals themselves. But that is not all. Once his special knowledge enabled the orientalist and his countrymen to gain trade concessions, conquer, colonize, rule, and punish in the East. Now it authorizes the area studies specialist and his colleagues in government and business to aid and advise, develop and modernize, arm and stabilize the countries of the so-called third world. In many respects the intellectual activities of the orientalist have even produced in India the very Orient which it constructed in its discourse. I doubt very much, for example, if Gandhi's concept of non-violence would have played the central part it did in Indian nationalism had it not been singled out long ago as a defining trait of the Hindu character.

A genuine critique of Orientalism does *not* revolve around the question of prejudice or bias, of the like or dislike of the peoples and cultures of Asia, or of a lack either of objectivity or of empathy. Emotions, attitudes, and values are, to be sure, an important part of orientalist discourse, but they are not coterminous with the structure of ideas that constitutes orientalism or with the relationship of dominance embedded in that structure. Any serious criticism of orientalist discourse in the many variant forms it has taken spatially and temporally must not be content simply to rectify 'attitudes' toward the Other. It must also penetrate the emotional minefield surrounding scholarship on Others. And it must directly confront the central question of knowledge and its multiple relations to power in orientalist representations of Asians.

Such in brief is the bold message of Said's *Orientalism*, with the difference that I have made India rather than the Middle East the primary referent in my summary of his portrayal. To a large extent I agree with Said's critique and so, too, perhaps do many other scholars of Asia. My intention here is not to interpret Said's book, to defend it against its detractors, or to attack them.[40] Instead, I would like to turn to a discussion of the peculiar form in which these experts on the Other have presented their knowledge of alien cultures.

1.3.2   Commentative Accounts

Fundamental to the form of Indological discourse is a distinction between what I shall refer to as the 'descriptive' and 'commentative' aspects of its texts. The descriptive aspect of an Indological account is that which claims to represent the thoughts and acts of Indians to the reader. The commentative aspect of an account is its frame, often isolable in distinct passages. It represents those same thoughts and actions by characterizing them, by indicating their general nature or essence. Goodman has argued that it is not possible to represent something

---

[40] Informative from a Marxian perspective is the review by Robert Irwin (1981).

as it is (or was). Even the most narrowly descriptive work of scholarship on South Asia thus necessarily contains (or at least presupposes) a framing commentary, representing its subject-matter *as* something (Goodman, 1976: 27–43). Many accounts go on to give explanation or interpretation (which I shall turn to next). Let me begin with those that stop with commentary.

It will be my contention that Indological texts (or their affiliates in the social sciences) place their strange and seemingly inexplicable descriptive contents in surrounding comments that have the effect of re-presenting them as distorted portrayals of reality. That is, they function to depict the thoughts and institutions of Indians as distortions of normal and natural thoughts and institutions (according to the dominant Western discourse of the period in question). They represent them as manifestations of an 'alien' mentality. Here, for example, is a passage from an account of Brahmanism by Louis Renou (1896–1966), one of this century's leading Sanskritists.[41] Brahmanism is the name Indologists have given to the religion that was based on the *Veda*, supposed to be the oldest and most sacred text in an Aryan language (see 3.3.1). Renou's first two sentences intentionally comment:

The Vedic rites are made to conform to a systematic arrangement; mythology may be lacking in system, but ritual is overburdened with it. It appears that originally separate rites were grouped together in vast systems in response to new demands that had arisen in the course of time, and under the influence of an advancing scholasticism. (Renou, 1968: 29)

The rest of the paragraph purports 'simply' to describe, yet here, too, commentary surfaces. Renou tells his reader that the 'two series' of 'great public rites, called Śrauta' and 'domestic rites, called Gṛhya' are 'entirely different in character, in spite of the resemblances that arise from borrowings'. He goes on, saying that all the sacrifices 'are variations of a single archetype' and that some 'are too complicated to be actually carried out, and are intended rather as intellectual exercises'. The beginning of the next paragraph intention-ally shifts back to the commentative, but what Renou says here is already implicit in his description above:

I do not intend to engage in a theoretical consideration of the nature of the ritual. Ritual has a strong attraction for the Indian mind, which tends to see everything in terms of the formulae and methods of procedure, even when such adjuncts no longer seem really necessary for its religious experience. (29–30)

Renou illustrates this and then returns to what he thinks is pure description, laying out the parts of the Vedic ritual.

What does this Indological text accomplish with this representation of Brahmanism? It transforms the thoughts and actions of ancient Indians into a distortion of reality. Renou might have shown that the apparently irrational minds and disconnected acts of Vedic priests were parts of a coherent and rational whole, that they participated in a real world, but that the real world of

[41] For a brief biography and a bibliography of his works, see *Mélanges* (1968: ix–xxix, 1–5).

the Vedic Indian was based on presuppositions differing from those of nineteenth-century European thought. Renou, however, does not do so, for he, like many Indologists, holds certain presuppositions about the relationship of knowledge to reality that precludes this. He assumes that there is a single, determinate, external reality 'out there' which human knowledge merely 'copies', 'represents', or 'mirrors'. Western science, claiming to be empiricist (or rationalist) in its epistemology and realist in its ontology, has privileged access to that reality. Vedic thought, characterized as mystical and idealist, does not. For Renou and most other Indologists, the knowledges of those whom they studied were, thus, what Foucault refers to as 'subjugated knowledges'. These comprised, according to Foucault, 'a whole set of knowledges that have been disqualified as inadequate to their task or insufficiently elaborated: naïve knowledges located low down on the hierarchy, beneath the required level of cognition or scientificity' (1980: 82).

The question of what assumptions one makes about the relationship of knowledge to reality is a crucial one for Indology and for orientalism as a whole, as well as for the affiliated human sciences, and I shall return to it in my conclusion. But there is more to say about the commentative text in Indology.

Certain metaphors appear in these Indological texts as constitutive of India and the West. The most important of these, from the standpoint of trying to understand how these commentative texts do their work, is the metaphor used to depict Indian thought itself. That metaphor, implicit in the text of Renou and other Indologists and used again and again, is the metaphor of the Other as a dreamer, as a neurotic, insane or mad man, one whose own representations of reality are made by his imagination rather than his reason. What better guide to this metaphoric realm can we find than Freud himself? His work on the dreams of his patients can help us to understand the ways in which orientalists from Hegel onward have constructed Indian thought as dream (3.2.2).

Freud argued that the report a person gives of his dreams is, in fact, a distorted representation of reality. It is a distorted reflection both of the external world of the dreamer and of his internal emotional world. The report of a dream, the 'manifest content' of a dream text, is a distorted representation of reality because the conscious reasoning which during waking hours represents the outer world to itself has, during sleep, ceased to do this. It has, at the same time, also lessened its grip on the unconscious emotions. The rational or intellectual operations of the mind are, as a result, pushed this way and that by its own irrational wishes (Freud, 1952: 93–6). Although Freud formulated this idea of a reasoning faculty dominated by desires in relation to dreams, he later extended it to cover not only the waking representations of neurotics but of the prescientific religious (or animistic) mind in general (Stevens, 1983: 30–4, 44, 56). It is here, of course, that the subject-matter of Freud and the orientalists overlap. Many Indologists would no doubt reject the more extravagant claims that Freud made about myth and religion, but that should not obscure the similarities in their discourses.

What is the precise nature of the distortions attributed to Indian thought in Indological accounts? Again, Freud furnishes useful terms. The distortions of a dream-text are the product of two primary sorts of mental activity, 'condensation' and 'displacement', and a secondary mental operation called, appropriately, 'secondary revision'. The first of these, condensation, causes each element in the manifest content of a dream to represent several elements in the latent content, the 'real' thoughts of the dream. At the same time, it also causes each thought in the latent content to be represented in several of the elements of the manifest content. The elements of the dream are 'overdetermined': the same part appears again and again. The second mental activity, displacement, the shifting of psychic intensity from the ideas to which it properly belongs, causes less important parts of the latent content to appear as more important than they really are in the manifest content and, conversely, makes the more important thoughts in the latent content seem almost inconsequential in the manifest dream text. Parts appear as wholes (synecdoche), associated elements appear as the entities with which they are associated (metonymy), and ideas are expressed not in their own form but in analogical form (metaphor) (Freud, 1952: 40–59; 1965: 312–44).

Let me return now to our Indological example. The Indian classification of rituals, as Renou construes it, is not a scientific, rational one. The product of a mind that leaps between the extremes of an occult mysticism and a finicky scholasticism, it is characterized by both of the forms of distortion described by Freud. All of the rites are but variations, one recalls, of a single archetype. The elements of one type of rite appear again and again in other types. The classification scheme is, in other words, overdetermined, uneconomical and incoherent in its organization.

The whole scheme also suffers from the other major form of distortion, displacement. Ritual texts, one assumes, contain the procedures for acts meant to be performed in order to obtain some religious objective. But not in Vedic India. There, the priestly mind makes up rituals which are not meant to be enacted while the priestly hand performs rituals that have no religious rationale. Thoughts that should have acts as their objects are displaced from those objects and turned back on to themselves, and ritual acts that should have goals are displaced from those goals and turned back on to the rites themselves. Where thoughts ought to be there are rites and where rites ought to be there are thoughts.

1.3.3 Explanatory or Interpretive Accounts

Many Indological texts do not go beyond the commentative in their representations. Many others, however, claim also to 'explain' or 'interpret'. This process, I would suggest, closely resembles what Freud called 'secondary revision' (or 'elaboration'). Operating after the condensation and displacement have done their work, it provides the confused dream text with an orderly façade (1952: 73–82; 1965: 526–46). Just as passages of comment frame those of description in an Indological account, so those of secondary revision frame, in turn, the commentative aspects of these texts. The condensation and displacement which Indologists attribute to the Indian mind in the characterizing passages of their texts make the thoughts and practices of the ancient Indian seem alien and stress his difference from the man of the West. Secondary revision in an account of

South Asia goes just the other way. It makes the strange and incoherent seem rational or normal. That rationality is, however, not attributed to the Indian mind. The Indologists themselves take credit for providing the orderly façade for Indian practices. Here scientific theorists – physical anthropologists, racial historians, historical materialists, comparative mythologists, social psychologists, historians of religion, structural-functional anthropologists, Parsonian sociologists, development economists, and psychoanalysts, too – truly come into their own. They all claim *their* ordering of the patient's material to be rational and not merely a rationalization.

Nearly all of these secondary revisions tend to be monistic, to concentrate on one sort of 'cause' or 'factor' to the exclusion of others. Which is to say that they are also almost invariably reductionist. Philosophical thought is reduced to the mythical, religion to psychology, the social or political to the economic, the cultural to the biological. The most important of these rationalizations for Indological discourse entails what I refer to as 'naturalist' assumptions. Evolutionism and functionalism, utilitarianism and a modern variant of that, behaviourism, are some of the strains of naturalism that have held sway in British and American studies of India.

As I have already indicated, not every Indologist has explicitly included secondary revisions in his account. Renou himself, although fully prepared to present the theories of others, remained rather sceptical of most such efforts, largely because he considered them too reductionist (Renou, 1968: 19–20, 47–8). On the whole, he preferred to leave his reader face to face with his representation of the disorderly Indian mind and its products unrationalized. Renou's refusal to theorize does not mean, however, that he avoided the naturalist assumptions of these reductionist theories. Renou consistently depicted Hinduism as a religion that has been unable to transcend the false knowledge and inferior practices of 'primitivism' (52–3, 109). Furthermore, the very fact that he did not provide his own secondary revisions or challenge those of others had the effect of permitting the theories of others to hold sway in the discipline. The point that Lorenzen makes about the empiricism of the early British orientalists applies also to the later Renou. Their works 'are characterized by a meticulous concern for accuracy, an exhaustive collection of all available facts, and an almost obsessive avoidance of systematic generalization and evaluation'. The difficulty with this profusion of 'factual' scholarship was, as Lorenzen correctly indicates, that 'Virtually none of them even tried to mount an effective counterattack against more popular imperialist interpretations of ancient Indian history and society' (Lorenzen, 1982: 86). The result is that the curious reader has had to turn elsewhere, to the work of others, to find those full 'interpretations', those texts that I refer to as secondary revisions. But this is, perhaps, beside the point, for the following reason. Renou, we have seen, attributed the same dreaming irrationality to the Indian mind that Hegel did.[42]

To summarize, the effect of the discursive work within Indology and the affiliated human sciences is first to present the reader in a supposedly descriptive passage with some 'facts' on the Other. The account then (or

[42] For the 'enlightenment' background of French Indology, see Murr (1983).

concurrently) represents the Other in commentative terms as radically different from the Self. It is a gross distortion of Self or the opposite of Self. Commentators articulate this difference with a metaphor, usually implicit, that of Indian thought as a dream. But this is itself disturbing, given the premise in orientalist (and social scientific) discourse of a unity of human nature, one that is exemplified or realized in Euro-American man. So these threatening differences are not allowed to remain. The Indological text also goes on to provide (or evoke) an explanation for the differences. These explanations or interpretations are almost always naturalistic (despite the fact that the most important explicator of things Indian in the world at large, Hegel, attributed these differences to the will of a Spirit). That is, they lie beyond, behind, or outside the consciousness and activity of the Others involved. It is necessary for the Other to be the way he or she is because of his or her environment, racial composition, or (inferior) place on the evolutionary scale. Once the reader comes to know the natural reason for the Other's otherness, the threat it poses is neutralized. The explanation is, thus, one that restores the unity of mankind, with Western man, essence of essences, as its perfect embodiment. It does this by hierarchizing the Others of the world, by placing them in a spatial, biological, or temporal scale of forms, one which always culminates in Homo Euro-Americanus.

1.3.4   Hegemonic Accounts

Every discipline has, within its particular historic formations, texts or accounts that can be dubbed 'hegemonic' in a Gramscian sense. They are the texts scholars and their administrative doubles in the world have used to build and maintain the hegemony of their discourses over other knowledges.

Although Collingwood's eristical relations are present within academic disciplines, in the form of 'required reading', and the examined syllabus (not to mention less savoury exploitations and threats), and, in the relationship of the academic to the lay public, in the form of expert mystification, much of the work that a hegemonic text does is dialectical. Description and commentary are not just self-reflections. They speak to others. Hegemonic texts appear to speak for, and to, not only the interests of the rulers but also those of the ruled, those of the authoritative philosopher or Indologist, as well as those of the lay reader and the beginning student. That is, the hegemonic text is an instrument not simply for browbeating those who demur but also for exercising a positive intellectual and moral leadership both within the educational institutions and in the other institutions that make and remake imperial formations. Even here, we need not assume that a hegemonic text is primarily designed or has the effect of maintaining the dominance of one class over another. Hegemonic texts are just as often as not used by fractions of the ruled against one another and are often taken as positions by the ruled among themselves around which to rally.

An Indological text that attains hegemonic status is, therefore, not concerned exclusively with the narrow issues internal to one of the pertinent disciplines, but with the broader questions of India's place in the world and in history, issues in which those outside a discipline, the active subjects of the world – business and government leaders – and the more passive subjects of the world's history, the populace at large, are interested. A hegemonic text is also totalizing – it provides an account of every aspect of Indian life even though its own focus may be on one topic such as caste or Hinduism or political history. It accounts for all the elements that the relevant knowing public wants to know about (Mouffe, 1979: 168–204). It is, finally, explanatory or interpretive as well as commentative (and descriptive) in its approach.

Certain accounts within the discipline of Indology or South Asian studies can, as I shall show, be considered as exercising hegemony therein under various circumstances. The question is, how does one decide which among the texts that meet these criteria of content, scope, and approach is hegemonic? It is usually one that is published (at least in this century) by a prestigious and authoritative press, such as a university or government press, and one that is bought in relatively large numbers and goes through several editions. One conventional way for determining importance (that appeals to positivists) is to count footnotes or references to it in other works. This might do up to a point, but it would be naïve to assume that the major assumptions and presuppositions traceable to Mill (or Hegel) are going to be footnoted. I would rather say that one must make this determination by seeing what position a text occupies in the field of knowledge (or more widely within a discursive formation) construed as a scale of forms. From this angle, a hegemonic text is one that has dialectically placed itself at the top of a scale of forms and is accorded that position. It is the account that contemporary and immediately subsequent scholarship deems to have created or transformed or summed up a particular field or topic, the one said to be most 'influential', the one with which would-be alternatives will have to contend. It is not, however, necessarily the one on which a more remote posterity settles. The members of a discipline have a well-known tendency, when they make historical statements about it, to sanitize its past. To end this chapter, I mention some of the main characters whose work has exercised hegemony among the knowers of India. I begin with the Indologists proper and then turn to those who hegemonized their work.

Sir William Jones (1746–94) was a lawyer and Persianist who received appointment as Judge of the Supreme Court at Calcutta and was an intimate of Warren Hastings (1732–1818), first Governor-General of Bengal, and is considered the first Englishman to have learnt Sanskrit. He is the man usually credited with first suggesting that Persian and the European languages were related to one another and not descended from Hebrew, as most had assumed. He was also the person largely responsible for founding the first Indological institution, the Asiatic Society of Bengal, in 1784. If any one person can be named as the founder of Indology, if any one man can be called the 'knowing subject' of the East India Company within the rising Anglo-French imperial formation, it is certainly he (Mukherjee, 1968: 80–90). Because he advocated the importance of studying Eastern languages and texts in India, he and some of his colleagues, most notably Henry Thomas Colebrooke (1765–1837), Professor of Hindu Law and Sanskrit at Fort William College in Calcutta, were dubbed 'orientalists'.[43]

---

[43] For Jones, see his *Works* (1807); and for Colebrooke, see his *Miscellaneous Essays* (1873).

Those who opposed these orientalists came to be known as 'Anglicists' because they argued that Western knowledge in English should displace the Eastern. The most notable of these opponents was the Utilitarian journalist, James Mill (1773–1836). Completed in 1817, his *The History of British India* is a model explanatory text of Utilitarian reductionism (Stokes, 1959: 47–80) and pre-Darwinian evolutionism (Burrow, 1970; 27–9, 42–9), and altogether a prime example of imperial knowledge (Iyer, 1983: 39–48, 115–24). It was, in large part, written as a refutation of some of Jones's ideas. The victory which Mill and his colleagues gained over the 'orientalists' in shaping the policies of the East India Company had the effect (hardly surprising given the convergence of Utilitarian thought with commercial and colonial objectives) of securing dominance for the views of Whigs and of the newer, more radical Utilitarians and political economists both in government practice and in the fledgling discipline of Indology. It is ironic that the founder of the European study of the civilization whose destiny was to be conquered should himself be overcome.

That victory had its effects within the small but growing group of scholars concerned with India. Jones, in addition to being grouped with the losing orientalists, failed to produce a single, comprehensive account of India. So his essays, well-written and rhetorically persuasive as many of them were, hardly constituted a hegemonic text. Mill's work, on the other hand, fulfilled those criteria without exception. Even though Mill himself (who worked for the East India Company but never visited India) can hardly be considered the founder of Indology, I would consider his *History* the oldest hegemonic account of India within the Anglo-French imperial formation.

Throughout the nineteenth century, Mill's *History* remained the hegemonic textbook of Indian history. Later Indologists have either (wittingly or not) reiterated his construct of India or they have (directly or indirectly) written their accounts as responses to it. To see both reiteration and response together in the same book, one has only to pick up a later edition of this work, the fifth (Mill, 1858), edited by the Sanskritist and orientalist, Horace Hayman Wilson (1789–1860).[44] Not the political radical that Mill was, Wilson took the stand of a post-Enlightenment Christian. He attempted in his long qualifying notes to 'claw back' this formative text not only to a more 'scholarly', removed position, but also to one which (like Jones's) saw parallels between the ancient religions of India and of Europe. Mill's text was not confined, however, to the studies of scholarly gentlemen. It was 'required reading' at Haileybury College, where, until 1855, civil servants of the East India Company were trained and where, incidentally, the first chair in political economy was established (Stokes, 1959: 87). It held sway within Indology, fending off the challenge posed to it by Mountstuart Elphinstone's *The History of India* (left unfinished in 1841) (1905), until 1904. That was the year in which Vincent Smith published his *Early*

[44] Reprinted by the University of Chicago Press in 1975 as a 'classic of British historical literature'. Arriving in Calcutta in 1808, Wilson studied Sanskrit and acted as Secretary to the Asiatic Society of Bengal. When he returned to England, he became the first Boden Professor of Sanskrit at Oxford in 1833, and Director of the Royal Asiatic Society in 1837. Something like a French equivalent of Mill's work is the account supposedly written by the Abbé J. A. Dubois (1906), on the authorship of which see Murr (1977).

History of India (1924). Smith's book became the hegemonic secondary revision of 'ancient' and 'early medieval' history of India for the next fifty years. But Mill's work was not completely set aside even then. Smith himself included selections from it in his chronologically more comprehensive *Oxford History of India* (1919) (Basham, 1961a: 217–29; 1961b: 266–74). If one were to name a successor to Smith, it would have to be the late A. L. Basham. His *The Wonder That Was India* (1954) acts as a bridge between the older condescending discourse of a Smith and the more egalitarian, euphemistic style of a post-imperialist era.[45] Indian attempts to counter the smaller Oxford and larger, multi-authored Cambridge History, never finished (1922–), such as the *An Advanced History of India* of R. C. Majumdar, H. C. Raychaudhuri, and K. K. Datta (1961) and *The History and Culture of the Indian People*, edited by R. C. Majumdar and still incomplete (1951–), might also be taken as hegemonic accounts, though they are confined mostly to the circle of Indian scholars.[46]

Here, just to give a taste of the way Mill depicted India, is a passage in which he talks about the topic Renou later dealt with, Hindu ceremonies:

To the rude mind, no other rule suggests itself for paying court to the Divine, than that for paying court to the Human Majesty; and as among a barbarous people, the forms of address, of respect, and compliment, are generally multiplied into a great variety of grotesque and frivolous ceremonies, so it happens with regard to their religious service. An endless succession of observances, in compliment to the god, is supposed to afford him the most exquisite delight; while the common discharge of the beneficent duties of life is regarded as an object of comparative indifference. It is unnecessary to cite instances in support of a representation, of which the whole history of the religion of most nations is a continual proof. (1858: I, 276–7)

Although more blunt than the later Renou, Mill was no different in resorting to the underlying metaphor of Indian thought as imaginary rather than empirical. The rationalization for Hindu 'excess' woven into his commentary consists of Mill's placement of Hindu civilization at an earlier time and lower 'stage' of evolution, the 'barbaric', than some (e.g. Jones) thought.

Bengali villagers say, in speaking of authority relations in their families, that 'Father has a father too.' So it is with hegemonic texts. Mill's History is to be counted the hegemonic text on India from within Indology, though he himself was not an Indologist. But there are still other works we must name, those that place India in a global scale of civilizations and cultures with the West at its apex. Those who performed this work were not the intellectually more insular

[45] He was Professor of South Asian History at the School of Oriental and African Studies, University of London, and then of Ancient Indian History at the Australian National University until his retirement in 1969. His *Wonder* is, he claimed, modelled after the *Antiquities of India* (1913) of his teacher, Lionel Barnett (1871–1960), Lecturer in Sanskrit and Ancient Indian History and Epigraphy at the School until 1948. Basham himself had helped to revise Smith's *Oxford History of India* for its third edition (1919).

[46] Majumdar was himself critical of many Indian practices from what we might call a Hindu Utilitarian perspective. More accessible is the two-volume *A History of India* (1966). Also a piece of bridgework, the first volume was written by Romila Thapar, the second by Percival Spear.

British but the Germans. The ringleader here was Hegel (1770–1831), who used Mill's account in his world history (1956). Cast into outer darkness by Bertrand Russell (1872–1970), the logical positivists, and Karl Popper (b. 1902), Hegel, a rationalist and idealist, has had a very bad reputation among the mostly empiricist and realist scholars of Britain and the US in this century. That is, he has been relegated to a low, negative, and marginal, yet dangerous position in the mid-twentieth-century scale of philosophical forms.[47] It is, therefore, not implausible to suggest that most Indologists in those countries have probably not read his lectures on the philosophy of history, which were first delivered in 1822–3.[48] Claiming to hierarchize Kant (who had claimed to synthesize the French rationalists and British empiricists), Hegel also found a place in his philosophical scale of ideas for the Romantics (see 2.3), though he rejected their dichotomy between an outer physical world and an inner mental life and claimed to see all the cultures of the world as manifesting an inner rationality in their outer institutions in an ever-developing rationality. Indeed, he was the thinker most explicitly to depict Indian thought as dream, as just prior to the awakening of subjective reason in human history, where India has remained ever since (see 3.2.2). He and Mill, along with other political economists, were also the intellectual ancestors of another hegemonic figure, Marx, who reproduced much of what they said but with an emphasis on the economic rather than the political. From their different peaks in overlapping scales of discursive forms, they consolidated and dispensed a discourse on oriental despotism and the Asiatic mode of production (see 2.2.1).

Thought-as-dream has been a constitutive metaphor in the study of India. Hegel's bold enunciation of the Indian imagination in his world history, in which he likens it to the working of the mind asleep, provides, therefore, an appropriate introduction to Indological discourse. The question I would ask, even at this juncture, is: whose thought is it that is dream-like in these commentative and explanatory texts, the Indians', to whom it is attributed, or the Indologists' themselves? It could well be that careful, empirical study of Indian texts and practices has indeed disclosed to us a culture whose bearers are lost in an irrational dream state. This is a difficult proposition to defend, however, because Europeans took dreaming irrationality as a distinctive trait of Indian thought *before* the field of Indological research was even established. I am not just referring to Hegel, with whose characterization I prefaced this chapter. The portrayal of India as a land of fabulous wealth, of miracles, of wishes fulfilled, a paradise of sensual pleasures and exotic philosophers, apparently constituted a reiterated theme in medieval thought. As Jacques Le

[47] For a brief review of Hegel's views and his treatment earlier in this century, see Cottingham (1984: 91–108). More extensive is the 'reading' of Taylor (1975: 389–427). On Hegel and Indian philosophy, consult Halbfass (1981: 104–21).
[48] Basham (1954: 487) mentions Hegel only in connection with the part his reading of Indian texts may have had in the development of his 'monism'. He does not, however, refer to him in his discussion of Indology (1954: 4–8). I rely on the admittedly bad English translation of Sibree (completed in 1857) because it is highly likely that the Indologists who have read Hegel on India have read this and not the German original. See also the recent edition and translation (Hegel, 1975).

48 *Knowledge of India and Human Agency*

Goff put it, 'A poor and limited world formed for itself an extravagant combinatoric dream of disquieting juxtapositions and concatenations' (Le Goff, 1980: 197). I am claiming that it is wrong to see Indian thought as essentially dreamlike and to view Indian civilization as inherently irrational. So it would be equally wrong to suggest that an unchanging dream of India as an exotic land is an essential feature of a hypostatized West. The dreams or images of medieval Europeans differed from those of the nineteenth-century scholar and imperialist. The medieval Europeans did not see India as an *inferior* land of the *past*, but as a *superior* land of the *future*, a paradisiac kingdom ruled by a priest-king, Prester John, who might, it was hoped, come to save Christendom (Rau, 1983: 205–6). Even so, this prehistory of Indology should make one sceptical of any argument that Indology has only represented Indian thought to the European and American 'as it really is'. But then how could the spokesmen for a politically ambitious West constitute themselves as possessors of a transcendent reason, as the instrument of an all-knowing spirit or nature, unless they could separate the Self's reason from its own imagination and dominate it in the form of a dreaming, riches-laden, effeminate Other?

2
India in Asia: The Caste Society

If it were possible to invent a method by which a few men sent from a distant country could hold such masses of people as the Hindoos in subjection, that method would be the institution of castes. There is no institution which can so effectually curb the ambition of genius, reconcile the individual more completely to his stations, and reduce the varieties of human character to such a state of insipid and monotonous tameness. (Reverend Sydney Smith, *Edinburgh Review* XIV, 1814)[1]

2.1 THE ORIENTS

The idea of India as the Asian land governed by a disorderly imagination instead of a world-ordering rationality has taken many forms and gone through many lives. Caste, the distinctive social institution attributed to India, is assumed to be its outer manifestation. Depictions of India's predominant religion, 'Hinduism', presuppose it. The picture of a 'medieval' Indian history as one of prolonged economic stagnation and political fragmentation has been theorized as its result (or, for some, its cause).

The idea of an India lost in dreams and divided into castes is not an isolate based on empirical research. It exists as part of a wider 'orientalist' discourse that not only distinguishes between India and the West but also among the lands in Asia itself that are still reproduced in the discourse of scholars today. To understand the India of this discourse we need to look briefly at the larger Orients in which scholarship and officialdom have embedded their Indias.

Europeans and North Americans have produced many overlapping images of 'the Orient' (*l'Orient, das Morgenland*) or 'the East' as the Other. Hegel was hardly the first European to construct a picture of Asia or the Orient as the Other in the medium of academic discourse. He and his contemporaries, particularly Friedrich Schlegel (1772–1828), amplifying on Johann Gottfried

---

[1] Quoted in Fisch (1985: 51–2).

Herder (1744–1803), were, however, the first, so far as I know, who made sharp and essential distinctions between the different parts of Asia.

Nowadays, terms like 'the Orient' or 'the East' are used very loosely, as in the past, to refer to Asia (which term itself has no Asian equivalents), but this is only one use to which these terms are put. The first of these terms (but not the second) is also employed at present to distinguish a 'Communist world', also known as 'the second world', from 'the free world'. The former, 'the East', dominated by the Soviet Union and including the nations of Eastern Europe and China, straddles both Europe and Asia. The latter, 'the West', assumed by its own leaders to be 'the first world', the part of the globe dominated by the United States and the countries of Western Europe, also includes (anomalously) an increasingly powerful nation of the East, Japan. The term 'the Orient' itself seems to have become something of a pejorative expression since the Second World War, especially among scholars and government officials. It continues to appear, though, in tourist brochures, where it is apparently meant to conjure up images of appropriately exotic opulence. This is the situation today. In the past, however, there was no reluctance on the part of European colonial administrators to use the term 'the Orient' and scholars spoke proudly of themselves as 'orientalists'.

They used the expression 'the Orient' (or 'the East') to paint two rather different pictures. One picture of the Orient, the older of the two, the one associated with the Hispano-Portuguese imperial formation, crudely but sharply distinguished a Christian Europe from an Islamic Asia. Here Europeans used the term 'the Orient' primarily to designate the peoples and lands dominated by the Ottoman Turks (1520–1807). This Orient embraced not only the lands of Anatolia ('Asia Minor'), the Levant and the Arabian Peninsula in Asia, but also Egypt in Africa. Parts of 'Christian' Europe – Albania, Bulgaria, and Greece itself, the *fons et origo* of European civilization – were also included within this Orient. The other parts of Asia, particularly Persia or Iran of the Safavids (1501–1736) and India of the Great Moguls (1526–1707), could be seen as vague extensions of this 'conception' in so far as they were constituted as Islamic polities, even though they lay outside the Ottoman sphere of influence. This is the Orient that was known as 'the Near East' (le proche Orient). With the addition of Iran and even Pakistan and Afghanistan to the east and of those parts of Muslim-dominated North Africa (Algeria and Tunisia) that lay outside the Ottoman domains to the west, it has come to be known today as 'the Middle East' (le moyen Orient).

The Hispano-Portuguese imperial presence in Asia, the Estado da India (from 1505 on), had been maritime and dispersive. With the rise of the Anglo-French imperial formation, dominance was greatly extended and knowledge of Asia changed. The German philosophers articulated another picture of the Orient which took its place beside the older one. It saw the Semitic Near East and Aryan Persia as sharing a fundamentally monotheistic and individualist culture with Christian Europe (and America) and contrasted this world with a more distant East, that comprising India and China (along with Japan and Central and South-East Asia). Hegel makes this distinction in no uncertain terms:

Asia separates itself into two parts – Hither [*hinter*] and Farther [*vorder*] Asia; which are essentially different from each other. While the Chinese and Hindoos – the two great nations of Farther Asia, already considered – belong to the strictly Asiatic, namely the Mongolian Race, and consequently possess a quite peculiar character, discrepant from ours; the nations of Hither Asia belong to the Caucasian, i.e., the European Stock. They are related to the West, while the Farther-asiatic peoples are perfectly isolated. The European who goes from Persia to India, observes, therefore, a prodigious contrast. Whereas in the former country he finds himself still somewhat at home, and meets with European dispositions, human virtues and human passions – as soon as he crosses the Indus (i.e., in the *latter* region), he encounters the most repellent characteristics, pervading every single feature of society. (1956: 173)[2]

This 'Farther Asia' is the Orient that has come to be known as 'the Far East' (l'extrême Orient), the Asia that is seen by Europeans and Americans as dominated by China (and, since the Second World War, by Japan). It is on this Orient I focus here.

Although India is integral to this construct of the Orient, she is only ambiguously included in the more restrictive idea of the Far East. India and her neighbours have for long been said to form a 'subcontinent' unto themselves within the larger Asian continent. It is very common today in academic and official circles to speak of the Indian subcontinent as 'South Asia', thereby distinguishing it from an 'East Asia' consisting of China, Japan, and Korea.

The features supposed to distinguish one region of Asia from the others in the imperial knowledges of Hegel and his successors depend on one another and interact in forming our images of Asia. We cannot, therefore, change our picture of one of the civilizations of the Orient without altering our picture of the others. This chapter is given over to a sketch of the place of India in Asia and of the feature – caste – alleged to distinguish it from the other Asian civilizations as well as from the West. I begin with a summary of the discourse that positioned India in the world from the point of view that predominated in Indology, as in the other branches of orientalism, that of empirical realism. Although Hegel was not himself an empirical realist, he occupies such an important place in the scale of forms that orientalists constructed that I include him here and in my treatment of the 'loyal opposition', that of the Romantic idealists.

2.2 EMPIRICAL, REAL INDIA: THE RULING IDEAS

2.2.1 Oriental Despotism and the Asiatic Mode of Production

The 'political economy' of Asia has a prominence in orientalist discourse second only to that given to the knowledges of the Orientals themelves. This

[2] Elsewhere in his essay (1956: 141–2) Hegel contradicts this neat division between Caucasian and Mongolian when he states that 'In recent times the discovery has been made that the Sanscrit lies at the foundation of all those further developments which form the languages of Europe', and even adds that 'India, moreover, was the centre of emigration for all the western world.' Hegel extracts himself from this philological embarrassment by declaiming that 'the diffusion of Indian culture is only a dumb, deedless expansion; that is, it presents no political action.' On the contrary, it has been the object of repeated conquest (see 2.2.2). The term Caucasian was itself relatively new, traceable to 1795 (Bernal, 1987: 219–20).

was not simply a matter of curiosity. Knowledge of the Asian states and economies was held essential to the project of that discourse in the eighteenth and nineteenth centuries – the removal of human agency from the autonomous Others of the East and placing it in the hands of the scholars and leaders of the West. This task was accomplished through the deployment of two ideas, 'oriental despotism' and the 'Asiatic mode of production', the very names of which seem to say that a place automatically gives rise to a distinctive type of state and economy. The concept of the Asian state as a despotic empire receives its first full formulation in Montesquieu (1949). To Marx (1964; 1968), who reproduced much of Hegel's view of the Orient, we owe of course the concept of the 'Asiatic mode of production'. There is a vast literature on these two related ideas.[3] For present purposes, I wish only to direct the reader to the excellent critique of the Asiatic mode by Hindess and Hirst (1975: 178–220) and especially of the Hegelian – and essentialist – aspects of the theory (203–6).[4]

The writings on these two troublesome examples of imperial knowledge are, in my analysis, both commentative and explanatory texts. They represent the peoples of Asia (and North Africa) as irrational and defective versions of their Western equivalents. Their major political and economic institutions all suffer from condensation and displacement (gods are made into kings and kings into gods: see chapter 5). At the same time, however, these accounts also rationalize or explain the practices of the East by resorting to naturalist and pre-Darwinian evolutionary arguments: Asiatic institutions are the outcome of racial conquests (or admixtures) and original adaptations to the environment peculiar to Asia.[5] The determinist assumption here is that past causes have their necessary present effects. So knowing the origin of something explains its essence. A more recent variant of these etiologies is functionalism. Strange political and economic practices are not so strange when one 'discovers' that they perform 'useful functions', filling a wide variety of psychological and social 'needs' or functions.

Here, in much abbreviated form, is a summary of the commentative and explanatory text of orientalist discourse relating to Eastern despotism.

Characterized by a salubrious mixture of topographic zones and a temperate climate, Western Europe is inhabited by temperate peoples of wide-ranging skills and organized into nations of a moderate to small size. Asia, with vast river valleys juxtaposed to its uplands and a climate either hot or cold, is inhabited by peoples of extreme temperament and organized into large empires. Because of these inherent differences, the political and economic institutions of Europe and Asia, and their accompanying religions, are also bound to be correspondingly

---

[3] The most accessible introduction to both ideas is to be found, with references, in Anderson (1979: 462–549). On India itself, see the rather disappointing essays by Thorner (1966) and Dumont (1966).

[4] Well worthwhile (and a complement to Said) is Turner's critique, following Hindess and Hirst, of the Asiatic mode in relation to Islam and developmental sociology (1978).

[5] Mandelbaum (1971: 97) points out, regarding the method of tracing resemblances to indicate common origins, that 'In fact, in philology it had already been used before Darwin in tracing genealogical connections among the Aryan (Indo-European) languages, and Darwin had cited this example in connection with the theory of organic evolution itself.'

and inherently different. A constitutional monarchy or republic is the characteristic political institution of the moderate or small nations of Europe and the
capitalist mode of production its characteristic economic institution. Despotism, the arbitrary or capricious rule by fear of an all-powerful autocrat over a
docile and servile populace, is the normal and distinctive political institution of
the East.[6] That elusive mode of production whereby the peasantry of the
immense Asian plains, distributed over innumerable, self-sufficient villages,
engages in a mixture of low-grade agriculture and handicrafts, makes over to
the despot the surplus of what it produces in the form of a tax, subsisting on the
remainder, is, as its name Asiatic proclaims, the distinctive economic (and
social) institution of the East.

If it makes sense for people to think and act in this apparently irrational
manner because, so runs our secondary revision, they are in a different place,
Asia, it also makes sense because they also belong to an earlier time, a prior
stage on the human developmental or evolutionary scale. Oriental despotism
and the Asiatic mode of production were, when they first appeared among the
peoples of the Nile, the Fertile Crescent, the Levant, and Persia, at the
forefront of the evolution of human civilization. They were the *Lux ex Oriente*
that is emblazoned on the old Oriental Institute at the University of Chicago.
After Alexander the Great's conquest of Asia, however, that Hegelian light
passed to the West itself. Europe continued to develop and change while Asia
remained, with the exception of a few dangerous outbursts on the part of Huns,
Arabs, Turks, and Mongols, more or less static. Changes there were, we read,
repetitive, and not, as in the West, cumulative or directional.

Fabian (1983: 31) argues that the 'denial of coevalness' has been a major
device of anthropological discourse to define the otherness of the peoples or
cultures at the very time that they are increasingly being brought into relation
with the European states. Here we have, in the 'primordialization' of an entire
continent, Asia, the most spectacular instance of this temporal distancing. A
temporal distinction is also made with respect to the two major divisions of
civilized Asia, the Middle East of Hither Asia and the Far East or Farther Asia.
Hegel made this distinction in his discussion of Persia:

With the Persian Empire we first enter on continuous History. The Persians are the first
Historical People; Persia was the first Empire that passed away. While China and India
remain stationary, and perpetuate a natural vegetative existence even to the present time,
this land has been subject to those developments and revolutions, which alone manifest a
historical condition. (1956: 173)

Although most of the earlier orientalists believed that Chinese and Indian
civilizations had arisen at about the same time as the Near Eastern, they also
held, with Hegel, that only the civilizations of the Near East had a major
contribution to make to world, that is Western, civilization. The civilizations of
China and India, despite their contributions of paper, printing, and gunpowder

---

[6] Talal Asad (1973: 103–18) shows how colonialist images of the Islamic states (which they
did not rule) emphasized repression, while those of the 'tribal' African states (over which they
did rule) emphasized consent as the essence of those states.

or of the zero and chess, lay to a large extent outside this evolutionary scheme. The Ottoman was a potentially dangerous Alter Ego of the European. His religion, Islam, was a false, fanatical cousin of Christianity and he continued to rule over parts of eastern Europe. But the Chinaman and Hindoo were the true Others. Both China and India were, thus, the opposites of the West. The traditions of each of these civilizations were, compared to those of the West, irrational formations. Yet China and India were also opposites in relation to one another, for the one was never truly conquered and dominated by another civilization, while the other was overrun again and again. The one was able to establish a political empire but could not (apart from Korea, Japan and Vietnam) export her culture; the other was able to extend a 'cultural empire' over all of Further Asia but was not able to achieve political unity (Lohuizen de Leeuw, 1970).

2.2.2   Conquest and the Unmaking of India

China, say the Sinologists, reached its fundamental shape under the early Han in the third century BC and continued to unfold, ever so slowly, until Sung times in the thirteenth century. Then came the failed attempt of the Mongols to govern China after conquering it. Subsequently, that civilization remained static, or even declined, falling way 'behind' the West.[7] Compare this with the pattern into which India's history has been cast by Indologists. India's history begins with the arrival there of the Aryans during the second millennium BC. No sooner, however, had India reached her full flower under the Mauryas in the fourth century BC, as an oriental despotism, than she – and recall that India is often considered feminine – began her decline. This downward turn was exacerbated (if not actually caused) by the invasions of the Hellenes, Scythians, and Turks during the first and second centuries BC and the first century AD. Although there was a renascence under the Guptas in the fourth and fifth centuries AD, the decline that set in after the intrusions of the Huns in the sixth century was never reversed. China was, in other words, the oriental despotism that mostly fended off conquest and succeeded; India was the oriental despotism that succumbed to conquest and failed.

It is worth pausing over this feature of conquest. It became an important part of the discourses on philology, ethnology, and world history in the nineteenth century. The myth of an original race of Aryan language speakers fanning out from the steppes of Central Asia to conquer not only India and Persia, but Mediterranean Europe as well was, for example, crucial in the attempt to construct Greece as a pure Aryan culture (Bernal, 1987: 330–6). But let us return to India. Mill had made this observation: 'It appears that the people of Hindustan have at all times been subject to incursions and conquest, by the nations contiguous to them on the north-west' (1858: II, 165). Conquerability thus appears to have been the feature that has distinguished India from China in orientalist discourse, but that is not quite the whole of it.

The Arab conquest of the Levant, North Africa, and Persia had virtually

---

[7] Consult, for example, the multi-authored 'China, History of' (1974); and Pulleybank (1970).

overwhelmed and destroyed the previously existing cultures of those places. But India was remarkable, for the repeated conquests of that subcontinent did not bring an end to her civilization or even, for that matter, produce any fundamental change in it. Mill asserted that Muslim rule in India 'had introduced new forms into some of the principal departments of state', but said that 'it had not greatly altered the texture of native society' (1858: II, 165). Similar statements are repeated many times over. Jawaharlal Nehru, writing more than 125 years later, cited with approval this statement of the Sanskritist Arthur Anthony Macdonell (1854–1930):

And in spite of successive waves of invasion and conquest by Persians, Greeks, Scythians, Muhammadans, the national development of the life and literature of the Indo-Aryan race remained practically unchecked and unmodified from without down to the era of British occupation. No other branch of the Indo-European stock has experienced an isolated evolution like this. (1951: 71)

What differentiated India, then, from China and the Near East was this paradoxical fact: outsiders beginning with the Aryans and ending with the British had conquered India again and again, but her ancient civilization had survived into the present more or less unchanged.

No better depiction of this paradox can, in my opinion, be found than in the painting of the French symbolist painter, Gustave Moreau (1826–98). Entitled 'The Triumph of Alexander the Great (Le Triomphe d'Alexandre le Grand)', it was apparently begun between 1880 and 1884 and left incomplete[8] (like all of the conquests of India themselves?).[9] The unfinished state of the canvas adds to the dream-like quality of the artist's depiction. It also makes the painting difficult for the camera, that ideal mirroring instrument of the representational theory of knowledge, to capture. Despite this difficulty, I think we can use it to see how the European *fin-de-siècle* visualized itself representing its own relation to an Other (keeping in mind that any interpretation of a painting will be underdetermined by its content). All of the features which Freud attributed to dreams are to be found at work here. The 'temple' in the background, with its 'idols', is itself a condensation of all the religious building and images of ancient India (Hindu, Buddhist, and Jain), combined together (from drawings of monuments at Elephanta, Sanchi, Ajanta, Mount Abu, Bhubaneshwar, and elsewhere) in a single structure. At the same time, these religions of mysticism and dread are all summed up in the giant, dark statue[10] that stands menacingly at the centre of the picture on a pedestal – he seems almost to levitate –

---

[8] This is why the captive people and the elephants at the centre of the canvas are indicated only in outline. Généviève Lacambre, Chief Conservationist of the Musée Gustave Moreau, has supplied the date, a correction of Mathieu (1976: 176).

[9] The painting, mostly in oil, is 1.55 metres square; number 70 in the Musée (Musée Gustave Moreau, Paris, 1983: 46). It 'borrows' from several sources, including the 'Triumph of Caesar' by Mantegna and, among works on India, James Burgess (1871); and Moreau had in his library Le Bon (1887: 200–2), which recounts Alexander's conquest.

[10] A Jaina image rather than one from Hinduism, the religion of India most Indologists considered her mental essence, but we can forgive this slight error.

separating the foreground scene of homage from the temple behind it. Alexander himself, whose white-clad figure dominates the foreground, at the right, is the only one seated. His throne, apparently assembled out of available materials on top of a small Buddhist chaitya (congregational hall) and surmounted by a Winged Victory, must be one of the most overdetermined chairs ever painted! The whole ensemble completely dwarfs the figure of the defeated King Porus, who stands, arm upraised in salute, in his chariot before his youthful, new overlord.

The Indian idol can be seen as displaying from within itself the lower, emotional depths of the human mind, the imagination that, Indology tells us, dominates in India. The figure of Alexander, on the other hand, can be taken to exemplify the world-ordering rationality of the West. We see in this canvas the triumph of the latter over the former. There is, however, something disturbing about this dream of the West (as there is in many of his works) that Moreau has depicted. The kings of India, the instruments of her mind, have clearly submitted; the women of India, the embodiment of her sensuous beauty and riches, have laid themselves at the feet of a triumphant West. Yet the immense monolith that embodies the mentality of the East, broad-shouldered and standing erect, faces serenely out over this passing moment of conquest, seemingly unaffected by it.[11] We can also see how in Moreau's notebook and on his easel the metaphor of Indian though as dream collapses back on itself. Is it *his* dreamy image of India that we see or does he simply mirror what is *there*?

2.2.3   Caste as Race

What in the nature of this civilization could possibly explain this seeming paradox? The answer discourses on India have given from at least the time of the Rev. Smith and the Utilitarian James Mill has been 'Caste', that institution considered peculiar to India, and particularly to India's distinctive religion, Hinduism. As one Indologist put it in his monograph on the subject, 'It has

---

[11] We might also ask how secure the position of this reason is when the imagination that depicts its triumph, itself a European institution, is able to master and subsume, as did Moreau, the classical skills – here he is the empiricist and rationalist – of drawing and composition? The artist himself made these notes about the work one year before his death:

> The young, victorious king commands a view of all the captive people, vanquished and cringing at his feet, overcome with fear and admiration. The little Indian valley where the immense and splendid throne is set up contains all of India, the temples with fantastic spires, the terrible idols, the sacred lakes, the caves full of mysteries and awes, this entire unknown and disturbing civilization, the great elephants surmounted by pagodas in which sacred dancing-girls are enclosed, all this mysterious and disquieting opulence, the priests, phantoms similar to the idols, the woman diviners, those thrown up by destiny, this entire people, spectral and silent, prostrates itself. And then one sees with it, in the distance, those great mountains of azure tinted with pink. There are those stony masses in the form of architecture (carved). There are those huge clumps of vegetation with the poisonous fragrances, and the young Greek holds out his sceptre toward the vanquished king as a sign of favour (mercy) and of sovereign protection.
>   And the soul of a radiant and proud Greece triumphs far off in the unexplored regions of dream and of mystery. (Mathieu, 1984: 107)

been found possible ... to regard it as the very soul of this somewhat indeterminate fluid collection of customs and beliefs which is called Hinduism' (Senart, 1930: 13). The hope here is that by 'finding' a permanent, stable, unitary nature, an essence, in that which appeared as just the opposite, knowledge and control would be forthcoming. The fact that the word for this Indian essence is, as almost every introduction to the subject points out, derived from the Portuguese, *casta*, seems not to disturb its solidity as the foundation of an entire civilization.[12]

This is not the place for a detailed history of intellectual practices regarding caste. What I will do in the remainder of this chapter is give an indication of how and why caste has been turned into an essence, into the substantialized agent of Indian society. I begin with the empiricist version of caste. I then look at the other of the two major perspectives in Indology, the Romantic idealist, and the hyper-rationalist perspective of Hegel. I have reserved some aspects of my critique for chapters 3, 4, and 5 because what Indological accounts say about caste is inseparable from what they say about Hinduism, villages, and the state, the other pillars of ancient India.

Mill asserted in his chapter on caste that 'The classification instituted by the author of the Hindu law is the first and simplest form of the division of labour and employments' (1858: I, 126). After listing off the four *varnas* – Brahman or priest, Kshatriya or warrior, Vaishya or merchant, and Shudra or servant (1858: I, 126–7) – Mill tells his reader that we have in caste the key to understanding India: 'On this division of the people, and the privileges or disadvantages annexed to the several castes, the whole frame of Hindu society so much depends that it is an object of primary importance and merits a full elucidation' (127). His description of the castes conflates the observations of European travellers with an ancient Indian text the Laws of Manu, the Adam of Hinduism. Composed 'in reality' by Brahman priests, this code-book (variously dated, but earlier than the 3rd century) was first translated into English by William Jones. Indologists ever since have taken it as seminal and authoritative. Mill pays most attention to these Brahmans, for he has the theory that the priesthood holds the 'greatest authority' in the 'lowest state of society' (128). Because India was a peculiarly unenlightened primitive society, one that had remained unchanged since the four castes and the thirty-six mixed castes appeared, one could only expect that it would exhibit a social order dominated by priests:

As the greater part of life among the Hindus is engrossed by the performance of an infinite and burdensome ritual, which extends to almost every hour of the day, and every function of nature and society, the Brahmens, who are the sole judges and directors in these complicated and endless duties, are rendered the uncontrollable masters of human life. (1858: I, 131)

As I shall show later in relation to the state (5.2), Mill thought of castes as group individuals motivated, in his theory of human nature, by endless desires

---

[12] One should not, however, conflate the earlier Portuguese ideas of race with those of the nineteenth-century British, French, and Germans.

to maximize their pleasures and especially to minimize the sensations of pain that might bombard them. Because India had no checks and balances built into its system of government, a despotic theocracy of those enemies of enlightened society, the greedy and deceitful priests (who, curiously enough, always come across as exemplary Utilitarian individuals) and of caste held sway. We are already familiar with the metaphor that animates Mill's discourse, that which likens the individual to the atom of a Newtonian cosmos. I will say no more about it here and pass on to a brief account of the high baroque in the empirical rendering of caste.

Not all of the early British concerned with India saw caste as exploitative and chaotic. Some of the more conservative, romantically inclined administrators early in the nineteenth century looked on caste as encapsulated in texts or villages as just the opposite, a marvellously cohesive if primitive form of social order (see 2.3.2 and 4.1). By the end of the century, however, the secular, empiricist view, infused with new life by racialist ideology, came to prevail (see also 3.5 and 4.2.3).[13]

The high-water mark in the empiricist study of caste was surely reached toward the end of this period, in those decades from 1891 to 1931, in which the Census of India came into its own.[14] Herbert H. Risley (1851–1911), Commissioner for the 1901 Census,[15] wrote the section of the Report of that Census on caste. Large portions of it (*Census of India, 1901*, 1903: I (Pt. 1, Report), 489–557) are reprinted in his *People of India* (1915) (published in 1908 one year after he was knighted) and in the widely distributed official *Imperial Gazetteer of India* (1907–9: I, 238–348). Within narrower academic and administrative confines, his surveys, with a Superintendent of Ethnography appointed for each of the Presidencies and Provinces, were the progenitors of a large brood of studies, 'The Tribes and Castes of . . . [Virtually Everywhere]'. His own study of Bengal (1891b) was the model eldest son for the project.[16] Cadet lines of this ethnological horde invariably found their way into the regional Gazetteers. Students can be seen to this day seriously poring over these volumes as they prepare their research papers. Here in these tomes of alphabetized empiricism, then, is to be found what I would refer to as the hegemonic discourse on caste of the Anglo-French imperial formation. Previous accounts of caste had been drawn from texts composed by the self-serving

[13] On the British construction of caste, see the excellent article by Richard Saumarez Smith (1985).

[14] The Censuses of 1872 and 1881 were very tentative affairs; that of 1941 was very much truncated by the War; the first Census taken by the government of India under Indian leadership decided to abandon 'caste' as a category, although retaining the notion of 'backward' or 'scheduled' classes and tribes.

[15] Arriving in India in 1873, he soon established himself as an expert in ethnology, becoming Honorary Director of the Ethnological Survey of the Indian Empire in 1903.

[16] It consisted of an Ethnographic Glossary and Anthropometric Data, each in 2 vols; the 'Introductory Essay' appears to have been the basis for his longer essay in the Census Report. On the background to the survey, see the introductory essay, pp. ii–xv; he says in the preface: 'The following volumes contain the results of what is I believe, the first attempt to apply to Indian ethnography the methods of systematic research sanctioned by the authority of European anthropologists.'

Brahmans or had been anecdotal, penned by Western travellers, missionaries, or revenue collectors. Now we were to have truly systematic and scientific, that is, quantitative knowledge of India's essence.[17]

Earlier writers on caste had imagined that the caste system they saw before them was either a remarkably preserved descendant of the ancient Aryan system of four *varnas*, caste in the sense of what I call estate, or a degenerate form of it that had turned into a caste society as a result of its isolation in the subcontinent or of finding itself in a tropical climate. Risley agreed with his predecessors on the importance of caste, but he was concerned to get at the real, empirical castes. These, he thought, were the localized, hereditary, endogamous (in-marrying) groups the *jātis*, rather than the bookish *varnas*. Risley also agreed with the view that caste was a stunted and strange post-tribal growth, but he departed from the older environmentalist idea that it was essentially an Aryan institution gone astray in the jungles of India. He argued instead that caste was the result of interactions between two racial types, a white and a black.[18]

Philologists had already concluded that many of the inhabitants of India, especially in the south and in the remoter parts of central India, were speakers of languages that were non-Aryan in origin and inferior in linguistic terms. The Rev. Robert Caldwell (1814–91) used the term Dravidian (from the Sanskrit, Dravida, used to name a country or people in south India and to distinguish peninsular India north India or Uttarāpatha or south India from the Deccan or Daksiṇapātha and the north) to designate, one might say invent, a new family of languages. He argued that the Dravidian languages are 'essentially different from, and independent of, Sanskrit' (1875/1913: 67). They are, he held, affiliated

[17] Risley describes (195: 109–10) the process whereby the results on caste in the Census were obtained. Assuming that language ought to refer to or mirror external realities, he tells his reader that 'In a country where the accident of birth determines irrevocably the whole course of a man's social and domestic relations … one is tempted at first sight to assume that the one thing he may be expected to know with certainty, and to disclose without much reluctance, is the name of the caste, tribe, or race to which he belongs' (109). Determinate social realities in India do not, however, seem to have had determinate linguistic effects. Risley declares that 'no column in the Census schedule displays a more bewildering variety of entries, or gives so much trouble to the enumerating and testing staff and to the central offices which compile the results' (109). The science of ethnology was not, however, to be thwarted. It would produce the knowledge that would not automatically reflect itself in ethnology's mirror: '[the] various alternatives, which are far from exhausting the possibilities of the situation undergo a series of transformations at the hands of the more or less illiterate enumerator who writes them down in his own vernacular, and of the abstractor in the central office who transliterates them into English. Then begins a laborious and most difficult process of sorting, referencing, cross-referencing, and corresponding with local authorities, which ultimately result in the compilation of a table …' (109–10). The results: 2,378 main castes and tribes and 43 races or nationalities were recorded. As if the Census authorities had not created enough trouble for themselves, Risley decided to arrange the castes in the Census not in alphabetic or some other order, but by 'social precedence as recognized by native public opinion …' (111). The mountain of petitions and polemical literature concerning caste standing that this act generated continues to have its effect to this day.

[18] The evolutionary ideas of the philosopher Herbert Spencer (1820–1903), and of the Social Darwinists (whose ideas are sometimes at odds with Darwin's), translated on to competing or warring castes and races, may, indirectly, be at work here. For context, see Howard (1982) and Mandelbaum (1971: 77–92).

with what he calls the Scythian more than with the Indo-European languages. Apart from his use of the term Scythian, Caldwell seems to have accepted the theory of language classification and development advocated by, among others, Max Müller. He distinguished three kinds of language or three stages in the formation of speech. First is one where roots are used as words; these are also called monosyllabic or isolating languages; this kind is equivalent to the radical stage in the formation of speech; of it Chinese is the best representative. Speakers of the second kind join two roots to form words, and in these compounds one root may lose its independence; these are also called agglutinative languages; this kind is equivalent to the terminational stage in the formation of speech; of it the Turanian languages are the representatives. In the third kind of language, two roots are joined, and both may lose their independence; this kind is equivalent to the inflectional stage in the formation of speech; of it the best representatives are the Aryan and Semitic language families (1864: I, 298–300).

Caldwell could be cautious in his speculations about the relations of the Aryan and Dravidian races (1875/1913: 107–11) and Müller could criticize Risley and others for conflating racial and philological terms (1898b: I, 230; 1898a: I, 257). But we should not be misled by this into thinking that these scholars were anti-racist'.[19] They did not have to rely on a theory of race as such, for they had their own global theory that was fully able to inferiorize the languages (and by implication the cultures) of the Other purely on linguistic grounds. Müller's linguistic taxonomy was a Hegelian hierarchy in which kinds (in space) are equated with stages (in time), making cultural geography the same as world history. One should also note that languages became more rational and spiritual as one moved to the top of this hierarchy.

Risley, though unwilling to abandon the use of linguistic terms as racial designations, was quite prepared to argue that language might be reducible to race.[20] His contribution to ethnology construes non-Aryans as inferior races responsible for the origin of caste. He opens his explanatory account with a description of a carved relief at Sanchi reputed to show racial consciousness on the part of ancient Indians (which, notes Crooke, his editor, is disputed). Risley then tells his readers what his project is:

An attempt is made in the following pages to show that the race sentiment which inspired this curious sculpture, rests upon a foundation of facts which can be verified by scientific methods; that it supplied the motive principle of caste; that it continues, in the form of fiction or tradition, to shape the most modern developments of the system; and, finally, that its influence has tended to preserve in comparative purity the types which it favours. (1908/1915: 5)

This passage is typical of the way Risley proceeds. Scientist though he is, he is not a crude positivist; he does not leave out of his account Indian ideas and

---

[19] Müller allowed that: 'It may be that in time the classification of skulls, hair, eyes, and skin may be brought into harmony with the classification of language. We may even go so far as to admit, as a postulate, that the two must have run parallel, at least in the beginning of all things' (1898a: I, 241).
[20] 'That some races produce sounds which other races can only imitate imperfectly is a matter of common observation, and may reasonably be ascribed to differences of vocal machinery' (1915: 9).

perceptions. These, too, are part of his object of study – not, however, as parts of Indian discourse that have their own objects, but as distorted or partial representations of reality.

Risley was an enthusiastic proponent of the science of anthropometry, now called physical anthropology, a science adhering to the theory that the 'proportions of the head serve to mark off important groups' (1915: 26). The quest of that science, to discover the biological essence of society,[21] was paralleled by the widely practiced science of phrenology, which claimed to be able to locate the biological essence of the individual in the various parts of his or her brain (Hedderly, 1970). Risley's science, which seems objectionable today, does not seem so strange if we keep this background in mind. India was, in his view, an ideal place for carrying out anthropometry which, like phrenology, was centred on measuring the human head, because of the 'operation of the caste system', which he held to be confined to India in its 'most highly developed form'. Its effect there was that 'differences of physical type ... may be expected to manifest a high degree of persistence' (1915: 25). This is how Risley compares India's racial history with Europe's:

all the recognized nations of Europe are the result of a process of unrestricted crossing which has fused a number of distinct tribal types into a more or less definable national type. In India the process of fusion has long ago been arrested, and the degree of progress which it had made up to the point at which it ceased to operate is expressed in the physical characteristics of the groups which have been formed. There is consequently no national type and no nation or even nationality in the ordinary sense of these words. (1915: 26)

Risley asserts that his racial types are not to be equated with the languages after which he names them, and cautions his readers not to see correlations between head shapes and intelligence. None the less, the retarded racial history that he has provided for India enables him to reach conclusions such as this, with respect to racial characteristics and their social manifestations:

Thus, for those parts of India where there is an appreciable strain of Dravidian blood it is scarcely a paradox to lay down, as a law of the caste organization, that the social status of the members of a particular group varies in inverse ratio to the mean relative width of their noses. (1915: 29)

Risley went even further than this in an earlier essay, stating that 'The remarkable correspondence between the gradations of type as brought out by certain indices and the gradations of social precedence further enables us to conclude that *community of race*, and not, as has frequently been argued, *community of function*, is the real determining principle, the true *causa causans*, of the caste system' (1891a: 259).

Not everyone involved in the Census agreed with Risley. There were sharp

[21] Müller pronounced in this regard that 'The skull, as the shell of the brain, has by many students been supposed to betray something of the spiritual essence of man; and who can doubt that the general features of the skull, if taken in large averages, do correspond to the general features of human character?' (1898a: I, 233).

differences of opinion on many issues, including Risley's racialist hypothesis. For example, one Surgeon Captain Drake-Brockman, who undertook detailed anthropometric measurements in the United Provinces, concluded that the differences between higher and lower castes were slight, 'a fact which tends to prove beyond doubt that the racial origin of all must have been similar, and that the foundation upon which the whole caste system in India is based, is that of function and not upon any real or appreciable difference of blood' (Crooke, 1896: I, xxxiii). Apparently, those with divergent theories about the origin and essence of caste could come up through this 'exact' science with equally divergent nasal indices.

Such objections made Risley tread more lightly, but they did not stop him. He first describes, after his introduction to the subject, the seven racial or ethnic types that he has 'scientifically' established. He works with a simple taxonomy that constitutes the Dravidian and the Aryan as the opposite racial types of India (with a dog's leg of a type called Mongoloid that is partly intermediate between the two and partly not Indian at all). The one is snub-nosed, shorter, and darker, the other sharp-nosed, taller, and fairer.

He then turns to an account of the 'social' types. These are also seven in number. Risley is careful (as a good scientist ought to be) not to push his claims too far, so he issues the usual warning about complexities and exceptions. Nevertheless, asserts the Census Commissioner, resorting to a hidden metaphor of caste as a sponge, the 'correspondence between the two sets of groupings is sufficiently close to warrant the conjecture, that each type was originally organized on a character-istic tribal basis and that, where tribes have disappeared, their disappearance has been effected by caste insensibly absorbing and transforming the tribal divisions which it found in possession of particular localities' (1915: 62). So, continues our intrepid researcher, 'In describing the varieties of tribes I shall therefore follow the ethnic types already determined by physical character-istics.' Risley then describes these tribal types, in the order of their primitive-ness, beginning with the Dravidian who, we have earlier been told, has 'labour' as his 'birthright' and who does human sacrifices to an earth goddess (45).

Risley proceeds up his chain of racial being, turning to caste when he gets to the highest or Aryan type.[22] The 'definition' of caste that he provides is one he wrote against his definition of tribe. Both consist of 'a collection of families or groups of families bearing a common name' and 'claiming common descent from a mythical ancestor'. The differences between the two may be summar-ized as follows. Tribes have distinct territories; castes have distinct professions. The former may, as groups, not be 'endogamous', the latter definitely are (1915: 62, 68). Risley did this, of course, because he believed that just as tribe was a development out of race, so caste was a development out of tribe. There is nothing strange in this, given the evolutionary thinking of the day.[23]

---

[22] There are also seven types of caste: (1) tribal, including Gujar, Jat, Rajput, Maratha, Chandal (Namasudra), Kaibartta, Nayar, Vellala; (2) functional; (3) sectarian; (4) by crossing, cf. Manu; (5) national (a puzzler, this, since castes are supposed to preclude nationality); (6) by migration; and (7) by changes of custom (1915: 69–91).

[23] Compare the definition of the French Indologist Senart (1847–1928), who saw castes as closed corporations which developed into city-states in Europe, castes in India (1930).

What is strange, however, is that the development of caste in India differed from developments elsewhere. 'When tribes are left to themselves', Risley pronounces, 'they exhibit no inborn tendency to crystallize into castes.' Then comes the contrast: 'In Europe, indeed, the movement has been all in the opposite direction. The tribes consolidated into nations; they did not sink into the political impotence of caste' (1915: 272–3). Risley implies here that caste retains the divided, natural form of the preceding tribal organization, while the nation becomes united and consciously political. Indian civilization, the caste society, remains, in a word, post-tribal. But we do not any longer see it as an Aryan and superior form of social organization frozen in time because it got lost in the tropics. We see a type of society that is decidedly inferior because of its repeated contamination by the polar opposites of the Aryans, the Dravidians. This was an important shift which I take up again in looking at religion (3.5) and at the institution which Indology made almost inseparable from caste, the village (4.2.3).

So now we come to the Big Question: why should this unique and politically divisive caste have become India's essence? The empiricist Risley will not provide us with a grand origin; we will have to settle for decisive factors or elements. Two of these operated, according to Risley, in the growth of caste sentiment, 'a basis of fact and a superstructure of fiction. The former is widespread if not universal; the latter is peculiar to India' (1915: 273). Risley then rehearses the theory, which he shared with others of his day, of the conquest of one race by another, the notion of 'hypergamy' or the acceptance of daughters from the inferior by the men of the superior race, and the formation of half-breeds that results from this practice. Here he concludes:

This is a rough statement of what may be taken to be the ultimate basis of caste, a basis of fact common to India and to certain stages of society all over the world. The principle upon which the system rests is the sense of distinctions of race indicated by differences of colour: a sense which, while too weak to preclude the men of the dominant race from intercourse with the women whom they have captured, is still strong enough to make it out of the question that they should admit the men whom they have conquered to equal rights in the matter of marriage. (1915: 275)

In his earlier book on Bengal, Risley had been bolder and more specific, arguing that 'in India alone were the Aryans brought into close contact with an unequivocally black race', and, after citing evidence from the *Vedas*, supposedly the earliest texts of the Aryans, in his support, he had concluded that 'the motive principle of Indian caste is to be sought in the antipathy of the higher race for the lower, of the fair-skinned Aryan for the black Dravidian' (1891b: I, xxxviii). For Risley, then, it was the antagonism between dichotomously opposed races, the Aryan and Dravidian, that distinguished the racial history of India from elsewhere and accounted for the rise of its peculiar institution.

This was the 'fact'. The fictional superstructure (which idea he took from Henry Maine (1907: 56–7, 219–20)) consisted of the 'myth' of four castes (*varnas*), the distorted Brahmanical representation of caste. The fiction embodied in this myth, says Risley, in a satement that constitutes a classic example of the displacement of nineteenth-century European racism on to those who are its victims, is that all social differences are reducible to racial differences:

Once started in India, the principle was strengthened, perpetuated, and extended to all ranks of society by the fiction that people who speak a different language, dwell in a different district, worship different gods, eat different food, observe different social customs, follow a different profession, or practise the same profession in a slightly different way must be so unmistakably aliens by blood that intermarriage with them is a thing not to be thought of. (Risley, 1915: 275)

So far, Risley has not strayed from the Social Darwinian path. The fictions to which he refers are not autonomous mental facts; they are themselves part of the material, evolutionary process.[24] Risley is not, however, quite finished.

The very next thing he does is distance himself a little from the evolutionist cosmology to which he was primarily committed and turn to that favourite topic of Indologists, the Brahmanical mind:

However this may be, it is clear that the growth of the caste instinct must have been greatly promoted and stimulated by certain characteristic peculiarities of the Indian intellect – its lax hold of facts, its indifference to action, its absorption in dreams, its exaggerated reverence for tradition, its passion for endless division and subdivision, its acute sense of minute technical distinctions, its pedantic tendency to press a principle to its farthest logical conclusion, and its remarkable capacity for imitating and adapting social ideas and usages of whatever origin. (Risley, 1908/1915: 275–6)

Like that of so many of his contemporaries, Risley's discourse presupposes a dichotomy of the material and ideal, the empirical and the metaphysical, base and superstructure. As a scientist and materialist, Risley would like to make his reductionist move and tell his readers that the imaginative Indian mind was largely the outcome of India's arrested racial development, but he has got cold feet and apparently decided, perhaps unconsciously, to placate those of an idealist bent, such as the philologist Max Müller. We shall see in a moment of what the idealist views consisted, and how the idealists constructed their image of caste. Let me here, however, conclude by asking what the point of Risley's discourse was.

Risley himself tells us when he turns in his book to the question of caste and nationality (1915: 278–301). Ever the empiricist and realist, Risley was suspicious of the 'idea of nationality' as the basis of national unity. He considered that it 'is in itself nothing more than an impalpable mental attitude, a subjective conviction, which may subsist independently of any objective reality, a fine flower of sentiment, springing from an unknown germ and nourished on Māyā or illusion'. However idealist, it was not to be dismissed, for 'once planted on Indian soil it may spread far and wide as its seeds are blown hither and thither by the breath of popular imagination' (1915: 299). To the extent that

---

[24] Risley had, in the earlier version of the essay, taken this position, arguing 'that the Indian caste system is a highly developed expression of the primitive principle of *taboo*', which principle 'derived its initial force from the sense of difference of race', but whose 'subsequent development' was due to 'a series of fictions' (1891a: 260).

there was any national feeling in India, he held, it was due to the use of the English language and the employment of Indians in the English administration. These were the very people who were trying to disseminate a fake notion of nationality, which he compares to the false idea of the four castes propagated by the Brahmans. What he refers to as 'genuine nationalities' had to be the 'product of common character and common experience' (1915: 299–300). This, in turn, was to be arrived at in India, as in Japan, by development of village communities and institutions – 'common property of the Aryan people both in Europe and in India' (1915: 300–1).

This would, however, be a difficult goal to accomplish because of the form of government necessitated by the caste type of society. Drawing upon an article of the philologist A. M. T. Jackson, Risley declaimed that:

exclusion of most of the castes from politics left little room for the growth of feelings of common interest and public spirit; secondly, the efficiency of the governing section became of immense importance. Only if this section were strong could it perform its function of keeping each caste to its proper duties, and thereby combine the parts into an organic whole; while if it were weak, society would fall apart into disconnected atoms. Anarchy is the particular peril of a society that is organized on the basis of caste, and the dread of anarchy leads to monarchy as the strongest defence against it. (1915: 285)

The problem implicit in this solution, of course, was that monarchy could not come from inside India. The Rev. Sydney Smyth (at the head of this chapter) had revealed this to his readers one hundred years before Risley when he asserted that the 'invention' of caste made Indians the pliable subjects of conquerors. Fortunately, the paternal, centralized administration that the British themselves had established in the subcontinent by Risley's time would provide the way out of India's developmental impasse. Vincent Smith, the historian, would even provide this alien monarchy with an ancient pedigree (5.4).

Time and again the message that caste equalled political impotence was hammered home, not just by academics looking over their shoulders at other academics with other reductionist axes to grind, but by administrators and journalists. Let us look at one fairly typical statement. Valentine Chirol (1852–1929), traveller and journalist who wrote on Indian 'problems' between the world wars, stated that 'Hinduism could not build up a nation because the one vital structure which it did build up was the negation of everything that constitutes a nation' (1926: 33). He spells this out, making it quite clear that caste membership precluded or displaced citizenship:

The fundamental laws which governed Hindu society as a whole were personal laws bound up with caste, which took no account of the territorial limits of the many states into which it was from time to time politically split up. The allegiance rendered to the rulers of those states by their Hindu subjects was secondary to the loyalty each owed to his caste since his caste was his *Karma*, determining much more than his present life, namely, all his lives still to come.

Caste caused perennial fragmentation at the interstatal level, making India easy prey for the unified Muslims as the earlier part of her 'middle ages' drew to a close:

There could never grow up between states, each made up of an infinity of separate and to a great extent independent and even conflicting units, any real sense of paramount national solidarity, and because Hinduism failed to create an Indian nation, the peoples of India were helpless to resist the first great onslaught of foreign invaders professing a very different creed, which at least taught Mohammedans of every race and class and condition that they were all equal and one in the great brotherhood of Islam. (1926: 33–4)

We cannot be sure that castes had multiplied and crystallized by the time India gained independence, but I think we can safely say that empiricist accounts of caste had. Caste had become essentialized and turned into the substantialized agent of India's history. In order to see how this latter process was effected, we should turn from the hegemonic view of caste, which incorporates this notion, to an examination of the Romantic idealist vision of India and of its construct of caste.

2.3   ROMANTIC INDIA

2.3.1   The Loyal Opposition

So far I have concentrated on the hegemonic scholarly views in Indology, those that might loosely be labelled – Hegel apart – empiricist in their epistemological assumptions and realist in their ontological assumptions. Given the British presence, they were also often Utilitarian and secularist in outlook. These were hardly all consistent with one another. One variant of them, for instance, was the position of post-Enlightenment Christian scholars who, while mostly assuming the epistemology and ontology of the secularists, superimposed a religious idealism. Quite often the presuppositions shifted, in different contexts even within the same work, from one of these epistemologies to the other. None the less, there is a definite thread in this discursive formation, the one I have referred to, following Bhaskar (1979: 25), as 'empirical realism'. Its strongest proponents, to be found in economics and psychology, dealt with constructing a positive science of the determinate – those external forces (social structures) or inner urges (human nature) that stand outside (underneath, behind?) agents' consciousness.

There have, however, always been seemingly opposed views within Indology. They parallel, within the human sciences, a minority position to which Bhaskar attaches the label of 'sociological individualism' (1979: 25–6). This perspective is to be found among those in sociology and anthropology, and the history of religions, who deal with the indeterminate – conscious intentions and meanings. The alternative views of India can be referred to as Romantic and spiritualist. One could also distinguish them as philosophical idealist rather than religious idealist because they do not usually involve the advocacy of denominational Christianity. I say that these views are seemingly opposed because their adherents do not, by and large, disagree with the empirical realists over the content of the construction itself. The German Sanskritist whose views on philology, mythology, and India were most often heard by an English-speaking public in the latter half of the nineteenth century, Max Müller, was, as we have seen (1.1.2), as much an empiricist or positivist as he was an idealist (Halbfass, 1981: 151–3).

The Romantics, too, agree that India is Europe's opposite. Where the Romantics do differ is in the evaluation placed upon India's civilization by the adherents of the secularist, empiricist view. The Romantics take those very features of Indian civilization which the utilitarian-minded find wasteful, deluded, or even repulsive and criticize – ascetic practices, philosophies, cosmologies, customs, visual art forms – and find them worthy of study and perhaps even of praise.

The Romantic image of India is no latecomer to Indology. On the contrary, it was there at the very creation of it. Sir William Jones, the founder of the discipline of Indology and chief of the 'orientalists', was not himself a Romantic, as the critical discussion of S. N. Mukherjee shows (1959: 42–4). Peter Marshall likewise distinguishes Jones and his eighteenth-century colleagues from the Romantics when he says:

As Europeans have always tended to do, they created Hinduism in their own image. Their study of Hinduism confirmed their beliefs, and Hindus emerged from their work as adhering to something akin to undogmatic Protestantism. Later generations of Europeans, interested themselves in mysticism, were able to portray the Hindus as mystics. (1970: 43–4)

Jones can, none the less, be seen as the founder of the minority view within his own discipline.

The first full-fledged Romantics among the Indologists are to be found not in England, but in Germany, where interest in pantheism on the part of post-Kantian idealists and in the work of Johann Gottfried Herder in the philosophy of history converged with the knowledge of the Indian ancients that the early Sanskritists thought they had discovered.[25]

Foremost among these was Friedrich Schlegel, whose older brother, August Wilhelm (1767–1845), was an orientalist.[26] Romantics typically took the stance not of supporters of Western values and institutions, but of critics of them. Yet Romantics do not necessarily (or usually) accept those of the East as ready-made substitutes. Rather, they situate themselves between or outside of *either*, considering both as somehow embodying the antinomies of 'human nature', the extremes to which men have gone. So the younger Schlegel begins his assessment of Indian philosophy in his world history, delivered as a series of lectures in Vienna in 1828, with praise, saying that 'this philosophy contains a multitude of the sublimest reflections on the separation from all earthly things,

[25] On the earlier French scholars, whom I have neglected here, see Schwab (1984). More recent is Biès (1973). For a (philosophically) critical review of the various American, mostly idealist, appropriations of Indian philosophy, see Riepe (1970).
[26] Consult, for Herder and the early German Romantics, Glasenapp (1960: 14–32) and Halbfass (1981: 86–103); for Schlegel, see Bernal (1987: 227–33).

and on the union with the God-head; and there is no high conception in this department of metaphysics, unknown to the Hindoos'. He then issues a mental health warning: 'But this absorption of all thought and all consciousness in God – this solitary enduring feeling of internal and eternal union with the Deity, they have carried to a pitch and extreme that may almost be called a moral and intellectual self-annihilation. This is the same philosophy, though in a different form, which in the history of European intellect and science, has received the denomination of *mysticism*' (1890: 160).

Like the empirical realists, the Romantics also held that there is a single reality, a single human nature or a single typology of human societies. They differed, however, on two major points. First, they held that it was not something abstract and fixed but something specific and changing. Second, they argued that neither the West nor the East exemplified it to the exclusion of the other. The features that constitute human nature are, for the Romantics, distributive and not, as they are for the empiricist and rationalist, cumulative in Western man. It would seem, therefore, that no society as such could embody the whole of human nature, unless all its members had first become transformed by understanding of the Eastern or Western Other. Accordingly, we find Schlegel arguing that humanity had a common origin, but that when it divided into separate nations, each with its own language, the four primary faculties of the human mind came to predominate in each of what he saw as the four major nations of the 'primitive' world, in the first epoch of human history, that is, before the rise of the universal empire of the Persians, in whom the four faculties were, for a time, reunited (Schlegel, 1890: 162–6, 172–3).

One might think that the Romantic views of India would be less substantialist with respect to human agency than that of the positivists, but this is not so. The Romantics disagreed with the empiricist or materialist in seeing human life as shaped in the last instance by a *material* reality that is *external* to it. They argued instead that it is shaped by a *spiritual* reality that is *internal*. That is why Schlegel has already focused not on institutions, but on faculties of mind as the defining features of the four nations of ancient world. The four faculties, ordered in two pairs, were Understanding and Will, Reason and Imagination, and the four nations were the Egyptian, Hebrew, Chinese, and Indian. Among the Egyptians and Hebrews, Understanding and Will were, respectively, the predominating faculties, while among the Chinese and Indians, they were, respectively, Reason and Imagination. China, the land of Reason, was seen as an example of benevolent despotism by enlightenment thinkers. But Schlegel considered it a nation where reason had become egoistical. India, on the other hand, was the land of Imagination. The preponderance of that faculty over reason is used by Schlegel to 'explain' the distinctive attributes of that nation, initially comparing India with China and, in passing, Egypt and Greece:

Equally, and even more strongly, apparent is the predominance of the imaginative faculty among the Indians, as is seen even in their science and that peculiar tendency to mysticism which this faculty has imparted to the whole Indian philosophy. The creative fulness of a bold poetical imagination is evinced by those gigantic works of architecture which may well sustain a comparison with the monuments of Egypt; by a poetry, which in the manifold richness of invention is not inferior to that of the Greeks, while it often approximates to the beauty of its forms; and above all, by a mythology which, in its leading features, its profound import, and its general connexion, resembles the Egyptian, while in its rich clothing of poetry, in its attractive and bewitching representations, it bears a strong similarity to the Greeks. This decided and peculiar character of the whole intellectual culture of the Indians will not permit us to doubt which of the various faculties of the soul is there the ruling and preponderant element. (1890: 165–6).

The idea of a mentality dominated by imagination has been a major constitutive element in idealist constructs of India and particularly of her major religion, Hinduism, as will be seen in chapter 3.

Of equal importance in essentializing an Indian imagination was the work of Georg Friedrich Creuzer (1771–1858). It presents us with the image of 'archaic civilizations', of which India was a leading example, as expressing their religious knowledge in 'symbolic' and 'mythic' rather than rational and discursive forms (1818–23). He and some of his contemporaries saw this as opening up a valuable part of the human experience of 'the divine' (Mitter, 1977: 202–7).[27]

2.3.2 Caste as Idea

This imagination that Schlegel and the other Romantics held in such high esteem was central to his version of caste. For Schlegel, as for the empiricist Mill and his successors, India was perennially open to conquest yet was also resistant to total conquest and incorporation by any outside culture, standing 'unchanged, like the one surviving monument of the primitive world'. The reason for this was that India was politically disunited (comparable in part to the feudal constitution of Germany): 'In the administration and government of this country, the absolute monarchical sway which exists in China, and the unlimited despotism of other Oriental countries, could never be realised' (1890: 142). Mill held that caste led to despotism. Schlegel took the opposite tack. India was no despotism, 'for that hereditary division of classes, and those hereditary rights belonging to each which, as they form a part of the Indian constitution, have taken such deep root in the soil'. These, in turn, 'as they rest on the immoveable basis of ancient faith, have become as it were, the second nature of this people – all these present an unassailable rampart, which not even a foreign conqueror could ever succeed in overthrowing' (1890: 142).

Schlegel paints a rather attractive picture. Caste is presented as kind of primitive example of civil society, one which, based on the principle of imagination that predominated in Indian religion, was able to withstand the imposition of despotic rule even if it was unable to prevent conquest.

Hegel, a contemporary of Schlegel and Creuzer, took a rather different stance. Just as the Sanskritist, H. H. Wilson, 'clawed back' the more extreme statements of Mill, so Hegel moved the views of these earlier Romantics back to a more central (that is, rationalist) position. He accepted the notion of archaic civilizations as symbolic (in his work on aesthetics) and he agreed that the imagination was central to India as the symbolic civilization *par excellence*, but

[27] For Creuzer's treatment of myth and religion, see Kramer (1977: 15–38). On his relationship to the other Romantic theorists of the symbol, see Todorov (1977: 216–18).

instead of viewing the symbolic as *complementary* to the modern, he argued the symbolic forms were *antecedent* to succeeding 'classical' (Greek) and modern (Romantic) forms (Mitter, 1977: 208–20). Each of these was, in its own time, rational (and not nonrational as the Romantics thought) but was overcome by the later, more rational forms. The importance of the Romantic theory of a symbol (both in its earlier Romantic form and its later rationalist or Hegelian appropriation) can hardly be overstated. It is deployed for the study of Others not only in Indian art history and, more widely, in Indology, but in the history of religions and anthropology as well, and we shall have several occasions to look at its effects later in this book (3.2.2, 3.6).

Just as Hegel hierarchized the Indian imagination in his rationalization of world history, so, too, did he place caste on his scale of forms. For Hegel, India's conquerability was no accident; it was an essential feature of India's civilization:

On the whole, the diffusion of Indian culture is only a dumb, deedless expansion; that is, it presents no political action. The people of India have achieved no foreign conquests, but have been on every occasion vanquished themselves. And as in this silent way, Northern India has been a centre of emigration, productive of merely physical diffusion, India as a *Land of Desire* forms an essential [*sic*!] element in General History. (1956: 141–2)

The desire to which Hegel referred is the desire of outsiders to possess the wealth and wisdom of India:

From the most ancient times downwards, all nations have directed their wishes and longings to gaining access to the treasures of this land of marvels, the most costly which the Earth presents; treasures of Nature – pearls, diamonds, perfumes, rose-essences, elephants, lions, etc. – as also treasures of wisdom. The way by which these treasures have passed to the West, has at all times been a matter of World-historical importance, bound up with the fate of nations. Those wishes have been realized; this Land of Desire has been attained; there is scarcely any great nation of the East, nor of the Modern European West, that has not gained for itself a smaller or larger portion of it. (1956: 142)

Hegel concludes this depiction of India as a treasure-trove with this pronouncement: 'The English, or rather the East India Company, are the lords of the land; for it is the necessary fate of Asiatic Empires to be subjected to Europeans; and China will, some day or other, be obliged to submit to this fate' (1956: 142–3).

The overall reason Hegel provided for this proneness to conquest differs from that given by Mill or Schlegel. It is forthcoming in his terse account of the Hindu state:

A State is a realization of Spirit, such that in it the self-conscious being of Spirit – the freedom of the Will – is realized as law. Such an institution then, necessarily presupposes the consciousness of free will. In the Chinese State the moral will of the Emperor is the law: but so that subjective inward freedom is thereby repressed, and the Law of Freedom governs individuals only as from without. In India the primary aspect of subjectivity – viz., that of the imagination – presents a union of the Natural and Spiritual, in which Nature on the one hand, does not present itself as a world embodying Reason, nor the Spiritual on the other hand, as a consciousness in contrast with Nature. Here the antithesis in the (above-stated) principle is wanting. Freedom both as *abstract* will and as *subjective* freedom is absent. The proper basis of the State, the principle of freedom is altogether absent: there cannot therefore be any State in the true sense of the term. This is the first point to be observed: if China may be regarded as nothing else but a State, Hindoo political existence presents us with a people, but *no State*. (1956: 160–1).

Let me restate in plain English the proposition that Hegel has presented here, for it is fundamental not only to Indology but also to Sinology. Western civilization is a highly rational formation: it sustains a healthy dialectic between the state and civil society, between what Hegel calls the principles of Unity and Difference. Out native informant says: 'An organic life requires in the first place One Soul, and in the second place, a divergence into differences, which become organic members, and in their several offices develop themselves to a complete system; in such a way, however, that their activity reconstitutes that one soul' (1956: 144).

Indian and Chinese civilizations are both in this fundamental regard neither irrational (Mill) nor excessively rational (Schlegel's China) or nonrational (his India). Both were rather pre-rational formations. India is represented as a distorted civilization because in it an incipient civil society (Difference) has engulfed the state (Unity). China, too, is represented as a misshapen civilization, but for almost precisely the reverse reason – there, the state (Unity) has swallowed up civil society (Difference).

The pre-rational form of civil society that engulfs the state in India is, of course, none other than caste, India's 'unique institution', and its supporting or constituting religion, Hinduism. Continuing his account of India's malformation, Hegel says that in India,

independent members ramify from the unity of despotic power. Yet the distinctions which these imply are referred to Nature. Instead of stimulating the activity of a soul as their centre of union, and spontaneously realizing that soul – as is the case in organic life – they petrify and become rigid, and by their stereotyped character condemn the Indian people to the most degrading spiritual serfdom. The distinctions in question are the *castes*. (1956: 144)

Caste is, thus, in Hegel's representation, not merely a form of social order peculiar to India either as exemplifying the most extreme of the unenlightened ancient societies (Mill) or as exemplifying a nation that had carried imaginative forms to excess. It has become, in Hegel's pages, the necessary and distinctive nucleus of India, logically integral to the whole of Indian civilization. It has, so far as human agency is concerned, become the substantialized agent of Indian history, from the time of its appearance down to the present.[28] To be sure, it gave India a brief glint of sunshine, but then petrified, causing India itself to spend the rest of time as the passive recipient of acts by other, more assertive essences from the West. As Hegel puts it, again metaphorically, 'A chain binds

---

[28] This idea of caste as a substantialized agent is to be sharply distinguished from the notion of 'code and substance' in my own earlier work.

down the life that was just upon the point of breaking forth' (1956: 145). Like Roma in the ancient histories of Rome (Collingwood, 1956: 43–4), caste appears at the dawn of Indian history, but it is not a part of that history, one that people in India, acting together or on their own, shape and reshape. Caste stands, fully formed before and outside of India's history. Her people and institutions, caste apart, are not even partially autonomous agents. Rather they are the patients of that villain, the social institution of caste.

The empiricist discourses which proliferated in British India after the Hegelian synthesis had, as we have seen in Risley, some difficulty in accepting what they saw as the dichotomously opposed idea or representation of caste as the product of an imaginative mentality, yet they did not seem to flinch at accepting Hegel's rationalization of caste as necessarily antithetical to the development of a strong nation-state.

Probably the most important of the Romantic idealist writings from 1875 to Independence are those not of Western scholars but of many of the Indian nationalists, including Gandhi and Nehru themselves. The rulers of India by and large held views that converged with the empiricist interpretations of Mill, Smith, and Risley, so it is no surprise to find that the nationalists often found themselves keeping company with the members of the loyal opposition within intellectual circles. The philosopher Radhakrishnan's discussion of caste under the rubric of the individual and social order is an excellent example of this Indian nationalist stance. He emphasizes the scheme of four *varṇas*, which he calls classes rather than castes, over the myriad smaller groups fetishized by the empiricists. That model of order was a logical and complete system for the division of labour and, even more, of man's nature. It was also one of organic solidarity and universal, applying to all mankind and not just to India; and Radhakrishnan argues that for many centuries foreigners were accepted into its folds.

Like so many of the nationalists (see 4.4.1, 5.4.2), he provides India neither with a static past (as Mill did) nor with the progressive history of the West, but with a regress or decline from a golden moment. This permits him to make his idea of the four classes the origin and essence of India and to locate the unwanted caste in a medieval period when India departed from her true self. He takes the position that although India had been actually organized along the lines of the ideal scheme of classes, these later 'degenerated into castes' (1959: 371). This, he argues, like others, took place during the period of the Guptas (where he places the ubiquitous Laws of Manu), in the fourth and fifth centuries. So what had been a dynamic, vital, organic, and open system of classes goes through a process of 'crystallization' and becomes separatist. He even accepts the empiricists' characterization of these castes as inimical to national unity, though, following another Indian student of caste, he says that this being the case, the British have an interest in keeping India divided into castes (1959: 376).

He differs, however, from the empiricists' and colonialists' view that these castes are integral to Indian civilization. What is essential is the old idea of four classes which, since it was universalist, can hardly be taken permanently to contrast an India with a West or a China. Yet Radhakrishnan does not escape from the world of essences. Far from it. By essentializing his version of caste, by making it an unchanging ideal that precedes human history and stands outside it, he too makes it into a substantialized agent, one that not only made India but that could or can make the whole of humanity in its image.

To sum up, the views of the Romantics have differed less sharply than one might first suppose from those of the Utilitarian empiricists with whom they have disagreed. As Hacking says of such disputes: 'whenever we find two philosophers who line up exactly opposite on a series of half a dozen points, we know that in fact they agree about almost everything' (Hacking, 1983: 5). The fact that Hegel could swoop down and combine both, with important altera- tions, into his world history bears witness to this. Both of the views in Indology agree that there is a single, absolute reality and both displace human agency on to it. The major difference is that the dominant view, that of the empiricist, has displaced it on to an external social structure or materially grounded human nature which he has tended to think of as determinate (fully knowable by human reason), while the idealist has displaced it on to an internal, spiritual nature which he or she has wanted to see as ineffable (or at least elusive and captured only in the human imagination). The former sees human acts as shaped by external material institutions over which ordinary humans have little control. The latter sees human acts as the product of a partly unconscious agency that lies embedded deep in man's soul. Yet the Romantic idealists have not, for the most part, objected to the metaphysics of science itself. They have mostly been concerned with salvaging some space for human subjectivity and free will. They have largely been content to see their views as complementing those of the empirical realists rather than replacing them, much as in the 'modern' world, the private, personal realm of the home and of pleasure has been placed in a relationship of complementation to the public, impersonal realm of work. They have, thus, tended to think with a number of oppositions – between 'nature' and 'history' (or 'society' or 'culture'), 'cause' and 'meaning', the 'instrumental' and the 'expressive' – that reduplicated the divide that separated their subject-matter from that of the absolutists.

Indeed, orientalists have often combined the two. Although they see themselves as scientists first, they also claim that it is important to sympathize with the Other, to try and see things from his point of view. To do this latter is not a question of scientific reason. It is more a question of intuition and of emotional stance. The hegemony of the metaphysics of textbook science in orientalism can be seen quite clearly. Even the adherents of a Romantic point of view often adduce scientific evidence for their position or claim to use the methods of science in their studies, turning meanings into determinate substances. What the members of the loyal opposition do reject is the notion that human subjectivity can be reduced to the phenomena of an external material nature. A science of ineffable Inner Man, if such there be, would not, therefore, necessarily follow the same rules as the sciences of Outer Man. Within Indology, adherents of this strain represent India as the space where an Other has somehow managed to preserve these human qualities.

When it comes to caste, there have been considerable differences between the empiricist and the idealist perspectives, extending even to the question of what caste is. For the empiricist it is the myriad of *jātis*, of 'real' caste groups, conceived of as in conflict; for the idealist it is the idea of the four *varṇas*. They have also differed in the value they place on their differing versions of caste. The hard-headed empiricist has seen caste as an obstacle to progress, while the dreamy idealist has considered it the embodiment of a holist, organic vision of human community. Both camps, have, however, agreed that caste is the defining institution of India and both have tied it in with the racial theory of Aryan conquest. Both have also agreed that caste is anti-individualist and tightly bounded – there are 'rigid barriers' between them – and both have agreed that caste is the opposite of the West's civil society. Finally, although they differed on what the essence of caste is – the empiricist looked to an external, observable something (racial composition, division of labour) while the idealist looked to an internal idea of a total man – they have both presupposed an essence for it. Caste for both points of view becomes a substantialized agent, the unitary, unchanging subject of India's history. To the extent that accounts write of change at all it is within a natural history framework of degeneration and petrification.

2.4   DISSENTING AND CHANGING VIEWS

Now, it would be wrong to insist that all texts produced by Indologists and anthropologists on caste have conformed precisely to the empiricist or idealist modes of discourse that emerged in the early nineteenth century. There have always been dissenting voices. Important changes have also taken place since the eclipse of the Anglo-French imperial formation by its US–USSR successor.

One dissenter was the anthropologist A. M. Hocart (1883–1939). He departs from other orientalists in his refusal to subscribe to the metaphysics which constructs a West and an East that are polar opposites. He argued that castes should be seen as a hierarchy of ritual offices centred on a king (or local lord) and having as their purpose the performance of the royal ritual for the benefit of the entire community. His evolutionism causes fewer difficulties than one would expect precisely because he emphasizes the *similarities* of Western, Eastern, and 'primitive' cultures without reducing them all to variants of 'Western rational man'. Castes, according to Hocart (1950: 17–19), were not a peculiar, irrational social institution confined to India; nor had they at their very point of origin swallowed up kingship; on the contrary, they were themselves offices of the state, a point to which I return (6.1.2).[29]

Hocart was quite conscious of the ways in which Indological discourse belittled Indians as it re-presented them, and seems to have taken delight in

[29] Hutton in his hegemonic work (1963: 176–7) reduces Hocart's views to one theory of 'origin' to be mentioned among the many and then passed over. Dumont and Pocock (1958) wrongly, in my view, reject Hocart's focus on the king. Needham in his new edition of Hocart's *Kings and Councillors* (1970) effectively 'rehabilitates' his work.

exposing Western institutions to the same treatment. Regarding the 'fiction' of four *varṇas*, he says:

This, we are constantly told, bears no resemblance to reality. The reality is to be found in Indian censuses, in the dictionaries of castes and tribes, and in the daily experience of Indian civil servants. What do we find there? Not four castes, but an infinitude, with an endless variety of customs, of mutual relations, and even of racial types. Therefore the four-caste system is a pure figment, the invention of priests for their own glorification. (1950: 23–4)

He then shows how the analogous idea of estates in Britain could be accorded similar treatment:

Before we apply an argument to a people whose ways are remote and little known (for, in spite of all the books about it, India remains an unknown country), before we take such risks it is well to test the argument on our own society which we do know. Our constitution divides the people into lords and commons. When, however, we examine the reality we find that the lords are a collection of families of different ranks – dukes, marquesses, and so on. We can also distinguish among them different sets which have little to do with one another. We can even distinguish different racial types, notably the Jewish. Among the commons the variety is even greater: it ranges from baronets, who come near to being peers, down to horny-handed navvies. Do we on that account reject the classification into lords and commons as a figment of our constitutional theorists? Why, we can see them any day sitting in separate houses with different procedures and privileges. It is a theory, but it is a theory translated into practice. Such is any social organization. (1950: 24)

Hocart ends this parry of Western scientific reason with one final thrust:

Why then should an Indian classification of the people into four be unreal because it gathers together into one group such heterogeneous elements as barbers, mat-makers, and sometimes even aborigines? Why should not such a classification be just as important in the state as ours? As a matter of fact, it is much more important since it runs through the daily life of the masses. (1950: 24)

It is worth noting *en passant* that Hocart's transcendence of the dichotomy between the empiricist and idealist versions of caste, implicit in his criticisms, is one of the many virtues of his work.

Certain shifts in the orientalist constructs have occurred since the Second World War. It is important to point these out, as Said does (1978: 284–328). Nearly all of the peoples previously incorporated into European imperial formations are now constituted as legally and formally independent and sovereign nations. At the same time, the United States has replaced Britain as the dominant Western power within a new US–USSR imperial formation. These changes have been accompanied in academic circles by the rise of 'area studies'. A survey completed in the US as this reached its crest in the late sixties reported that there were more than 1,000 specialists offering nearly 650 courses with over 14,000 undergraduate and almost 4,000 graduate enrolments (Lambert, 1973: table 9.3). The study of Indian civilization has also been boosted in the Soviet Union (Bongard-Levin and Vigasin, 1984), the major rival of the United States, for in the imperial formation of the 'three worlds' it has to compete with the US for followers and allies in the 'third world'.

Along with these shifts there has arisen an atomistic (and, in my view, specious) doctrine of cultural relativism (see also above, 1.2.4). Mimicking the notions of the 'individual' and of national sovereignty, it claims to accord equal respect to all cultures and minority or ethnic 'heritages' while largely ignoring the relations of domination that have existed and still do exist among them. It is no longer possible to speak openly of cultural, never mind racial, inferiority and superiority in an international forum. The strong, confident language of the nineteenth century has given way to the euphemistic language of United Nations reports and Asian Civilization Course syllabuses.[30] The best example of this American reworking so far as caste goes is probably Mandelbaum's two-volume anthropological survey of Indian society (1970). Like so many of his predecessors, he opens his account by citing the evidence of an early Greek ambassador, the 'observant' Megasthenes (5.4.1), and uses this to bolster the assertion that caste is the 'distinctive social order' of India.

It would, however, be rash to say that the representation of the Other as irrational and naturalism (in the form of evolutionism and functionalism) no longer dominate Indological discourse. The oppositions of East and West, traditional and modern, civilized and primitive, have been transformed and have reappeared as the idea of the 'three worlds'. As Pletsch has convincingly shown (1981), naturalist assumptions are integral to this post-war cosmology. Nations of the first world are the most 'developed' or 'advanced' because they are shaped in accord with scientific knowledge of nature; those of the second world are, although developed, held back by their distorting socialist ideology; the third world, where religion and superstition still run rife, are 'underdeveloped' or 'developing'.

India is still regarded as a civilization in which a distorted form of civil society long ago engulfed the economy and state. Barrington Moore, Jr. could still write of caste in his widely read book:

In pre-British Indian society, and still today in much of the countryside, the fact of being born in a particular caste determined for the individual the entire span of existence, quite literally from before conception until after death. It gave the range of choice for a marital partner in the case of parents, the type of upbringing the offspring would have and their choice of mate in marriage, the work he or she could legitimately undertake, the appropriate religious ceremonies, food, dress, rules of evacuation (which are very important), down to most details of daily living, all organized around a conception of disgust. (1967: 337–8)

Confident in his knowledge, the professor continues, as Hegel had almost 140 years previously, to describe India as a place where 'Government above the village was an excrescence generally imposed by an outsider.... The structural contrast with China is quite striking. There the imperial bureaucracy gave

---

[30] Typical of this shift with respect to India is Brown (1953), successively updated.

cohesion to the society.... At the local level such an arrangement was unnecessary in India. Caste regulations took its place' (1967: 339).[31]

Barrington Moore can perhaps be criticized because he is not an 'expert' on things Indian, but one can hardly offer that as an excuse for A. L. Basham. Predictaby, his *Wonder* softens its language, referring to *varṇa* as 'class' rather than 'caste'. None the less, it still rehearses unambiguously the old Hegelian proposition that caste, here 'society', ever had the upper hand in its dealings with the state: 'Society, the age-old divinely ordained way of Indian life, transcended the state and was independent of it. The king's function was the protection of society, and the state was merely an extension of the king for the furtherance of that end' (1954: 88). One might think that Hocart had put an end to the racial theory of caste, but no, it is integral to the predominant constructs of India, so it persists. Basham tells his reader, in speaking of the four *varṇas*, that 'In India class stratification grew more rigid when, in the Vedic period, a situation arose rather like that prevailing in South Africa today, with a dominant fair minority striving to maintain its purity and its supremacy over a darker majority' (1954: 137). He also continues to adhere to the notion that caste is a primitive, post-tribal form of society, just as Mill had, and uses the metaphor of petrification so favoured in retailing its history: 'Tribal class-divisions hardened, and the dark-skinned aboriginal found a place only in the basement of the Aryan social structure, as a serf with few rights and many disabilities' (1954: 137). British racialism has been shifted in his representation from the British on to the Indians and naturalized: 'Soon the idea of varna had become so deeply embedded in the Indian mind that its terminology was even used for the classification of precious commodities such as pearls, and useful materials like timber' (1954: 137–8). Not even the South Africans, presumably, are racist in their treatment of plant and animal products. Basham did not, of course, write in isolation. The empiricist, racialist study of caste soldiered on into the sixties, with J. H. Hutton (1885–1968), the anthropologist who directed the 1931 Census of India, as its spokesman (Hutton, 1963).

The major post-war sociological statement on caste is undoubtedly Louis Dumont's *Homo Hierarchicus* (1980b; first published in 1966), the book to which intellectuals, but non-Indianists, turn when they want to learn about the subject. He is explicit in his criticism of the empiricist and racialist approach of

[31] Nor, should I add, have we transcended the sort of global rationalization of the present order of things that Hegel provided us. I have before me one pygmy update of his philosophy of history, a book by a sociologist, John A. Hall. Not only does Hall claim to give Adam Smith and Karl Marx intellectual facelifts, he also improves on that totem of post-Second World War conserative liberalism, Max Weber himself (1986: 17–23). His startling and original conclusion regarding India is that 'Indian civilisation' is held together by 'Hindu culture', that is, by the Brahmans. India seems 'peculiar', he says, to 'Western eyes', because the '"community" created by the Brahmans was based on division and hierarchy'. Parroting Weber, he proclaims that 'Such a system did not allow for the autonomous emergence of any economic dynamism of a capitalist kind. It is likely that the hierarchical effect of caste was to diminish the social participation ratio, and thereby to block economic interchanges. Equally important, however, was the instability of political rule that resulted from Brahman withdrawal from power. This encouraged predatory interference with, and prevented the provision of services for, economic life' (1986: 83).

the Risley construct.[32] Yet he, too, presses the same point about civil society and the state that Moore made very hard. The difference is that for him it is not just an empirical finding, it is integral to his theory. What distinguishes Indian (that is, Hindu) society from that of the West, according to this Durkheimian and structuralist reformulation, is that in the former, 'purity' (caste hierarchy) encompasses 'power' (kingship) (1980b: 33–49, 65–72, 152–8, 235–8, and especially 1980a: 287–313). Here the fascination is no longer with India as a type of society that is a deviation from the economic individualism of the older British view. Rather it is with an India that seems to embody the social holism of Durkheim (not to mention the conservative idealist) in an almost paradigmatic form. A study of Indian society from this standpoint, where the organic is the model rather than the machine, has, thus, an educative value. It helps us to see that the individual, the *homo aequalis* of the modern West, is not as free as he might think and that the individualist theories of the Western economists and political philosophers can indeed benefit from the corrective of a Durkheimian holism. Yet Dumont, who revives the Hegelian, rationalist view of India, does not break with the notion of caste as the substantialized agent of Indian civilization. If anything, he comes closer than anyone else in equating caste, as a principle of social order, with that civilization. Since I criticize Dumont's views below (4.4.2, 5.6.2), I will say no more here and pass on to the Weberians.[33]

The family of views that has probably predominated in the US in the last two decades when it comes to the study of the 'underdeveloped' countries is that of the followers of Max Weber (1864–1920). Scholars have taken this German intellectual as their hero, one suspects, precisely because he has been seen as somehow transcending the two dominant approaches of the nineteenth century, those I have tagged as empirical realism and Romantic or idealist (Hughes, 1958: 287–335), although I prefer to see him as a sociological individualist or idealist who also wanted to be an empiricist. Weber himself, of course, wrote on Indian civilization (1958), asking why it had not developed 'an ethic that endorsed and encouraged the life of rationally oriented business activity', as had the West (Hughes, 1958: 322).[34] Some of the sociologists – Edward Shils (1961), S. N. Eisenstadt (1969: 4, 11), and Reinhard Bendix (1969: 256–356) – and anthropologists – Robert Redfield (1956), Clifford Geertz (1963: 139–42), and Milton Singer (1972) – most closely connected with the establishment of the Weberian position have also, to varying degrees, had things to say about India. The most important of the Weberians among Indologists in recent years has been the Dutch Sanskritist, J. C. Heesterman, whose work, more focused on the state, I discuss later (5.6.3).

If Dumont can be taken as giving Marx's materialist and Hegel's idealist reworking of Mill's India an update, with Durkheim providing the sociology, Weber can be seen as doing the same thing, with the difference that he did so

[32] The interest in the origin and evolution of caste is not, however, dead. Klass (1980) has revived it.
[33] For some criticisms of Dumont and more recent literature that parallels mine, see Appadurai (1986).
[34] For a discussion of Weber's work on India, badly translated into English, and of alleged Indo-American misappropriations of Weber, see Kantowsky (1982).

from the standpoint of his appropriation of liberal Austrian economics (Therborn, 1980: 270–315). The German version is situated at the crossroads of an imperialist struggle between the capitalist nation-states and of a class struggle between capitalist polities and socialist movements. The American version is to be read in the post-Second World War setting of the 'three worlds'. According to this translated and transposed Weber, Indian social and religious forms did exhibit rationality (in his sense of 'systematic arrangement') but they did not possess its essence, what I have labelled as a 'world-ordering rationality', that which the Weberians associate with capitalism, cities, legal-bureaucratic forms of domination, and protestant Christianity.

Like so many others, Weber zeroes in on caste. Relying heavily on the Census of India, he tells his reader that 'the caste order is oriented religiously and ritually, to a degree not even partially attained elsewhere' (1958: 44). He uncannily reiterates Risley's mix of materialist and idealist explanations for the rise of caste in India, except that for Weber it is the idea of caste and its bearers, the unitary Brahmans, that, in the last instance, 'conquer' India: 'this well-integrated, unique social system could not have originated or at least could not have conquered and lasted without the pervasive and all-powerful influence of the Brahmans. It must have existed as a finished idea long before it conquered even the greater part of North India' (1958: 131). The extremeness of Indian 'traditionalism' counted most, of course, in the area of life with which Weber was most concerned, the economic. 'Modern capitalism', he tells his reader, 'undoubtedly would never have originated from the circles of the completely traditionalist Indian trades'. This is so despite the fact that the 'Hindu artisan is known for his extreme industry' (1958: 113). The reason for this extreme traditionalism in India is none other than the essence of Indian civilization, the 'caste order' (1958: 112). The Occident had – we should note that the perspective throughout is that of the capital accumulator – also suffered from this difficulty. So when the British introduce factories, great resistance is met, as it had been in Europe. Note that what Weber seems to see in his account of this is not resistance by formerly autonomous agents to selling their labour (and themselves) for wages but resistance to the development of a truly rational world:

The workers want to earn some money quickly in order to establish themselves independently. An increase in wage rate does not mean for them an incentive for more work or for a higher standard of living, but the reverse. They then take longer holidays because they can afford to do so, or their wives decorate themselves with ornaments. To stay away from work as one pleases is recognized as a matter of course, and the worker retires with his meagre savings to his home town as soon as possible. He is simply a casual labourer. 'Discipline' in the European sense is an unknown idea to him. (1958: 114)

Here we have, laid bare for a moment, that which has been a major concern of social scientific discourses since at least the time of James Mill, ancestor of the discourse to which Weber contributes: the production not so much of a hard-working labour force, but of one that can be 'controlled' and 'managed'. Weber has much to say about magic. It was, he argues, the inability to transcend magic that largely constituted India's traditionality (1958: 336). But Weber seems not to realize that it was precisely the magic of 'management' and 'administration', of turning agents into the seemingly willing instruments of a capitalist economy, that was largely constitutive of his 'science' in its more practical applications and of the 'rational' world its practitioners wished to bring about.

Not to be ignored here are the later Romantics. They overlap with the Weberians, the major difference being the concern of the former with the mental in *personal* rather than in *public* life. Together, the two can be seen as reproducing under a neo-Kantian umbrella the wider divide between the empiricists and idealists. Among the more prominent of these Romantic views of India are to be counted those of certain art historians, to wit, Ananda Coomaraswamy (1877–1947) (Lipsey, 1977: III)[35] and Stella Kramrisch (Miller, 1983: 3–29), and of many historians of religion, most notably Mircea Eliade (1907–86).

The most important of the Romantic views, though, are probably those of the associates or followers of Carl Gustav Jung (1875–1961) (who was well acquainted with the work of Creuzer) (Brome, 1980: 120, 290), and German Weberians (who also reproduce post-Rankean elements in their work). Those I would name among the Jungians are Heinrich Zimmer (1890–1943) and his disciple, Joseph Campbell (born 1904), whose work has been generously supported by the Bollingen Foundation, set up to assist Jungian projects (Brome, 1980: 236).[36] I would consider Hermann Goetz (1898–1976) and his pupil, Hermann Kulke, of the South Asia Institute at the University of Heidelberg, the foremost among the latter.[37]

Here is a passage from Joseph Campbell's widely read work on mythology, which rather elegantly exemplifies the position of the Romantic as outside or between East and West:

Two completely opposed mythologies of the destiny and virtue of man, therefore, have come together in the modern world. And they are contributing in discord to whatever new society may be in the process of formation. For, of the tree that grows in the garden where God walks in the cool of the day, the wise men westward of Iran have partaken of the fruit of knowledge of good and evil, whereas those on the other side of that cultural divide, in India and the Far East, have relished only the fruit of eternal life. However, the two limbs, we are informed [in a study of Jewish legends], come together in the center of the garden, where they form a single tree at the base, branching out when they reach a certain height. Likewise, the two mythologies spring from one base in the Near East. And if man should taste of both fruits he would become, we have been told, as God himself (Genesis 3:22) – which is the boon that the meeting of East and West today is offering to us all. (1962: 9)

[35] A good example of his views is Coomaraswamy (1977), where he opposed 'traditional' to 'modern' instead of 'Oriental' to 'Christian'.
[36] For an excellent brief discussion of Campbell, see Riepe (1970: 227–8), who criticizes him for not talking about the naturalist, realist, and materialist traditions of India.
[37] For some of the connections of Jung and of Goetz, Zimmer, and Eliade with Coomaraswamy, see Lipsey (1977, III, 203–4, 210–13). And for a brief account of Goetz's career by Kulke, see Deppert (1983: 13–23). For the work of Kulke and his associates, see Eschmann, Kulke and Tripathi (1978).

Like the earlier Romantics Campbell and his colleagues continue to assume that there is, ultimately, a single humanity, albeit not a fixed, universal human nature. That is why Campbell uses the metaphor of human mythology as a single tree – a metaphor for racial and linguistic history as well – and is at pains to assert that it has a single origin in the Near East.

The message here is that the authoritative guide in these matters can help his readers (or patients) to become whole persons by reuniting in themselves the best of these two worlds. These latter-day Romantics are, however, voluntarists. So, within our society anyone who puts into practice the teachings of the appropriate Romantic master can come to partake of human totality and acquire a balanced personality. No major changes in his or her social circumstances are required. A person can somehow look into his or herself and step mentally outside his or her social world (while at the same time appearing to conform to its strictures) in order to create for themself a new person. India here becomes a living museum (and keen market-place) of religious humanism, of New Age psychic phenomena, yogic health practices, and ultimate experiences.[38]

Campbell's image of caste is also consistent with the position of a Romantic idealist and comparable to Radhakrishnan's. While the empiricist student of India would see the external, empirical institution of caste as the substantialized agent that has shaped persons in India, the idealist would consider the internal, the substantialized idea of caste in the form of 'orthodox' Hinduism, as the agent. Campbell, for example, opens his short account of caste by pronouncing that 'There is therefore in Hinduism an essential [*sic!*] affirmation of the cosmic order as divine. And since society is conceived to be a part of the cosmic order, there is an affirmation, equally, of the orthodox Indian social order as divine.' The Jungians themselves promise great freedom to their adherents, but this is not allowed to the people whose culture is going to make this possible: 'Furthermore, as the order of nature is eternal, so also is this of the orthodox society. There is no tolerance of human freedom or invention in the social field; for society is not conceived to be an order evolved by human beings, subject to intelligence and change, as it was in advanced Greece and Rome and as it is in the modern West.' He continues, attributing the Enlightenment idea of an immutable natural order to the ancient Indians: 'Its laws are of nature, not to be voted on, improved upon, or devised. Precisely as the sun, moon, plants and animals follow laws inherent in their natures, so therefore must the individual the nature of his birth. . . . Each is conceived to be a species' (Campbell, 1962: 339–40).

[38] The British *Observer* (Sunday, 18 May 1986) provides insight into the voluntarist bottom line here when it reports that a 'rich and mysterious guru', Shri Chandra Swamiji Maharaj, was involved in the sale of Harrods, the London store, to the Egyptian Fayed brothers. We read that: 'The Swami, a giant bearded figure in flowing white, claims to advise a number of leading political figures around the world, including King Hussein of Jordan, President Mobutu, Rajiv Gandhi and Richard Nixon. He is currently on his way to visit ex-President Marcos in Honolulu. He has met Mrs. Thatcher several times.' A later article (Sunday, 20 July 1986) reported on attempts to 'expose' the Swami in the Indian press. In an interview in the *Illustrated Weekly* of India, the Swami says, 'I have at least 60 to 70 heads of state who would do anything I tell them.'

He concludes with that other favourite image of the conservative idealist, that of society as a hierarchic, organic whole. He claims to derive it from the Indian notion of the 'great man' without telling his unknowing readers that the same notion is also used by Indians to talk about their great heroes:

The Greek or Renaissance idea of the great individual simply does not exist within the pale of the system. One is to be, rather, a *dividuum*, divided man, a man who represents one limb or function of the great man (*purusa*), which is society itself: the Brahmin, priestly caste, being its head; the Kshatriya, governing caste, its arms; the Vaishya, financial caste, the belly and torso; while the Shudras, workers, are its legs and feet. The Pariahs, outcastes, meanwhile, are of another natural order entirely, and in connection with the human community can perform only inhuman, beastly chores. (1962: 340)

The same mental 'fiction' that Risley and other empiricists have dismissed as a false representation of Indian social reality has become, in the eyes of the later Romantics, like Radhakrishnan and Campbell, its innermost reality.

I, too, was lured in earlier research by the siren of caste. This is not the place to review or criticize recent work on caste as such. Some of it no doubt represents a partial break with the old Indological paradigm. Yet it must be said that the very importance given to caste has in itself tended to have the effect of reproducing the Indological axiom regarding caste and the state. Marriott and Inden state, for example, that,

It is the moral duty of the ruler (properly a Ksatriya) to use force (*danda*) so as to establish the moral order, especially in order to maintain the rank and separation of the castes, so that their internal self-government and their proper exchanges may continue. (Marriott and Inden, 1974: III, 989).

I now reject the idea that makes caste rather than kingship or a polity the constitutive institution of Indian civilization from its very inception down into the present. My own research on the history of caste and clan formations in Bengal is in large part and, perhaps ironically, responsible for this rejection. There I showed that it was the collapse of Hindu kingship which led to the formation of 'castes' in something resembling their modern form (albeit not as usually described). That is, the distinctive institution of Indian civilization does not appear until the thirteenth or fourteenth century, at the earliest; and castes are not the *cause* of the weakness and collapse of Hindu kingship, but the *effect* of it (Inden, 1976: 73–82).

To summarize, virtually all of the hegemonic accounts of India, beginning with Mill and Hegel, have made caste into the central pillar of their constructs. Caste, they have held, is the type of society characteristic of India, the institution that distinguishes it from the other civilizations of Asia as well as from the West. The representations of India as a civilization dominated by caste are legion. Commentative texts that portray caste as suffering from the distortions of condensation and displacement abound, never mind the explanatory accounts which claim to reveal the origin of caste. Indian society is overdetermined by caste, proliferating separate castes and subcastes by the hundred and thousand for no good reason, while at the same time becoming more rigid and impermeable. Caste is, furthermore, displaced in this discourse on to every area of Indian life; it is associated with race and occupation, religion and status, land control, and psychic security, with birth and death, marriage and education. Indian thoughts and actions are separated from each other; there are always discrepancies between caste rules and actual behaviour.

The two ways of knowing about India, the empirical realist and the Romantic idealist, have not of course agreed on what caste is. The multiplicity of *jātis*, castes and subcastes which the former tried to entomb in the Census is ever at odds with the ideal, Brahmanical scheme of four *varṇas* or classes which the latter have resurrected from ancient Indian texts. Is it a fundamentally Aryan institution or a fundamentally Dravidian one? Is it inherently and excessively divisive and centrifugal and therefore antithetical to economic and political progress, or is it inherently and excessively cohesive and centripetal and therefore the exemplary conservative social order? Does caste originate in racial conflict (and remain a matter of status and purity) or is it the product of the division of labour (and therefore essentially economic)?

Caste, considered the essence of Indian civilization, has often been treated as though it were the unchanging (substantialized) agent of the civilization, from the rise of the Indus Valley culture and the arrival of the Aryans down to the present day of regionalism and caste in electoral politics. It is, thus, deeply embedded in Indological discourse. Many of the more recent accounts of caste have dropped the racialist explanation, but they have not broken with the notion that caste is a unique type of society, one that displaces the economically oriented polities of the West. Some, like Dumont, have supplanted the predominantly atomistic perspective of the British empiricists by returning to the rationalizing holism of Hegel. Others, like Heesterman, substituting one essence for another, have argued that clan or kinship inside the dominant castes was more important than intercaste ties (see 5.6.3, 5.6.4). Nearly all, however, have continued to look on their version of caste as a post-tribal society of 'natural' ties that constitutes the distinctive essence of India.[39]

The multiple effects that this essentialism has had on the study of Indian politics, religion, and history is the major focus of the rest of this book. I will later suggest (chapter 6) how 'caste' can be thought of as a form of citizenship, refashioned over and over in different circumstances, rather than as an excessive and perduring 'natural' society. In a moment I will turn to Hinduism and the mind which Indologists have fitted into this agent of Indian civilization. Let me conclude here, however, with a thought about the importance of these discourses on caste for the European and American Self.

Accounts of caste can and have been used as a foil to build up the West's image of itself. To simplify, the more staunch, secular, and reform-minded empiricists have wished to see caste society as the very hypostasis of a pre-enlightened world where superstition and darkness reign, with poverty, exploitation, and political chaos as the result. The more conservative and idealist have wished to see in caste an organic, hierarchical social order, even if static and stifling of individual initiative. The makers of both of these images give us a

---

[39] For a different approach to the 'problem' of caste and tribe, see Galey (1986).

picture of caste as a type of society that has gone to extremes. They have done this, I believe, because both are worried about what political philosophers refer to as civil society, the attempt to build a society of individuals on the analogy of a machine (or a machine-like organism) while yet retaining the freedom of its divine maker for all its inhabitants (or at least its rulers), a world of competition that is yet populated by patriotic and caring citizens. I suspect that much of what we say about caste is motivated by the impossibility of realizing this utopian dream. Our discourses on caste, thus, not only have the effect of stripping Indians of their agency; they also have the effect of blinding us to this difficulty. When we read or talk about the excesses of caste, we are able to think that we *have* realized this dream. Or at least we can remind ourselves of what the unpleasant alternatives are.

3
Hinduism: The Mind of India

Hinduism has been likened to a vast sponge, which absorbs all that enters it without ceasing to be itself. The simile is not quite exact, because Hinduism has shown a remarkable power of assimilating as well as absorbing; the water becomes part of the sponge. Like a sponge it has no very clear outline on its borders and no apparent core at its centre. An approach to Hinduism provides a first lesson in the 'otherness' of Hindu ideas from those of Europe. The Western love of definition and neat pigeon-holing receives its first shock, and also its first experience of definition by means of negatives. For a while it is not at all clear what Hinduism is, it is clear that is is not many things with which it may be superficially compared. (Spear, 1958: 57)[1]

3.1 MALE MANAGER, FEMALE JUNGLE: EUROPEAN SCIENCE AND INDIAN RELIGION

British, French, and German scholars asserted again and again as they helped draw India into the Anglo-French imperial formation of the nineteenth century that because of its radically otherworldly or spiritual orientation, the key to understanding the thinking of that civilization lay in understanding its religious basis. But which of the myriad of religions found there was to be their guide in this quest? Not Buddhism, for that religion was practically nonexistent in nineteenth-century India, nor Jainism, the faith of a very small minority, nor, of course, Islam. The religion they wanted was the one that they considered integral to caste, India's essential institution, the religion that was itself fundamentally concerned both with the maintenance of a 'natural' society which transcended the economic and political and, at the same time, with escape from it.

The symptom of that predominance of the otherworldly over the worldly in

[1] T. G. Percival Spear (1901–82) taught in India and worked for the Information Department of the government of India before returning as a Fellow to Cambridge. Revisor, with Basham, of Smith's *Oxford History of India*, he wrote as the sun set on the British empire.

the land of caste was the superior position of the Brahmans, the caste of priests, those concerned above all with representing the social and religious in their texts. The essential religion of India must, therefore, be the religion (and philosophy) in the charge of these priests. One name that men of letters gave to this religion was, appropriately enough, Brahmanism. More generally, however, they have designated the religion they have invented by the term (from the Persian, as one is always told) Hinduism. Significantly, it is the only world religion (apart from Judaism) that is named after a place rather than a founder or doctrine. Vincent Smith spoke for many when he told the would-be reformers of the Indian government: 'If all reference to Islam, Christianity, and other foreign religions be put aside for a moment, it may be said that India, excepting uncultured tribes, is essentially [!] Hindu, the land of the Brahmans. The unity underlying the obvious diversity of India may be summed up in the word Hinduism' (Smith, 1919: 26). Simply put, the proposition is this: the essence of the religions of India is the religion of the Brahmans. To understand their religion is, therefore, to grasp the mind of the entire civilization. Hinduism, then, is another pillar in the construct of India.

Those who claim special knowledge of India almost invariably introduce Hinduism to the wider public in a summary commentative account that displays that religion's strange way of ordering its world. Such is the portrait by the historian, Spear, at the head of this chapter. The very use of the metaphor of Hinduism as a sponge indicates that we will be dealing here with what Spear calls a 'mysterious amorphous entity', one that is palpable yet lacks something. What is the essence that Hinduism – and, therefore, India – lacks? It is what I refer to as a 'world-ordering rationality'. But it is not just an absence that Spear conveys with this metaphor. Implicit here is also the idea that Hinduism is a *female* presence who is able, through her very amorphousness and absorptive powers, to baffle and perhaps even threaten Western rationality, clearly a male in this encounter. European reason penetrates the womb of Indian unreason but always at the risk of being engulfed by her.

Probably the most widely used metaphor, though, is that of Hinduism as a jungle. Sir Charles Eliot (1862–1931), diplomat and orientalist, states in his 'authoritative' history of Indian religions that 'Hinduism has often and justly been compared to a jungle.' He continues:

As in the jungle every particle of soil seems to put forth its spirit in vegetable life and plants grown on plants, creepers and parasites on their more stalwart brethren, so in India art, commerce, warfare and crime, every human interest and aspiration seek for a manifestation in religion, and since men and women of all classes and occupations, all stages of education and civilization, have contributed to Hinduism, much of it seems low, foolish and even immoral. The jungle is not a park or garden. Whatever can grow in it, does grow. The Brahmans are not gardeners but forest officers. (1954: II, 166)

This metaphor of the Brahmans as forest officers is an apt one. Like their Aryan ancestors and British cousins (who, it should be emphasized, do not belong to the jungle, but come from outside) they do not constitute an order out of the jungle, for it is inherently disorderly, but they can, it would seem, introduce a certain degree of rationality into it.

That there is no apparent order in Hinduism should not be taken to mean that it has no knowable essence. It is, after all, a part of the orderly world in which the jungle officer of the Indian mind, the Indologist, wishes to live. So, like any other phenomenon that comes under the close scrutiny of a positive science, it must have an essence. That essence is not, however, to be seen at work in a system of parts making a whole, but rather as Freud did in analysing the overdetermined dreams of his patients. 'Yet in spite of their exuberance Hinduism and the jungle have considerable uniformity', says Eliot. He continues:

Here and there in a tropical forest some well-grown tree or brilliant flower attracts attention, but the general impression left on the traveller by the vegetation as he passes through it mile after mile is infinite repetition as well as infinite luxuriance. And so it is in Hinduism. A monograph on one god or one teacher is an interesting study. But if we continue the experiment, different gods and different teachers are found to be much the same. (1954: 167)

These different movements and the religion in different places in India are uniform because – mark the geographic determinism – 'it smacks of the soil and nothing like it can be found outside India'.

Not surprisingly, the essence which Eliot is about to pull from the soil for his reader is the self-same mentality of extremes on which Spear had focused:

Hinduism is an unusual combination of animism and pantheism, which are commonly regarded as the extremes of savage and of philosophic belief. In India both may be found separately but frequently they are combined in startling juxtaposition. The same person who worships Vishnu as identical with the universe also worships him in the form of a pebble or plant. The average Hindu who cannot live permanently in the altitudes of pantheistic thought, regards his gods as great natural forces akin to the mighty rivers which he also worships, irresistible and often beneficent but also capricious and destructive. (1954: 167)

There is, thus, little doubt here that this jungle with its soil, is, like Spear's sponge, also a female, one that can be managed by its male masters and known so long as they don't become entwined in its embraces.

When Indologists, historians, and anthropologists depict Hindu thought as opposed to a Western, male rationality, they have mostly had in mind as their exemplar of world-ordering rationality the science of the heavens or natural philosophy that their Enlightenment forebears had fashioned. The ordered world produced by that rationality was the mechanical and deist image of the universe and of the human mind itself.[2] Although many natural scientists have abandoned the metaphysical principles involved here, human scientists continue to be the guardians of this dinosaur metaphysics. They do so because they and the leaders of European polities have tried, since Hobbes, not only to study the human world through his metaphor of the mechanical body, but also to

---

[2] Even so, Quine, the analytic philosopher, can conclude his discussion of metaphor thus: 'The neatly worked inner stretches of science are an open space in the tropical jungle, created by clearing tropes away' (1978).

fashion its institutions, the nation-state (Macpherson, 1962: 17–46, 70–106), the church, and the joint-stock company[3] in accord with its principles of order. Even the model of the homeostatic organism, used in racial and evolutionary theories as the *fin de siècle* approached, has the notion of mechanism as its central principle.

Those principles of order are, let us recall, those of mutual exclusion, unity, centredness, determinacy, and uniformity. The transcendent knower of Indological discourse proceeds by discovering mutually exclusive categories, as in a taxonomy, and reducing them to a single order. The universe that is so constituted is centred (on the immanent sun, and on the transcendent God, its maker) and it is stable and uniform (and therefore predictable) in its movements. It is a determinate world, where there is a place for everything and where single events can be explained by single causes. It is also a moderate and reasonable world. This ordering is no mere mental exercise. The 'enlightened' governing agent also attempts to order the human world itself along these lines (or, perhaps most often, simply assumes that it is or 'naturally' ought to be so ordered). It is also one that has pretended, in its more triumphant moments, to exclude disorder itself from the world that it manages.

The phenomenon of Hinduism is in its essence, we are led to believe, a negativity of that sort of order. That is the effect that the use of organic metaphors, lacking the essence of mechanism have had on discourses about Hinduism and on the subject itself. Hinduism does not consist of a system of opposed but interdependent parts, but of a wild tangle of overlapping and merely juxtaposed pieces. It is uncentred (having not one high god, but two), unstable (new sects and castes are constantly sprouting up), and lacking in uniformity (it indiscriminately mixes magic and pantheism, the intellectual and the emotional). If Hinduism has a positive essence, it consists of its feminine imaginativeness, its ability to absorb and include, to move from one extreme to the other, and to tolerate inconsistencies.

The Hinduism we shall examine is the outcome of differing European commercial and political projects of the nineteenth century and involved the placing of Hinduism in relationship to European systems of thought and religious practice. One of these was the attempt to remove cosmology from the province of theology and place it in the hands of natural philosophy or science. Concomitant with that was the effort directed at reconstituting some kind of space for the human and moral, either by reforming Christianity so that it could be compatible with the new knowledge, or by constructing personal philosophies that could provide meaning in a world dominated by science. Another project, more diffuse than these two, was the attempt to redefine gender relations in Europe, to constitute women simultaneously as pure, submissive symbols of domesticity and as seductive ruiners of 'man' (Lloyd, 1984: especially 74–85; Dijkstra, 1986: 160–73, 210–25, 237–8).

A final movement, which appears to have been integral to the building or rationalization of the European imperial polities in the later half of the century,

---

[3] For the work done by the presupposition of a unitary agency in a business corporation, see Thompson (1982).

consisted of the attempt to order and explain differences by constituting races as the major agents of an evolutionary history. Two explanatory texts hold sway here. The older holds that Hinduism was primarily a development of the earlier religion of the Aryans. The other argues that it was the outcome of the interaction between the religions of the Aryans and the indigenous populations of the subcontinent, in particular, the Dravidians.

The first section of this chapter deals with the way in which the founders of Indological discourse, English Utilitarians, committed to the advance of a secularized world, Christian idealists, bent on reforming their own religion, and philosophical idealists from the Continent, all systematized by Hegel's Spirit, constituted Hinduism and brought it in relationship to the religion and science of Europe.

The major device scholars used in their efforts to rationalize their untidy Hindu jungle was that of sorting its elements into religions that they mapped on to contrasting 'levels' of Indian society, providing each with its own mental essence. Sections 3–6 of the chapter are concerned with these 'religions' and with their 'history'. I look first at their construct of 'Brahmanism', religion of the Aryans or of the highest level, that of the 'intellectual' priesthood, the essence of which is an impersonal pantheism. Historically, it developed in the millennium before Christ. Next I deal with its lower opposite, the depiction of a wider or 'popular' Hinduism as the religion of a lower level, that of the emotional laity, the essential feature of which is a devotional theism. Indologists have construed this Hinduism in its 'classical' phase, fourth to sixth centuries AD, as a reaction to, and (somewhat contradictorily) a symbolization of, its superior opposite. Beneath this level Indologists and ethnologists have placed a third religion, one opposed to the religion of both the Brahman and the educated, urbane laity. They characterized this, a religion of the illiterate folk level, as a changeless, animistic religion of survival and as the religion of a Dravidian or pre-Aryan race. Then I turn to the 'decline' of Hinduism during what historians have termed a 'medieval' or 'sectarian' phase of excesses, one lasting from the seventh century until the eighteenth. We witness here the attempt to construe this degeneration as the triumph of a basically Dravidian or non-Aryan religion. At each turn, I argue, Hinduism has been constituted as exemplifying a mentality which privileges the 'imagination' and the 'passions' rather than 'reason' and the 'will', the two inevitable components of world-ordering rationality.

I follow with a look at post-Independence constructions of Jungians and structuralists. The former have, with their emphasis on a racial or archaic unconscious, I contend, made our picture of Hinduism, if anything, even worse. The latter have given prominence to holism, which is laudable, but still laden with difficulties from the standpoint of agency. The chapter ends with a critical summary.

3.2 PSYCHIC ORIGINS

3.2.1 Utilitarian and Anglican Distortions

The predominant construct of Hinduism was the one fashioned by Utilitarians and Christian idealists. The Utilitarians were empiricist or (later in the century) positivist in epistemology and secular or materialist in ontology. The Christian idealists adhered to the Utilitarian position with the difference that they added a God and tended, therefore, to be idealists when push came to shove. On the whole, the economists, anthropologists, and sociologists of India have tended to be secularists while British Sanskritists and historians of religion, many of them Anglican and government servants, have tended to be idealists. They have more or less consistently taken the position, at odds with the notion of Hinduism as a totally other religion, that Hinduism, in the ancient past was closely similar to that other religion of the Aryans, paganism.

James Mill's *History of British India* contains a long chapter entitled 'Religion of the Hindus'. If read with the commentary of the Indologist, H. H. Wilson, written well after Hegel had placed India in his world history, it can be taken as setting the terms and providing the framework of presuppositions within which both the predominant positivist scholarship of Indology, whether secular or religious in ontology, and the opposed views of the German philosophical idealists, were formulated.

At the beginning of his chapter on religion Mill opposes the 'constitution of the government and the provisions of law' to 'Religion' and wonders which had the 'greatest influence' on Hindus (1858: I, 228–9). Mill had no doubt, however, that 'the order of priests obtained a greater authority in India than in any other region of the globe.' That superiority 'they employed with astonishing success in multiplying and corroborating the ideas on which their power and consequence depended' (I, 229). As a result, their God was as far from the noninterventionist clockmaker of the Enlightenment as one could get:

Every thing in Hindustan was transacted by the Deity. The laws were promulgated, the people were classified, the government was established, by the Divine Being. The astonishing exploits of the Divinity were endless in that sacred land. For every stage of life from the cradle to the grave; for every hour of the day; for every function of nature; for every social transaction, God prescribed a number of religious observances. And meditation upon his incomprehensible attributes, as it was by far the most difficult of all human operations, so was it that glorious occupation which alone prepared the intense votary for the participation of the divine nature. (I, 229)

This overdetermining religion was not easy to apprehend because of 'the unparalleled vagueness which marks the language of the Brahmens'. From their 'wild eulogies and legends' it was possible to extract 'no coherent system of belief'. This was the result of building a faith on 'imagination'. Like other Anglo-Saxon philosophers of a secular stripe, he used a theory of mind as a machine. This theory privileged the sense impressions (and especially for the Utilitarians, the reception of quantifiable doses of pain and pleasure). The imagination of this theory had the job of displaying images delivered by the senses. To the extent that it stabilized these images, its function was approved; to the extent that it rearranged them without regard to those sense impressions from which they derived, its use was simply a matter of distortion. So distorted was Hindu knowledge that the relationship between language and object was reversed. Instead of 'representing' reality, language among the Brahmans concealed it.

Hinduism: The Mind of India 91

The major difference between religion before the Enlightenment and afterward, according to Mill, was that religion before that time had attempted to explain the causes of events and the origins of things (1858: I, 230). Given, however, the 'imperfect state' of society, man – the knowing subject here is always the lone male individual – was unable to think of natural events as a unified body of phenomena subject to scientific explanation. Instead, he endowed natural events with a life or agency. When these early religious thinkers tried to account for the whole of nature, they eventually came, especially in Asia, to focus on the god of the sun. This explanation of traditional religion, later known as 'intellectualist', appears again and again in the Indological accounts of Hinduism (Skorupski, 1976: 1–11).

Mill's intellectualism is most vivid in his commentary on Hindu cosmology. In the Hindu conception of the universe 'no coherence, wisdom, or beauty, ever appears: all is disorder, caprice, passion, contest, portents, prodigies, violence, and deformity'. It was at its irrational worst when held up against the pride and joy of the Englightenment, the mechanistic image of the cosmos provided by Descartes and Newton: 'It is perfectly evident that the Hindus never contemplated the universe as a connected and perfect system, governed by general laws, and directed to benevolent ends' (1858: I, 267–8). Ignorant of the laws of nature and especially of the Utilitarian laws of human nature, the natural world is nothing for the Hindus, in Mill's depiction, but a distorted image of the world in which they lived. Their religion consisted of the 'primary worship' of 'the designing and invisible beings who preside over the powers of nature, according to their own arbitrary will, and act only for some private and selfish gratification' (1858: I, 268). Within that world of self-aggrandizing, divine aristocrats (is Mill describing India or England?), it was no wonder that the language of servile men was hyperbolic and that interactions between the two were grounded in fear and expressed in flattery (1858: I, 268).

Wilson, orientalist and commentator on Mill, was not the secularist that Mill was. The ontological assumptions he made appear to have been those I refer to as religious idealist. He was certainly no missionary and indeed kept rather quiet about his religious stance. He does, however, provide us with a clue in the closing passage of his major work on Hinduism, where he remarks that the 'tendency of many widely diffused divisions is decidedly monotheistical ...'. Up to this point we might see Wilson as a secularist. But, quite obliquely, he makes it clear that the 'germ' of monotheism that will grow in India, encouraged not by missionaries but through the educational institutions, such as those of which he had charge as an official, will be a post-Enlightenment form of Christianity (1846: 238). Wilson was also quite happy to see the pre-Christian forms of Hinduism, some of which the privileged gaze of the scientist could see in the practices of present-day Hindus, as similar to the religion of European antiquity. This was a major justification for the study of Hinduism. We could peer into the past of our own religion in the Indian present.

From the standpoint of a post-Enlightenment Christian, however, the differences between Hinduism and European or Christian thought were almost as great as they were for Mill. Wilson shared Mill's intellectualist assumptions about traditional religion and agreed that the 'notions' of the Hindus are

irrational and erroneous', and 'are therefore offensive to minds better informed'. His disagreement was, therefore, not over the basic construction of the
Hindu religion, but over Mill's moral condemnation of it, saying that his
'designations of degrading, gross, and disgusting, are scarcely applicable'
(1858: I, 266). Wilson did accuse Mill of not distinguishing between mythology
and 'philosophical doctrines'. The latter, says Wilson, citing Rammohun Roy
(1772–1833), the contemporary Bengali apologist for Hinduism, do use reason.
Wilson states that those doctrines 'invariably enjoin disregard of all external,
and merely temporal existence, and the exclusive direction of the powers of the
mind to the study of man's own soul', and he agrees that they 'may be
condemned as unwise and ill-directed, but they can scarcely be termed, with
justice, mean and degrading' (1858: I, 266). So, here again Wilson challenges
Mill only in his evaluation of Hinduism, not in his construction of it as a
distorted picture of the world resulting from a mind whose imagination was not
engaged with external reality.

Mill was prepared to concede that he and the orientalists, Jones and
Colebrooke, might disagree in their evaluation of Hindu thought. But, asserted
Mill, 'there is an universal agreement respecting the meanness, the absurdity,
the folly, of the endless ceremonies, in which the practical part of the Hindu
religion consists' (1858: I, 274–5). Compared with that of any other nation,
none is 'more tedious, minute, and burdensome' (275) than the 'ritual' of the
Hindus. A rational religion ought, argued Mill, to emphasize the moral and
useful and shun 'wasteful' rites. Within Hinduism, however, 'The precepts,
which are lavished upon its ceremonies, bury, in their exorbitant mass, the
pittance bestowed upon all other duties taken together. On all occasions
ceremonies meet the attention as the pre-eminent duties of the Hindu' (1858: I,
277). Mill accordingly gives over a great deal of space to these ritual excesses.
He rehearses long lists of 'pollutions' (1858: I, 278–9) and 'penances' (279–
87), reports 'human sacrifices' (287–8), takes note of devotees throwing
themselves under the chariot wheels of Juggernaut and drowning themselves in
the Ganges (289), and concludes with accounts of suttee, the 'burning of the
wives on the funeral piles of their husbands' (289).

The picture Mill painted of a Hindu god and his worshipper was that of the
aristocrat whose power is unchecked, on the one hand, and of the flattering
courtier or servant, on the other. Given this, it is easy to see why he takes the
worship of images in temples as the epitome of Hindu ceremonial:

To the rude mind, no other rule suggests itself for paying court to the Divine, than that
for paying court to the Human Majesty; and as among a barbarous people, the forms of
address, of respect, and compliment, are generally multiplied into a great variety of
grotesque and frivolous ceremonies, so it happens with regard to their religious service.
An endless succession of observances, in compliment to the god, is supposed to afford
him the most exquisite delight; while the common discharge of the beneficent duties of
life is regarded as an object of comparative indifference. (1858: I, 276–7)

Wilson, wishing to save ancient religion, points out that the 'observances' of
the early Hindus were 'all personal and domestic', and compare favourably with
the public worship of Greece and Rome so far as waste of time and

offensiveness is concerned. The 'public observances' were not, according to Wilson, ancient, and hence not essential to it (276). Wilson does not, however, deny the motivation that Mill attributes to this form of worship. Nor does he find troublesome the idea that image-worship is a displaced form of royal attendance, an idea that persists in studies of Hinduism.

This Utilitarian polemic against Hinduism ends with an account of morality, of the 'duties' supposed to be carried out by the Hindus. As elsewhere, Hindu morality is characterized as beset by extremes. Mill wonders how, for example, 'a religion which subjects to the eyes of its votaries the grossest images of sensual pleasure, and renders even the emblems of generation objects of worship', could promote 'chastity' (1858: I, 294). The chapter concludes with a brief discussion of 'metempsychosis' in which he argues, once again, that worldly life has been mistakenly displaced on to an afterlife. The enjoyment of material pleasures and pains by a mind whose job was to mirror reality through the medium of the senses on a daily ongoing basis was what, in Utilitarianism, kept men sociable. According to Mill, 'the doctrine of future rewards and punishments has, in no situation, and among no people, a power to make men virtuous' (1858: I, 302).

Given his commitment to the universality of a mechanical mind, Mill was hard put to explain how or why the imagination of that mind in India had come so consistently to override its foundation in the senses. To attribute it to the bad intentions of the Brahman priests simply deferred this problem of his account. Help was, however, near at hand. The German Romantics who were concerned with fashioning world histories had already come up with one explanation for the mentality they and the British wanted to find in Hinduism. Hegel, the arch-rationalist, would come up with another.

3.2.2   Romantic and Rationalist Dreams

The writing of Romantic idealists and of their rationalist critic, Hegel, in Germany was probably more important than that of the early British scholars in constructing Indology's Hinduism. More ambitious than the Christian idealists, these metaphysicians were intent on uncovering an absolute that would transcend both science and religion. They held, in their attempts to account for differences in a world that was coming to be centred on Europe, that the abstract, static, and universal rationality which the Enlightenment thinkers (and early Utilitarians) called human nature did not exist. Rather human nature was a mixture of the rational and irrational; it was specific to circumstances; it was dynamic, changing from period to period; and it also varied from place to place (Collingwood, 1956: 90–1, 116–17). There existed different human natures for each of the 'nations' of the world, in each of which different mental faculties predominated. The idea that the essence of Hinduism was an idealist or illusionary pantheism derives, I argue, from their theory of a divided human nature and from the contrast between a sensual imagination and spiritual reason presupposed in that division.

Hegel classed the religion of the Hindu (along with other oriental and Egyptian religions), with its cult of sun, fire, water, moon, trees, and so on, as a 'natural' religion and distinguished it from the 'later' religions of 'freedom' (among which were those of the Jews and Greeks, and, of course, Christianity) (Hegel, 1895). The philosophy that he and other idealists thought constituted the mind of this earlier religion was an illusionary variety of pantheism.

The Romantic Schlegel held that Vedānta, the teachings explanatory of the religion of the Veda (see 3.3.2), India's oldest and most authoritative text, is the one of the 'six systems' of Indian philosophy that 'exerts the greatest influence' (1890: 188) and equated that with what he refers to as a 'complete system of Pantheism' (189). He distinguished it from the 'rigid, mathematical, abstract, negative Pantheism' of some of his contemporaries, claiming that it is a 'modified, poetical, and half-mythological system', one that does not deny the 'personal existence of the human soul'. None the less, he repeatedly referred to a 'general inclination of the Indian philosophers to regard the whole external world of sense as vain illusion, and to represent individual personality as absorbed in the God-head by the most intimate union' (187–8). Hegel, too, considered this illusionary pantheism the complement of India's natural religion. For both it was the product of a mind that was dominated by the imagination.

Hegel reappropriated the ancient European notion of a multi-layered soul, reworked over the centuries by differing schools of Aristotelians and Platonists. The imagination or, more generally, in Hegel's scheme, representation (*Vorstellung*, feminine), was the premier faculty of the material, sentient or organic level of the mind, while reason or understanding (*Verstand*, masculine), thought proper, was the spiritual. Representation, thinking in images, was, for Hegel, the mode of knowing for religion, while conceptual thought was that of philosophy. The imagination takes sensual images that it experiences or recollects. It reproduces them or, more complexly, associates them. In its highest form, that of the 'creative imagination' (*Phantasie*, also feminine), it makes up images without recourse to recollection or experience (1971: 206–13).

Fantasy or fancy is thus not simply an imagining mechanism which, when detached from the senses, has ceased to function in a useful way. She is an inferior form of reason that attempts theoretical thought but can do so only by the use of sensual images. The symbol (by which is meant icon, a concrete, sensual image that has an inherent resemblance to that which it represents) does it in a plastic or material form (architecture, sculpture, painting), and the myth in language, especially in poetic language.

Thought in which the reason of spirit (*Geist*, masculine) predominates is, according to Hegel, both subjective and objective (1971: 224). It is oriented toward truth and produces a fully 'rational' knowledge of the world and orders the world in conformity with it by use of an accompanying 'will'. Fantasy, in which the subjective aspect of mind is 'severed' from the objective, is by definition lacking in realism.[4] Wild instead of stable, extreme instead of moderate, obscure instead of clear, and repetitive instead of economical, it is only dimly rational. What is more, it is accompanied not by a rational will, but by appropriately inferior passions, which pull it hither and yon. Because its

---

[4] As Taylor points out (1975: 466), this epistemology 'has a notion of conceptual thought as self-transparent which we find it hard to share today'.

imaging of reality is unstable and unrealistic, the imaginative mind is also unconscious of its operations, unaware not only of the difference between symbol and referent but wanting in a theory of representation.

Indian mysticism – 'this absorption of all thought and all consciousness in God – this solitary enduring feeling of internal and eternal union with the Deity, they have carried to a pitch and extreme that they may almost be called a moral and intellectual self-annihilation' – proceeded logically, according to Schlegel, from this imaginative mentality (1890: 160). He explicitly compares the 'excesses' or 'aberrations' of this mysticism, which 'have been carried to such a fearful extent, not only in speculation, but in real life and practice; and which, transcending as they do all the limits of human nature, far exceed the bounds of possibility, or what men have in general considered as such', with the 'more temperate and harmonious constitution' of the European 'mind' (1890: 160–1).

Hegel also conjured a Hinduism of extremes as entailed by its epistemology of imagination: 'The Indian view of things is a Universal Pantheism, a Pantheism, however, of Imagination, not of Thought'. Spirit is everywhere in the world: 'One substance pervades the Whole of things, and all individualizations are directly vitalized and animated into particular Powers' (1956: 141). But this did not effect a theophany of unitary order and beauty because the Hindu absolute is not a free, ordering subject. It has no subjectivity, no active will. It is a passive, empty, neutral substance. The only way a person can attain to unity with that substance is to deprive himself also of subjectivity and activity, to completely denaturalize or dematerialize himself. Whence the extreme asceticism of Hinduism on the part of those who set out to obtain unity with that absolute. On the other hand, the realm of nature itself remains chaotic, wild and disorderly, held in thrall by the passions. Whence the multi-limbed, protean depictions of the divinity 'made bizarre, confused and ridiculous' (1956: 141) in Hinduism, and the voluptuousness of image-worship on the part of those who remain in the world.

Hegel thus explains why the religion of the Indians suffers, in Freudian terms, from displacement and condensation. Everything in it is divine, but nothing partakes of divinity. The soul, he says, 'is delivered over to these limited objects as to its Lords and Gods. Everything, therefore – Sun, Moon, Stars, the Ganges, the Indus, beasts, Flowers – everything is a God to it. And while, in this deification, the finite loses its consistency and substantiality, intelligent conception of it is impossible' (1956: 141). The divine which ought to be transcendent yet active in the world is instead immanent but inoperative.

Creative imagination or fantasy was not for Hegel, as for Schlegel, an opposed, but complementary mental activity. It was, rather, an inferior form of thought but one that is continuous with the higher form, one that anticipates the higher and superseding form, and, as such, merits study. It was, he alleged, the state of mind of humanity when civilization dawned in the East, when the mind of man thought as in a dream.

Hegel held that there is no fundamental difference between the essence of the 'inner' (spirit) and the 'outer' (nature, matter) (Taylor, 1975: 496). One consequence of this is that the epistemology (inner, subjective knowledge) and ontology (outer, objective reality) of the religion and philosophy of a given period of history and region of the world are productive of one another. If knowledge of the world is the product of a 'creative imagination', a way of knowing disengaged from external reality, it must be the case – given the unity of inner and outer – that the spirit or mind inside that external reality is itself disengaged from its human knowers.

Precisely because Hegel insisted on this unity of inner and outer, he considered India's moment in the history of human rationality as one in which spirit must itself have been in a dreaming state. Hegel often correlated the history of mankind and the life of a man. He also saw an analogy between dreaming and the activity of the creative imagination. Hindu India had the same characteristics in the spiritual development of man as the mental condition of a man dreaming just before he awakened (1956: 140–1). Whence the importance of the dream in Hegel's India and in so much of discourse on the religions of that subcontinent. It is this which Moreau so brilliantly depicts in his 'Triumph of Alexander'. Not only can we see his portrayal as a dream, but in that dream we can see the two main figures, Alexander and the colossal Indian statue, as the embodiments of Europe's Spirit or Reason, on the one hand, and of India's Imagination, on the other (see 2.2.2). Men in later times and other civilizations might produce dream-like knowledge when they were asleep, but in India, men produced it when they were fully awake. The dreams of the Hindu 'are not mere fables', they constitute, for him, a real world (1956: 141). Contemporary psychologists, Mill's heirs, refer to this as 'autistic thinking' (Thomson, 1959: 197).

To conclude, by replacing the universal, mechanical mind of the Anglo-Saxons with a varying or dialectically developing one, these Germans were able to rationalize Mill's Hindu mind. The intellectual architects of the first imperial formation that would reach to every corner of the earth, the Germans also gave Indian thought a place within this new global framework. What were more or less disconnected examples of Hindu irrationality and superstition for Mill, the empiricist, were, for the German idealists, including Hegel, instances of the core metaphysics of that religion, of its double displacement of the ideal and material, the subjective and objective and of the predominance in it of creative imagination or fantasy over true thought or reason. That becomes the positive inner essence of the female India that a masculine Europe with its inner essence of reason was coming to dominate. Ironically, the German's own dream, that this world civilization would have a unified German state as its hegemonic polity, was not to be realized in the nineteenth century. The British and the French became the hegemonic powers in this new imperial formation. They, especially the British, were, however, quite happy to divert the German rationalizations of a world order and append them, piecemeal and often unknowingly, to their own Utilitarian or Christian views. We would not have those later British depictions of India as a feminine sponge or jungle animated by a feminine imagination had the Romantics and Hegel not done their work. The endless stream of studies of myths and the myriad portrayals of a mysterious India that reveals layers of the psyche, all have their ancestry here. The later structuralist, Lévi-Strauss, reinvents this lower form of reason and attributes it to the minds of 'primitive' men (1966).[5] Lacan, the psychoanalyst, can be taken as extending it to the unconscious of all people (Harland, 1987: 33). I shall look at the parallels in structuralist studies of Hinduism below (3.6).[6]

3.3 BRAHMANISM, THE ARYAN MIND IN THE TROPICS

Mysticism is the religion of feminine natures. Enthusiastic surrender, a delicate capacity for feeling, soft passiveness are its characteristics. Prophetic religion, on the contrary, has an unmistakably masculine character, ethical severity, bold resoluteness, and disregard of consequence, energetic activity. (Professor Heiler, theologian)[7]

3.3.1 Vedic Sacrifice as Displaced Materialism

The Utilitarian and deist concept of religion that Mill and Wilson tried to impose on Hinduism continued to predominate throughout the nineteenth and into the twentieth centuries, now contradicted, now supplemented by the views of the Romantic idealists and the rationalist Hegel. Scholars soon began to distinguish a religion called Brahmanism from within Hinduism. H. H. Wilson's account of 'sects' in India is itself as responsible as any other single work of scholarship for promulgating this notion:

An early division of the Hindu system, and one conformable to the genius of all Polytheism, separated the practical and popular belief, from the speculative or philosophical doctrines. Whilst the common people addressed their hopes and fears to stocks and stones, and multiplied by their credulity and superstition the grotesque objects of their veneration, some few, of deeper thought and wider contemplation, plunged into the mysteries of man and nature, endeavoured assiduously, if not successfully, to obtain just notions of the cause, the character and consequence of existence. (1846: 1)

The 'few' were the adherents of the six 'schools of philosophy' (*darśana*), while the many were the worshippers of different divinities separated into distinct 'associations'.

---

[5] Commenting on what he calls primitive man's 'science of the concrete', in which he likens the difference between the thinking of the neolithic and that of the scientist to the difference between the *bricoleur* and the engineer (1966: 16–22), Lévi-Strauss says 'that there are two distinct modes of scientific thought. These are certainly not a function of different stages of development of the human mind [contrast Hegel's stance] but rather of two strategic levels at which nature is accessible to scientific enquiry: one roughly adapted to that of perception and the imagination: the other at a remove from it' (15).
[6] Although Harland points to the importance of Hegel's objective ideas, stripped of their older religious connotations, for structuralism (1987: 70–6), and discusses Lévi-Strauss's characterization of the thought of primitive man as a form of conceptual understanding different from that of modern science (29–31), and suggests that the psychoanalyst, Lacan, extends to his idea of the unconscious of all men (33), he does not point to the parallel here with Hegel.
[7] From his 1932 book, *Prayer*, cited by S. Radhakrishnan (1959: 65–6).

Wilson also tried to discover the opposition he imagined to exist between the elite and the popular duplicated among the Brahmans themselves. 'Few Brahmans of learning, if they have any religion at all, will acknowledge themselves to belong to any of the popular divisions of the Hindu faith', says Wilson, but then immediately concedes that, 'although, as a matter of simple preference, they more especially worship some individual deity, as their chosen, or *Ishta Devata*' (1846: 20). Which is to say, that these Brahmans, whom he and others have referred to by the indigenous term, Smārta, 'traditional', are also, at least nominally, theistic.

What emerges from the oppositions in Wilson's 'secondary revision' is a religion of two levels and two periods. Brahmanism is the earlier, pre-Christian religion of the Aryan elite, the Brahmans, while Hinduism is the later, post-Christian religion of the populace at large. I begin here with Brahmanism, the Indian branch of Aryan paganism.

The two focal points in the study of Brahmanism and its construction have been the 'sacrifice' (*yajña*) and the quest for 'emancipation' (*moksha*) through 'knowledge' or 'gnosis' (*jñāna*). While commentators adhering to both the Utilitarian and idealist views of Indian religion have written on both of these subjects, there has been a strong tendency for the former to concentrate on the sacrifice and the latter to stress liberation. Both, however, have been fascinated by the texts or 'scriptures' they considered the basis of this religion, the *Vedas*. Scholars quickly came to realize that the term 'veda', usually translated as 'knowledge' in keeping with the highest religious goal to be reached through the use of these texts, embraced a number of different but related texts. The *Vedas* proper consisted of four 'collections' (*saṃhitā*) of 'hymns' or prayers' (*mantra*), the *Rig, Yajur, Sama*, and *Atharva* made by different 'schools' (*śākhā*) of priests. Composed in verse in the earliest form of Sanskrit (called Vedic), they were organized for different purposes in the performance of the Vedic sacrifice. Supplementing them were texts in prose, the 'ritualistic precepts' (*brāhmaṇas*), called *Brāhmaṇas*, of the different schools, compared with the Hebrew Talmud. Still other texts in both prose and verse, the *Upanishads*, 'mystical or secret doctrines' concerned with knowledge and liberation (see next section) rather than sacrifice, completed the *Vedas*.

The amazing thing about the earliest of the Vedas was the 'discovery' that they had been preserved and transmitted intact as oral texts since the time of Aryan settlement in India (1500 BC). They were not only the oldest texts from India and the most authoritative in its religious tradition – that would not have had too much appeal – they were the oldest religious texts of the Aryans, of both the Europeans and the Indians, older than the Bible itself. To edit and translate these texts using the methods of the new science of comparative philology[8] would, thus, lay bare not simply the origins of Indian religion, but reveal the beliefs of man at his moment of origin, the 'natural' religion people practiced before they lived in cities.

This is not the place to undertake a history of scholarship on the two topics constitutive of Brahmanism. What I shall do here, in keeping with my objective

---

[8] Max Müller was the first to do this (1849–74; 1869—; 1877).

of producing a history of intellectual practices, is to look at two examples, one a Utilitarian treatment of sacrifice, the other an idealist treatment of emancipation. For the sacrifice I will rely on the summary depiction of the British Indologist, A. L. Basham, written as Britain's empire turned into a commonwealth.

That sacrifice was taken to be of crucial importance in these primordial scriptures had its effect. Sacrifice became the centre of a scholarly industry around the turn of the century,[9] at its busiest in philology (including classics) and overlapping with the history of religions, but with important branches in anthropology and psychology. The more secularist approach has, as already indicated, wished to see the sacrifice as a form of false technology, a displaced form of scientific thinking. The perspective of the post-Enlightenment Christian idealist differs from the intellectualist primarily in its wish to discover in the pre-Christian sacrifice an anticipation of Christ's sacrifice, while at the same time pointing to its aberration, human sacrifice.

Like the earlier scholars who wrote on sacrifice in India, Basham proceeds 'historically' by looking first at the 'earliest' form of Brahmanism in the 'oldest' text, the *Rig Veda*. On his reading, the Indic Aryans were presumably settled in the Panjab region. Organized into tribes, they subsisted largely by herding cattle. Their religion centred on an 'aristocratic' cult of sacrifices made into a fire. Although Basham does not explicitly call it a natural religion, he does point out that the gods of early Brahmanism 'were chiefly connected with the sky' and (preparing the way for the later rise of mother goddesses) 'were predominantly male' (1954: 233). Not depicted in icons, those invisible gods came to partake of the offerings.

Basham's predecessor, Monier Monier-Williams, a Christian idealist, was much less vague.[10] He was sure that the religion in the *Vedas* was the same in origin as the religion of Ourselves. He asks, 'To what deities, then, did the Vedic poets address their prayers and hymns?' The answer he gives is that 'these were probably the very deities worshipped under similar names by our Aryan progenitors in their primeval home somewhere on the table-land of Central Asia.' As to the nature of their deities, he says: 'The answer is, they worshipped those physical forces before which all nations, if guided solely by the light of nature, have in the early period of their life instinctively bowed down, and before which even the more civilized and enlightened have always been compelled to bend in awe and reverence, if not in adoration' (1894/1951: 14–15). Here we have not simply commentated description, but explanation: pre-Christian Aryans worshipped nature because the Christian truth about a

[9] The founder of this as an explanatory industry was the work, apparently inspired by Frazer, of a scholar of the Semitic languages, W. Robertson Smith (1972). The major work on sacrifice in India was that of Louis Renou's teacher, Sylvain Lévi (1898). The formalist work of Durkheimians Hubert and Mauss (1898), critical of Robertson Smith's evolutionary approach, relies heavily on Vedic materials, including Vedic classifications themselves. Monographs on particular Vedic sacrifices, highly formalist, abound.

[10] One of the most important of the British students of Hinduism in the latter part of the nineteenth century, Monier-Williams was born in Bombay and was the Professor of Sanskrit, Persian, and Hindustani at Haileybury, the training school for East India Company 'executives', from 1844 to 1858, before succeeding H. H. Wilson at Oxford, where he founded an important Indian Institute in 1883.

God had not yet been revealed. This explanation has not stood up well. So Basham simply omit it, reiterating the commentative representations that these older explanatory accounts animated. His account is one that has, so to speak, been given a prefrontal lobotomy.[11]

Basham represents the sacrifice as a Utilitarians' feast. Mostly 'good natured', the gods 'descended to the sacred straw (*barhis*) on the sacrificial field, drank and ate with the worshippers, and duly rewarded them with success in war, progeny, increase of cattle, and long life, on a *quid pro quo* basis' (1954: 239). The crude materialist view of 'tribal' religion that pervades his text comes to the fore when, after seeming to accord the sacrifice respect by saying that it 'must have had its element of awe and wonder', Basham implies that the origin of those features of 'mystery' that constitute the core of Brahmanism were induced by drink: 'The worshippers, inebriated with soma, saw wondrous visions of the gods; they experienced strange sensations of power; they could reach up and touch the heavens; they became immortal; they were gods themselves.' The priests had a scarce commodity in this, which they were to convert into their privileged position: 'The priests, who alone knew the rituals whereby the gods were brought to the sacrifice, were masters of a great mystery' (1954: 239). He then goes on to enumerate some of the 'less obvious' (that is, less Utilitarian and more Indian) ideas that arose in connection with the sacrifice; those of a 'mysterious entity called *brahman*' (which is 'magical power' in the form of 'sacred utterances (*mantra*)' and, more diffusely, 'a sort of supernatural electricity, known to students of primitive religion as *mana*', of the 'mystical identification of god, victim and sacrificer', and of a 'creator-god' or 'primeval man' (1954: 239–40). Having thus guided us through the *Vedas* proper, Basham then turns to the development of Brahmanism in the next oldest Vedic texts, the *Brāhmaṇas*.

As the Aryans settled, according to Basham, in the Gangetic valley and adopted a more sedentary way of life based on agriculture, changes occurred in the 'natural' religion common to both Indians and Europeans. An extreme ritualism, in which the sacrifice became a 'supernal mystery', developed: 'the priests mystically repeated the primeval sacrifice, and the world was born anew. Without regular sacrifices all cosmic processes would cease, and chaos would come again.' There was a shift of power away from gods to the Brahman priests, 'who by the magic of the sacrifice maintained and compelled them'. That left the Brahmans in the superior position that has been theirs ever since: 'The brahman was more powerful than any earthly king, or any god; by his accurate performance of sacrifice he maintained all things, and was therefore the supreme social servant; by the slightest variation of ritual he could turn the sacrifice against his patrons and destroy them, and was therefore the most dangerous of enemies' (1954: 241).

There is much in this characterization that is questionable. If tribes were, as Basham also argues, turning into states and kingship was becoming a more important institution, might it not be more plausible to read the *Brāhmaṇa*

[11] Consult for a more extended and differentiated version of a religion of nature, quasi-Kantian in approach, F. Max Müller's chapter, 'The Worship of Tangible, Semi-tangible, and Intangible Objects' (1880: 168–217).

texts, given that they are religious texts, as exalting *both* kingship and the officiants of the Vedic sacrifice? Equally dubious is his conversion of the Brahman priest into a cosmic magician and the related idea that the sacrifice is a kind of false technology or displaced materialism shrouded in a maze of rationalizations. But there is a desire embedded in the discourse to produce an India dominated by priests and by a religion that is extreme both in its worldly magic and its otherworldly mysticism. Hence, the original religion of the Aryans, which Indologists had pulled free of Mill's undifferentiated Hinduism and made into the ancestor of both European and Indian religions, they had now to Indianize. They have obligingly turned Vedic sacrifice into a contra-dictory excess. They have transformed it into a complex of overdetermined magical acts which is at the same time overly intellectualized. Here, then, according to Basham, is the earliest manifestation of an Indian tendency to go too far. What should follow this original 'thesis' of ritualism in the crude dialectic imposed on Indian religious history, where ordering and moderating syntheses are in short supply? Why nothing but its opposite, a rush to mysticism of the most radical sort.[12]

3.3.2 Upanishadic Mysticism as Misguided Idealism

Indologists tell us that the Upanishads are the texts that contain the origins of Indian philosophy. They are the texts in which the 'soul' or 'self' (*ātman*) appears as the essence of the person. In these also, we are told, the famous doctrines of metempsychosis or the transmigration of souls (*saṃsāra*) and of emancipation or liberation from that process, synonymous with the soul's absorption into an 'impersonal' or 'neuter' Brahman, make their appearance. They constitute the basis of Vedānta, the 'end' or 'completion' (*anta*) of 'knowledge' (*veda*) and provide the justification for caste inequality. Reading these counterparts of Plato's Dialogues will, thus, reveal to us the inner recesses of the Indian mind and of the society it animated.

To get us to this point our guides have already had to make some careful selections. Vedānta was, they inform us, one of the 'six systems' of philosophy in Brahmanism, the Mīmāṃsā. That was divided into two schools, an 'earlier' Mīmāṃsā, that concerned with interpretation of scriptures, the 'section on sacrifices' (*kārma-kāṇḍa*), and a 'later' Mīmāṃsā, devoted to interpretations of the doctrine of liberation, the 'section on knowledge' (*jñāna-kāṇḍa*), otherwise known as Vedānta. There were and still are many schools of Vedānta, distinguished by the relation of God or absolute to man to which they adhere. The three major positions to which the schools have gravitated are Advaita or 'nondualist', Bhedābheda or 'identity-in-difference', and Dvaita or 'dualist'. Most scholars have, however, directed our attention to just one, the *advaita*, characterized as a 'monist', 'metaphysical', 'religious', or 'mystical' philosophy. Translators and interpreters assert that this monist philosophy is the core of the *Upanishads*. They almost invariably rely for their reading of them on the

---

[12] Monier-Williams, comparing this to a pendulum's swing, says 'a process of action and reaction has marked the whole course of Hinduism' (1894/1951: 35).

commentary of Sankara on Bādarāyaṇa's earlier *Vedānta-sūtra*, itself an interpretation of the Upanishads which the latter considered most important. Since
this Sankara was, we are assured, India's greatest philosopher, we are on the
right track.

Most scholars, whether empiricist or idealist, have considered the doctrines
of the *Upanishads* themselves a development in reaction to the excessive
ritualism of the earlier Vedic texts. The Brahmans who first preached these
doctrines were presumably also the first of the Smārta or 'traditional' Brahmans,
observing, as a part of this reaction, a simplified householder's version of the
more elaborate Vedic, or Śrauta, cult of sacrifice. There are, as I have
indicated, two theories which explain why both the excessive ritualism and its
response, an extreme form of mysticism, should have developed out of the
earlier Aryan religion. Throughout much of the nineteenth century, the theory
that most Indologists adhered to was environmental. Maurice Bloomfield
(1855–1928), for example, asserted that when the Aryans first arrived in India,
they were 'a sturdy, life-loving people'. They continued to push their way
eastward in India, 'until they had overrun the plain of the Ganges – the hottest
civilized land on the face of the earth'. Reminding his reader that it was there
rather than in the northwest that the 'pessimistic' philosophies were composed,
he declares: 'There in the land of Bengal, if anywhere on the face of the
civilized earth, the doubts and misgivings that beset human life at its best might
permanently harden into the belief that life is a sorry affair.' The universal
human mind embodied in the Aryan did not decline there, but his body did:
'Hypochondria, melancholia, dyspepsia – call it what we may – conquered the
conquering Aryan, whose stock was no doubt the product of a more northerly
and invigorating climate' (Bloomfield, 1908: 265–6).[13] Whence the illusionist,
otherworldly direction taken by our ancient cousin's thought.

Other scholars, plumping for the racial theory of High Empire, have argued
that Brahmanism itself, the core religion of India's intellectual elite, was
also the result of interaction between Aryan and pre-Aryan races or cultures. Even one of its 'basic' tenets, transmigration, 'seems to rest', according
to Basham, 'on a primitive belief that conception occurred through the eating by
one of the parents of a fruit or vegetable containing the latent soul of the
offspring' (1954: 242). Less satisfying, but still more up-to-date, Basham
gives as the reason for the 'growth of pessimism, asceticism and mysticism' a
'deep psychological uneasiness' brought on by the 'breaking up' of the 'old
tribal units' and the removal of 'the feeling of group solidarity which the tribe
gave ...' (1954: 246). So much for the rise of India's mental essence. Let us
turn to its content.

The successors of Schlegel in Germany took much more readily to the
Upanishads than they did to the sacrificial texts, so it is only appropriate that we
should concentrate on their handiwork in reviewing what nearly everyone has
come to consider the most important texts of Brahmanism. The example I have
chosen is the study by Paul Deussen (1845–1919), certainly one of the finest

[13] Bloomfield was Professor of Sanskrit and Comparative Philology at Johns Hopkins
University, USA.

products of Indology's idealist wing.[14] He argues very forcefully that the 'fundamental conception' of those texts in relating the 'first principle of things to created nature', popularly referred to, says Deussen, as the relation of God to the universe, is idealist. By this he means that 'God alone and nothing besides him is real. The universe as regards its extension in space and bodily consistence is in truth not real; it is mere illusion, as used to be said, mere appearance, as we say today' (1966: 160–1).

He contrasts this position with three other positions – realism, theism, and pantheism – which he says are to be found in the *Upanishads*. Of them, the prevalent one is, according to him, the pantheist. Yet that is 'but an unconscious concession made to the empirical that demands a real universe held together by causal connections of time and space' (185). In other words, pantheism is itself reducible to idealism. Given his own metaphysical equation of essence with origin, Deussen is convinced that 'the older the texts of the *Upanishads* are, the more uncompromisingly and expressly do they maintain this illusory character of the world of experience' (228). He admits in the next breath that 'this peculiar and far-fetched idea is seldom expressed in absolute simplicity', but he explains this, once again, as a concession to the 'empirical modes of knowledge'.

There is, however, more at issue here than simply a study of difficult texts. Deussen, who himself held it 'in the nature of a philosophical principle to be a unity' (244), desires to show, through his analysis of the *Upanishads*, that the philosophical sun does indeed rise in the East. He wishes to argue that these texts are older than those of Plato and that they contain the origin and essence of all philosophy, namely, a quest for a 'first principle of the universe' and a 'more or less clear consciousness that the entire empirical reality is not the true essence [*sic*] of things' (41). Concerning the *Upanishads*, Deussen therefore proclaims that 'the world-wide historical significance of these documents cannot, in our judgement, be more clearly indicated than by showing how the deep fundamental conception of Plato and Kant was precisely that which already formed the basis of Upanishad teaching' (1966: 42). Like Hegel, Deussen assumes here that the idealism of early Indian thought is the product of an imaginative faculty, and he also places it before the rise of the West, where symbolical thought may safely be allowed to roam, instead of placing it side by side with Christian or European thought. The reader may rest assured that Western reason, in the form of Plato and ultimately of Kant will develop this universal idealism, and not the later Indians. Indeed, Deussen had rather harsh things to say of them, referring to the dualist system of Sānkhya, another of the six systems of Indian philosophy, as the 'husk' which caused the kernel to perish (239–44) and to Vedānta as an attempt to separate the one from the other (400).

Thus, Deussen continued to adhere to the idea that the essence of Hinduism was an illusionary pantheism, with this difference. Deussen has refined the essence, declaring the illusionary part of it (rather than the pantheist) to be the

---

[14] Deussen, the Professor of Philosophy at Kiel, was himself a proponent of the transcendental idealism of Immanuel Kant (1724–1804) and of Arthur Schopenhauer (1788–1860), a rival of Hegel whose collected works Deussen edited.

'kernel' of Brahmanism and even of 'the entire religious and philosophical belief of India' (400).[15]

The secular priests who guarded the imperial talisman in British India early in this century were not pleased with the idea that the inner, imaginative thought of the *Upanishads* was the origin of both Eastern and Western philosophy. One of these, A. B. Keith (1879–1944), argued that Deussen's Kantian interpretation of the *Upanishads* could not be sustained. He criticized the *Upanishads* for what he considered to be their confused thinking and fatalism and believed that, 'regarded as serious contributions to the solution of the fundamental problems of philosophy, the value of the *Upanishads* must be considered to be comparatively small.' While he did not disagree that 'the *Upanishads* are essentially pantheistic', he was careful to add, 'with a strong theistic leaning'. Of what value were the *Upanishads*? They were valuable for their universalist mysticism (over and against the personalist mysticism of Christianity). Keith then went on to repeat what we have been told innumerable times:

The chief distinction, however, between the standpoint of the *Upanishads* in this regard and that of Western theories of the absolute is that the *Upanishads* do not feel any serious necessity for finding a place for morality and political life, while in the West from Hegel onwards, heroic, if unsuccessful, efforts have been made by the followers of this ideal to establish morality and civil life as an essential [sic] element in the absolute. (1925: 592–600)[16]

So, even the absolutist philosophers of the West, wrong though they may be when compared to their more successful Anglo-Saxon cousins, cannot help but deploy the world-ordering rationality that is theirs. Mill's heir, Keith dismissed mysticism as a 'tendency to see things cloudily, in a golden or sentimental haze, to justify the habit of the human mind to entertain contradictory beliefs at the same time, to exalt confusion of thought'. He will not allow early Indian thought even one moment in the sun. Like his ancestors and contemporaries, he is a materialist. Just as ideas were supposed to be caused by the data of the senses, so he is also more readily prepared to see caste as the cause for India's mysticism rather than, as the German idealists, the other way around.

Despite these differences, both the idealists and the materialists assumed the existence of essences and all agreed on what the double essence of Brahmanism is. In the first instance, it is an over-elaborated cosmic ritualism; in the final instance it is a radical idealism or mysticism. Theirs is not the orderly world made by King Reason and his prime minister, Will. It is the disordered, extreme world conjured by the mistress of the senses, Imagination.

[15] Another idealist, Heinrich Zimmer, who taught at Heidelberg and Oxford before coming to the US in 1941, treats the *Upanishads* in much the same way, stating that the philosophers of India turned, in those texts, not to science, but inward to the 'mystery of the Self' (1956: 356). Later, he makes this wider comment: 'The force of the conceptions and paradoxes of Advaita Vedānta in the life and history of the Hindu consciousness, and even today in the civilization of modern India, is simply immeasurable' (1956: 458).

[16] Arthur Berriedale Keith was a constitutional lawyer and acting Professor of Sanskrit at Oxford.

The essentialism of these accounts did not go completely unchallenged. At least one Indian scholar, a theist, argued against Deussen's equation of the Vedānta with pantheism.[17] Those who supported an Advaita or nondualist position tended to find Deussen's essentialist position attractive (Hiriyanna, 1932: 256).[18] They did not always agree, however, with the Westerners on what the content of that essence was. Christian idealists such as Albert Schweitzer never tired of drawing a dichotomy between an ethical, life-affirming Christianity and a Hindu mysticism indifferent to ethics and life-negating. The former, they assumed, was the product of a masculine, 'prophetic' rationality, the latter of a feminine imagination. The famous Indian philosopher, S. Radhakrishnan, himself an apologist for Advaita Vedānta, had effectively criticized this contrast, arguing that there are positive and negative forms of mysticism in both Christianity and Hinduism, and that it is a mistake to characterize Advaita Vēdanta as a negative form (1959: 61–114).[19]

Such quibbles have tended to confuse the neat dichotomies of Indological discourse, but not for long. The Sankritist and historian of religion, Friedrich Max Müller, formed a bridge between the largely British empiricist approach to India and the most German idealist apprehension of it (Halbfass, 1981: 151–3). Though he never visited India, he was probably the premier spokesman on things Indian to a nineteenth-century European audience. He, therefore, spoke for almost everyone when he represented an illusionist pantheism as 'fundamental' to Vedānta (1973: 114–17). He observed that all the systems of Indian philosophy 'share so much in common, with but slight modifications'. And he was convinced, he tells his reader, 'that there is behind the variety of the six systems a common fund of what may be called national or popular philosophy, a large Manasa lake of philosophical thought and language' (1973: xiv). This metaphor of a still, sacred lake as a shared source of ideas sums up rather well the essentialist tendencies of nearly all these Indologists.[20]

3.3.3 Sankara, Hero of the Imagination

Whatever their interpretations of the Vedic ritual and Upanishadic philosophy, both the secularists and Christian idealists on the one hand, and the philosophical idealists on the other, have on the whole agreed that the monism embodied in Advaita Vedānta constituted the essence of Indian thought and the mentality of the caste society. They have also agreed in the later 'history' that they provide for Brahmanism. Buddhism, India's 'heterodox' religion, arises at about the same time as the Brahmanism of the *Upanishads*, or somewhat later (sixth century BC?), and it comes to predominate in India over Brahmanism from the

[17] R. G. Bhandarkar (see below, 3.4.1).

[18] M. Hiriyanna (1871–1950) obtained his MA degree at Christian College, Madras, and worked as a government clerk, school teacher, and librarian before joining Mysore University, where, urged by S. Radhakrishnan, he began to teach philosophy in 1918. He retired in 1927 as Professor of Sanskrit.

[19] For a good critical account of approaches to mysticism, try Staal (1975).

[20] Basham reiterates this point: 'Where in other religions mysticism is of varying importance, in those of India it is fundamental' (1954: 246).

time of Asoka (third century BC) down to the time of the Gupta 'revival' of Brahmanism (fourth century AD). The philosophy of the Indian thinker, Sankara, was, according to the historians, the culmination of Brahmanism. The most famous of the proponents of Advaita Vedānta, he was the hero of Brahmans known as Smārta, the supposed guardians of the traditional householder relgion of the *Vedas*. Sankara's efforts on behalf of these Indologists' Brahmans were, at least in part, responsible for the final 'decline' of Buddhism and the 'revival' of Brahmanism. Said to have been born in 788 and to have died young in 820 (though more likely he flourished between 700 and 750), Sankara travelled throughout India, besting in debate not only the philosopher of the Mīmāṃsā system of sacrificial exegesis, Kumārila, but more importantly, the defenders of a later form of Buddhism, the Mahāyāna or 'great vehicle'.

Basham highlights the close relationship of his philosophy to that of Mahāyāna Buddhism and his formulation of the doctrine of *māyā*, which he summarizes as follows: 'on the highest level of truth the whole phenomenal universe, including the gods themselves, was unreal – the world was *Māyā*, illusion, a dream, a mirage, a figment of the imagination' (1954: 328). He concludes by telling the reader that the comparison of Sankara with Thomas Aquinas is fair, for the system which the Indian thinker rationalized in his interpretation of the *Upanishads*, 'though not unchallenged, has remained the standard philosophy of intellectual Hinduism to this day' (1954: 327–8).[21]

Sankara's triumph was not unqualified, however, for the same scholars also see this 'early medieval' period as the one in which a theistic Hinduism, comprising the 'sects' of Vaishnavism and Saivism, rises to prominence, the period when their monumental temples come to dominate the landscape. This is more than a little confusing, for these scholars are asking us to believe that the moment of Brahmanism's triumph over Buddhism is but one of a series involving the decline of Brahmanism itself (Barth, 1963: 87–100). European scholars have, consequently, attempted to portray Sankara as the icon of the ideal Brahman, a man who is simultaneously swimming with and against the tide of Indology's history. For example, Eliot accounts for the fact that Sankara, the hypostasis of Brahmanical values, should hail from Kerala, a relatively isolated part of the Dravidian south, and not the Aryan north by asking us to look behind Hindu appearances – 'This is not the land of giant gopurams [tower gateways of the south Indian temples] and multitudinous sculpture.' No, it is in essence the land of Brahmanism, 'of lives dedicated to the acquisition of traditional learning and the daily performance of complicated but inconspicuous rites' (1954: II, 207–8). His Sankara was, accordingly, the 'champion not of Vishnuism or Sivaism but of the ancient Brahmanic religion, amplified by many changes which the ages had brought but holding up as the religious ideal a manhood occupied with ritual observances, followed by an old age devoted to philosophy' (1954: I, xl). The earlier scholar, Barth, tried to resolve this contradiction by portraying the Brahman of the Indologists as a beleaguered

---

[21] More cautious in his later article, Basham says, 'The Sankaran system has sounded the keynote of intellectual Hinduism down to the present, but later teachers founded sub-schools of Vedanta, which are perhaps equally important' (1974: 914).

upholder of ancient Vedic tradition who simply shuts out the world around him (1963: 89–90). His rather poignant picture of the changeless ancient Indian Brahman, a man who learns nothing from experience and forgets nothing of his heritage, carefully preserving it until Western scholarship can take hold of it and make something out of it, reproduces all of the assumptions and presuppositions of the metaphysics on which it is based.

There would be nothing wrong with the framing of Indian religions in this metaphysics if it engaged the discursive texts of those religions. But this is not the case. Eliot's and Barth's representation of Sankara and of the ideal Brahman are in many respects quite at odds with the representations of Sankara's life that are made in the same Indian texts from which they and others have drawn their data on his life. Those texts depict Sankara (Potter, 1981: 14–16, 115–19) as the champion not of the withdrawn life of the Brahman scholar, but of an active and sometimes militant monastic organization, called Daśnāmi, one that seems to have been intent on occupying the ontological space over which the Buddhists were losing command (Sarkar, n.d.: 123–44). One of these texts depicts Sankara as an avatar of the deity Siva whose early life incorporates but transcends the childhood of Krishna, his rival (Lorenzen, 1976: 87–107). It portrays his travels and debates as a 'conquest of the quarters' in the course of which Sankara establishes the Daśnāmi monastic order. He founds four monasteries, ascetical command-posts for each of the four quarters of India, the foremost of which was in the south, at Śringeri. The heads of these are known in recent times as Sankaracharyas (implying the presence in these *acharyas* or 'teachers' of the original Sankara). To this day, those same 'orthodox' Brahmans in south India who call themselves Smārta also acknowledge the Sankaracharya at Śringeri as their head (Eliot, 1954: II, 209–10).

Although this might seem to corroborate the construction placed upon the orthodox Brahman by Indologists, it does not hold up under closer scrutiny. In the first place, the supposedly purist Smārta Brahmans are not distinguished from both Śaiva and Vaishnava Brahmans, but only from the latter, implying that Śaiva and Smārta are one and the same.[22] Those Smārtas who join the Daśnāmi orders do not have to be men who have completed themselves as householders, as 'orthodoxy' would require. Furthermore, these texts do not view the 'sectarian' Hinduism we are about to discuss as the negation of some pure Brahmanism, but as a necessary and lay stage of their 'traditional' religion. That religion, as they describe it, is not some isolated and hoary monism, but a form of Saivism. Not only has it enveloped the daily Smārta liturgy it has appropriated in the worship of Siva,[23] it has also claimed to account for and incorporate within itself the best of all other religions, including its own version of Advaita philosophy.

Nor was this monastic religion scornful of the world. On the contrary, the rise to prominence of the Daśnāmis seems to have been closely connected with

---

[22] On the classification of Brahmans, see Bhattacharya (1896: 94–5).
[23] For an early European account of the daily liturgy of these Brahmans in south India, see the so-called Abbé Dubois (1906: 147–8).

the position the Sankaracharyas held as the royal preceptors of the emperors at Vijayanagar, capital of the largest Hindu kingdom, near Śringeri, in the fourteenth to sixteenth centuries. We can, to conclude our look at these texts, see that their project was the fashioning of a scale of forms that placed a monastic form of Saivism at its top, with its heads, the Sankaracharyas, in command of a hierarchy comprising all of the 'acceptable' religions of India. Within it, the Smārta householder Brahmans were one grade of devotees, and not the highest at that.

Sankara cannot, thus, be made to embody a social level consisting of Brahman gnostics who have stood firmly above a changing illusory world, preserving a perennial mysticism. But perhaps the depiction of his philosophy as an illusionary idealism or pantheism assumed to constitute the mental essence of Brahmanism still stands? Alas, even here all is not a peaceful, meditative slumber.

The simplified characterizations of *māyā*, supposed to be the very heart of Sankara's idealism, as 'illusion', do not stand up well. S. Radhakrishnan and his protégé, Hiriyanna, among others, have argued for a 'phenomenal' rather than an 'illusionist' interpretation of Sankara's world. Hiriyanna concludes his explication of Sankara's metaphysics with this understatement:

For the present we merely note that the foregoing account shows how mistaken is the common belief that Samkara views the objects of everyday experience to be false or unreal. So far from doing this, he claims some kind of reality even for objects of illusion. To be perceived is for him *to be*, and this theory may therefore be described as an inversion of the one associated in western philosophy with the name of Berkeley. (1932: 351; Radhakrishnan, 1928: 144–56)[24]

We are, I think, entitled to infer from Hiriyanna's approach that the dichotomy between knowledge and the world presupposed in many of the accounts of Indian thought in general and of Sankara in particular is not sustained by a careful reading of Sankara, who, according to Hiriyanna, seems to have presupposed a continuity between the two. I am no expert on Sankara and I will leave it to the philosopher to work out this important question of interpretation. If we may suppose that the accounts of Radhakrishnan and Hiriyanna were to prove correct, the implications would be immense. If Sankara's philosophy does not treat the world as an illusion, then the very core of the essentialist construction of Hinduism or Brahmanism as a 'world-renouncing' rather than a 'world-accepting' religion is seriously weakened. At the same time, Hiriyanna's interpretation would open the way for Sankarites to be active in the world, and this in its turn would help explain how the world-ordering Daśnāmi Śaivas could have taken to this philosophy in constructing their religion.

I now wish to turn to a discussion of Hinduism, the religion of the laity or the people, to those urbane Hindu sects and to those vulgar village cults which have disturbed the Indologist's dream of a pure unchanging Aryan tradition, yet have been necessary as a foil to it.

[24] Deussen himself shows that the term *māyā* first appears in the Śvetāśvatara, an admittedly theistic *Upanishad* (1921/1966: 42).

3.4 HINDUISM, SYMBOLS FOR THE PEOPLE

3.4.1 The Theistic Creeds and Image-worship of the Laity

Indologists have used the term Hinduism not only in a wider sense to refer to any Indian religion that attaches itself to the *Vedas*, but also in a restricted sense to distinguish a theistic religion from the earlier polytheistic and pantheistic religion of Brahmanism, just discussed. This Hinduism is, we are told, a religion of a lower level of the population, of the laity rather than of the priesthood, of the people rather than of an intellectual elite. Indologists have also considered Brahmanism and Hinduism to be religions related to one another in time. Brahmanism develops in the centuries before Christ while Hinduism develops afterward. The later religion, however, never fully supplants the earlier in this jungly growth, as the narrative on Sankara evidences.

As a religion of the laity, Hinduism is said to emphasize the worship (*pūjā*) of 'images' or 'symbols' of one god rather than sacrifice (*yajña*) in a fire to a number of unrepresented gods. It is also supposed to stress devotion, or *bhakti*, as the means for emancipation from transmigration; and final union with one of two 'personal' gods called Vishnu or Siva instead of gnosis or knowledge (*jñāna*) as the means to absorption in a single 'impersonal' Brahman.

The texts of this religion are, accordingly, not the Vedas or Upanishads, the preserve of the Brahman priests, but the Sanskrit *Epics*, the *Mahābhārata* and *Rāmāyaṇa*, the *Purāṇas*, the 'books of Sacred Law', and collections of hymns and poems, and these 'were available to all, even to men of low caste and to women' (Basham, 1954: 299). Originally secular histories and cosmologies, these texts become sacred by virtue of receiving religious interpolations. The most famous of these is the *Bhagavad-gītā*.

The primary mental property which Indologists attributed to Brahmanism was either an errant imagination deluded by its metaphysical wanderings or the creative imagination of a lower, sensual soul. Neither of these was derived from the study of Indian texts and practices but rather were supplied from a European psychology. The devotional mentality attributed to Hinduism is, I argue, similary derived. The core of that mind was assumed to consist not of the imagination but of the passions, the emotions that comprised the 'appetitive' faculty of the sensual soul. Broadly speaking, scholars distinguish two historical stages of this religion, an Epic and Puranic or classical, associated with the Gupta empire (fourth to sevenths centuries) and a sectarian or medieval, which I turn to in the next section.

Who were these two gods, Siva and Vishnu, whom the laity worshipped? Wilson's hegemonic heir, Monier-Williams, says of the first that 'the worship of the composite deity Rudra-Siva is nothing but the expression of the awe felt by human beings in the presence of the two mutually complementary forces of disintegration and reintegration.' As for the other, 'the worship of the personal god Vishnu in his descents upon earth in human form is nothing but the expression of the very natural interest felt by man in his own preservation and in the working of the physical forces which resist dissolution' (Monier-Williams,

1891: 64–5). Which is to say that we have here the two gods of a 'natural' religion rather than the single god of a religion of 'freedom'. Neither is a god to be apprehended by the cognitive faculty of the sentient soul, the imagination (never mind the higher understanding), but rather by the goal-seeking faculty that operated in conjunction with the senses, that of the passions, the emotions that tend the person toward the good and away from evil. The mainspring of these was, of course, love.

Now, it might seem that the mental essence of Hinduism is the same as in Christianity, but that is not so, for scholars assumed that the passion that constituted the emotional core of this lay religion was not guided by scientific reason or divine will. Its devotees have 'no stern belief in the unity of God'. Presumably dominated by the imagination, their emotions were divided between dread (Siva) and love (Vishnu). Fundamentally unstable, like its source, the imagination, their theism 'constantly tends to pantheistic or polytheistic superstitions'. The most worrying aspect of the direction its devotion took, according to Monier-Williams, was 'the mystical theory of a duality in unity' (1891: 224). Here he is referring to the dualism of the Sānkhya theory. This he believed to be as old as the doctrine of pantheism in Vedānta and traceable, like it, to the Veda itself (1891: 29–30). What disturbed him about this dualism was its recourse to male–female relations to constitute its cosmology. The presence of sexual relations within a religion was bound, he assumed, to be a source of mischief rivalled only by that other passion, greed. Together with the other passions of envy and hate, they would, without a Christian God to referee, prevent the proper development of ethics.

The distinctive attribute of this bifurcated classical Hinduism was devotion, and the most important of its practices were, we are told, the worship or adoration of images in a shrine or a permanently established temple. Earlier observers had, of course, referred to this as idol-worship or idolatry. Hegel had argued that the extreme opposition of an abstract and impersonal unity of the Hindu absolute to the concrete multiplicity of nature was the result of a mind dominated by the imagination. This tendency to extremes had its counterpart in the 'Hindu' forms of worship as well. The worship of what comes to be called Brahmanism he construed as internal and extremely self-denying. On the one hand, it involved the 'attainment of torpid unconsciousness' or even 'suicide and the extinction of all that is worth calling life, by self-inflicted tortures'. On the other hand, that worship also 'consists in a wild tumult of excess; when all sense of individuality has vanished from consciousness by immersion in the merely natural' (Hegel, 1956: 157).

Hegel's idea that Hindu image-worship is the consequence of fantasy, of a mentality that is sensual rather than rational has remained a leading assumption of Indology. Here is how Auguste Barth, the French counterpart of Monier-Williams, commented on it around 1900:

The worship which is celebrated in these temples is but slightly addressed to the understanding; but according to the evidence of all those who have had occasion to witness it, it has especially in the great sanctuaries, an impressive effect on the senses and on the imagination. The essential part [sic] of it is the service of the idol and of the temple, which is his dwelling. (1963: 273)

The result of such construals is that *pūjā* becomes an expression of the overly stimulated passions of the people which the Brahmans have merely rationalized, *rather* than, as in Christianity, a constructed liturgy that is *both* cognitive and emotive.

Retailers of images of Hinduism had tried to persuade their readers that the earlier Brahmanism was a religion of the individual householder and not congregational. This was also the case for Hinduism. Monier-Williams insists that:

A Hindu never enters a place of worship with the object of offering up common prayer in company with his fellow-men. He has no conception of performing the kind of religious act which a Christian performs when he 'goes to church.' Occasionally, it is true, and on stated days, he visits idol shrines. But he does not go there with any idea of praying with others. He goes to the temple to perform what is called Darsana; that is, to look at the idol, the sight of which, when duly dressed and decorated by the priest, is supposed to confer merit. After viewing the image he may endeavour to propitiate the favour or avert the anger of the god it represents, by prostrations of the body, repetitions of its name, or presentation of offerings. But this is not an essential [*sic*] duty. His real religion is an affair of family usage, domestic ritual, and private observance. (1891: 351–2)

The tack taken here is to assert that *pūjā* in a temple was not social and not fundamental to Hindu worship. It was only an appearance. The essence of that religion consisted of the practices of the natural units of society, those performed by the Smārta Brahmans.

The idealist cultural historian, Ananda Coomaraswamy, has tried to reconcile image-worship and Brahmanism in a different way. He concedes that 'opening the eyes' of the image in the course of its consecration after the 'real presence' of the deity is invited into it certainly lends credence to the criticism of idolatry that worshippers of such images believe the god to be present (Coomaraswamy, 1956: 155–69). He gets around this by asserting that it is 'human nature' for the mass of people to be superstitious, to attribute material reality to entities that are actually ideal or spiritual.

Coomaraswamy argues, *contra* Barth, that Hindu image-worship is actually a manifestation of Indian 'religious philosophy as a whole', by which he, of course, means his idealist rendering of Advaita. This was by no means a new position. It is the one that most accounts of classical Hinduism have taken for almost one hundred years. Coomaraswamy's differs primarily in its sophistication. He invokes the concept of *māyā*, saying that it is not '*de*lusion' but 'creative power' and the 'principle of manifestation'. Thus, images are appearances; they are symbols used to aid the worshipper in his or her devotion. Once one no longer needs this aid, one can presumably dispense with it. Coomaraswamy brings in Sankara himself, supposed advocate of 'pure monism', to support his theory of image-worship. He was, we are told, 'a devout worshipper of images, a visitor to shrines, a singer of devotional hymns'. Because he saw the 'inevitability of the use of imagery, verbal and visual', our hero 'sanctions the service of images' (1956: 160).

Coomaraswamy is, thus, able to reconstitute an extreme form of worship, that of an enlivened image, as a rational, conscious theological practice, but he can only do this by normalizing it, by treating it as a concession to the emotional masses and by making the devotion of Hinduism inferior to the knowledge of Brahmanism. He has reduced it to a symbolic husk around the kernel of Deussen's radical idealism. There is, however, no winning here: for that knowledge consists of the extreme mysticism of a removed intellectual elite, itself not the offspring of a spiritual reason but of a sensuous imagination. There is, furthermore, a hitch in this notion of an appeal to popular emotions, for most Indologists will also tell us (see the next section) that the devotion to an image is not in fact the mode of worship for the bulk of the populace!

The theory scholars first used to account for the origin of Hinduism was a social variation of the environmentalist explanation that they used to derive a mystical Brahmanism from the earlier natural religon of the Aryans. It held that the individualist, cognitive religion of the priesthood had to meet the needs of a laity. The more secularist (and evangelist!) versions, always castigating the clergy for their self-seeking motives, explained the rise of Hinduism as the result of the Brahmans' development of theologies and rituals that catered to the superstitions of the masses. The more liberal Christian and Romantic versions, assuming that the people of India were instinctively loving, argued that Hinduism was a popularization of Brahmanism, designed by the Brahmans to meet the religious needs of the people.

The development of the two-headed theism of Hinduism in its classical phase was, we are told, a reaction to the pessimism or nihilism of Buddhism. Monier-Williams considered Hinduism a direct development out of the earlier Brahmanism (1891: 71). Buddhism, flawed because it 'substituted a blank for God', had none the less centred on the life and teachings of a heroic figure, Gautama Buddha. It had, consequently, become more popular with the people than had the austere and impersonal pantheism of Brahmanism, the abstract religion of nature that had preceded it:

Of course the religious instincts of the mass of Hindus found no real satisfaction in the propitiation of the forces of nature and spirits of the air, or in the cold philosophy of pantheism, or in homage paid to the memory of a teacher held to be nowhere existent. They needed devotion (*bhakti*) to personal and human gods, and these they were led to find in their own heroes. (1891: 42-3)

What, then, did the Brahmans do in responding to the Buddha's pre-Christian appeal to the emotions of the populace for a hero? Apparently they had learned how to distinguish symbol from reality, for they took the heroes of the people and deified them, made them out to be suffused with the universal absolute of their elite religion. They thus transformed popular heroes into objects of personal devotion. A split religion with two gods emerged from this process. According to Monier-Williams, 'Siva was the Buddha in his monastic character. Vishnu was the Buddha in his character of a beneficent and unselfish lover and friend of the human race' (1891: 58-9).

The vehicle for effecting this change was the Epic: 'Myths and stories confirmatory of the divine origin of every great hero were invented and inserted into the body of the poems. In this manner a kind of anthropomorphic religion, well adapted to the popular mind, was devised' (1891: 43). The two creeds of the lay elite of India with their idol-worship are thus reduced to illusions, the 'symbolizations' of a higher truth, one that is the preserve of the priestly or philosophical elite. With our omniscient gaze, we Indologists can see that they are 'really' worshipping the impersonal absolute.

There was, furthermore, no real synthesis in this development, only an apparent one: 'Yet we must guard against the idea that theistic Hinduism has superseded pantheistic Brahmanism; for in India forms of pantheism, theism, and polytheism are ever interwoven with each other' (1891: 54). Deploying that jungle metaphor, here in a processual rather than structural sense, the Sanskritist constitutes Hinduism as the product of the Aryan mind gone astray because it is in a tropical setting: 'Hinduism grew out of Brahmanism. It is Brahmanism, so to speak, run to seed and spread out into a confused tangle of divine personalities and incarnations. The one system is the rank and luxuriant outcome of the other' (1891: 3). Instead of being an improvement on the past, as Christianity was on paganism, this growth was a 'degeneration'.

The idea that classical Hinduism was the abstract doctrine of pantheism or monism in symbolic clothing, whether presented by the Utilitarian intellectualist or the Romantic idealist, has not gone without criticism. Most of these criticisms centre on the nature of Vedānta and hence of the *Upanishads*. One of the earliest critics was R. G. Bhandarkar (1837–1925),[25] who argued that theist and atheist tendencies were also present in the *Upanishads* and that it was, therefore, a mistake to equate Vedānta with the doctrine of pantheism. He offers in his conclusion this acerbic criticism of the intellectualistic treatment of God in Hinduism:

If they mean by Theism the Deism of the eighteenth century according to which the world is a machine constructed and set in motion by God who remains apart from it, with perhaps the additional doctrine that he enters into relations with men who worship him, they are probably right. But this is not Hindu Theism. The immanence of God in the external world and in the heart of man is its essential [*sic*] doctrine. But that is perfectly consistent with the belief in God's transcendency. (R. G. Bhandarkar, 1913: 157)[26]

The later philosopher, S. N. Dasgupta, made some passing comments regarding the relation of God and man in the early texts of Hinduism that strengthen Bhandarkar's critical insight. He stated that the position assumed in the Bhagavad-gītā and in the older *Purāṇas* was not that of Advaita, 'monism' but of Bhedābheda, 'identity-within-difference'.

Now, we could simply take this as a confirmation of the construct of Hinduism of which I am so sceptical. For are not the philosophical texts of

[25] Educated in his home 'province', Bombay Presidency, he went on to become Professor of Sanskrit at the Deccan College, Poona, one of India's leading centres of Indology. Charles Lanman, Sanskritist at Harvard, pronounced him 'the first great Indianist of India to combine the native learning in which they must ever excel us, with the knowledge of the Occidental methods which gave us in some ways important advantages over them' (1920: 236).

[26] His argument is not without problems of its own, in the form of an inherent theistic 'need'. He assumed, in making his case, that these religions were developed by a theological elite in response to the spiritual needs of their clientele, and he assumed that the theistic religions ultimately triumphed because they were best able to meet those needs.

Brahmanism monist? Dasgupta, however, provides us with two reasons for taking a different stance. He argues that a Bhedābheda interpretation of the *Brahma-sūtras*, the early explications of the *Upanishads*, probably antedates Sankara's monistic treatment. He also points out that the position implicit in the *Vedānta-sūtra* of the authoritative Bādarāyaṇa himself, by the light of Sankara's own commentary on him, was not 'monist' but that of 'identity-within-difference' (1922–55: II, 42–4, 524; III, 105). The implication here (which Dasgupta did not himself follow up) takes us much further than the Indian attempts to refute the Western interpretation of Sankara's philosophy as illusionist. It enables us to suggest that the philosophy embedded in the creeds of classical Hinduism (and especially of Vaishnavism) is not a monism or radical idealism, but an ontology of plurality-with-unity that treats the world as real. *Bhakti*, which I prefer to translate in many contexts as 'conscious participation', does not seem logical as the highest state of a mysticism in which the human soul will be reabsorbed into the world soul. When a theology that takes *bhakti* as its highest goal is accompanied by the notion that both the God in whom the devotee participates and the devotee are real and retain distinct (yet not opposed) identities, it makes a good deal of sense. If, as Dasgupta indicates, the early Vaishnavas and Saivas also had their philosophers, we do not have to assume that they were intellectually dependent on early Advaitins. They had constituted themselves as religions fully agentive with respect to their knowledge of the world.

We need not, thus, see that fundamental Hindu text, the *Gītā*, as a mere 'compilation' of diverse views. Nor do we have to view it either as the expression of a popular religion that has as its essence a pre-given devotion opposed to or without cognitive content or as a lower-level symbolization of an ethereal illusionary pantheism. Some ancient Indians said that it was one of three methods or systems (*prasthāna*) that constituted the Vedānta (the other two being the *Upanishads* and the *Brahma-sūtra*). The text of which the *Bhagavad-gītā* is part, the *Mahābhārata*, itself claims to be the fifth *Veda*. So we are perfectly entitled to see the *Gītā* as a guide to the reading and interpretation of the *Upanishads*. We may see it as a consciously constructed, rational theology or world-view, one that differs from other, earlier as well as contemporary ones, and needs to be justified. The point of its discourse is to show not just logically but also in 'realistic', narrative form, why its religion of action and devotion, concerned with the problem of order in the human world, is superior to its contemporaries. We might argue that other doctrines appear in it not as *membra disjecta* but as recognizably distinct yet transformed parts of a larger whole. The *Gītā* has placed them within a scale of forms in what it considered the proper relationship to the doctrine of participation it advocates.

I cannot resist adding here that this religion was not something confined to texts. Most Indologists agree that the Guptas, the imperial rulers who were supposed to have presided over a classical synthesis in the fourth to sixth centuries AD, actively and openly supported the religious order of the Bhāgavatas, those who advocated the religion preached in the *Gītā* (Sircar, 1954: III, 419). The picture is, however, complicated, because some of those rulers seem also, passively and covertly, to have supported the Yogācāra tendency among the Buddhists (viz. the older ruins at their monastic centre, Nālāndā, in Bihar) (Dutt, 1954: III, 390, 394). We may tentatively infer from this that the Guptas placed Vaishnavism in the position of the premier religion of their empire, according second position to that of the Yogācāra Buddhists. The former, an activist householder's religion, provided the world-ordering rationality for the Gupta imperial formation as a whole, while the latter, subjective idealist, as its doctrinal name, *vijñānavādin*, 'propounding the doctrine that knowledge alone exists', implies, provided the rationale for those who wished to retreat from life in the world. The idealism of the Yogācārins and the identity-in-difference philosophy of the Bhāgavatas were taken as the primary and secondary targets of Sankara's discourses in the eighth century, but it is difficult to argue that an Advaita philosophy constituted orthodoxy under the Guptas.

The continued depiction of Hinduism as a religion of two dichotomously related levels of the Indian populace and of its sensual mind has still other problems. Its own inventors undermine it by imagining into existence another religion of the people, one that is opposed in its mental essence both to the pantheism of the imagination and to the theism of the passions. Let us look now at this still lower level of the Indian mass and its mentality.

3.4.2 The Animistic Cults and Blood Sacrifices of the Peasants

Scholars of the nineteenth century often gave the impression that the populace at large, subsumed in its lay leaders, worships either Siva or Vishnu. At other times, however, they asserted otherwise. Monier-Williams, for example, held in places that the gods of the 'ordinary peasant's religion' were exclusively 'tutelary' in nature; that is, they were conceived of not as saviours taking their worshippers to a desired goal, but simply as protectors from harm (1891: 209), the major causes of which were demons of various sorts. He states that 'the great majority of the inhabitants of India are, from the cradle to the burning-ground, victims of a form of disease which is best expressed by the term demonophobia.' Villagers are, he continues, 'firmly convinced that evil spirits of all kinds, from malignant fiends to merely mischievous imps and elves, are ever on the watch to harm, harass and torment them, to cause plague, sickness, famine and disaster, to impede, injure and mar every good work' (210–11). Monier-Williams describes some of these gods, noting that they are included in the Hindu fold as, for example, sons of Siva and leaders of troops of demons (211–18).

The major deities the peasant worshipped, however, were not, according to Monier-Williams, male, but female: 'Every village', he says in his account of 'mother-worship' (222–9), 'has its own special guardian mother, called Mātā or Ambā.' He attributed the greater attention paid to female deities to what he thought was a weaker, erratic 'thoroughly feminine nature' (222). Projecting his Victorian notion of the female, he asserted that on the one hand, 'She is more easily propitiated by prayer, flattery, and offerings; more ready to defend from evil.' On the other, she is 'more irritable, uncertain, and wayward in her temper and moods; more dangerously spiteful, and prone to inflict diseases, if offended by neglect' (222–3). Peasants, thus, did not worship a single impersonal absolute or one of the two male personal gods of salvation; they worshipped a host of lesser deities, mostly female, which were more demonic than divine.

First we were initiated into a religion of the intellectual Brahmanical elite, the psychic essence of which was an impersonal monistic pantheism spawned by a creative imagination. Then we were introduced to its opposite, a personal, dualist theism of the laity. The defining attribute of that religion was not cognitive but emotional, the devotion directed toward a saviour. Now, we have revealed to us still another religion opposed to both of these, a religion neither of cognition nor of devotion, but of prevention directed primarily at troublesome, irresponsible mother-goddesses, one that is simply a negation of the other two. This was, if I may invoke Europe's ancient psychology, a mentality of the vegetative soul, concerned with food and fertility.[27]

The making of votive offerings of flowers, lamps, fruits and milk products to an idol, though far from desirable, could at least be seen as an extreme or displaced version of the human impulse to Christianity. Post-enlightened Christians' treatment of the peasants' form of worship was different. They looked on the village cult as the opposite of the theistic cult of Siva or, especially, of Vishnu. It took the form of the worship of a 'rude fetish', that is, of a symbol actually equated by these ignorant folk with the spirit in question, with bloody sacrifices of animals, the largest of which was the buffalo. Furthermore, the priests who performed these rites were not, as with the Vedic rites and the temple rites of Vishnu and Siva, symbolizing Brahmans, but men of the lower castes. Such rites were, observers assumed, not grounded in the passions. They were not motivated by an inherent love, however misdirected. Rather they were 'propitiatory', aimed at removing the obstacles to the growth of children and crops, the domain of that lowest part of the feminine Indian soul, the vegetative.

We have, then, two forms of worship at issue in this depiction of a popular Hinduism. One, the devotional worship of idols, was seen as a reaction, coincident with the rise of the personal gods Siva and Vishnu, to the excessive ritualism and radical idealism of Brahmanism and the equally extreme nihilism of Buddhism. The form of worship that emerged was itself excessive. It was the worship of a mind that required the flamboyant and erotic symbols of fantasy to focus its passionate essence on an impersonal absolute, a need that the Brahmans were well suited to supply. The other form of worship that this discourse constitutes, the violent sacrifice of animals to rough-hewn fetishes by demon-fearing villagers, was not a development at all, since it was held to pre-exist the arrival of the Aryans in India. In that sense we cannot rightly include it within a classical phase of Hinduism any more than we might within the earlier Brahmanical or later medieval. It was at best the activity of a primitive mind preoccupied with subsistence in a world filled with hostile spirits, one lurking beneath the cognitive pantheism of a Brahman elite and of the emotive, theistic Hinduism of the laity. By the turn of the century, more and more scholars began to take the position that this perennial peasant religion was not simply an untransformed survival of the primordial past. According to the

[27] For the connection made with Near Eastern mother-goddesses, see 3.5.

Dravidian or substratum hypothesis they supported, that religion had itself shaped Hinduism and was perhaps more responsible for the shape that Hinduism took in 'early medieval' India than the earlier Sanskritists would have wanted to imagine.

3.5 MEDIEVAL DECLINE, THE DRAVIDIAN MIND TRIUMPHANT

The historians of Hinduism repeatedly tell us that the unity or tolerance of Hinduism, its classical glow in the age of the so-called Gupta revival (fourth to seventh centuries), gave way in a subsequent 'medieval' period (eight to eighteenth centuries) to disunity. Each of the major creeds of this already bifurcated religion divided into numerous 'sects', named after either its distinctive practice or its founder. The texts of these sects are the *Āgamas* (Śaiva), the *Saṃhitās* (Vaishnava), and the *Tantras* (Śākta) (Dandekar, 1979: 34–5). The use of non-vedic *mantras* is supposed to mark these texts off from the earlier Hindu texts. Theological treatises and commentaries also appear and devotional texts in the vernacular languages make their début. The sectarian rivalry that is supposed to have been endemic in this period contributed to the Islamic political conquest of India and helped perpetuate Muslim dominance until the arrival of the Europeans.

The religion the scholars represent to have emerged in this prolonged Middle Ages is, thus, the religion with which they themselves had to contend in making India part of their imperial formation. What is the nature of the theologies and philosophies said to proliferate under the rubric of Vedānta in it? With almost no exception, they are hostile to the supposed orthodoxy of Advaita. Monier-Williams, for example, states that 'all the Vaishnava sects are more or less opposed to the non-duality (*advaita*) doctrine of Sankaracarya' (1894: 116).[28] The mental core of these sects was, however, not so much their philosophy as their intense devotion. Like the two creeds themselves these sects were, as we have learnt, the products not of the cognitive faculty of the imagination, but of the emotive faculty and its passions. Basham says that the earlier notion of devotion in the *Gītā* was 'respectful' and 'stern', more the religion of an elite. The 'ecstatic love' of God, 'reflected by the worshipper in love for his fellows', that he sees in the Tamil word for devotion, was mostly without parallel in the 'Aryan religious literature' (1954: 330–1). This deeper devotionalism was perhaps to be admired. But there was another, uglier side to it. This was the worship of 'mother-goddesses' in various Tantric sects. According to Basham, 'the goddess was the *śakti*, the strength or potency of her male counterpart. It was thought the god was inactive and transcendent, while

---

[28] The Pāñcarātra Vaishnavas, according to the later Basham, conceived the relation between god and worshipper as an 'eternal paradox', Rāmānuja advocated a doctrine of 'qualified monism', and the later Madhva, dualism itself. Among the earlier Śaivas, only the Trika or Kashmiri Śaivas were monist. The later Śaiva-siddhānta adopted a kind of dualism. The Lingāyats adhered to a 'qualified monism', even 'opposed image worship' and 'rejected the Vedas and the authority of the brahman class' and 'instituted complete equality' (1954: 329–35). The Daśnāmis alone, I would point out, claimed to adhere to the nondualism of Sankara.

his female element was active and immanent' (1954: 311). What happened as Aryan imagination faded was what Christian idealists had suspected all along: 'With the spread of these ideas sexual symbolism, and even sexual intercourse as a religious rite, were incorporated into the teachings of some schools of both Hinduism and Buddhism' (1954: 280).

The image-worship integral to this religion of the senses also changed. The rites were no longer simple. The priests treated the immense and numerous images in these temples not just as honoured guests but as great kings living lives of oriental luxury in their palaces (1954: 335–6). To house these cults, small shrines were made to give way to monumental temples increasingly complex in design. People and their rulers diverted vast sums of wealth into the support of these establishments. Here we see the displacement of the secular on to the sacred that Indologists thought characteristic of Hinduism carried to its extreme.

Indologists have been able to persuade themselves that the rites inside the temple, controlled by Brahmans, were (even in their own time) an attenuation of the old individualist rites of the Veda. Here somehow the radical idealism of old continues, appearances notwithstanding. What went on outside the central chambers, however, both fascinated and worried them. There, they noted, the secretive goings-on around the idol were counterbalanced by an extreme form of congregation, glossed in the literature under the rubric of 'pilgrimage'. The activities which occasioned the gathering of these crowds were the 'festivals' that continued in the nineteenth century to be celebrated at the temples or at other 'sacred' sites (Barth, 1963: 270, 283–4). Many of these included religious processions of the idols, in which thousands of pilgrims participated. The most famous of these was, of course, the procession of the god Jagannath, a form of Vishnu. From the relentless movement of the giant wheels on the car of that idol, crushing his devotees (vividly reported by missionaries), we have obtained our word juggernaut (now applied to large lorries that hurtle down the inadequate roads in Britain).

The artistic quality on exhibit in temples also changed for the worse. James Fergusson, patriarch of Indian architectural history, had argued that even the so-called Indo-Aryan type of temple in north India was largely the result of the Aryans being swamped by the aboriginal tribes there (1899: I, 45; II, 86). Ernest B. Havell (1861–1934), something of a philosophical idealist and advocate of his version of Aryan culture, attempted to salvage the temple of the Gupta period by arguing, against Fergusson, that it was largely an Aryan symbolic form.[29] Yet even he would not stretch his own sensibilities so far as to encompass the monumental temple in what he, too, considered a period of 'Hindu decadence'. The austere symbolism of an earlier age became reified as the result of a growing belief in the reality of the gods installed in temples (Havell, 1915: 204–6). That is, the mind behind the building of these temples was no longer, like that of the classical Brahman, capable of distinguishing a symbol from its referent. He says of art in the south that it 'vibrates with intense

[29] He was Principal of the Government Art School and Keeper of the Art Galleries in Calcutta.

creative energy; yet it lacks neither coherency nor self-restraint. Then, as in a forest choked with undergrowth, it gradually runs riot in a maze of elaboration and pedantic artifice.' The situation in the north was no different (Havell, 1924: 121).

Indological discourse has represented classical Hinduism rather ambiguously as a decline of the earlier mystical religion and also as a popularization or emotionalization of it. Either perspective none the less left the religion of the Brahmans and its quasi-reason in command. That ambiguity disappears in their depictions of this second, medieval phase. Clearly, the classical, imperial lid is off. The imagination of the Indian Aryan, itself a weak form of reason, is being overcome by the passions. What semblance of unity there was has collapsed into sectarian bickering. Male Aryan spirit is being strangled by the overheated female matter of India.

How were the Indologists and others to explain this degeneration or decline? Scholarship earlier in the nineteenth century had assumed that the 'natural' religion of the Vedic Aryans was the earliest form of religion. When they looked at the religion of the Vedas they assumed they were looking at an ancestor of their own religion. They had thus looked on Indian civilization as fundamentally Aryan and had attributed the rise of India's excessive mentality to isolation and climate. Later, attempts to construct an explicitly imperial polity centred on London and to account for new historical and ethnological evidence led them to postulate the existence of still earlier and more primitive stages of society and forms of religion and to associate these with different 'races'. With this shift in focus came a change in the causes for India's peculiarities.

Observers began to see Indian institutions as the outcome of interaction between a higher Aryan and lower pre-Aryan races. We have already seen how Risley derived caste from the opposition he construed to exist between a white Aryan and a black Dravidian. Ethnologists deployed two other dichotomies to generate other theories, the one an opposition between male and female, the other an opposition between a 'natural' religion of cosmic forces and a religion of material objects. One was the theory of 'mother-right' (for which evidence on the matrilineal Nayars of Malabar was integral). It held that there was a barbaric stage of human society in which descent was through women and property was held communally.[30] The other was the theory that 'stone age' peoples with 'fetishistic', 'animistic', and 'totemistic' religions preceded the Aryans and their natural religion.[31]

One of the first attempts to explain the development of Hinduism as the result of the interaction of Aryan and pre-Aryan was that of Gustav Oppert (1836–1908).[32] Responding to the discovery that the Aryans and Semites were not the originators of civilization in the Near East, he argued that the 'original inhabitants' of India, also civilized, were not Aryan. They belonged to a race he called Gauda-Dravidian, itself a branch of the Turanian race. Earlier, Max

[30] For a discussion of Maine, Morgan, Bachofen, Engels, and others, see Coward: (1983: 17–74, 130–62).
[31] On Indology's reception of this discovery, see Oldenberg (1898: 51–66).
[32] A student at Leipzig, Halle, and Berlin, he became Professor of Sanskrit at Presidency College, Madras, in 1872 and, after his return to Germany in 1893, Professor of Sanskrit at Berlin University in 1894.

Müller had held that 'the name Turanian is used in opposition to Aryan and is applied to the nomadic races of Asia as opposed to the agricultural or Aryan races' (1864: I, 301). Oppert, trying to accommodate the recent archaeological evidence, reversed this proposition. He stated that the Turanians were an agricultural, matriarchal people who lived in the early civilizations of the Near East before their conquest by our pastoralist Aryan and Semitic ancestors. The religions of these two racial families (like their agglutinative and inflected languages) were opposed to each other. The Turanians gave preference in their worship to a 'Mother Earth' over a Supreme Spirit of heaven as their principal deity, while the Aryans worshipped deities that were almost exclusively male (Oppert, 1893: 387–8, 457). The village goddesses of India (see 3.4.2) were, in his eyes, the parallels, degraded by the Brahmans (1893: 508), of the city goddesses of Babylonia (327, 398).[33]

The external differences between the Aryan and non-Aryan forms of worship were themselves due to inner, mental ones. The former, he contended, revered 'the *Forces of Nature*, while the latter adored the *Manifestations of the Forces of Nature*'. This distinction, according to Oppert,

> explains the higher status which characterises the Aryan belief when compared with the non-Aryan. It expresses the gulf which separates the Male from the Female Principle, and it explains the superiority in position and conception maintained by the Aryan over the non-Aryan divinities. It is also manifested by the tendency towards abstractness so fully developed among the so-called Aryan and Semitic races, in contrast to the predilection towards concreteness so apparent among the non-Aryan tribes. (1893: 553–4)

The Aryan's capacity for abstract thought coincided with superior physical power and made it possible for the inherently masculine Aryan (and Semite) to conquer the essentially feminine Dravidian (1893: 622). Here then we have a mind that is, in Hegelian terms, more primitive in its highest form than the Aryan at the dawn of its history. The mind of India, as exemplified in Hinduism, was no longer in essence Our mind, lost in time and modified by the Indian jungle. It was now a mind that was in essence fundamentally Other, different not in degree but in kind. To the extent that it resembled the Self's mind, it was because it (she?) had been modified by the 'influence' of the Aryan.

While Dravidian hypotheses have been used to account for the origin of some of the main features of Brahmanism itself, especially since John Marshall's Dravidianist interpretation of the Indus Valley civilization (1931: I, 48–78), their main deployment has been in the construction of a medieval Hinduism.[34] Empiricists and idealists, both British and Indian, have looked on it as the result of a triumph of Dravidian features. Basham summarizes this depiction no longer (of course) as a hypothesis but as a conclusion:

> The final form of Hinduism was largely the result of influence from the Dravidian South. Here, on the basis of indigenous cults fertilized [*sic!*] by Aryan influences, theistic

---

[33] This connection has, no doubt, been confirmed by the 'hard' evidence of the numerous figurines of female figures excavated in the Near East (Clark and Piggott, 1985: 177–8).

[34] For a brief historical review of the theory of Aryan and Dravidian interaction, see Nilakanta Sastri (1967).

schools had arisen, characterized by intense ecstatic piety. It was this devotional Hinduism, propagated by many wandering preachers and hymn-singers in the medieval period, which had the greatest effect on Hinduism as it exists today. (1954: 298)[35]

What was the consequence of the construction of Hinduism and of the mind it expressed as Dravidian? On first sight, the shift of essences, from a masculine Aryan mentality that had been tropicalized, to a feminine Dravidian or aboriginal mind that had been Aryanized, does not seem to have entailed a change in the assumptions about what constituted the essence of the Hindu mind itself. On second glance, however, there is a major change involved here. The change from depicting an Indian mind that was the same in its racial origin as that of the Self to one that was fundamentally different was significant. It was a shift from a mind that once had been on a par with that of the Self and could perhaps be again some day to one that never had been and never could be. Here was a perennially post-tribal people who would always be dominated by or dependent upon mentally and physically superior foreigners or on their national heirs, the Westernized Indians and the protean Congress presided over by the Nehrus. Some of the Utilitarians would have bred the Indian plants in their care back to their original vigour. Not so for the imperial jungle officers that took charge after the Mutiny. They came to imagine themselves as presiding over an India comprised of Dravidian plants that could only be managed. So long as they did their job with reasonable care and avoided stirring up the primitive, emotional, violent elements of these Aryanized Dravidians and especially their presumed tendency to swarm around a heroic figure, whether the idol of a god or a nationalist leader, they could dream of keeping their charges in a more or less permanent state of tutelage.

For over ten years I have been at work on the *Vishnudharmottara Purāṇa*. That 'early medieval' text of Kashmir, which places itself in somewhat the same relationship to its predecessors as the *Gītā* does, as overall enunciator of what religion is and what to do about it, urges its major readers, a 'king of kings' and his court, to construct a world empire after becoming endowed with the 'luminous will' (*tejas*) of a form of Vishnu taken by the Pāñcarātra 'sect' as the overlord of the cosmos. They are to build a large temple for the performance of his liturgy in celebration of their joint triumph over the quarters. The theology and practices of this sect – we could just as well call it an 'order' (as in Roman Catholic or Eastern Orthodox Christianity) – all presupposed not the monist, illusionist, and quietist philosophy considered the core of Advaita, but the pluralist, realist, and activist philosophy of the Bhedābheda. The contents of this text are, thus, almost completely at odds with the picture of a medieval India that the Indological history of Hinduism provides for its readership. The mind that is made to preside over a divisive Middle Ages is not the mind of the West, of will governed by reason. It is a perversion of that mind, one in which the passions were ruled by the ever-volatile imagination. In its Advaita Vedānta philosophy and during the classical or Gupta period of its history, the

---

[35] Nilakanta Sastri speaks, in work based on a lecture delivered while he was Visiting Professor at the University of Chicago in 1959, of a decline from a 'golden' to a 'silver' age and of the increasing influence of a Dravidian 'little tradition' on the 'great' (1963).

imagination had more or less stayed on top. Now, however, after the death of Harsha in the seventh century, the passions of erotic attraction, greed, and glory have emerged triumphant. Unable to tell symbol from reality, this visceral mind confuses the local with the global, the spiritual with the temporal. Inhabiting an essentially rural India, it is concerned primarily with agricultural and human fertility and obsessed with their female sources, the Mother.

The moral of this narrative of decline in its earlier pro-Aryan version is the warning of what could happen to the mind of the Self in the threatening Indian climate and to the mental and religious life of the Self apart from Christian guidance. The lesson to be learned in its Dravidian recension is what happens when the mind or culture of a lower race or lower layer of the human mind, or the lesser of the two sexes, gains the upper hand over the higher.

3.6   JUNGIANS AND STRUCTURALISTS: TODAY'S VARIANTS

Since the displacement of the Anglo-French imperial formation by that of the US and USSR, the views of Jungians and structuralists, descendants of the philosophical idealists of the nineteenth century (2.3.1), have become more important than the empiricist and Christian liberal views. Both tend to focus their attention on 'myths' and 'symbols'. Among the Jungians, whom I consider first, I include Mircea Eliade, a historian of religion,[36] the Indologist Heinrich Zimmer, and his student, the mythologist Joseph Campbell.[37]

The Jungians draw a sharp dichotomy between Aryan and pre-Aryan. The life-affirming, optimistic, activist, pantheistic religion of the Vedic Aryans is antithetical to the originally present religions of the non-Aryans, which were all life-denying, pessimistic, quietist, and dualistic. But they do not stop there. The 'upgrading' of the Dravidians tended to undermine one of the reasons for invoking them in the first place, namely, to explain why the civilization of India, nominally produced by Aryans, differed so sharply from its Western counterparts. Once the Dravidians had been turned into a branch of the Near Eastern people as part of a uniform Neolithic Asia, India's distinctiveness ran the risk of evaporating. So the ethnologists and Jungians invoke the jungle metaphor and invent a still earlier 'layer', that of the Kolarian or Proto-Australoid, primitive hunters and gatherers.

On to these 'tribals' the Jungians then offload the savagery, animal sacrifice, and general fetishism and animism formerly attributed to the Dravidian. Campbell conjures up this essence: 'For the calmly ruthless power of the jungle and consequent orientation of its folk (the Proto-Australoid aborigines of that world of static vistas, with no history but duration) has supplied the drone base of whatever song has ever been sung in India of man, his destiny, and escape

---

[36] Though not an Indologist, Mircea Eliade, late Professor of the History of Religions at the University of Chicago, studied in India at the University of Calcutta with the philosopher, Surendranath Dasgupta, and wrote that some have considered his very 'influential' book on yoga (1969). The successor to Eliade as retailer of the sacred is W. D. O'Flaherty, in numerous books such as *Dreams, Illusions, and Other Realities* (1984).

[37] Also, tangentially, the Tibetologist Giuseppe Tucci (1970).

from destiny.' This defining essence consists of nothing more than the female side of the mind, that which threatens to overcome man's consciousness and reason. There has, to be sure, been a beneficent side to this femininity: 'New civilizations, races, philosophies, and great mythologies have poured into India and have been not only assmilated but greatly developed, enriched, and sophisticated.' But the goddess Kali, condensation of this jungle essence, is always there: 'Yet, in the end (and in fact, even secretly throughout), the enduring power in that land has always been the same old dark goddess of the long red tongue who turns everything into her own everlasting, awesome, yet finally somewhat tedious, self' (Campbell, 1962: 164; Eliade, 1969: 293–364).

Thus have the Jungians pushed the Romantic idea of Hinduism as an ambivalent feminine entity to its extreme. The basement of the Hindu mind would seem to make India the place where the mentality of primitive man has strangely developed into a civilized form, one that seems opposed to that developed in the West. India is the land where the imagination reigns supreme. Its 'metaphysically oriented tradition', in which 'there is therefore nothing to be gained, either for the universe or for man, through individual originality and effort', is ever at odds with the ethical, historical, and political orientation of the West (Campbell, 1962: 3–8). India is also a place where, given the Jungians' theory of mental and racial stratification, the more primitive unconscious elements of earlier races remain ever present, never being overcome, as in the West, by the later, more progressive and conscious elements of the later races. Finally, India is the civilization in which, since the unconscious of a man is a female entity known as the *anima*, the feminine predominates over the masculine.[38]

This notion of a feminine Hindu mind has even been taken over by some Indian psychoanalysts. Sudhir Kakar, who styles himself a Freudian, states as a matter of fact that Indian culture is one 'in which mother-religions and the worship of Kali in her many manifestations ... forms the deepest layer of Hindu religiosity' (1978: 173).[39] India is, thus, important for the psychoanalyst and historian of religion because it is where the female layer of the human unconscious is most in evidence. Whereas the West has developed the conscious scientific rationality of man, the East in India (equated by sleight of hand now with the 'primitives', then with the 'archaic', here with the pre-Christian, there with the pre-Enlightenment) has developed its unconscious, mystical, symbolical side. The 'material' values of the West and the 'spiritual' values of the East are not, however, quite complementary in their Jungian rendering; they are, separated from one another, extreme. Properly integrated in the individual, however, an uplifted and balanced 'new' Western man emerges. The guide in this personal quest is the discourse of the Jungian analyst and historian of religion, both in print and in expensive, authoritative treatment or education. The 'primitive' or 'archaic' man does not know he is continually being drawn toward 'archetypal man', while the 'modern' can, by signing up with the Jungians or other gurus of the New Age movement, come to

[38] The importance of these views may perhaps be gauged by the fact that the main article on 'Hinduism' in the current edition of *Encyclopaedia Britannica* (1974), anonymously authored, is clearly Jungian or, if one wishes, Eliadean.

[39] Much closer to Freud's secularism is Masson (1980).

know this and, as a result, fine-tune his psyche. Not only can the harassed corporate executive adjust to the stress he suffers, he can cultivate a part of his self that stands outside the modern world, expressing itself in those exotic anti-commodities, the vacation to the Orient or the Tibetan sculpture on the coffee table.

Most troublesome, from the standpoint of human agency, is the idea of the human 'collective unconscious', the bottom-most 'layer' of the primitive mind, below even the racial. Here is buried the essence of man, in a Grecian urn of 'archetypes'. These are (so far as one can tell) the 'primordial images', 'principal ideas', resembling Platonic forms, except, we are told, that these contain a 'dark' as well as a 'light' side. What are these the images of? Well, they are images of a Great Father, a Great Mother, and a Child, and so on (Jacobi, 1973: 39–51). Whatever one may think of this theory, one must at least give credit to Jung for arguing the case for his archetypes. His followers, however, make no such argument. They simply assume them to exist. Eliade, churning the ocean of natural religion, even extends the list to include the sky, sun, moon, water, and the like (1963). These are the true agents of people's actions which themselves are also archetypal.

Just as this collective unconscious precedes human history, so the true agents and actions of archaic people are in reality also timeless. Eliade can, thus, tell us that 'the rite always consists in the repetition of an archetypal action performed *in illo tempore* (before 'history' began) by ancestors or gods', and that 'by its repetition, the act coincides with its archetype, and time is abolished.' This is not just the case, however, with 'rites'. It applies to the whole range of actions. Eliade promises to show us that 'the greater part of primitive man's actions were, so he thought, simply the repetition of a primeval action accomplished at the beginning of time by a divine being, or mythical figure.' He is quite explicit about the relationship of act to essence: 'Now, every action performed by the primitive supposes a transcendent model – his actions are effective only in so far as they are real, as they follow the pattern (1963: 32–3).

The Jungians have claimed or assumed that their irrationalist, Neo-Kantian, quasi-Neoplatonic ontology is that of the primitive or, in at least one instance, that of Indian yoga.[40] This is nothing more than an updated repetition of the claims by the earlier Romantic idealists that they had discovered their idea of the imagination in Indian (or Egyptian) myth and philosophy. Perhaps there are archetypal acts after all. They are not, however, the actions performed by Indians and other primitives, but the acts of these keepers of the secularized sacred, perpetually revealing the mysterious, feminine Hindu mind to themselves and their devotees.

Dumont, who challenged the empiricist and evolutionist voice in Indological discourse on caste, has also questioned what it has said about the religion or ideology that is supposed to accompany the institution of caste, Hinduism. In a brilliant article on a village deity, he argues that the 'divergent opinions' about the god 'result first of all from hasty interpretations rooted in the idea, which

[40] For an attempt to salvage this salvation of religion from the Enlightenment, see Dudley (1977: 105–18).

has done so much harm, that Indian culture is merely a juxtaposition of Aryan and so-called Dravidian or other elements'. Arguing for a 'structural' or 'relational' approach, he states that instead of looking for the 'essence' of the god, 'we shall attempt to get a more reliable view of the data by insisting upon the god's double relation on the one hand with the "demons" and with the goddesses on the other' (Dumont, 1970: 21).[41] Two prominent followers of Dumont's approach are the Sanskritist, Madeleine Biardeau,[42] and the anthropologist, Veena Das (1977).

These structuralists differ from the British and Indian empiricists in that they assume an inherent rationality in Hinduism. The rationality at issue here, though, is not that of mistaken scientific or practical reason applied by the individual to the natural world, as with the intellectualists (see 3.2.1), but of a socially shared, unconscious symbolic reason that provides people with a morally and emotionally ordered world. The approach of the structuralists is holistic rather than atomistic. Biardeau, for example, replaces the disparate cultures of the Aryan, Dravidian, and Proto-Australoid with a single Indian or Hindu culture which she conceives of as an integrity comprised of inter-related parts. Differences between sects are set aside in order to get at the 'level' where this unity is to be found. She prefers to see Vishnu and Siva as complements (the one royal, the other ascetic) rather than as sectarian rivals and imperfect attempts to conceptualize a Christian god. Yet she does not go quite so far as to reduce those gods to symbolizations of an impersonal absolute.

Similarly, when Biardeau turns to the goddess she eschews the notion that she is the essence of a pre-Aryan Hinduism that has survived into the present. The goddess is, we are told, 'a fundamental category of Hindu consciousness as such'. She is, in her various forms, an integral part of the Hindu ensemble of deities and complements Vishnu and Siva as much as they do each other. Nor does Biardeau account for the worship of the goddess with a buffalo sacrifice by seeing it as propitiatory. Rather, 'It symbolizes the struggle of the goddess against the buffalo-demon, and perhaps more profoundly still, the essential relation of the Goddess with the most impure, and thus the most formidable, demon' (1981b: 9–16).

Although she associates the goddess with the soil, she does not see that association as the reappearance in a male, sky-oriented Aryan religion, of a different and earlier female religion, one of small farmers. Rather, she considers the opposition as internal to Hinduism itself: 'The soil, from which humanity – and the gods of the sky who receive offerings from it – draws its sustenance, belongs to the demons, those subterranean gods who withhold the source of all fecundity. The sky has need of the demons, the Brahmans likewise, as they need the "untouchables" for whom the demons are the gods.' The goddess, she concludes, is also a 'necessary mediator' between these opposed pairs of 'pure and impure, divine and human' (1981b: 15–16).

Hinduism thus becomes, in her hands, a system of coherent symbols and

[41] Quite different is his repetition of the opposition originally imposed on India by Hegel, between individual and society (1980c).
[42] Her work (1981a; 1986: I, 17–43) also relies on the philologist and historian of religions, Georges Dumézil.

meanings, taking on the aspect of a rational theology in its textual manifestations. It is a system – not her concern for Dumont's fundamental social pair of the pure and impure – that mirrors and expresses social relations (or is it the other way round?).

I certainly welcome the approach of Biardeau and other like-minded structuralists with enthusiasm; indeed, some of my own work has an affinity with theirs. The move away from the atomist and evolutionist history of Hinduism has, however, also created two problems. First, the atomism characteristic of the earlier intellectualists has not been altogether expelled. To a certain extent it has been translated from the parts on to the whole: Hinduism itself has become a unitary, dare I say, molecule, sealed off from other religions within India and from interactions with other religions outside the subcontinent. The second problem is closely related to the first. Hinduism has been liberated from the largely specious evolutionist history, but in the process it has been left without any history at all.

While this bracketing out of history by Biardeau (and most of the contemporary anthropologists and Indologists who share her point of view) can be seen as an over-reaction against evolutionism, it is also, in my opinion, partially a result of certain assumptions made in common with the Jungians. To the extent that Biardeau and her sympathizers retain a strong empirical bent and avoid seeing India and its mother goddess as representative of archetypes, they are able to keep their distance from them. When it comes to the question of subject, consciousness, and of myth and symbol, however, there are certain difficulties that remain unresolved.

The method of Biardeau privileges the unconscious of structuralism. It maintains that while certain 'surface features' of the general structures at issue may manifest themselves in texts or in rites, these reside largely at an unconscious level of the minds of those people to whom they are attributed. The problem I have here is this: Who is or are the subjects of these unconscious structures? It seems to me that the quest for a general unity of structure implies that there is a single subject. The danger here is that Hinduism runs the risk of being treated as the true (underlying) subject of the specific thoughts of Hindus and of being taken as the unchanging agent of the acts that they have performed and do perform, leaving the Indians themselves as the unconscious instruments or patients of those acts. In so far as one equates consciousness with rationality, one would have to say that these Indian actors are hardly rational.

Closely connected with the idea of a floating subject, indeed, integral to it, is this further complication. The subject of a structuralist Hinduism itself has no object. There is a strong tendency to see people here not as people who act in consequential ways, whose acts actually make their world, including their consciousness. Rather the tendency is to see them as more narrowly concerned with meanings that are themselves part of the underlying structure and not of the problematically conscious minds of particular persons. The acts that go on around the specific actors become, as it were, givens, as do, I might add, the texts that are mined for meanings.

It is hard to avoid the conclusion that the largely unconscious reason attributed to the minds of Indians in these structuralist analyses bears a certain resemblance to the 'creative imagination' or 'fantasy' of Hegel (3.2.2). He did, after all, see it as a lower, more visceral, less 'spiritual' (in Hegel's sense, less conceptual) form of reason. So while Biardeau and her colleagues have helped to restore rationality to Hinduism, it is a rationality that remains largely confined to symbolic representations – at worst to an 'inner' realm of meanings and at best to an 'outer' realm of rituals. By those circularities of thought that appear in the history of intellectual practices and differentiate it from the history of ideas where only critical advances are proclaimed, we find present-day scholars using Lévi-Straussian structuralism to make studies of Indian myths and rituals, seemingly unaware that they are applying a notion of mind to the very culture where that type of thinking first makes its appearance on the world stage and reaches its fullest, most extreme development.

3.7 CRITICAL SUMMARY

The 'mind' which the differing constructs of Hinduism have implicitly or explicitly attributed to that religion is closely connected to the issue of human agency that runs throughout this book. Most of the studies of Hinduism rest on the assumption that it has an essence consisting of an ambiguous and inferior form of reason associated with the senses and called the imagination. The predominant construction of Hinduism during the Anglo-French imperial formation was 'empirical realist'. The more Utilitarian, secular in outlook, simply looked at Hindu thought as unenlightened, that is, as the universal mind whose imagination had been diverted from its natural task of mirroring accurate pictures, composed of the sense-impressions, to itself. Christian liberals, conceding knowledge of the material world to the scientists, agreed that the Hindu mind was led by imagination rather than reason, but added that because the passions that constituted man, the foremost of which is love, were also unguided by revelation, it did not yield up an ethical orderly religion of the good.

The Romantic, idealist voice enthusiastically construed Hindu thought as emanating not from a reason of spirit but from a 'creative imagination' or 'fantasy' of the senses. The essence of Hinduism was a form of thinking that was not simply the absence of the 'conceptual', but rather the presence and predominance in it of the 'symbolical'. It was not that the Hindu does not think rationally. It was, rather, that he thinks in icons or images. Since this is a form of thinking which Western, scientific man has largely outgrown or pushed into its subconscious, its presence and development in the East is of great importance, for it may provide the mind of Western man which is, for the Romantics, as one-sided as that of the Easterner, with direct access to that part of himself that he has 'lost'. Hence, the Romantics and idealists and their Jungian descendants in no way disagree that Hinduism is a religion constituted by a mentality of extremes that is in essence imaginative. Indeed, it is precisely this 'central feature' of Hinduism that has made it of such interest to them. All alike, however, have agreed that Hinduism lacked that heir of the rational soul, the transcendent scientific mind capable of apprehending the world as a separate object and observing the centred, hierarchic, clear, uniform, and moderate order present in the world.

The Hinduisms the scholars have produced were construed as dominated by imagination rather than reason. They depict for us religions related to one another as levels of the human mind that were opposed to one another in their essences. The priestly elite adhered, as isolated individuals, to an essentially cognitive mysticism, consisting of a domesticated version of the Vedic fire sacrifice and a pantheism that treated external reality as an illusion. The urban educated adhered to a form of theism that was emotive (or even erotic) but not ethical in its essence. Divided into the cults of two principal gods and ever splitting into sects, it was, with its idol worship, phallic cults, temples adorned with lewd sculptures, and processions swarming with thousands of devotees, the excessive opposite of the extreme self-denial of the Brahmans. Opposed to both of these religions or conflated with that of the well-off laity, was still another, the animist religion of the villagers. While this faith was also emotional, it was not a misplaced love but a fear of disease and disaster-bearing demons and an obsession with fertility in the gift of mother goddesses that motivated its bloody sacrifices. Its essence, however, was not sensual either in the cognitive or emotive sense. Peasants were concerned neither with mystical nor moral knowledge, but fundamentally with the knowledge of survival, with food and reproduction. That is, theirs was a religion of mere existence. All three 'levels' of Hinduism – and of the Hindu mind – were, thus, assumed to be bodily or organic rather than spiritual or rational in their essence.

The Hindu mind similarly lacked that instrument of the scientific intellect, a governing or ordering will. It was deficient in the capacity to form voluntary associations and carry out joint activities. That is why the religion of the Brahman philosopher had no church and was not congregational, requiring no organization, and yet it remained a religion of the 'natural' units of society, the joint family, clan, caste, and village. That is, the individual was either completely absorbed in the natural units of society or stood completely outside them.

Implicit in this notion of Hinduism as exemplifying a mind that is imaginative and passionate rather than rational and wilful was, of course, the idea that the Indian mind requires an externally imported world-ordering rationality. This was important for the imperial project of the British as it appeared, piecemeal, in the course of the nineteenth century. Why? Because the theist creeds and sects, activist and realist, were the world-ordering religions of precisely those in the Indian populace, among the Hindus, that the British themselves were in the process of displacing as the rulers of India. To provide India with a polarized religion, one that was, where rational thought was in evidence, cosmically idealist or parochially materialist, acted not simply to justify the presence of the conquering outsiders in some abstract way. Indology was as a discipline not merely reflective but agentive; it actually fashioned the ontological space that a British Indian empire occupied. Its leaders would, as had others before them beginning with the Aryans, inject the rational intellect and world-ordering will that the Indians themselves could not provide.

The 'scientific' explanations for the existence of the Hindu mind, when offered, were either environmental or racial. Earlier scholars, apparently combining Montesquieu with Hegel, construed it as the result of a masculine Aryan mind which started out with the same germ of rationality as the Self. Instead of developing as it did in ancient Greece and the West, however, it went to seed because its originators, the Brahmans, had been planted in the extreme environment of the tropics. Later scholars, melding Herder and Spencer, came increasingly to see the Hindu mind not as a branch of the universal or Western mind that had gone astray but as one that was fundamentally different. It was an inferior mind inherently ruled by an imagination incapable of distinguishing concrete symbol from abstract referent, a feminine presence, that of the impassionate Dravidian or Kolarian race or culture, which had become 'Aryanized' or 'humanized' by interaction with the Aryan. The Brahmans were, hence, only the intellectual managers of this jungle of a mentality. Either way, Brahmanism, the earlier and pre-Christian form of Hinduism, took its ritual and mystical turn. The mind of India was set.

When we turn to the historical narratives of this religion, we behold a degenerative psychohistory masterminded by Hegel. The Hindu mind, directed by a sensuous imagination that cannot properly relate subject and object, lurches first from one extreme to the other, from a bonkers ritualism to a solipsistic mysticism, then to a nihilistic salvationsim of the Buddha, then to the schizophrenic religion of Siva and Vishnu. Instead of witnessing the triumph of man, reason, and spirit, however, we see the triumph of the effeminate, the sensuous, and the parochial. After the Gupta 'synthesis', the Aryan has spent himself, and by the end of the twelfth century it is time for a hopelessly divided civilization, already overwhelmed by a symbolical mind, to fall prey to the world-destroying will of a fanatical Islam.

The mind that Indologists have provided for the 'caste society' through their studies of Hinduism has had important consquences for the way in which they and others have depicted Indian civilization as a whole. This will be the subject of the next two chapters. Not many today would feel comfortable with the metaphor of Hinduism as a jungle or sponge (although I am told that the jungle recently sent up new shoots at a conference on materials for teaching Hinduism). There is no longer much point in arguing that Hinduism did not (or did) conform with the mechanical image of the world implicit in that metaphor, for the major presuppositions on which that image rested have been critically damaged, especially in physics, the science where that metaphysics was supposed to reign supreme. (Two years ago I came across a science column in a newspaper reporting that some physicists, attempting to break with their mechanistic past, now analogized the universe with, well, a sponge.) Made aware of the equally problematic psychology presupposed in the idea of the imaginary Hindu mind, few would, I suspect, be ready to defend it. Indeed, it would not be unfair I believe to characterize the present state of affairs in the study of Indian religions as one of uncertainty, in which there is a widening gap between monographic studies and the increasingly derivative surveys that frame them. Yet precisely because we have not made ourselves aware of the major assumptions and presuppositions built into Indology, we continue to produce and validate studies of Hinduism that have failed to struggle free of the construct I have outlined. We continue, with perhaps a sometimes uneasy feeling of their inadequacy, to reproduce the notions of Hinduism animated by this metaphysics and its imperial politics. There are alternatives. Some of these are to be found dispersed in the already existing scholarship. I myself take up certain aspects of them as a part of my discussion of agency in medieval Indian polities in chapter 6.

Let me conclude here, however, by stressing that the changes called for are not minor ones. We would have to give up the major presupposition of this discourse – that there is some essence called the Hindu mind that can be captured and summed up in a 'nonwestern' civilization or world religions course syllabus. Conjointly we would also want to get out of the habit of equating Indian thought with Hinduism and equating Hinduism with the monist pantheism and idealism attributed to Advaita Vedānta. People on the subcontinent have constructed many systems of thought. There is no reason why most of these – the 'sects' of Hinduism, the 'schools' of Buddhism, Jainism altogether, the forms of Indian Islam, and 'village' practices – should be treated either as popularizations of, deviations from, or the ultimate origin of a permanent orthodoxy consisting of an illusionary pantheism, that of Advaita Vedānta. Scepticism here is especially prudent when we consider that that orthodoxy is itself as much the product of the Anglo-German imagination and of its shifting desires in the nineteenth century. Among these was a wish to create a purely masculine, spiritual, transcendent Reason for itself. This construct implied its opposite, a feminine, visceral, immanent Imagination, one that remained ever necessary to Reason, but also always a threat to it. Without India to act upon, without a civilization in which this internal Other could be externalized, and worked upon, it is hard to see how our ancestors could have convinced themselves they had succeeded to the extent that they did.

4

Village India, Living Essence of the Ancient

4.1 IDYLLIC COMMUNITIES

India has been called a land of villages, and if proof is needed of the truth of the description, it is found in the census figures which show that the rural population numbers over 300 million or nine-tenths of the total population. Practically the whole country is parcelled out among villages, about half a million in number. A more vivid impression of the predominance of village life is obtained from a railway journey through India. For hundreds of miles at a stretch village succeeds village, towns are few and far between, and many of the small towns are more like overgrown villages, in the midst of which the cattle are driven afield and from which the peasant goes out with his simple plough on his shoulder to till the neighbouring lands. (O'Malley, 1934: 100)

Scholars and rulers of the Anglo-French imperial formation of the nine-teenth century took the village in their discourses to be the irreducible unit, the 'atom' of the state in the nations and empires of Asia, not only in India, but in the Ottoman empire or Persia and China as well. Perhaps more than in the others, however, the village in India came to be viewed as the quintessential Asian village. China, they said, has been a unified, centralized empire for most of her history. The essential feature of Chinese civilization is, therefore, the Chinese state, by which is usually meant the 'bureaucracy', and the jostlings for power and status by her privileged elite families. Orientalists have characterized the Middle East again and again as a civilization not of settled agricultural villages, but of sedentary trading towns, on the one hand, and of the desert, nomadic pastoralists, on the other.

When we come to India, however, we find ourselves confronted with a civilization that is, in the eyes of the Asian studies specialist, truly rural in nature. That is what L. S. S. O'Malley (1874–1941), civil servant and Census Commissioner, proudly said (at the head of the chapter) after British officers had been surveying and classifying these villages for some one hundred years. If the Ottoman empire provided in its caliph the capricious autocrat of the oriental state and China the overbearing official in her mandarins, India supplied Asia with its traditional peasants in the ryots of her village settlements. Indeed, throughout much of the nineteenth century the Indian village was even taken as typical of both Europe and Asia. Many of the earlier orientalists, envisioning an original Aryan religion and society that were more or less isomorphic with an original Aryan language, believed it to be the living descendant of the Aryan village. Looking upon it with a condescending fondness that borders on the romantic, they supposed the Indian village was analogous with the post-tribal, agricultural village of the Teutons or Germanic branches of the Aryans in ancient and medieval Western Europe, an area of historical enquiry that was being formed at the very same time that the British were settling the revenue in Indian villages. That village in Europe had all but disappeared as it became a 'modern' society. India, however, was still an 'ancient' society. The ancient Aryan village still survived there.

Now, it could well be that the importance of the village in the study of India may be due not only to the supposed pre-eminence of the village in Indian civilization but also to this noble quest for our own origins. I will argue that the constitution of India as a land of villages was also due to the efforts of the British to deconstitute the Indian state. As they were composing their discourses on India's villages, they were displacing a complex polity with an 'ancient' India that they could appropriate as an external appanage of a 'modern' Britain. The essence of the ancient was the division of societies into self-contained, inwardly turned communities consisting of cooperative communal agents. The essence of the modern was the unification of societies consisting of outwardly turned, competitive individuals. Just as the modern succeeded the ancient in time, so the modern would dominate the ancient in space.

Nearly every book that tries to capture the fundamental characteristics of India for its readers in whatever sphere of human activity, includes a statement about the Indian village. It is one of the pillars of these imperial constructs of India. Most of these are capsule representations which trace their descent back to the statement of a prestigious servant of the East India Company, Sir Charles Metcalfe (1785–1846). His description of a 'village republic' first appeared in a British Parliamentary inquiry of 1810. Not surprisingly, Mill, Utilitarian advocate of political economy, began this tradition, first reproducing the passage in his discussion of revenue, the category under which most accounts of villages were classed in nineteenth-century discourse (Mill, 1848: I, 217–18). It is a tradition that has been kept up all too well. Elphinstone included it in his would-be replacement for Mill's *History* in 1841, the first part of which was updated by E. B. Cowell, H. H. Wilson's student, early in this century (1905: 63).[1] And it has appeared in varying renditions countless times since. Even Marx, relying on the writings of two on-the-spot commentators, Colonel Mark Wilks (1760?–1831), Company servant in Madras from 1782 to 1801, and Sir George Campbell (1824–92), who held high posts in India between 1842 and 1874, produced a text on the Indian village in *Das Kapital* (Marx, 1968: 39–40).

The discourse on Indian villages, whether in these thumbnail sketches or in

[1] Louis Dumont has traced the genealogy of this multi-authored piece (1966).

the longer accounts, has depicted the village as the locale where caste, the essential institution of India, appears in the form of a strange community of collective actors and a peculiar political economy of subsistence exchanges, the so-called 'jajmani system'. The smallest unit of the Indian state, it was, of course, also the site where government revenue was generated and collected.

Let us look at one example of a cameo portrait. The hegemonic voice in the making of discourses on village India throughout most of the nineteenth century was neither that of the philologist nor of the missionary, those mainly responsible for Hinduism and India's mind. Men interested in political economy and legal history, but who had no direct knowledge of their object, combined intellectually with those who did make this claim, the settlement officers of the Company (and Crown) and their supervisors, to hold sway here. To show how much these disciplines overlapped and depended on one another, I have purposely selected the derivative portrayal of the Sanskritist, Monier-Williams, from the chapter on caste and occupation in one of his books on Hinduism, first published in 1883. He prefaces his description with this reminder of the significance that Indian villages are made to have, one that transcends their position as objects in Indological discourse:

And here I may observe that no circumstance in the history of India is more worthy of investigation than the antiquity and permanence of her village and municipal institutions. The importance of the study lies in the light thereby thrown on the parcelling out of rural society into autonomous divisions, like those of our own English parishes, wherever Aryan races have occupied the soil in Asia or in Europe. (1891: 455)

With this promise that we shall see reflected in the mirror of the Indian village our own origins, Monier-Williams proceeded.

Like the other accounts of the village we shall examine, his emphasized certain features which the Indian village possesses:

The Indian village or township, meaning thereby not merely a collection of houses forming a village or town, but a division of territory, perhaps three or four square miles or more in extent, with its careful distribution of fixed occupations for the common good, with its intertwining and inter-dependence of individuals, family, and communal interests, with its perfect provision for political independence and autonomy, is the original type [of Aryan rural society] – the first germ of all the divisions of rural and civic society in medieval and modern Europe. (1891: 455)

Silently positioned in such accounts as these is the presupposition of a dichotomy between inner and outer. Villages were not overlapping agents interacting with and reshaping one another. Each village was an inner world, a traditional organic community, self-sufficient in its economy, patriarchal in its governance, surrounded by an outer one of other hostile villages and despotic governments.

Coupled with this and just as important is the notion that the Indian village was in many ways opposed in its 'essence' to that of the Indian state, which together constitute the two levels of Indian society. The lower one is portrayed as a natural, organic, and stable community of subsisting peasants. The higher is considered an artificial, disorganized, and unstable institution of personal aggrandizement and opulence. This opposition is embedded in the Indological snapshots of 'the' village. Monier-Williams, again:

It has existed almost unaltered since the description of its organization in Manu's code, two or three centuries before the Christian era. It has survived all the religious, political, and physical convulsions from which India has suffered from time immemorial. Invader after invader has ravaged the country with fire and sword; internal wars have carried devastation into every corner of the land; tyrannical oppressors have desolated its homesteads; famine has decimated its peasantry; pestilence has depopulated entire districts; floods and earthquakes have changed the face of nature; folly, superstition, and delusion have made havoc of all religion and morality – but the simple, self-contained Indian township has preserved its constitution intact, its customs, precedents, and peculiar institutions unchanged and unchangeable amid all other changes. (1891: 455)

It is as though, in this bilevel Indian world, the possessive individual of the political economists and Utilitarians had been split. The rational, ordering part has been inserted in the village while the insatiable desire part has been inserted in the traditional Indian state. That is why the former constituted an ordered whole capable of meeting its needs, but one that was static because it had no desires. The latter, on the other hand, possessed the insatiable desire of the capitalist individual, but lacked the ordering reason required to convert that into the accumulation of capital.

What follows is an attempt to bring out the presuppositions embedded in the Indological construct of the village and the place it occupies in the construction of Indian civilization as a whole. My concern will be to show how accounts of villages are informed by an essentialist dichotomy drawn between the 'ancient' and the 'modern', one that was primarily concerned with the constitution of economic agents at home and the deconstitution of political agents abroad. The knowing subjects of this schema used it to place the village into relations both with their image of the Indian state and with the modern one they were fashioning in India. Simultaneously they also tried to position the Indian village with respect to a unitary developmental history.[2]

4.2 ORGANIC INSIDE, ATOMIC OUTSIDE

4.2.1 Marx: Asiatic Communes and Rural Mentalities

An issue that dogged discourses on rural India in the nineteenth century was the question of whether the village holds or owns its lands in common or whether the cultivating households of an Indian village hold them severally. The writings of Marx and Engels were central to this debate, either directly or indirectly, because of the role they gave to the village in their idea of an Asiatic mode of production. While I agree with the view (Hindess and Hirst) that

---

[2] For the changing British setting in which these constructions were formulated, I draw on Dewey (1972).

criticizes later scholars for reading too much theoretical consistency and elaboration into the partial, inchoate, and changing statements of Marx on Asia, it cannot be denied that those statements formed a part of nineteenth-century discourse on 'society' and its 'origins' and that much of what they had to say overlaps in some of its major presuppositions with Indological, legal, and fiscal discourses of the period. One can also see Marx as extending Hegel's philosophy of history in the economic direction as much as inverting its major elements. Nor should it be forgotten that much of what Marx and Engels had to say about Asian villages was supposedly based on evidence provided by British administrators of India, and that since Independence a socialist view has come to shape recent works of South Asian history.

Marx distinguished three modes of production apart from the capitalist. The first and earliest of these was the communal or tribal. The Asiatic mode, which does not appear in the 'earlier' Marx, seems always to be classed by him as a variant of the communal, a direct development out of the primitive mode that accompanied the rise of agriculture. The Asiatic land form was, thus, clearly distinguished from the two other pre-capitalist forms, both confined to Europe, the ancient or Roman and the Germanic. Clans (*Stamm*) were present in all of the precapitalist formations, but they were of primary importance in the earliest or tribal mode and, hence, in the Asiatic mode.

Persons of the clan community (when it lived by pastoralism) saw the clan not as the result of their cooperative efforts, but as its 'presupposition'. Consistent with this is a further presupposition: the members of the community thought of the land not as their personal property, but as the property of the community. They were merely its possessors; hence the displacement of ownership on to a fictional entity, the clan ancestor or deity (Marx, 1973: 472; 1964).

The primitive society, one characterized by a gentile constitution, that is, one consisting of a confederation of descent groups, was not divided into classes and possessed, therefore, no state, the instrument (in this theory) for the furthering of class interests. Within the Asiatic states that arose out of such earlier tribal societies, a division into classes took place, but this was synonymous with the division into villages and the state. Concurring with the view of Mill (1858: I, 208–17), Marx argued that the surplus that it extracted was, consistent with this lack of differentiation, both a tax and a rent. The same displacement of thought that had occurred within the primitive community was, correspondingly, carried one step further. The ownership of the landed property of the various communes became, in its turn, displaced on to the oriental despot and his divine double, an imagined god (1973: 473).

The village is, thus, a strange world and the villager a strange sort of human, for he thinks that the village lands on which he labours belong not to him who plows them but to the village as a whole. He merely possesses his land and only then by virtue of his descent from an ancestor and patriarch of the clan, who is at the same time founder of the village. The village itself belongs, in the 'metaleptic' thought of the villager, to a remote owner or state in the form of an oriental despot. The unity of that state is based in his mind not on real activities and relations, but on imaginary ones, the 'presence' of the spirit of a clan or village deity and of a despot-and-god couple.

Marx was not content simply to comment on this fundamentally irrational state of affairs, namely the existence in India of self-contained village communities that have not changed since the Dark Ages. He also attempted to explain it. Marx did this through an evolutionary or developmental scheme which placed the Indian village in a stage just above the barbaric or primitive.

The Asiatic village and its form of property was, according to him, a development or variant of the first (and earliest) form of property. It appears before the other two forms of property, those entailed in the ancient or Roman and feudal or Germanic mode of production, and is logically more distant than they from the capitalist form.[3] Each of the other forms had, because of its inner workings, a tendency to dissolve itself and proceed to the next and higher form, including even the communal (1973: 486).

For Marx, the agent of history was not, as it was for Hegel, a transcendent Spirit that was also immanent in the state. It was a purely immanent agent, the relations and forces of production. In so far as these are made the subject of a history that is seen to be moving in a certain direction, it can be said that this theory turns the relations and forces of production into a substantialized agent. A mode of production is, then, a particular form of that agency. The Asiatic mode, however, was one that deviated from the others in that it had no forward movement. Because the structure of the Eastern social formations lacked certain fundamental distinctions found in the Western forms, the Indian (Asian) village was condemned to perpetuate itself without change. They remained stranded at what we might call the 'early ancient' stage of civilization.

What were these absent distinctions? First, there was no separation of the cultivating householder (by virtue of his owning his own land) from the village, the clan or commune, to which he belonged. Second, there was an absence of a division of labour among villages. Or, to put it another way, all of the trades and crafts necessary for the agricultural community to survive and reproduce itself were encapsulated within each village. This was the second major reason for the changelessness of the Indian (and, more generally, Asiatic) village. There was, finally, no separation of the village from its lands (1973: 486, 494). Echoing Hegel on the individual, but with the accent on 'property' rather than 'spirit', Marx asserted that the community is, then, for the Asiatic (as for the tribal) form, 'the substance of which the individuals are mere accidents, or of which they form purely natural component parts' (1973: 474; Hegel, 1975: 198).

The main reason for the changelessness of the Asian village was not, however, simply immanent in the clan itself. There was also a reason that lay outside these. Hegel had explained why India and Asia as a whole should have remained static. For him, the unseen substantialized agent of history was Spirit in the form of Reason. That agent had decided that history, the development of man's freedom, his self-consciousness, would begin in the East and end in the West. It would endow the latter but not the former with the inner capacity to transform itself. Hence, Asia's moment would come with the rise of substantial freedom on its soil; it would then give way to the West where genuine subjective freedom would evolve.

---

[3] This is so, I believe, whether one takes Marx as having advocated a unilineal scheme of development or not.

Marx and his partner, Engels, seem to have agreed with Hegel that Asiatic society was static, but they did not agree, of course, that it was some presumed Spirit that was the cause. Engels, consistent with the Marxian 'inversion' of Hegel's ontology, offered a different agent as the cause for Asia's inability to reach even the feudal form of property. It is not Spirit, but Matter, here in the form of a supposedly 'desert' environment and the 'artificial irrigation' that Asian agriculture required.[4] Those waterworks were, thus, the feature that distinguished the Asian village and the Asian state from other ancient communities and states.[5]

In India itself, the transition to a state-organized society centred, needless to say, on India's peculiar institution, caste. For Marx, castes were clans transformed from exogamous units into endogamous ones. Villages are clans transformed from units, virtually all of whose men engage in the same livelihood, into those characterized by the division of labour and the exchange of goods and services among them. Of these, 'the most extreme, strictest form is the caste-order, in which one is separated from the other, without the right of intermarriage, quite different in [degree of] privilege; each with an exclusive, irrevocable occupation' (1973: 478).

It is clear, then, that within Marx's scheme of historical materialism, clans are transposed into castes[6] in order to obtain the *essentially* Hindu village community in which Indians have lived down to the present. Since castes are, however, nothing but a peculiar subspecies of clan in this discourse, it is easy to see why the people of India, though not primitive, have nearly the same mentality as those who remained in a barbaric or primitive state. Marxism thus turns caste, as the forces and relations of production peculiar to India, into the agent *par excellence* of the Indian village community. Combined with irrigation, it not only causes Indian villages to be self-contained and organic but also makes them into its patients, the recipients of others' actions. They are non-social communities, only more so than villages elsewhere.

Now, one might assume that the views of a conservative English legal scholar and civil servant would be sharply at odds with the Marxist account of the Indian village, and in some respects they are. The amazing thing, though, is the extent to which they agree in the major presuppositions they hold.

4.2.2 Maine and the Aryan Village Brotherhood

Two sets of texts from the latter part of the nineteenth century (both of which relied on the earlier accounts, among which are those of Metcalfe, Wilks,

---

[4] Engels, letter to Marx, 6 June 1853 (Marx, 1968: 451–2); incorporated in Marx's *New York Daily Tribune* article of 25 June 1853 (Marx, 1968: 88–95).

[5] Karl Wittfogel and others have used such statements, made, I suspect, more to counter Hegel's spiritualism than to reduce the Asiatic mode to a single, environmental 'cause', as warrants for the functionalist thesis that the totalitarian states of the East have arisen as a result of the 'need' for the centralized control of water supplies. I will say nothing more here about the idea, easy to discredit but ever popular, of Asia as a 'hydraulic' society. See Hindess and Hirst, 1975: 207–20).

[6] A perennial 'theory', see 2.2.3, 4.2.2, and Senart (1930: 188–206), Lévi-Strauss (1966: 109–35), and Klass (1980: 135–60).

Elphinstone, and Campbell) can be said to constitute together the 'hegemonic' text on Indian villages. The earlier of these were the books of that comparative historian of jurisprudence, Sir Henry Sumner Maine (1822–88) (1888; 1907). The later were the works of B. H. Baden-Powell (1841–1901) (1892; 1896; 1899). His text stands in somewhat the same relation to that of Henry Maine as H. H. Wilson's text does to that of James Mill.[7] I begin with the legal scholar. Although Maine focuses not so much on property and production as on the question of authority and legality and community solidarity, it is striking how close some of his major presuppositions are to those of Marx and Hegel, not to mention Mill (whom Maine read).

Maine, trained as a classical scholar, took up the study of Indian law (but without learning Sanskrit) around the time of the Mutiny – he wrote in defence of the East India Company – thinking, like the philologists, that it would provide the missing link between the Roman and Anglo-Saxon legal traditions.[8] Politically, Maine was a conservative, but one who also supported *laissez-faire* as right for modern Britain.

Maine saw the Aryans as establishing full Aryan villages in north India consisting of the territories of their clans or septs. Their lands were originally held in common – here he agrees with Marx – and they were governed by councils or panchayats. Maine repeatedly referred to these villages as 'brother-hoods', even though he was well aware of the diversity to be found in many or even most Indian villages. Maine believed that this Indian village antedated the feudal manor, remaining as an institution where the Germanic village community, the mark, was in the early Middle Ages (Dewey, 1972: 300–7).[9]

India was, thus, in Maine's eyes, a living museum not just of the ancient, but of those ancients destined to rule the world, the Aryans (1907: 210–11). The villages held jointly by Rajputs, Jats, and Gujars in the nineteenth century were, he therefore assumed, direct continuations down into the present of those earlier Aryan communal or clan villages.

Although Maine agreed with Marx that ownership of the land in India was communal, belonging to the village brotherhood, he rejected the view that the land there, as in other Asiatic despotisms, belonged to the despot or to the state.

---

[7] For a critical analysis of British classifications of land tenures and a preliminary attempt to reconstruct these by relating them to caste and kinship, see Galey (1973).

[8] He served as Law Member of the Governor-General's Council in India from 1862 until 1869 (including four years as Vice-Chancellor of Calcutta University), when he became the first Professor of Comparative Jurisprudence at Oxford, a year after Max Müller had been made Professor of Comparative Philology. As J. D. M. Derrett, leading scholar of Anglo-Indian law in Britain, says in his intellectual assessment (1977): 'Maine owed *Ancient Law*, his subsequent (and resultant) career in India, his chairs at Oxford and Cambridge, and his immense celebrity, in a very significant, if not preponderant degree, to his "discovering" Indian legal material, and to the timely chance of the Indian Mutiny which put that material in his way.'

[9] What he says of the relationship of English to German medieval historical scholarship could be repeated, without much change, as a description of the relationship of the two nations' Indologists: 'Every phase of the subsequent German idealization of the Teutonic village community was duly echoed in the English literature: English historians, aware of their own technical inferiority, accepted German findings in toto, and preserved them in a patriotic jelly of their own' (1972: 305).

That, he argues, was a mistaken view which the English, confusing the 'Mahometan' practice with the older Hindu, had unwisely adopted. The correct view, which he only alludes to, is that the ancient Indian ruler had a right only to a 'share' of the produce, albeit 'a far larger share of the produce of the land than any western ruler has ever claimed' (1907: 104). Maine, an Aryanist who believed that a 'natural aristocracy' was the agent of human history (Dewey, 1972: 310–11), seems to imply here that full-fledged oriental despotism, in which the sovereign is owner of the soil, was an Islamic invention. The earlier or Hindu ruler was not the sole proprietor of the land. Those kingdoms were, in other words, closer to the primitive stage than Marx and Engels argued. In them, the Aryan community or tribe, that is, the confederation of Aryan warrior clans (ancestors of the English aristocrats distributed round Victoria's empire?), was the collective owner of the soil. The eldest male of the senior-most branch was the rightful king and it was in his capacity as king, by virtue of his genealogical position, that he received his share of the village produce.[10]

Maine made a sharp distinction between two types of society, the 'ancient' and 'modern', each of which is constructed of opposed features generated by manipulating two entities – the Communal, which has kinship (status) as its essence, and the Individual, which has contract (association) as its. Within the ancient the Communal encompasses the Individual while within the modern world the reverse is true; the Individual encompasses the Communal. Concurring with Marx and Hegel, Maine assumed that the members of communities in an ancient society thought metaleptically. Because the Individual is the truer of the two principles, the ancient villager mistakes the true agent, the individual, for the community in which he is submerged. Second, his community is really based on local contiguity but he has to think of it as based on blood or descent, even when it is not. In language reminiscent of Hegel, Maine says there is:

one peculiarity invariably distinguishing the infancy of society. Men are regarded and treated, not as individuals, but always as members of a particular group. Everybody is first a citizen, and then, as a citizen, he is a member of his order – of an aristocracy or a democracy, of an order of patricians or plebeians.

What Maine said so far could easily have applied to Rome or Greece. When he refers to India, it is with the disdain he has for a society that has not developed 'naturally' in the way the West has. Note how citizenship and caste are mutually exclusive: 'Or, in those societies which an unhappy fate has afflicted with a special perversion in their course of development, [he is the member of] a caste.' Finally, all of these ancient communities consisted of smaller descent units nested, as in a taxonomy, within the larger ones, the family within the 'gens, house, or clan' and the latter within the order (1888: 177–8).

Authority in this hierarchically ordered society was, predictably, patriarchal: 'The eldest male parent – the eldest ascendant – is absolutely supreme in his household' (1888: 119). All ties of legality, authority, and solidarity were, in his

[10] Maine does not spell this out, but this is what A. C. Lyall (1899: 227–8), writing on the Rajput states before 1882, inferred, with considerable justification, as the Mainean position.

construal of early society, turned inward and focused on the patriarch, the nucleus of Maine's atomic household: 'Men are first seen distributed in perfectly insulated groups, held together by obedience to the parent' (1888: 121). The converse of this inward focusing was also operative. Relations outside the group were invariably ones of hostility. The Indian village itself, like the Teutonic mark, was accordingly seen by Maine to be organized into 'separate households, each despotically governed by its family chief, and never trespassed upon by the footstep of any person of different blood' (1907: 113). Thus, for Maine as for Marx and Hegel, the clan-based village was the basic community in earlier societies and the basic unit of that, its bedrock, was the patriarchal household. A principle of patrilineal descent (and of seniority) was for him the principle according to which those who had not yet 'discovered' the true principles of social order distributed authority and property and symbolized their solidarity or unity.

Along with Marx, Maine saw caste as the diacritic that distinguished the Aryans in India from those elsewhere, and like him, he also believed that caste was a transmutation of clan that had, because of its exclusiveness, prevented change in India (1907: 219–20). Maine was, however, not so subtle as Marx in explaining the changeless nature of the Indian village. The explanation which Maine invokes is a 'historical' one: 'The chief secret, a very simple one, lies in the extreme isolation of the country until it was opened by maritime adventure' (1907: 211–12). The inwardness of caste, he seems to be saying, was a feature of the entire civilization, the Mainean equivalent of Hegel's World Spirit or Engels's canals and waterwheels.

4.2.3 Baden-Powell and the Dravidian Severalty Village

Henry Baden-Powell was a civil servant in the Panjab from 1861 until 1889. While his younger brother was mobilizing the Boy Scouts and Girl Guides he had founded for the Empire, Henry took charge of immobilizing India's villages for the same cause. Baden-Powell reworked the Indian village at a point when the mass of evidence collected about both medieval European and contemporary Indian villages had begun to undermine the simple, unilinear evolutionary scheme of Maine and others. The centralization of European states was also occurring at this time, and the trend was toward the production of studies focused on the metropolitan and administrative. There was, as Dewey points out, another political angle here as well. This was the Irish Question, in the form of the Irish Land Act of 1881. English landowners perceived this as a direct threat to their interests. The analogy of the Irish with the ancient Aryans and their institutions was one that they and many of their compatriots found, to put it mildly, distasteful. The answer to this question was to pull apart the neat scheme which Maine had put together, and the result of this, at least in part, was to 'neutralize' the village community of both East and West in current political debate (Dewey, 1972: 316–28).

Baden-Powell was generally sceptical about the extent to which one can speak of Aryan villages at all. Citing the orientalist-administrator, W. W.

Hunter, he argued that the proportion of conquering and settling Aryans to the aboriginal population would have been small and that, as a result, the former would have been forced to come to terms with the latter (Baden-Powell, 1896: 84–5). He also criticized Maine's postulation of that type of village in which lands were held in common as necessarily the original and universal type. Villages of this type were, in the first place, more heterogeneous than Maine let on. 'The brotherhood', argues Baden-Powell, includes 'inferiors and dependants (tenants)' and 'in fact, forms a kind of "hierarchy," the degrees of which are determined by the order in which the various sets of cultivating families have been amalgamated with the community' (1896: 6–7). They were also not the most widely distributed 'type' of village, being confined mostly to north India (1896: 7–8).

Baden-Powell, like many of his contemporaries, saw India as a fundamentally Dravidian rather than Aryan culture. He made two connected arguments. One is clear. It is that there are two types of village in India. The other, less clear, is that the type of village thought by Maine and others to be the universally and essentially Indian type, the jointly held village of the Aryans, is not, in effect really a type of *village* holding. It is a form of *aristocratic* landholding superimposed on another type. The jointly held villages which Marx and Maine had mistaken as typical were, in fact, the holdings of the very landholding class that was not supposed to exist in an oriental despotism where, it will be recalled, state and ruling class are supposed to be isomorphic!

This other type of village, the more widely distributed one, was that which had come to be called 'raiyatwari'. It is one in which separate households have each their distinct lands, and no lands, cultivated *or* waste, are held in common by the village as a whole. Ownership in those households is vested in the patriarch or head; they are not joint families, in which male offspring automatically become coparceners. 'The raiyatwari village', Baden-Powell concludes, 'seems to depend originally on the idea that the house-father is the separate and sole owner, whilst the *joint-village* represents the more developed idea of the joint-family and the limitation (not to say extinction) of the *patria potestas*' (1896: 418).

Baden-Powell agrees that the raiyatwari village had originated in a 'tribal stage of society' (1896: 9), but he holds to the view that it had come into existence *before* the settlement of Aryans in north as well as south India. If the jointly held village was the result of a *continuation* into the present of an essentially Aryan clan system, the raiyatwari village was the result of the *decay* or *dissolution* of a pre-Aryan or Dravidian clan system. He speculates that before central governments had formed, 'there were clan-divisions of territory, containing a number of villages, each under its own headman or chief, who was a natural and essential [*sic!*] part of the institution' (1896: 9–10).

The matrix of the typical Indian village community was, thus, the Dravidian (or some other aboriginal) race. The Aryan race (together with other 'latecomer' races) was the matrix of the jointly held village, a form of landholding imposed on the earlier severalty form. Neither of these races, however, inscribed Village India on a *tabula rasa*. They developed it, during India's formative centuries, in interaction with one another and in response to 'needs' arising in the distinctive natural, social, and political environment of India. The essence he manufactured was, thus, not to be found so much in any one race as it was in the interactions of races with each other and their environments. If Baden-Powell's theory of determinate evolution is to be believed, then there was very little scope in the Indian village for human action that was not simply a natural adaptation either to hostile neighbours, Aryan conquerors, or a tropical environment. The village, whatever the race of its inhabitants, was compelled by 'necessity' – here it is the agent – to become the reality of the Indologist's representation. Since those simple needs had not changed after the moment of caste and state formation in ancient India, her village institutions therefore remained static (1899: 14–15).

Baden-Powell thus broke with the idea that the village was inherently democratic or republican in its constitution because it was a unit of communal landholding, all of whose members were, at least in origin, members of a single clan or brotherhood. For him, the village was, in its essence, a community of separate cultivating holders and other village functionaries organized as a small monarchy or oligarchy. He furthermore believed that the typical Indian village was not an Aryan institution. It was, more likely, a Dravidian (or aboriginal) one that existed, in a tribal form, before the arrival of the Aryans. These, 'our' ancestors, had, of course, gained ascendancy over the non-Aryan and even retained their own Western institutions as their landlords, but they can only be said to have modified the institutions of the latter and certainly not to have constituted them out of their own. They, like their British descendants at District Headquarters, were the managers, the 'jungle officers' of the Other, and no longer its progenitor. The main point, though, is that Indian villages were from now on to be seen as Indian problems. The Dravidian village, we are supposed to believe, had no analogue in Europe. It did not evolve from the same origin. Nothing, therefore, was to be learned from it that had application to any situation in Europe or Britain, especially Ireland. No Dravidians need apply.

The desire to quarantine Ireland was, however, only one reason for this changed vision of the Indian village that Baden-Powell and other officers of the jungle had conjured. That itself was part of the emergence of a con-sciously imperial framework for the overseas patchwork of possessions that the British had stitched together. Within that frame, ideas of racial conflict and conquest were decisive. The essences of nations were races and relations of political and economic domination were to be explained and justified as the triumph of one essence over the other in a natural evolutionary process. Europeans could not help it if nature had made them superior and named them rulers of the earth. One result of the rise to prominence of this imperial image was that the older, liberal notion of a unity of mankind as a family of sovereign nations would have to be postponed, perhaps indefinitely. The communities wanted for this empire were those of an inherently different and lower kind, belonging to an inferior race and not those of the superior race that had gone missing in the jungle but could be set right now they had been found by their distant cousins.

4.3 CASTE'S POLITICAL ECONOMY

4.3.1 Fixed Share Payments (*Jajmānī*)

The kind of economy that one would expect the caste village to have would meet the following theoretical requirements. It would not be socially undifferentiated as in 'tribal' society, yet neither would it have class divisions and class 'exploitation'. The surplus labour value, whether in the form of products (agricultural or manufactured), of cash, or of labour itself, would be appropriated, therefore, not by any exploiting class *within* the village, but by the state *outside* the village. The relations of the castes in the village would be characterized by ties of group cooperation and solidarity rather than of competition between individuals. The payments made for goods and services would be determined not by a market but by considerations internal to the village community. Scholarship has obligingly produced just such a village economy. It has been referred to as the '*jajmānī* system', after the relationship the village priest was supposed to have with his patrons or sacrificers (*yajamāna*, *jajmān*). The classic account of this economy is Wiser's (1958), but it is pioneering mostly in its empirical detail, not in its conception.

The Indian village is invariably described in discourses on it as containing, in principle if not in practice, a full complement of those occupations, hereditary and belonging to different castes, that were required for the meeting of its own 'needs'. According to Colonel Mark Wilks (upon whose work Marx and Engels drew), the full complement supposedly consisted, in the Deccan (upland area of peninsular India), of people engaged in twelve different occupations. Because they were due 'shares' (*baluta* or *ayam*) of the village's produce, they were known as the 'twelve balutedars' or 'ayagars'. After the requisite declaration that 'every Indian village' is a 'republic', he enumerates these 'officers', beginning with the headman (*gauḍa* or *paṭel*), whom he calls the 'judge and magistrate' and the accountant (*karnam* or *shānbhog*) whom he calls the 'registrar'.[11] Each of these 'village servants', whose 'offices were hereditary, going from father to son' (Rice, 1897: I, 581), received for the services he performed a fixed annual payment, calculated as a share of the crops harvested by his patron (also received in 'allotments of land from the corporate stock'). The patrons of these village servants were, typically, the heads of the cultivating households resident there.

Maine, like Marx and the earlier commentators, also held that Indian villages were economically 'organised and self-acting' (Maine, 1907: 125–6). Baden-Powell may have disagreed with Maine over the issue of forms of property and their origin, but he appears to have shared his assumption that the economy of the village was self-sufficient and that payments in fixed shares of grain or the equivalent were integral to it (Baden-Powell, 1896: 16). Maine considered

---

[11] Reproduced in a gazetteer (Rice, 1897: I, 574–5). The others were the village watchmen (*talāri* or *sthaliwar*, and *toṭi*); the water-distributor (*nīrganṭi*); the astrologer (*jotishya*, *joisa*); smith, carpenter, potter, washerman, barber, and goldsmith (who, Rice adds, is often replaced by the poet, who is also often the schoolmaster).

competition, 'that prodigious social force of which the action is measured by political economy', an inherent feature of modern societies, one that was closely linked with the individual and private property in land which, he said, 'is most unreservedly accepted in the United States, with little less reserve in England and France, but, as we proceed through eastern Europe, it fades gradually away, until in Asia it is wholly lost' (Maine, 1907: 227–8).

If Indian villages were ancient communities, then they could not possess any of these features, for they came together as a package. Thus, the absence of a free market, of individuals, of private property, and of a competitive spirit said to characterize the Indian village were not simply empirical findings for the nineteenth-century theorists; their absence was essential to the type of society itself. Those missing elements were tied to each other and constituted the essence of modern society. They were opposed to the features that formed the essence of ancient societies – reciprocal exchange of goods and services within a specialized but closed economy, collective actors, communal property, and total unity within the kin group and enmity between groups not so related.

The issue here is not whether such payments were made. There is little question that the British investigators did nearly everywhere in India confront village practices in which ideas of shares played an important part. Notions of shares were also important in Indian discourses at an early time. The question is, hence, not empirical. It is whether an economy of shares is to be seen as a determinate, unchanged essence of the village as an early ancient community.[12]

Lurking in the background of these accounts of the village economy and, indeed, motivating many of them, was also the vexed question of the revenue collected from the village by the state. This, as Maine and Baden-Powell both explicitly recognized, was also conceptualized as a 'share' of the produce of the village. They drew two inferences from this. One was that the 'authentic' Hindu state was itself a clan monarchy, the legitimate ruler of which was the genealogically senior-most Rajput or Kshatriya (see 5.3). He did not own the land; the clan to which he belonged did. The royal share of the produce, like that set aside for the headman of the village, was the payment for the services he rendered to the kingdom. The second inference was that many, if not most, of the imperial Hindu rulers, had in fact, where they were not usurpers, been badly motivated and collected too much revenue. Either way, it was considered an element of the village's economy that paradoxically operated to maintain its isolation.

The double idea of the revenue as an immutable share and as a violently extracted surplus had other uses. The first enabled the British government to 'depoliticize' the revenue-collecting relationship, to make it a purely administrative one by arguing that the payment of shares was customary, a social and not a political fact. The legitimate job of the British administrator was to determine what that immemorial custom was and to preserve it. The second idea, not inconsistent with the first, enabled the government of India to claim

---

[12] Neale (1957) extends Maine's concept and brings it to bear on the debate (still continuing) on the 'embeddedness' of economies in 'traditional' societies, on the question of whether economics can be a naturalist, universal, and formal science or has to be concerned with the historical, particular, and substantive.

that certain previous rulers, those who had engaged in conquests and in building centralized states, had necessarily been exploitative. The British, with their modern ways, would be able to establish a centralized state that was not oppressive in its revenue collections. With Political Economy at their side, they would determine scientifically (and not politically) what the land revenue should be.

4.3.2 Councils and Headmen

Closely connected with the issue of whether land was collective or individual property was the question of whether the essential political institution of the ancient and authentic Indian village was a council or a headman. Maine held that the brotherhood or jointly owned village was the true Indian village and argued that the council, an instrument of joint rule and hence isomorphic with that village type, was the essential institution of rulership in it, even though it might not seem so at first sight:

India has nothing answering to the assembly of adult males which is so remarkable a feature of the ancient Teutonic groups.... I have good authority for saying that, in those parts of India in which the village-community is most perfect and in which there are the clearest signs of an original proprietary equality between all the families composing the group, the authority exercised elsewhere by the Headman is lodged with the Village Council. It is always viewed as a representative body, and not as a body possessing inherent authority, and, whatever be its real number, it always bears a name which recalls its ancient constitution of five persons. (1907: 122–3)

Maine's successor and critic did not, however, agree.

For Baden-Powell, the 'typical' village of India was the severalty village rather than the jointly held village. Consistent with its form of property and division of labour, the essential political institution of that type of village was not the 'council of five' (*panchayat*), but the headman. Just as that type of village developed, according to Baden-Powell, out of a tribal ancestor, so too, his headman was the continuation of the earlier tribal headman and not an intrusion from a developing or conquering central government. There was, however, one village functionary who was just such an intruder, the village accountant, whose rise 'was inevitable when the plan of taking revenue by means of a share of the produce was introduced, and some kind of public administration was organised ...' (1896: 13–14). Thus did Need introduce a 'modern' administrative principle into the village alongside the 'ancient' principle of kin-relatedness. One might think that this village bureaucrat would have eventually replaced the older headman, but this was not so. He remained the nominally 'superior' head of the raiyatwari village, retaining 'small ... powers' and 'much-cherished privileges and precedence rights' (1896: 14–15). Beyond this early insertion of the administrative principle, the ruling institution of the Indian village apparently underwent little or no change. The persistence of the older office of hereditary headman was a symptom of the post-tribal nature of the Indian village community and its caste society.

The displacement of the little republic by the little monarchy as the 'atom' of

India's political economy has had important consequences. To some extent it can be seen as clearing away an egalitarian inconsistency in Marx and Maine of the primitive, stateless society. The idea that the Indian village was by nature a small monarchy seems much more congruent with the idea of an India divided into ranked or hierarchically related castes and patriarchal households. But Baden-Powell was not prepared in making this shift even to suggest that the headman and the other villagers were not related to each other by the 'natural' ties of descent, although it seems clear to me that this question did worry him.

He speculated that even after the intrusion of an outside state, the headman's office, as the focus of unity, was still ringed with the aura of tribal and natural wholeness (*Gemeinschaft*):

Probably at their first foundation the village families were more closely connected by clan ties than they are now; and there may have been some further feeling of 'community' on this ground. The nature of the revenue-system which early Governments adopted in dealing with these villages must have greatly influenced their solidarity. When the old custom of the State grain-share was quietly followed out, the headman managed the whole, and every holder in the village knew that he had to contribute. (1896: 18)

More important than this difference over the form of political office in the village was the answer these imperial scholars gave to the question of whether Indian villagers had the capacity to combine in associations for differing purposes. Both Maine and Baden-Powell, like Marx, were at pains to point out that the headman and the village officers and elders did not constitute an association. They were constituted by their 'natural' places in the community, by their descent, by their age and sex, and by their clan and caste. They did not in themselves have the power to constitute themselves as a complex agent. That power was, as Marx and others, including Durkheim, would have it, displaced in the minds of the villagers on to the village or clan deity, its ancestral founder. Baden-Powell has, thus, managed to replace the council with the headman without giving up the idea that the village was an apolitical, natural community. They were constituted merely as patients, as a non-social community, by some agent outside themselves.

But there is one more twist to this story of the Indian village's Indological degradation. Caste has been a jealous mistress and was not content to allow even the possibility that the petty realm of the village might be a political society and its headman an autonomous political authority. The officers of the 1911 *Census of India* undertook a survey to determine the distribution and strength of the village *panchayat*. The overall conclusion that the Census officers reached differed from the positions taken by both Maine and Baden-Powell. They argued that on the whole the village *panchayat* was, where it existed, not a village council. It was actually a *caste* council. By implication, the headman would also have to be counted as a *caste* rather than a *village* chief. The Bombay Census officer took the most extreme stance, concluding that 'There is *no* evidence that such organization as a village panchayat ever existed. All permanent panchayats, except the big trading guilds ... have been *caste* panchayats, and the myth of the village panchayat has probably arisen from the fact that a village is generally, if

Village India 147

not invariably, formed by several families of some one caste settling in one spot ...' (*Census of India, 1911, 1913*: VII, 200). What is more, some of the higher castes have no regular caste *panchayats*. The Marathas, for example, settled caste questions at meetings presided over by a *deshmukh* or *patil* (territorial headmen) or by a leading man of the locality appointed by the Sankaracharya of Śringeri (*Census of India, 1911, 1913*: VII, 289–90).

Maine's and Baden-Powell's representations of the Indian village, however constraining from the standpoint of human agency, still left it as something of a political unity. The Bombay Census would remove even this limited degree of the political from the village by reducing the *panchayat* to a caste *panchayat* whose jurisdiction was strictly confined to its own caste and in which the authority ultimately resides not with its own members, but with the highest caste, the Brahman. Caste had, thus, reduced the village to a mere residential and economic space.

The picture was, however, not quite so neat. Some *panchayats* (in the Punjab) were not confined to affairs of their own castes: 'in matters affecting the whole village the panchayats of the smaller groups merge into that representing the predominant caste of the village to form a tribunal whose decision is binding on the whole community' (*Census of India, 1911*, 1913: I (Report), 395). In certain hilly areas, on the other hand, 'the only panchayats are village panchayats, who exercise the functions which elsewhere are assigned to caste panchayats', just the opposite of what Bombay had reported.

The spokesman for the *Census of India* in all its glory, L. S. S. O'Malley, tried to harmonize these conflicting 'findings', but ended up undermining them instead. By referring to Maine's brotherhood as an 'oligarchy' he qualified its nature as the essence of a post-tribal community. By agreeing that joint villages must have existed as the rule, but had been destroyed by oppressive government (the implication of which was that under British rule *panchayats* or their local equivalent could again flourish), he snipped the major thread of Baden-Powell's argument about the headman as the essence of village rulership (O'Malley, 1934: 106, 108–9).

O'Malley confused matters still further when he argued elsewhere that the king in ancient India 'issued marriage regulations for castes, he fixed the social rank of different sub-castes, he promoted members of one caste to another, and he degraded them to a lower' (O'Malley, 1932: 56). What is more, 'Till lately the limits of caste do not seem to have been so immutably fixed in the hills as in the plains. The Raja was the fountain of honour and could do much as he liked' (O'Malley, 1932: 58). He concludes that whether Hindus were organized into village or caste councils was a function of whether they were under Hindu or Muslim rule. Since the larger part of the subcontinent had been under Muslim rule when the British acquired it, it is no wonder that the caste council and village headman predominate over the village *panchayat* (O'Malley, 1932: 59).[13] We have slowly drifted from the naturalist assumptions that pervade the work of the Census and scholarship on village and caste in general. We could take this

---

[13] Here he summarizes the work of Sir Denzil Ibbetson (1847–1908), Superintendent of the Punjab Census for 1881.

summary as arguing that the organization of people in the countryside was historically contingent and not inherent in caste itself as a peculiar form of society. Even further, it hints that there may have been a conscious political and religious dimension to the shifts in organization that took place. The rise of 'caste' assemblies and the increase in the importance of the Brahmans as arbiters of caste conduct in the regions where the larger polity was committed to Islam might even be construed as a form of resistance.

The knowing subjects of British imperial discourse did not, however, permit these growing inconsistencies to disturb the overall construct that they wished to impose on rural India. That construct, especially in its recently Dravidianized version, fit far too well the image of the Indian Empire that they had built. By the time the British had installed themselves in their imperial capital at New Delhi in 1912, they had come to imagine that the villages of India no longer mirrored their own origins back to them. Those villages (and perhaps even their traditional rulers, too: see 5.3.2), were truly the powerless opposites of themselves, abiding in natural communities that had only a natural history. The British themselves, however, were inhabitants of the national state that was (in the eyes of the discourse it spun) making not only its own history but that of the world. Indian villagers were the very essence of an older type of society, the early ancient, their rulers the quintessence of its opposite, the fully modern. The villages were confined to themselves. They did not have any political aims or ambitions (other than to be left alone). Their leaders did not formulate strategies for becoming towns or even district or principality centres. They grew naturally and not politically, each 'cell' expanding in size to fill up its own surrounding waste area and the whole cellular mass multiplying in number to make productive the unoccupied waste spaces of Indian subcontinent. The British nation was, by contrast, rapidly expanding, establishing the commercial and political empire with which a Utilitarian providence had blessed it. Finally, the villages had as their natural terrain the rural areas where they constitute the lowest 'level' of the Indian polity. The British, on the other hand, had as their points of purchase on the subcontinent the presidency towns, Calcutta, Bombay, and Madras, which they themselves had made into the commercial and administrative centres of their India.

This village India was not an Other that in any way threatened the European Self. It did not exist in the same time as the Self, nor did it occupy the same political and economic space. On the contrary, the two occupied complementary, hierarchically related 'spaces'. The modern in the form of the British Indian state had the power to know and to govern not only itself but also the Indian villagers, embodiments of the ancient incapable of any action on their own even in their own time, never mind in the 'present' where they now found themselves. The subject of the discourse had thus constituted for itself a patient, a non-social community that was both radically different from itself and easy to dominate. That subject alone, the essence of political society, the embodiment of the West's world-ordering rationality, could, if it wished, preserve these ancient communities; or, it could, alternatively, improve and reform them.

4.4   NATIONALIST AND POST-INDEPENDENCE DEPICTIONS

4.4.1   From Early Ancient Tribal to Late Ancient Socialist

The depiction of the traditional village in the Anglo-French imperial formation that had emerged by the end of the nineteenth century had changed not for the better but for the worse. As the embodiment of early Aryan institutions it had at least been a museum in which the European could gaze on his own origins. The reformation of the village as a Dravidian one modified by interaction with a conquering Aryan and a tropical environment left it as a jungle terrarium for Risley and other social biologists. Indian nationalists responded to this latter-day image primarily in the production of historical accounts. Written by Indians trained in a formal, political historiography, capable of sophistication in unravelling problems considered fundamental to dynastic history, they are often naïve or simplistic in their approach to 'economic' or 'social' history.

Of the earlier historical works that focus on the village in ancient India, the most important were probably those by certain young nationalists. That of R. C. Majumdar (1888–1980) (1918),[14] made a factually impressive, but theoretically flaccid attempt to correct the false impression that ancient India was bereft of associational forms. He claimed that he was the first to discuss the organization of the Brahman estate, Uttarameru, which example has been reproduced in almost every discussion of village government since.[15] The book of Radha Kumud Mookerji (1880–1963) (1919)[16] is more theoretically informed. Refer-ring to a dispute then current between political 'monists' and 'pluralists', he argued that the Indian polity was:

a balanced synthesis of three distinct and co-existing elements, the State with its jurisdiction as represented by the Danda, the individual on the Road to Freedom (*Mukti*), and the various intermediary groups, functional, local, or voluntary (e.g., in various types of Eastern monarchism), connecting these two poles by means of their own Dharma, their Special Codes, and Customaries. (1919: xxiv)

The great merit of his work, apart from his treatment of Indian texts as discursive, as constituting serious propositions about the world (rather than simply as dead bits of evidence), is its insistence on the existence of associational political forms that bridged the gap alleged to exist between the village and the imperial state. Probably inspired by his reading of syndicalist and pluralist political theory, which itself challenged both the atomist and absolutist theories of the state, it flies in the face of British assertions about India that such institutions were essentially absent. He criticizes the position taken by Baden-

[14] He was educated at Presidency College and the University of Calcutta.
[15] See the later, more detailed work of the pioneer of South Indian history, S. Krishnaswami Aiyangar (1931: 130–245).
[16] Professor of History at Banaras Hindu University, the University of Mysore, and Lucknow University, he had the same educational credentials as Majumdar.

Powell that Indian society was post-tribal: 'the Indian development of the local bodies really and fundamentally represents a distinctive type which must not be confounded with the rudiments of tribal self-government, invariably characteristic of primitive societies' (1919: 24). Turning the Aryan community of Maine back on its conservative owner, he argues that the Indian type was socialist in a positive sense, over and against the elitist and excessively individualist institutions of Rome (1919: 22–3). He even goes so far as to say in his conclusion that 'this pluralism of the group, as an intermediate body between the state and the individual units, has been the most characteristic feature of Indian polity through the ages, and indicates the lines on which Indian political development should proceed' (1919: 317). Mookerji thus rejected the image of India as a land of villages stalled at an 'early ancient' stage; for him, it was a 'late ancient' society of differing associational forms that were every bit as advanced as any in Rome, only they were socialist rather than individualist in their trajectory. Unfortunately, neither he nor anyone else of note elaborated on this perspective.[17] Indeed, Mookerji himself backs away from the implications of his pluralist position in later work (5.5.2).

Because they have had so little to say that is not simply reiterative of the image constructed by Maine and modified by the early nationalist historians, I shall say no more here about the work of the later formalist historians and philologists, into which category Basham, bridging the transition to a post-Independence period, falls (1954: 189–93). Nor, for the same reason, will I say anything about the views of the nationalist political leaders, who saw the cooperative spirit of the village as prefiguring a 'socialist' Inida.[18] The most important result of the work done by the national historians was not theoretical but empirical. Their researches on the large numbers of epigraphs that were coming to light led to the embarrassing conclusion that associational forms of governance had been most in evidence in South India and the Deccan in the 'early medieval' period. These 'findings', taken seriously, completely undermine the theories of Marx and of Maine and Baden-Powell. According to these, associational forms were supposed to be the property of the Aryans, presumed to have made their strongest impress in north India, and in ancient rather than medieval times.[19] The appearance of records showing that they were most elaborate in the medieval Dravidian south seems almost a wilful defiance on the part of the Other.[20]

We will look at the implications of the disturbing evidence from south of the

---

[17] A. S. Altekar (1898–1960), Manindra Chandra Nandi Professor of Ancient History and Culture, Banaras Hindu University and director of the K. P. Jayaswal Institute at Patna, argued against Mookerji (1927) that the village was not uniformly the same everywhere in India and that it was not unchanging, but ignored his major argument.

[18] On Gandhi, see Bose (1947: 57–9), and a collection of Gandhi's writings (1957), and on Nehru, Nehru (1951: 243–6).

[19] Altekar notes this (1927: 26–7, 28–9), but does not draw out the significance.

[20] The reader curious to see the contortions through which some of these discourses have gone in order to save their objects, in this case the idea of an Aryan polity in India, might wish to explore the theory of E. B. Havell, idealist critic of British views of India (1918: 10–28, 227–34).

Vindhyas at the end of this chapter. But it is not necessary to decipher these ancient documents. Not all discourse on Indian villages in the British Empire was fashioned in the form of revenue and settlement reports. One need only glance through the pages of the book first published under the name of its hero, Govinda Samanta, to discover just how different an account of a village could be. Written as a 'history' by the Rev. Lal Behari Day (to win a prize for a novel on the 'social and domestic life of the rural population and working classes of Bengal', by one of her 'enlightened' landowners, it claims to be a realistic depiction (1906: 1–4). In it, the commonsense discourse of villagers, by and large dismissed in more 'scientific' accounts as a distorted medium through which facts may pass, appears by the pageful. An analysis of it would raise serious questions about the treatment of villagers as the mere accidents of an ancient caste society.

4.4.2 Neo-Hegelian Anthropology

As Basham was writing about the village in his post-imperial summary of British Indology, a new spate of village studies conducted by American and British anthropologists began to appear. The British and Indian work, of which the monographs of Mayer (1960) and Srinivas (1952), are perhaps totemic, involved the intensive field study of particular villages rather than the massive surveys of the past. They were also 'structural-functionalist' in approach, attempting to bracket out the evolutionary aspect of the naturalism adhered to by Baden-Powell and the earlier Census anthropologists. US cultural anthropologists, concerned in a post-colonial world more with cultural than administrative unity (see 5.6.2), placed more emphasis on 'socialization' and 'personality formation', and, following Kroeber and Redfield, concerned themselves with tracing the links of 'little communities' to the other units of 'complex societies' or 'civilizations' (Redfield, 1955). The collection of essays, entitled, aptly enough, *Village India*, may be taken as inaugural here (Marriott, 1955). These and later studies have emphasized the connections of the village with the surrounding region, the 'little kingdom', the ethnically defined micro-region or (in caste terms) the marriage circle (what I refer to as a union of villages), discussing the relationships of villagers with the world outside largely in terms of the metaphors of 'exchange', 'transaction', 'network', or 'linkage'. We have also inserted villages into an Indian 'cultural system' that would somehow underlie their practices in both a 'little tradition' and the ideas of the texts in a 'great tradition'.

There has, thus, been a shift in Indological discourse with respect to villages since the dissolution of the Anglo-French imperial formation and the rise, after the Second World War, of the US (and USSR) to the position of world dominance. The village community as a distinct object in these discourses has gradually eroded at the same time that certain advocates, both in and outside the Indian government, have attempted to bring into existence the idealized villages of the nationalist movement. On the other hand, the picture of the Indian village as an idyllic but static rural community has also given way to one of that same village as the very epitome of the 'grinding' poverty and despair of the 'third world'. It is either ripe for 'community development' or a 'green revolution' or a hopeless victim of its own past and a relentless world system that has forever shattered its former self-sufficiency.[21]

The concern to look at villages in their wider settings is certainly to be welcomed, but it does not mean that we have totally transformed the predominant episteme for viewing the village. Old habits die hard among us moderns. The idea that there is a village community, transmuted into 'peasant society', still persists.[22] I would also argue that in its concern with the maintenance of order, its connections with functionalism, and its (mostly) Durkheimian view of religion, much of this work can be seen as *de facto* heir to the image of the Hindu village as natural and post-tribal. Dumont's *Homo Hierarchicus*, the currently hegemonic work on caste, partly reiterates that position, but it also goes back to Hegel (whence his similarity to structuralists). For the very reason that they have been seen as so completely intertwined, Dumont's treatment of the village is to be taken as seriously as his treatment of caste.

Dumont's discussion of villages takes place within a context where 'power' is already subordinated, in the 'structure' that comprises caste, to status or hierarchy. Dumont attempts to rationalize the 'facts' about villages with respect to that structure. He clearly breaks with the atomism of his predecessors, saying that:

one must not picture to oneself the functioning of village administration, in particular the greater or lesser extent to which its functions are articulated and formalized, as independent of the royal or central power. Everything we know tends to show that on the contrary all this depended, and still depends today, on the establishment of a satisfactory relationship with the central power. (1980b: 171–2)

In this respect his work is to be praised (*contra* that of some neo-evolutionists, like Klass, who continues to see castes as temporally contiguous with old clan and tribal units that predated the state).

Dumont begins by noting the 'fact' that castes were divided into territorial sections and that these were roughly coterminous with the units of larger polities, which he, following Bernard Cohn, refers to as 'little kingdoms' (Cohn, 1960: 422–4). Now, it might seem here that this was the result of political acts that have constituted castes as parts of kingdoms, providing each kingdom with its own 'caste system'. But this would begin to suggest that perhaps 'power' was not subordinated to 'hierarchy'. So this apparent coincidence of territorial and political units with castes and even caste systems must be accounted for. Dumont accomplishes this by arguing that the political acts themselves are, in the end, the result of an ideology that devalues territory and permits the

[21] For one ethnologist's photographic 'reinvention' of the South Asian village and an attempt to counter the 'inaccurate' image of India as 'poverty- or disaster-stricken' and 'retrograde', see Huyler (1985).

[22] Shanin, introducing a collection of readings edited by himself (1971), is able to conclude, after dealing with criticisms, that 'nevertheless, the definition of peasantry which views it as representing an aspect of the past surviving in the contemporary world seems, on the whole, to be valid.' (1971: 17).

fragmentation of what might otherwise have been a political unity into endlessly multiplying segments. Kingship, the very agency that might have been responsible for the divisions, is itself, thus, morselized and encapsulated within local caste systems. Dumont allows that political events have affected this process and that there is much regional variation. None the less, he says, in concluding his discussion of the 'little kingdom', that there was 'a *tendency* for regions to close in on themselves' (1980b: 156).

The ideology of caste is also to be seen in Indian land tenure systems. Dumont asserts, in a passage that reveals his rationalism, that 'what takes place in this domain could almost have been deduced *a priori* from the general characteristics of the system' (1980b: 158). Because of the predominance of caste and caste values, rights to land are inevitably fragmentary and always mutually complementary. Kings and outsiders in general can use force to interfere with these rights because, being a caste system, it is defenceless. Such interferences cause particular people to lose their land without affecting the system, one he refers to as a 'subtle' form of 'collectivism' (1980b: 158).

Regarding the economy of the village, it is doubly disadvantaged in comparison with that of a modern Western society: 'One can say that just as religion in a way encompasses politics, so politics encompasses economics within itself. The difference is that the politico-economic domain is separated, named, in a subordinate position as against religion, while economics remains undifferentiated within politics' (1980b: 165). Here, as elsewhere in his argument, activities that are so hierarchized tend to be seen by Dumont as 'historical' and 'empirical' rather than 'structural' (that is, contingent rather than necessary in their occurrence). Since economic activity has no place in the ideology, 'we are reduced to putting a question of pure fact' and 'various periods in history must then be explored . . .' (1980b: 166). When some sort of autonomous economic activity is uncovered at the ideological 'level', it is offloaded, following Weber, on to the religions such as Jainism that are, in Dumont's consideration, not essentially Indian, that is, Hindu (1980b: 166).

The idea of a village having a 'dominant caste', first argued by Srinivas, is enthusiastically endorsed by Dumont because it puts caste back in the centre of the discussion. He argues that the dominant caste replicates at the village or local 'level' the royal function. This apparently makes it possible, at least in principle, to understand the kingdom by looking at the village. It is also important in another respect, for it means that if one demonstrates the subordination of power to hierarchy at one 'level' in this segmented, holographic system, one has also shown it at the other levels.

Dumont continues, in discussing the 'village community', to deride the notion that there ever was such a thing in the sense of a territorial and political or civic unity governed by a headman and/or a *panchayat* or council representative of the villagers as such. He holds, echoing one of the more extreme conclusions reached in the *Census of India*, that what most investigators thought was the 'village assembly' was a 'semi-mythical being' (1980b: 168). It was really the *panchayat* of the dominant caste which, because of its caste superiority, was able to exercise authority over not only its own members but also over the inferior client castes (1980b: 171). That form of governance was inherently plural not because of any positive notion of equality but because of the friability of political institutions characteristic of a caste regime. Unlike Baden-Powell, he does not, therefore, see the position of village headman (where such exists) as the true replica in the village of the king. His is a contingent office. It originates not internally as part of a tribal society, but with external, state power. This headman is 'real' only 'if he appears to the members of the dominant caste as the link between them and political power' (1980b: 183).

The factions that are found to exist within the dominant castes, another phenomenon studied intensively by anthropologists, have only an 'empirical' (contingent) existence (1980b: 164) in the Dumontian scheme. They are yet another symptom of the disintegrating effect of the ideology of caste on the political unity of the dominant caste and its assembly. The very institution, this assembly, which Maine and Baden-Powell both saw as one of clan and community *strength*, is construed by Dumont as the sign of the inherent political *weakness* of a society made by caste.

Dumont leaves behind the atomic village, and he consciously steps around the naturalism of the earlier evolutionists. However, in harking back to the grandfather of Indology, Hegel, he goes even further than them and their structural-functionalist successors in displacing agency from Indian villagers on to a caste ideology. Subjected to his rationalist gaze, the village itself has all but dissolved. Village headmanship ('singular authority') is, in essence, reducible to village *panchayat* ('plural authority') and that in turn is reducible to the authority of the dominant caste. This, in turn, replicates that of the king or chief of the 'little kingdom' which, in its turn, mirrors the royal function in Hindu ideology where (as we shall see in chapter 5), it is clearly subordinated to the principle of purity or hierarchy. Particular villages do not, thus, have truncated political and economic institutions as a result of their particular circumstances or of their encounters with other villages and the greater and lesser polities with which they have been involved. The village is itself – never mind its headmen or assemblies – inherently weak as a polity (and economy) because of its hierarchization within a structure, that of caste society.

Dumont has also extracted a high price for adopting a theoretical stance that exalts a holistic type of society – caste – and downgrades history. Maine had seen the Indian village as the living ancestor of the Aryan community. Hegel had seen the caste society of India as a necessary phase in the gradual unfolding of a world history. Anxious to avoid the errors of the evolutionists who preceded him, Dumont does not even allow India its early moment in the sun. It simply appears on the world scene as the total embodiment of a principle of social and religious Hierarchy, the opposite of the West with its essence, Equality. Nor has Dumont transcended the atomism of the older construct. His villages may have dissolved, but the larger entity into which they have emerged, his image of a traditional Indian civilization, is itself construed as an isolate unaffected by historical interactions.

4.4.3   Neo-Marxist History

Turning from anthropology to history, the most important shift, especially in South Asia, has been the rise to prominence of scholarship that returns not to

Hegel but to Marx.[23] The most important of those dealing with ancient India have been Kosambi (1956), and the historian, Sharma (1965). An important minority of the village studies, notably those of Gough (1981) and Beidelman (1959), who brings to light the conflictive aspect of *jajmāni* relations, converge with the work of these neo-Marxist historians. Empiricist (if not always factual) in their approach, those who have taken this position have adhered to the 'scientific' historical materialism established under Soviet leadership. They have rejected the idea of an Asiatic mode of production, embarrassing to Eastern Marxists, replacing it with a 'feudal' mode. Their 'feudalism' differs from that of the nineteenth-century writers like Tod (see 5.3.1), who focused on the agonistic relations of king and king and the solidary relations of king and vassal. The emphasis of these Marxians is rather on the relations of the vassals or landlords and their tenants or serfs, the peasants or villagers of this chapter.

Kosambi and Sharma argue that the Indian village became 'nearly self-contained' by the end of the Gupta period owing mainly to the decline of trade and urban life which, in their view, had characterized the mostly Buddhist period down through the Mauryas. According to Kosambi, a first feudal period, marked by the post-Mauryan invasions (second century BC to first century AD), consisting of a closed peasant economy of the disturbed early centuries of the Christian era, constituted a 'feudalism from above'. Later, after the Guptas (seventh century onward), kings made grants to subordinates and this gave rise to a 'feudalism from below' in the form of a class of landowners that developed within the village and between the state and the peasantry. Crucial to the argument of both is the idea that political fragmentation and the concomitant rise of a landowning class were due not so much to foreign invasions and conquests but to a decline of foreign trade and Indian commodity production.

If the picture that these feudalists paint has a familiar look, that is because it is remarkably similar both to the earlier despoticist view of the village and state and to the later nationalist narratives of Hindu India's decline after the Mauryan or Gupta period. Comparing the Indian village not with the post-tribal, pre-feudal mark of the European Dark Ages, but with the later European manor, the feudalists have, for the most part, simply shifted from a centralized, 'Asiatic' despotism to a decentralized, 'feudal' form (Hindess and Hirst, 1975: 224). Instead of placing the village in a relation of opposition to a despotic state, they have turned it into the site for class conflict between an exploited peasantry and an oppressive class of landlords. The places of ruling class and state are, as one might predict, reversed. Whereas in the despotic construct, class was subsumed in a tax-gathering state, in the feudal construct the state becomes reduced to the mere instrument of this rent-collecting class. The Brahmans, who dominate in the more idealist constructs (such as that of Dumont), are here reduced to the position of ideological mouthpieces of the landlord 'interests'.

The main sources of change for both of these images of rural India are also external. The major difference between the 'new' and the old is that the new consistently looks for economic or technological 'causes' for the same sequence

---

[23] I will discuss Burton Stein's work on South Indian localities, more tribalist than feudalist, in chapter 5.

of events. The moral of the tale is, however, pretty much the same. The world-ordering rationality of the West, embodied in its economic structure, leads to capitalism and world dominance. The relative absence of that economic structure in India leads, after a promising beginning, to a protracted feudal period, one that lasts in much of the Indian countryside almost down to the present.[24]

This feudal characterization has nearly displaced the older, dynastic history, finding its way into textbooks written for both Indian and Western audiences (Thapar, 1966: I). It has also precipitated a great deal of debate among both South Asian and foreign scholars. The most persistent evidential challenges to this Indian-style Pirenne thesis have come from the prolific formal, dynastic historian and epigraphist, the late D. C. Sircar. He argues (1969) that trade did not decline and that coins did not become scarce and rightly contests many of the less than careful and contextual interpretations that the feudalists have placed upon the documents. The most important Indian criticisms from a Marxian or left-of-centre perspective have come from Harbans Mukhia, who extends Sircar, arguing that the peasantry in India was not servile but, in formal terms, free. The 'high level of exploitation' of the Indian peasants was due, in his view, not to the control of their labour through serfdom but to the 'high fertility of the land' and to the peasants' 'low subsistence needs'. This apparently permitted the peasant, under threat of force, to give up more because he could do with less.[25]

The emergence of this feudalist school has, despite the objections, been beneficial in so far as it has helped to break the hegemony within the discipline of ancient history of the narrow, formalist view. The focus on class is also, in principle, a step in the right direction. The proponents of an Indian feudalism have, however, a long way to go. Apart from some highly original but pre-liminary work by Frank Perlin (1985), they have not yet squarely confronted the problem of agency. They have, to a large extent, simply moved it around. Caste, transformed in their view into class, still remains the substantialized agent of

[24] One of the more ironic difficulties that arises from trying to shoehorn economic history into a teleological succession of modes of production has to do with the 'ancient' mode of production, slavery. A way out of this has been to propose that the development of modes could be 'multilinear' (rather than 'unilinear') and still remain under the umbrella of historical materialism. If one adheres to the unilinear approach, then there is difficulty (admitted even by the adherents) in teasing out a slave mode in ancient, pre-Gupta India. If one adopts the multilinear view, it would do away with the need to have a slave stage followed by a feudal one. This has the advantage of preserving the uniqueness of Western history, if one can accept the embarrassment that slavery is the West's unique contribution to man! (But then is not slavery the reverse side of the coin of freedom?) The problem in Indian history then becomes this: how can one talk about the rise or development of feudalism in India with and after the Guptas? Just what *was* the mode of production under the Mauryas and Kushanas and Satavahanas? Can one distinguish an ancient mode which doesn't have slavery as its key element? Or are we back to square one, forced to reinvent oriental despotism (with a new label) so that India can decline into a feudal period? But then, if Hindess and Hirst are correct, how different are these two?
[25] His and other criticisms and counter-criticisms that have appeared in the course of this debate are reiterated in Byres and Mukhia (1985), itself precipitated by Mukhia (1980). Also useful as a review is Jha (1979).

India's villages. The state has been turned into its instrument and the village its victim.

4.5   CRITIQUE

Recent attempts to mount a rescue of the village's economic essence face some of the same difficulties that post-Independence anthropology and history have failed to resolve. C. J. Fuller (1989) has criticized the tendency in anthropological accounts to reduce a number of historically and regionally different village economies to a single uniform '*jajmani* system'. He argues, mostly against Dumont, that there is no 'ancient' system which can be, in my terms, denominated the essence of the village or rural caste economy. He takes to task the assumption that money, markets, and trade have no place in 'traditional' India until the British arrive on the scene on evidential grounds, and rightly argues that the 'substantivist' position in economic anthropology largely reproduces the view of Asian society as static. But to argue, somewhat weakly, that modern economic forms are to be found in the traditional village or, more vigorously, that the Indian (or Asian) peasant has all along been the embodiment of an Adam Smithean economic rationality (to which we have been blinded by our prejudices) largely swaps a traditional peasant for a pre-modern one.

To a large extent, then, the presuppositions on which the earlier image of the village rested still remain in place. One of these presuppositions is the determinism assumed to characterize the social 'system' or 'structure' of a village. Every cause has one effect and one only. There is, or has been, no degree of indeterminacy in the formation and reproduction of villages or little kingdoms. One cannot, therefore, speak of them as having a history. That, in Collingwood's terms, would presuppose the possibility of freedom of action (without, at the same time, rushing to the opposite position of voluntarism or 'sociological individualism' (see 2.3.1, 2.4), which sees the free actor as a given and denies his or her shaping by complex agents that pre-exist him or her). One can only see these villages as naturally evolving to a post-tribal stage and then propagating themselves at that (low) level. The phrase, 'many factors contributed', often used by the empiricist and historian, while it may embody the intention to avoid determinism, does not necessarily succeed in doing so, because it does not provide a positive alternative to the deterministic position. It loosens the strings on the puppets, but leaves them as puppets none the less.

The presupposition of determinacy is at work in the assumptions made by virtually all of the contributors to our theory of the Indian village. It is at work when we assume that the settlement of the Aryans in the isolated subcontinent of India (Maine) was bound to cause the Indian village as a brotherhood to remain underdeveloped (compared to its Mediterranean and Teutonic cousins). Or, suppose the existence in India of Dravidians and let the Aryans be superimposed, and require that both have to meet the (mostly biological, species-survival) needs that are given in the tropical Indian environment (Baden-Powell), and the Indian village, severalty and joint, will be the result. Or, again, ask yourself what villages will look like under the firm rule of a caste ideology and you can, like Dumont, almost deduce the politically fragmented and ineffectual village that he construes as typical of Hindu India. The determinism silently presupposed in all these variants of the predominant theory is, of course, antithetical to a social science that would restore action because it does not permit actors, whether simple or complex, to exercise any choice with respect to how they construct their communities.

The second major presupposition is the essentialist one. It is the presupposition that some essence, in the sense of a stable, determinate nature or structure, underlies human institutions and even entire civilizations. This essence, present as identifiable properties or characteristics, is assumed to exist as an objective reality which constitutes an ancient or modern society. The recent tendency has been to deny the traditionality of the Indian village in 'factual' terms without questioning the essentialism that lies behind the dichotomy of traditional and modern. The result has been to see the villagers as anticipations of the rational men that some economic theorists have postulated as essential to modern (capitalist) economic activity. This is an easy trap to fall into, for most of the users of the traditional–modern dichotomy themselves explicitly or implicitly relate the two types teleologically in a global evolutionary scheme. One pertinent example of this is the assumption that, if the entire surplus had not been pumped out of the village, it would naturally have evolved in the direction of the modern capitalist West. There is no reason why such an assumption should be made. There are many ways in which villagers could have disposed of the 'surplus value' of their labour.

Similarly, the assumption that there are fixed, definite forms that money, markets, agricultural production, contracts, surplus disposal, and so on must take (unless prevented) is another deployment of an imperializing essentialism that I would want to avoid. It hinders an exploration of the genuine multiplicity of actions that one might want to constitute as forms of economic rationality. Even a brief examination of the attempt by economists who basically agree with one another, for example, monetarists, to decide what shall be counted as money in one contemporary economy should give pause to the anthropologist or historian in any discussion he or she might begin about money or monetization in the villages of a 'remote' hill area or a twelfth-century Hindu state.

The next presupposition of the Indological construct of a village India I would point to is that of a dichotomy between 'inner' and 'outer'. The insistence that the village was economically self-contained, the view that relations inside it were organic and hierarchic, while those outside it were antagonistic and anarchic, were and still are constitutive of the image of village community. The same mechanical (or organic) metaphors that commentators used to constitute the possessive individual and the sovereign nation-state they have also used to imagine the Indian village into existence. Combined with the assumption of homogeneity, that villages are everywhere in India pretty much the same, we are given our picture of a cellular rural society. Certainly sufficient evidence has been accumulated, especially in the post-Independence work, to show that there are great difficulties here. I suspect that it is possible to demonstrate that those villages which observers have taken as typical or representative (when they weren't simply mirroring their own ideal construct) have, in most cases, been the major villages within a circle or union of villages and not the average ones which, of course, presupposes that there were (and are) important differences among villages within even the same locality. Yet we are still not free of this presupposition, for, as I have indicated, we have largely deferred the problems by shifting the dichotomy of inner–outer to the 'level' of the little kingdom.

The epistemology that accompanies this essentialism pays no or little heed to the discourse of villagers. In so far as it does, it treats it positivistically either as a transparent medium by which one obtains 'data', or, since villagers think metaleptically, as a smokescreen to be penetrated or as a false consciousness that has to be translated into the rational, clear, scientific description-language of the ethnographer. Even Dumont, who, to his credit, does attend seriously to the discourse of Indians in the form of what he refers to as 'ideology', has difficulties here. By and large, he tends to hold to the view that the conscious thoughts are a partial representation of society, making it possible to use them as 'facts' in the same way as other evidence, but he also makes the essentialist assumption that 'there is a basic ideology, a kind of germinal ideology tied to common language and hence to the linguistic group or the global society' (1980b: 343). This essentialism is also antithetical to a theory that would revive action because it sees particular acts not as *constitutive* of social reality, but merely as *expressive* of it or *deviating* from it.

Most important, however, in this metaphysics of textbook science that has produced our village India, is the presupposition of a dichotomy between village and state. By this I mean that, so far as their characteristics are concerned, village and state are mutually exclusive 'levels' in Indian civilization, each the negation of the other. Probably the most important of the oppositions assumed to obtain between the two is the one that makes the 'state' the level of a peculiar politics (that of force, deceit, and exploitation) which is absent from the 'village', and at the same time makes the village that of an equally peculiar society and economy of communal cooperation which is absent from the state. The state, in other words, is essentially political while the village is essentially social and economic. Because they are so opposed, the one is a realm of aimless, non-developmental flux, while the other is a timeless, self-contained world of solidarities and reciprocities. The former is, so to speak, the level of meaningless change in Indian civilization. The latter is, on the contrary, the level of changeless meaning.

This dichotomy of state and village-cum-caste is not, however, the same dichotomy of state and individual, citizen, or civil society often postulated as characteristic of classical and post-classical Europe (and, by way of tracing an origin to this 'essential' feature of the West, of ancient Greece and Rome). As we have seen, the village and caste society is also opposed in Indological discourse to the 'civil society' of modern Europe, to the ideas of 'nationality' and 'citizenship' seen as so important to the modern nation-state. Not only are persons dissolved into their families, lineages, subcastes and castes, the principles by which these social units (one will pardon the expression) reproduce themselves are natural ones, those of birth and mating. Now, these joint families, lineages, and castes may have heads and/or councils, but these cannot be said to be associational, for membership is not contractual, a matter of rational deliberation and decision-taking, but determined by position. And the procedures followed are not those of a conscious, rational legislative body, but of men dominated by an irrevocable, unchanging custom. The village community consists not, then, in Collingwood's scheme, of any society, but purely of a system of non-social communities.

Suppose, however, that we substitute the idea of imperial formations for the notions of nation-state and empire. Because we would now be able to think of the agents making up a polity as overlapping classes of agents, instruments, and patients, we could collapse the dichotomy of state and village. We could then assume that politics is an aspect of, or a way of talking about, all human institutions and not the essence of one of them, the 'state'. We would begin to see changed notions of state and village as two of several overlapping jurisdictions within polities rather than as 'the' two complementary levels of Indian society. We would look upon the very constitution and renewal of these agents as the result of actions that take place not only within them but also of acts that position polities within a larger imperial formation and that relate one imperial formation to another.

If at the same time we were to collapse the dichotomous contrasts between a constraining 'kinship' and 'free' association that thinkers have used to oppose 'caste' to 'civil society' in the Indo-sociological accounts of the Indian 'village community', villages would then begin to look quite different. The idea of agency entailed in the idea of imperial formation would permit the villagers to shape and reshape themselves as complex political agents through headmen or councils. It would enable them to exhibit something of a world-ordering rationality. With its emphasis on underdetermination, it would allow economic activities that are classed in the bipartite scheme of ancient and modern as inherently modern (and Western) to be as much integral to so-called ancient and non-Western communities as they are to the modern. Yet it would not require that they be seen as inchoate or distorted versions of the determinate forms alleged to exist in the modern capitalist West. More generally, we would be able to provide the bulk of the people of an ancient India with the possibility that they could have consciousness of themselves, of their community, and of the larger polity to which they belonged, of the province or peripheral country in which they were situated, and of the city, king and court, to which they were attached, and of the contingencies in which these interacted.

If, finally, we gave up the assumption that the actions of villagers are simply expressions of or deviations from an underlying essence – the caste society as the extreme, isolated, and static instance of an Asian or peasant agrarian structure or fixed religious hierarchy (with its attendant mythic and metaleptic mentality) – we would want to focus more carefully on the actions themselves and on their outcomes. We would do this not, I should add, because, via a hermeneutic anthropology or social history, we want to discover the 'meanings' villagers attach to the strange traps in which they have been snared for centuries. This only combines the approaches of the naturalist and the idealist without changing the assumptions of either. No, we would do it because from our standpoint the acts of the villagers, performed in tandem with other agents, are the events that actually shape and reshape villages.

We would want to look in particular at those complex activities of rural political societies that have had as their purpose the renewal of the village or union of villages. Among these were the first plowing and planting of the fields, the negotiation of the revenue to be paid to those lords of whom the villagers are the subjects, the harvest at the end of the major growing season. And we would want to pay attention to the rites which have accompanied these complex acts. Examples of these activities can be found in the Anglo-French accounts of India, especially in those inclined to the romantic.[26] The major revision of our view of India that would emerge from the change of approach I recommend would relate to the supposed keystone of Indian civilization itself, caste. Before we turn to this, however, we must partake of the essence opposed to the village in Indological discourses, the divine kingship of the state.

[26] Alexander Kinloch Forbes (1821–64), educated as an architect and then at Haileybury, arrived in Bombay in 1843 and served first as Assistant Collector and Judge, in Ahmedabad, Gujarat, and then as Political Agent for one of the Western India princes. During this time he took an interest in the bardic chronicles of the area. The results of his research were published while he was back in England. We learn from his narrative that the day selected to mark the onset of the monsoons and the beginning of the agricultural year appears to have been one of the major occasions, for the locality or village, for the reiteration of the 'society' of ruler and ruled. That day in princely early nineteenth-century Gujarat was the Akshaya-tritīyā, the third lunar day of Vaiśākha. Forbes reports on the interaction that takes place on that day between the lord of the village, presumably a Rajput, and its principal householders, people called Koonbees (from *kuṭumbin*, 'householder') who, says Forbes, related themselves to the Rajputs:

> When the festival called Ukhaturee comes round, which it does early in Wyeshak (May), the chief of a village collects the cultivators, and tells them that it is time for them to commence work. They say, 'No! the assessment was too heavy last year, you laid too many taxes upon us; besides, we have in truth, no master over our heads; people burn our houses, and lay waste our lands, and you afford no protection, and do not go on the *wār* [battlefield?].' The chief makes sundry excuses, the most usual and convenient of which is, that everything is the fault of that rascal of a *mehtā* (his man of business), whom he protests his intention of dismissing at once. As to the cultivator, no one can have greater affection for them than he has; they are, in fact, his sons and daughters. Nor does the chief altogether over-state his feelings in this point; for he is well aware that his lands are of no value to him without the aid of the cultivators, and that in Goozerat, as in other countries of the east, 'In the multitude of people is the king's honour, but in the want of people is the destruction of the prince.' After much haggling, and when the chief has presented the head-men of the village with turbans, and made liberal promises of remission of rent, the auspicious day is at length fixed upon, and cultivation is commenced. (1924: II, 243–4)

5
Divine Kingship, the Hindu Type of Government

5.1 NATION STATE, NATURAL STATE

The best reason why monarchy is a strong government is that it is an intelligible government. The mass of mankind understand it, and they hardly anywhere in the world understand any other. It is often said that men are ruled by their imaginations; but it would be truer to say that they are governed by the weakness of their imaginations. (Bagehot, 1976: 83)

The Hindu 'state', government in the narrower sense of that term's usage, constituted the last pillar of the Indological construct of an ancient India and the complement of village and caste, her exotic substitute for the development of a true 'civil society'. Anyone interested in developing a theory of human agency, of focusing on the specifically instituted capacities of humans to order and fulfil their lives, must take into account the political societies into which peoples have been organized, for states in the wider sense of polities are, more than any other, the complex agents *par excellence*. Those governing agents more than other agents (but not, I hasten to add, to their exclusion) exercise the capacity to constitute and transform polities.[1] As a scholar interested in restoring human agency to the people of South Asia, the study of the 'Hindu state' is, therefore, of special interest to me.

Here, however, we come up against great difficulties. There is a persistent

---

[1] I do not hold that the state (government) need be seen as a work of art, humankind's highest achievement, nor do I consider it as inherently 'transcendent' or 'sovereign'. Other institutions may be seen to have rivalled (or currently rival) or even to dominate supposedly discrete nation-states or polities – the Roman Catholic Church, the multinational corporation, the international labour movement, the 'free world' led by the United States. Certain liberal advocates of *laissez-faire*, libertarians, and anarchists have, for different reasons, wished to see states as minimal organizations, obedient to the choices of 'individuals' or local, participatory polities. But both those who would see states as only one among a number of powerful institutions and those who would deny their desirability have had to take into account the existence and history of these entities.

strain in the social sciences and in Indological discourse which wants to reduce states or political agents to the status of instruments of one or the other of two essences. These essences, often dichotomized in social scientific and more explicitly ideological discourses, are the 'individual' and 'society'. The individualists, who would have society be the outcome of 'free' and 'rational' choices made by self-contained, fully equipped individuals (the 'human nature' option), will see the state primarily as the instrument of individuals, as the regulator of a market and provider of law and order. The socialists, holding that individuals are the products of a larger social totality which is the carrier of a world-ordering rationality, would see certain types of states as necessarily entailed in certain types of society (the 'social structure' option), in which case the state becomes the instrument of an 'industrial society' or the 'forces and relations of production'.

Either way, the tendency in these discourses has been to reduce the realm of the political in their own polities to a formal one of voting citizens representing themselves as 'individuals' and as 'interest groups' (civil society). Here writers after Locke have depicted the state as what I will call a 'representational polity'. Activities that fall outside that sphere are deemed nonpolitical and transferred elsewhere. Those (free marketeers) who want to see the abstract individual as supreme transfer them to the 'private sector' (mostly, these days, bureaucratically organized big businesses). Those wishing to privilege the 'social' translate these activities to the 'welfare state' (also bureaucratically organized). These retain the notion of a representational polity, but see it as culminating in what I shall refer to as the 'administered polity'. Giddens, the sociologist, attributes the persistent lack of interest in the state in the social sciences to the formation of those sciences at a time when its founders assumed that the realm of the political (which he sees as, ultimately, the exercise of violence) would shrink, dissolving into an industrialized world increasingly unified by ties of economic interdependence (Giddens, 1985: 26). I cannot agree. The major purpose of much of social scientific knowledge was precisely to advance the process by which human agency was displaced on to an increasingly centralized (in both the private and public sectors) but magically depoliticized, that is, scientifically administered, polity.[2]

If the tendency to reduce the political to the individual or social is widespread in the social sciences at large, it is no surprise to find that it is even more in evidence when it comes to the study of India, the land supposed to be dominated by the essences of caste and (even deeper) racial and regional conflict. The treatment of government or the state, of the polities into which South Asians were organized, has, to be sure, been shaped more than that of any other institution of the subcontinent by the stratagems and rationalizations of discourses on empire. The reason for this is not hard to find. The authors of political and economic discourses in the Anglo-French imperial formation were in the process of establishing themselves, of constructing or altering state practices and institutions in those parts of the world where they found themselves, or wished to insert themselves as superior or autonomous agencies.

---

[2] More on target are the comments of Crick (1982: 92–110).

Yet political society in 'ancient' India has seldom been the direct centre of focus in Indological discourse. Certain ideas about political society in India do indeed pervade it, but the Indian state as a specific topic, with a special scholarly tradition, is practically non-existent. To a large extent, of course, this is due to the efforts of most of these theorists to depoliticize their own polities in the name of a transcendent 'individual' or 'society'. But there was more to it than that. They were at the same time trying to come to terms with polities they took to be wrongly constituted. They considered the representational and administered polities of Europe as 'modern' and their ancestors, the absolutist monarchies of pre-revolutionary England and France, as 'ancient'. This is also how they classed the contemporary polities of large parts of the world, starting with the Holy Roman Empire and its penumbral successors and a Tsarist Russia and Ottoman Empire. There were also unenlightened men at home, such as Edmund Burke (1729–97). He did not look on political activity as due to ignorance, and did not look with scorn upon traditional monarchical forms of government, and had loudly criticized the East India Company's doings. So the battle against the Indian states had to be fought on many fronts.

Indological discourse partakes of the polemic against ancient and feudal regimes that Enlightenment advocates used both to constitute and defeat them. The constitution of the Indian state was, as we shall see, proportional to the defeat it would receive. The very absence of a world-ordering rationality claimed to be so central to a conquest-prone Indian civilization would preclude the development of separate discourses on the political and economic because there was, mostly, nothing 'there' to talk about. Instead of making a civilization in which a transcendent and developing state and economy were based on the 'individual' or the 'social', the Indians would make one in which a changeless 'caste' forever remained its transcendent essence. The government of the former 'type' of civilization could hardly be placed on the same footing with the latter, even though they seemed to have had a similar (Aryan) origin.

For the reason just given, I cannot say that any of the monographs devoted especially to the topic of the Hindu or pre-Islamic state has been a hegemonic text. Hegemonic assertions about Hindu states are to be found at every turn in Indological discourse, but they are, more often than not, nested in discourses about land tenure, caste, Hinduism, and, as pointed out in the previous chapter, villages. The discourses in which ideas about political activity have, of course, been most in evidence are historical narratives. Since these histories (under the varying rubrics of national, imperial, regional, or dynastic) are almost always organized around a chronology of political events, constructs of the Hindu state, whether implicit in the narrative itself or in separate topical chapters, are integral to them. Not surprisingly, the historical narrative that I have dubbed the ancestor of hegemonic texts for India as a whole, that of James Mill, can be taken also as 'authoritative' on the issue of the Indian state.

The main thing I wish to do in this chapter is to sketch in the ancestry of the two images of the Hindu state, the absolutist or despotic, and post-tribal or quasi-feudal. These images have not themselves been stable (despite the essentialist claims of their makers) because, as will become clear, the images of the European or American polity of which these images are distorted reflections have themselves undergone important shifts. Together, these two depictions constituted the hegemonic construct of the Hindu state within British imperial discourse. I will also review the nationalist constructions, which were pitched against this shifting imperial depiction, and criticize discursive developments since the rise of the US–USSR imperial formation.

Virtually everyone who has written on the Indian or (more narrowly) Hindu state has characterized it as a 'divine kingship', yet, with one partial exception, there has been no serious treatment of its 'political theology' of this as a problematic, changing set of practices. The main reason for this is that Indologists have considered the divinity of government a 'secondary attribute'. That is, they have taken it as an index of some pathological 'special' condition of the Indian body politic. Secular-minded reformers saw it as a symptom of false consciousness. More conservative, religiously inclined commentators looked on it, as they did in Europe (see Bagehot's apology for monarchy in Britain at the head of the chapter), as a symbol necessary to the maintenance of authority. Some have taken the divinity of kings to be the essential feature of Indian government from its very origin, while others have argued that it was imported into India. Nearly all, however, have agreed that a form of divine kingship (which most observers thought to be as excessive in its claims as it was in its ineptitude) triumphed in Indian political thought during its 'medieval' history and signalled the decline and collapse of Hindu civilization as a political reality.

5.2 ABSOLUTE MONARCHY, INSTRUMENT OF THE CASTE SOCIETY

5.2.1 Utilitarian Despotism

Mill, who had written his *History* in the hope of making money on its sales, succeeded not only in that; he obtained a post with the East India Company (as did his son, the more famous John Stuart) in 1819, eventually becoming Examiner of Correspondence in 1830. He tells his reader in his 'Essay on Government', one year after his appointment, that:

We have seen, that the very principle of human nature upon which the necessity of Government is founded, the propensity of one man to possess himself of the objects of desire at the cost of another, leads on, by infallible sequence, where power over a community is attained, and nothing checks it, not only to that degree of plunder which leaves the members (excepting always the recipients and instruments of the plunder) the bare means of subsistence, but to that degree of cruelty which is necessary to keep in existence the most intense terror. (Mill, 1978: 67)

Whether Mill had the East India Company and the conduct of its officers in mind, I cannot say. Given the theory of the individual which he espouses, however, we have every right to ask questions about 'interests' when we read his account of India.[3]

---

[3] Mill discusses the Hindu state in three consecutive chapters of his second book, 'Of the Hindus' (1858: I, 107–376; II, 1–164). These are entitled 'The Form of Government', The Laws of the Hindus', and 'The Taxes', respectively. After four chapters on religion, manners, the arts, and literature, he returns to the topic of the state in a concluding chapter of 'general reflections'.

Mill begins his account of the Hindus with a discussion of the transition from 'tribes' to the 'more regulated and artifical system of a monarchy' (1858: I, 123). For Mill, as for many others in Anglo-Saxon political philosophy, the state as a subject was a 'secondary growth'. The primary entities in a community were the individuals (male heads of households). The state, as government, was supposed to maintain the conditions necessary for these individuals to prosper. I refer to this theory of a polity as 'representational' because government in it was supposed to be dominated by a law-making body comprised of those who represented the interests of the ultimate constituents of the state, the individual householders. The heroic legislator (who was also, ambiguously, the decisive magistrate, maintainer of law and order) was the token of the type in this construct, the successful individual who was able to represent the interests of the whole. Such men 'are superior spirits, capable of seizing the best ideas of their times, and, if they are not opposed by circumstances, of accelerating the progress of the community to which they belong' (1858: I, 124). Consistent with this view, Jeremy Bentham, Mill's mentor, had offered his services 'as a sort of Indian Solon' to the East India Company in 1793.

Some may have imagined that the transcendent representational polity in which perfect utility is achieved was at hand in nineteenth-century Britain. But this was not the case for those Others who lived in earlier, darker times. The institutions for ordering the earlier, tribal peoples were typically held by their promulgators to have been 'founded upon divine authority' (1858: I, 124). This, however, was not because the leader himself believed in gods, but because the ignorant minds of the ruled, misled by their imaginations, required the invocation of divinity to persuade them: 'it is evidently the most effectual means which a great man, full of the spirit of improvement, can employ, to induce people, jealous and impatient of all restraint, to forego their boundless liberty, and submit to the curb of authority' (1858: I, 124). This structure – an enlightened ruler using theology to rule his complement, a superstitious mass – is to be found with some variation in almost all of the discussions of government in ancient India. It might be noted, even at this early point in our discussion, that the idea of a leader using religion to sway the people he rules presupposes the existence of a natural mind or reason which is the agent 'clothing' itself in religion. There is a 'possessive individual' hunkered down inside the mind of the Hindu monarch ever masking itself as the people's benefactor. Similarly, there is in every people a representational state which is trying to take shape.

Mill does not suppose the existence of a dichotomy between ruler and ruled only in India. It must have been characteristic, in his secularist view of the world, of all ancient societies. India, however, was not normal even by the abnormal standards of antiquity:

No where among mankind have the laws and ordinances been more exclusively referred to the Divinity, than by those who instituted the theocracy of Hindustan. The plan of society and government, the rights of persons and things, even the customs, arrangements, and manners, of private and domestic life; everything, in short, is established by divine prescription. (1858: I, 124–5)

Here, as in so many representations, the influence of religion is depicted as irrationally overdetermined in India. This, as we shall see, is a major feature in the construction of Hindu kingship. If claims to divinity are the symptoms, in the eyes of a rationalist, of an irrational order of things, then India must be the unique home of disorder.

The institutions that arose in India in the transition from tribal to monarchic were, according to Mill, those that make up caste. So he first presented his treatment of caste in a chapter that precedes the chapters on government. Only after it is firmly established that India is pregoverned by a priesthood do we arrive at an account of government. This priesthood 'is generally found to usurp the greatest authority, in the lowest state of society'. The men who make it up are ever and always self-interested and never to be trusted.

Mill consistently assumed that castes were extensions of that essence of utilitarian theory, the possessive individual. They are greedy, lazy, self-interested agents always on the lookout for what serves their material interests and not the interdependent parts of an organic whole (as with Hegel and Marx). As ignorance and superstition were at their greatest in India, so the priesthood there, the Brahmans, as a group individual, have been able not only to gain success over their Indian competitors, they 'have acquired and maintained an authority, more exalted, more commanding, and extensive, than the priests have been able to engross among any other portion of mankind' (1858: I, 128). The idea that the Hindu state is a theocracy in which the ruler is reduced to the status of the Brahmans' instrument thus throws a long shadow over Mill's discussion of the Hindu state before he even begins it. I shall return to the question of the state or the king's relation to the Brahmans and gods. Let me now, however, proceed to Mill's representation of the Hindu form of government.

Mill argued that the form of government adhered to by Hindus was, 'according to the Asiatic model', that of absolute monarchy, 'with the usual exception of religion and its ministers'. Citing Manu's statement of the king's formation out of particles of the guardian deities, Mill concluded: 'The pride of imperial greatness could not devise, hardly could it even desire, more extraordinary distinctions, or the sanction of a more unlimited authority' (1858: I, 141). The essence of the Indian or Hindu state was, thus, a sort of nightmarish version of absolutism, divine right and all.

Although despotic, the Asiatic state did not, according to Mill, possess a true central government. It was segmental rather than mechanical. The monarch had no other 'plan' than 'simply to divide his own authority and power into pieces or fragments, as numerous as the provinces into which it was deemed to be convenient to distribute the empire' (1858: I, 142). By contrast, in the government of a European state, 'officers are appointed for the discharge of particular duties in the different provinces of the empire; some for the decision of causes, some for the control of violence, some for collecting the contingents of the subjects, for the expense of the state.' Evoking Hobbes's *Leviathan*, Mill concludes that 'the powers of all centre immediately in the head of the government, and all together act as connected and subordinate wheels in one complicated and artful machine' (1858: I, 142).

It is easy to exaggerate the earlier Utilitarians' commitment to a democratic, representative form of government and, more generally, to politics. They had an instrumental view of both. This is no surprise, for their higher commitment was to the establishment of a society of individuals governed not (as most Whigs and Tories believed) through ongoing political debate and struggle, but by certain 'scientific' principles. It was these as much as any concern for personal freedom that seems to have animated utilitarian discourse. As Halevy says, 'What the Benthamites wanted was to found a social science on the model of the exact sciences, the sciences of measurement, geometry and mechanics.' They believed that 'the egoistical pleasures and pains which concern the well-being of our physical individuality, are the only ones which admit of objective equivalents, the only ones which can be measured' and saw science 'as an explanation by reduction, by decomposition into simple elements which were necessary for the organisation of their knowledge' (Halevy, 1928: I, 467).

So, where politics could be got round, as in the East India Company, Mill advocated reforms that were non-representational (Lively and Rees, 1978: 49–50). What we are seeing here, rather, is the rise of an administrative science, that whole congeries of practices which, Foucault has argued, is presupposed not just by the 'modern' state, but in the everyday life of school, office, and factory. The underside of legal and political freedom in a contracting political domain is a domain of expanding 'control', of micro-forms of power in the workplace. The 'architectural figure' of this new order, according to Foucault, was Bentham's notorious Panopticon, 'the diagram of a mechanism of power reduced to its ideal form; its functioning, abstracted from any obstacle, resistance or friction, must be represented as a pure architectural and optical system: it is in fact a figure of political technology that may and must be detached from any specific use' (Foucault, 1977: 205). No polity, it was a totalizing observatory:

But the Panopticon was also a laboratory; it could be used as a machine to carry out experiments, to alter behaviour, to train or correct individuals. To experiment with medicines and monitor their effects. To try out different punishments on prisoners, according to their crimes and character, and to seek the most effective ones. To teach different techniques simultaneously to the workers, to decide which is the best ... The Panopticon is a privileged place for experiments on men, and for analysing with complete certainty the transformations that may be obtained from them. (Foucault, 1977: 203–4)

India, if Bentham and Mill had their way, would become a realization of this Panopticon.

Consistent with his view of the Hindu state as despotic, Mill also held that 'The sovereigns in India had not only the ownership, but all the benefit of the land; the ryots had merely the privilege of employing their labour always upon the same soil, and of transferring that privilege to some other person' (1858: I, 224). Mill was not just making an idle claim in his discussion of landed revenue. He argued not only that it was rent, but that as such, it was, as Marx was to say, equivalent to the entire surplus value of the ryots' labour. But this was not, in India, calculated according to scientific methods. In theory, it was set at a fixed share of the produce; in practice, however, it was bound to be more: 'We may assume it as a principle, in which there is no room for mistake, that a government constituted and circumstanced as that of the Hindus, had only one limit to its exactions, the non-existence of any thing further to take' (1858: I, 222). The result of these exactions, predictably, was that the 'individual occupants' did not (as they increasingly did in Europe from medieval times on) prosper, and the population of India consequently stagnated at a low level.

Now, one might think that Mill would have advocated 'privatization' under British rule. But he did not. 'Mill's plan for India', reports Stokes, 'was for the State to be the sole landlord, with the immediate cultivators as the tenants' (Stokes, 1959: 92). Stokes argued that Mill 'was prepared to accept the oriental role of the State as landlord of the soil, because this happened to coincide with his views on taxation' (92). I would not quarrel with this, but I think we are also justified in considering Mill's characterization of the Indian state a stunning example of displacement. Mill would use the accusation of oriental despotism to transform the East India Company into the owner of an entire civilization. An entire subcontinent would be turned into the landed property of an 'individual' in the form of a trading company. Indeed, government in India, where Utilitarianism could succeed, was more like the management of a business firm than it could be at home, where politics prevented the very strong government, ruling in the name of a popular majority, that thoroughgoing or radical reform presupposed. Perhaps it is here, in the modern business firm, and not in an *ancien régime* (itself absolutist and mercantilist in practically the same breath) that the true source of the oriental despot is to be found.

5.2.2 Political Disunity, Priestly Tyranny

Mill begins his discussion of the relations between Hindu states and of the national or imperial unity of India with the argument that it was possible for a people lower in civilization 'to be united extensively, under one government, and to remain steady for a great length of time in that situation' (1858: II, 124), and cites China, Persia, the Ottoman empire, and Russia as examples. India, however, differed. It was more barbarous than these other nations of Asia:

Among uncivilized nations, however, it is most common to find a perpetual succession of revolutions, and communities in general small; though sometimes a prince or individual with uncommon talents arises; and, acquiring power, extends his authority over several of those communities; or even, as in the case of Charlemagne, over a great number; while, after his death the large empire which he had erected gradually dissolves, till the whole, or the great part, is re-divided into small communities, as before. Every thing which the Europeans have seen in Hindustan conspires to prove that such subdivision of communities, and occasional and temporary extensions of power in particular hands, have composed the history of that country. (1858: II, 125)

Mill then made his kill, ridiculing the attempt of Burke, opponent of the East India Company, to save the idea of India as a unified monarchy by analogizing the relations among its princes with those of feudal Europe (Burke, 1784: 14–15).

As interesting as Mill's denial of any true political unity in India is the reason he gave for it. He argued that 'There are two modes in which the subordination of a number of petty princes, to a great one, may take place' (1858: II, 139). The first of these, that constitutive of a centralized empire, is a relation of total subjection which Maine would later argue is the only one possible in the ancient type of society between communities or polities unrelated by kinship: 'The inferior states may exist merely as conquered, enslaved countries, paying tribute to a foreign government, obeying its mandates, and crouching under its lash' (139). The second mode is the one Maine would hold to be characteristic of modern society and developing out of European feudalism. It is one 'where the inferior states were connected together by confederacy, and acknowledged a common head for the sake of unity, but possessed the right of deliberating in common upon common concerns' (139–40). We can see, in what Mill next states, that the Hindu imperial state is ruled out not only empirically but also in theoretical terms: 'It may, with confidence, be pronounced, that in neither mode is the supposed effect compatible with the state of civilization in Hindustan' (140).

If India was less civilized than the ancient societies which did succeed in establishing enduring empires, how much less possible was it for the representational form of government that was supposed to typify the emerging modern society of Europe to have occurred in ancient India. It presupposes a self-restraint that hardly exists among the moderns, let alone among the barbarous Hindus. The ancient Hindus did not lack the motive to subject their neighbours. On the contrary, 'Wherever an Indian sovereign is able to take possession, he hastens to take it. Wherever he can make a plundering incursion, though unable to retain, he ravages and destroys' (40). What might seem like a compact between rulers is only, in Mill's view, a tactical ploy: 'Now it sometimes happens, that a neighbouring prince, too weak to prevent or chastise these injuries, endeavours to purchase exemption from them by a composition' (140).

Mill then trumpeted his conclusion, trying as he did to silence the still reverberating voice of Edmund Burke:

Of all the results of civilization, that of forming a combination of different states, and directing their powers to one common object, seems to be one of the least consistent with the mental habits and attainments of the Hindus. It is the want of this power of combination which has rendered India so easy a conquest to all invaders; and enables us to retain, so easily, that dominion over it which we have acquired. Where is there any vestige in India of that deliberative assembly of princes, which in Germany was known by the name of the Diet? (1858: II, 141)

For Mill, then, the normal relations of Hindu polities to one another was not that of provinces in an empire or of kingdoms and principalities in a feudal confederacy, but of petty states constantly at war with one another. The quintessential Hindu state Mill seems to have had before him as he wrote was that of the Marathas. A highly volatile confederacy led by a Brahman minister, the Peshwa, the Marathas were the major Indian rivals of the East India Company for hegemony in the subcontinent, apart from the Mogul emperor himself.

Just as the state was reducible to the human nature of the individuals making it up, so the political chaos of India was attributable to the internal constitution of Indian polities. Hence, Mill returns to this. Government was, for Mill, as with so many English and continental political philosophers, naturally divided into three branches, the legislative, judicial, and administrative (1858: I, 151). Since the Hindus attributed their laws not to themselves but to their gods, one can only speak, among them, of interpretation. The power to do this was in the hands of the Brahmans: 'The power of legislation, therefore, exclusively belongs to the priesthood' (151). With respect to judicial power, the situation was similar: 'The king, therefore, is so far from possessing the judicial power, that he is rather the executive officer by whom the decisions of the Brahmans are carried into effect' (152). So, according to Mill, 'the king was little more than an instrument in the hands of the Brahmans. He performed the laborious part of government, and sustained the responsibility, while they chiefly possessed the power' (152).

The difficulty with Mill's theory that the Hindu monarch is a despot, absolute in all matters except religion, would not seem to leave the Hindu king much scope for action if, as Mill himself has already argued, every institution of the Indian people was pervaded with religion. Mill was aware of the strain in his construction of the Hindu state: 'But with this inference the fact does not correspond ... their monarchs enjoyed no small share both of authority, and of that kind of splendour, which corresponded with their own state of society' (1858: I, 153). What, then, were the residual powers left to the Hindu king?

They had two engines entrusted to them, the power of which their history serves remarkably to display: they were masters of the army; and they were masters of the public revenue. These two circumstances, it appears, were sufficient to counterbalance the legislative, and the judicative, and even a great part of the executive power, reinforced by all the authority of an overbearing superstition, lodged in the hands of the Brahmens. These threw around the sovereign an external lustre, with which the eyes of uncultivated men are easily dazzled. (1858: I, 153–4)

The divinity of the Hindu king was, in Mill's treatment, no godly splendour. It was the glint of a steel sword and the glitter of gold coins, displaced by a superstitious mass on to a divine source. Nor was he the great heroic leader who rose above the ordinary man, for his greatness originated not out of any inner strength or rational awareness, but because of external necessity:

In dangerous and disorderly times, when every thing which the nation values depends upon the sword, the military commander exercises unlimited authority by universal consent; and so frequently is this the situation of a rude and uncivilized people, surrounded on all sides by rapacious and turbulent neighbours, that it becomes, in a great measure, the habitual order of things. The Hindu king, by commanding both the force, and the revenue of the state, had in his hands the distribution of gifts and favours; the potent instrument, in short, of patronage; and the jealousy and rivalship of the different sets of competitors, would, of their own accord, give him a great influence over the Brahmans themselves. The distribution of gifts and favours is an engine of so much power, that the man who enjoys it to a certain extent is absolute, with whatever checks he may appear to be surrounded. (1858: I, 154)

So, the Hindu king (and state) was accorded some autonomy after all. Yet it should immediately be noted that this autonomous capacity was highly limited.

He had the capacity to command force and distribute wealth. But he was not sufficiently constrained either by his own rational greatness or by institutional checks, so he did not act as the free agent that a truly utilitarian hero would. His distributions, made for his own personal advantage (as any Utilitarian would do), were arbitrary. They had the effect not of improving India but rather of perpetuating its despotic caste society. The king, furthermore, had no capacity to make rules or laws. His use of force and wealth did not, therefore, constitute or reconstitute the Hindu caste society which forever transcended Indian states and their atomized village economies. That capacity lay exclusively with the caste of Brahman priests. Yet because they, too, lacked true rationality, because their thinking was dominated by the Hindu religion and its exceedingly unempirical, imaginative way of apprehending reality, it was not really possible to consider even the Brahmans the agents of their own acts. Divine kingship in India, the most extreme the world had seen, was thus in reality a theocracy, but one that was marked as much by its greed as by its ineffectuality because of its excessive irrationality.

5.3   CLAN MONARCHY, THE POST-TRIBAL STATE

5.3.1   Oriental Feudalism: Tod's Rajputs

The men who dominated discourse on Indian and Hindu states throughout the nineteenth century were the builders of Britain's Indian Empire. A major concern for these men was not only the 'settlement' of the revenue, but the pacification and administration of areas and the ongoing problem of which areas to administer directly and which to leave in the hands of 'native princes'. As they engaged in these activities in different parts of India, with policies that were often discrepant and results that were not always those intended, they had also to justify what they were doing to Parliament and other interested agencies in their own country. What emerged from these activities was a number of distinctions between different regions of India, periods of time, and types of government that did not appear in the work of Mill.

The quarrel over whether Indian states were autocratic despotisms of the Asiatic variety or feudal states comparable to those of the Holy Roman Empire did not end with Mill. Some colonial scholars continued to fashion an image of the Indian state as feudal or post-tribal. Few of them were prepared to be as bold as Burke. The states that they came to take as exemplary of this feudalism were those hill states designated as Rajput and not the great empires of the plains. The 'seminal' work they pointed to was that of James Tod (1782–1835).[4]

Tod considered the Rajputs to be descendants of the Scyths, Dark Ages Aryans from Central Asia (1920: I, 24–9), and the same in origin as the tribes of early Europe (1920: I, 73). He assumed, in his opening comments on the

[4] Going to Bengal in the service of the East India Company in 1799, he was eventually appointed Political Agent in the Western Rajput States in 1818, retired in 1822–3, and first published his book on Rajasthan (1920) in 1829–32.

'feudal system' in Rajasthan, that the institutions of all these Scyths were analogous because they had the same origin (154). He wrote: 'It is in these remote regions, so little known to the Western world, and where original manners lie hidden under those of the conquerors, that we may search for the germs of the constitutions of European States' (155). Citing Hallam, historian of the Middle Ages in Europe, Tod argued that the feudal compact, which produced mutual sympathy or loyalty by way either of 'ancient prejudice' or 'acknowledged merit', relied almost exclusively on the former in Rajasthan (148), evidence, no doubt, of its earliness.

Tod depicted the Rajput ruler as a man who shared his sovereignty and divinity with other Rajput rulers and nobles by virtue of their common descent from the Sun or Moon (or Fire). These were, he asserted, the 'earliest objects of adoration' (1920: II, 623) in India, and he held that the Horse Sacrifice was the oldest and most important of the 'festivals' in honour of the Sun performed by the Indic branch of the Scyths (1920: I, 91–5). A Rajput performed it 'to signalise his reign and paramount sovereignty' (1920: I, 60). The descent of Indian royalty from *two* gods (rather than one), as laid down in the *Purāṇas*, the 'sacred volumes' of the Indians, was no accident. It set the stage for a system of 'feuds' in which warriors of the two 'races' descended from these deities, and the dynasties within these, were perennially related as rivals (43–4, 47, 60). As implied in the concept of feud, this rivalry was not simply a lawless war of each against all (as in Mill); it was, albeit barbaric, itself an inferior substitute for the legal resolution of disputes (210–12). Under a strong prince or a paramount king the incidence of feuds might be reduced, but it remained an essential feature of Rajput polity. Consistent with his tendency to equate the Rajputs of Mughal India with the Kshatriyas of ancient India, Tod took the rivalry of the Kurus and Panchalas, as narrated in the *Mahābhārata*, as the canonical expression of this system of feuds. The divine king of Tod was, thus, divided against himself by his divinity more than, as in the despotic view, he was set over his subjects.

The principle of government in these states was 'truly patriarchal' because in them 'the greater portion of the vassal chiefs, from the highest of the sixteen peers to the holders of a *chursa* [skin or hide] of land, claim affinity in blood to the sovereign' (1920: I, 155–6). The division of lands among the Rajputs reflected this sharing of authority. The 'best and richest' land, located 'in the heart of the country' (and known by the term *khalisa*) was reserved for the king himself. It was the 'nerve and sinew of sovereignty' (166). The lands around this were distributed to vassals of four grades, ranging from the 'sixteen', who 'appear in the presence only on special invitation, upon festivals and solemn ceremonies, and are the hereditary councillors of the crown' (167) to the 'offsets of the younger branches' of the king's family.

The Brahmans in Tod very much occupy a background role. They are not the all-powerful conspirators of Mill. They did not, claimed Tod, even form a separate priestly class until Hindu India declined. The mental hold that they had over the Rajputs and especially over the peasantry greatly increased then, but it was no stronger than in the 'dark ages' of Europe (1920: II, 594–7). Tod placed 'legislative authority' in his ideal Rajput state in the hands of the prince and not, as the despoticists did, in the hands of Brahmans. He described the prince, with the aid of his civic council, the four ministers of the crown and their deputies, as promulgating 'all the legislative enactments in which the general rights and wants of the community were involved'. This authority was exercised by all the Rajput councils in a kingdom, each of which was 'a miniature representation of the sovereign's', and not by a sovereign Crown in Parliament.

The ministers of a Rajput state, according to Tod, held lands on an 'official' and not a hereditary basis. This was so because they were not of the ruling race, which alone had hereditary rights, and not because they were the appointees of a despot, serving at his pleasure. The ministers were, however, assimilated to this model. All preferred land to cash salary (1920: I, 165). Yet it would be a mistake to characterize Tod's account as opposing in a simple fashion the 'appanage' system of the Asiatic despot to the 'central machinery' of Mill's European state or of seeing in it too close an anticipation of the 'segmentary' state (5.6.4). Here and there one obtains from Tod the idea that certain principles of complementation were brought to bear in the assignment of these offices. For example, in his description of the *purdhan* or premier, he states that he was a 'military minister' and a Rajput, who was distinguished from the 'civil minister' who was 'never of this caste' (150).

Tod held that the 'landed system' of the Rajputs exhibited 'greater purity' than those elsewhere in India because of its relative isolation. Tod marshalled varied evidence on land ownership, including discourse from the Rajasthani ryot:

He compares his right therein to the *akshay duba* [a tenacious grass that grows in all seasons and in the most intense heat], which no vicissitudes can destroy. He calls the land his *bapota* ['belonging to the father'], the most emphatic, the most ancient, the most cherished, and the most significant phrase his language commands for patrimonial inheritance. (1920: I, 572–3)

He backed these up with references to Manu and an 'ancient adage' of Rajputana: ' "The government is owner of the rent, but I am the master of the land" ' (573) and concluded that 'the ryot (cultivator) is the proprietor of the soil in Mewar' (572) and not any oriental despot.

Tod's account contains many relapses into political atomism and oriental despotism, including a self-contradictory description of 'village republics'. On the whole, however, if we give priority to his own descriptive passages and set aside the framing of his account, we do get glimpses of polities with complex constitutions that are autonomous agents and not just stereotyped Eastern autocracies. Any serious reader cannot but be impressed with the extent to which Tod's 'feudal' image addresses the discursive and non-discursive practices of the Rajputs. That, however, was not the point of his *Annals*.

Hunting bigger game, Tod contended that the feudal polity of the Rajputs was the essence of the Hindu state in general and not simply the outcome of Hindu states which reproduced themselves, with great effort, on the periphery of more powerful Islamic states in northern India. The scholar-administrator, lectured Tod, has observed to little purpose who does not trace a uniformity of design, which at one time had ramified wherever the name of Hindu prevailed: the language has been modified, and terms have been corrupted or changed, but the primary pervading principle is yet perceptible; and whether we examine the systems of Khandesh, the Carnatic, or Rajasthan, we shall discover the elements to be the same. (1920: I, 573–4)

Although he did not say so at length, Tod saw despotism as the essence of Muslim rather than Hindu rule. Slightly later writers, including the Sanskritist H. H. Wilson, commentator on Mill, were quite explicit about this (Mill, 1858: II, 127; Campbell, 1852: 75–6). Mill had had the right idea; he just had the wrong religion.

If Tod was indeed correct that the essence of the Indian state was feudal and not despotic, the implication for future courses of action that his acquisitive colleagues might take was serious. The very essence of the Rajput state that was so endearing was also the very source of its weakness. Hence:

In no country has the system ever proved efficient. It has been one of eternal excitement and irregular action; inimical to order, and the repose deemed necessary after conflict for recruiting the national strength. The absence of an external foe was but the signal for disorders within, which increased to a terrific height in the feuds of the great rival factions ... (1920: I, 174)

The corollary was that the Hindu state was not a threat to British imperial aims: 'We have nothing to apprehend from the Rajput States if raised to their ancient prosperity. The closest attention to their history proves beyond contradiction that they were never capable of uniting ...'. The British rulers could save, restore, and co-opt polities of this type. Tod was quite explicit about the relationship they could (and, as Tod's editor points out, did) have with them:

Let there exist between us the most perfect understanding and identity of interests; the foundation-step to which is to lessen or remit the galling, and to us contemptible tribute, now exacted, enfranchise them from our espionage and agency, and either unlock them altogether from our dangerous embrace, or let the ties between us be such only as would ensure grand results: such as general commercial freedom and protection, with treaties of friendly alliance. Then if a Tatar or a Russian invasion threatened our eastern empire, fifty thousand Rajputs would be no despicable allies. (1920: I, 223–4)

Tod's feudal clan monarchy was not Burke's Holy Roman Empire. Tod depicted the Rajput 'system' as an early, pristine form of governance, the essence of which was princely feuding, thin-skinned and hot-headed, and not as the late, over-ripe feudalism of Germany. The major difference between Tod's and Mill's Hindu monarchs was this: Tod's prince was the instrument of a transcendent structure of clan rivalries. The chivalric warrior, he was, as a result of the disunity inherent in that structure, the perennial patient (and sometime victim) of the despotic king who stood outside it. That despot was Mill's prince, the instrument of the Brahmanical caste sytem. The difference between him and Mill was over which of these, the feudal Rajput or the despotic autocrat, constituted the *essence* of Hindu, and hence Indian, government and not over whether there were despots of the sort described by Mill.

While both would have agreed that the Indian despot, whether the Hindu Maratha or the Mogul, would have to go, Tod, adumbrating the doctrine of 'indirect rule', would advocate the retention of a 'natural'– he called it 'feudal' – Rajput aristocracy as an instrument of British rule.

Indological discourse vacillated before the Sepoy or Indian Mutiny of 1857, between depicting the Hindu state as a despotism whose essence was the abuse of power (Mill) and as something of a feudalism whose essence was a tie of vassalage or vendetta (Tod, Wilson). From the very moment of its formation, however, Indological discourse, whichever of these positions its makers have taken, has agreed on one thing: Hindu kingship is the instrument of the transcendent post-tribal or ancient society typical of India, that of her castes, tribes, and clans. They differed primarily over whether that caste system was a form of disorder or inferior order, but not over its position as the true ruler of India.

The question that none of these pre-Mutiny writers had to face, however, was whether the Indian kingdoms were 'sovereign' nation-states. This became an issue when the British replaced the East India Company and the penumbral Mughal Empire with an empire of their own. It precipitated some rethinking about the essence of the ancient Indian state.

5.3.2   From Feudal to Tribal

One of the best examples of British discourse on the issue of sovereignty so far as India is concerned is to be found in the writings of Sir Alfred Comyn Lyall (1835–1911), who wrote a number of widely read essays, including one on Rajput states, after the Mutiny.[5] In that essay, Lyall called the comparison that Edmund Burke, arch-enemy of the East India Company, had made of India to the empire of Germany the 'great grandfather of all the false analogies that have since been current'. It had resulted in the 'popular notion' that a state in Asia denotes 'a territory occupied by a people of one nation under a king or ruler of their own nationality, as in France, England, or Spain at the present day'. If Asians were organized, like Europeans, into sovereign nation-states, then it would not be legitimate for the 'governing class' of another nation-state such as Britain, 'distinct in race and religion', the components of nationality, from the Asians, to impose its 'foreign rule' on them (Lyall, 1899: 221–2). Since, however, there were no nation-states in Asia, the question of their sovereignty did not arise:

But it cannot be too clearly understood that the unwilling subjection of one nationality to another, which in Europe is always supposed to constitute an oppression and a legitimate grievance, is a political condition absolutely different in kind from that forcible domination of one clan or family over other races or tribes which we so constantly find in Asia. (Lyall, 1899: 222)

Let us look more closely at this Asian essence that differed in kind and not just in degree from the sovereignty of the European nation-state.

[5] He was appointed Commissioner in Berar, central India, and Lieutenant-Governor of the Northwest Provinces, 1882–7.

Fundamental to this concoction was Maine's dichotomous scheme for classifying societies into ancient and modern. Ancient communities are defined by the attribute of kinship or blood. Modern nation-states are defined by association or contract. Sovereignty, not in the sense of the absolute capacity to exercise force, but in the sense of general will, was something implying contract or consent. This applied not only to internal relations within a state, but to external relations among states. Truly sovereign states could treat with one another. Sovereignty, so defined, can only be the property of the nation-state. It cannot be the property of a truly ancient state. There, internal relations (status) are defined by kinship, while external relations are defined by force. As Maine himself put it, 'The fundamental assumption is, that all men not united with you in blood are your enemies or your slaves. To associate on terms of equality or friendship with a man who is not in some sense your brother is an unnatural condition; if it be prolonged your neighbour grows into your brother' (Maine, 1883: 276).

We can now see where Lyall is heading in his discussion of Indian states. None of the Native States in India was a nationality. None was or ever had been constituted by the principle of territorial sovereignty. All were and had been under 'foreign' rule. None the less, there was an important distinction to be made with respect to the 'constitutions' of these states, once we had this major principle clear. A state, such as that of the Maratha prince, Sindia, did not consist of Marathas, but of the territories forcibly annexed in the recent past by a man and his son and their armies. It was an ancient state in the sense that it was constituted by the principle of force. Its ruler was, according to Lyall, a 'despot of the ordinary Asiatic species, ruling absolutely the lands which his ancestor seized by the power of a mercenary army' (Lyall, 1899: 224–5).

The Rajput states differed. Lyall accepted Tod's argument that the Rajput states which arose after the Muslim conquests were direct descendants of the ancient Hindu states and manifested within them the true nature of Hindu kingship.

Given his commitment to Maine's scheme, which was at once both classificatory and evolutionary, Lyall could not allow Tod's characterization of these kingships to stand. The idea that they were feudal implied that they were, or were about to become, as in Germany, modern sovereign states. So, Lyall proceeded to reconstitute the Rajput and thereby the Hindu state. Tod, he said, missed 'the radical distinction between the two forms of society, tribal and feudal'. According to Lyall, 'the cement of the system was something much stronger than feudalism' (Lyall, 1899: 243–4). Among the Rajputs, he contended, 'Land tenure is not the base of this noblesse, but their pure blood is the origin of their land tenure' (Lyall, 1899: 246). Maine himself fully endorsed Lyall's classification, declaiming that 'society' in Rajasthan was 'præ-feudal' or 'tribal' (Maine, 1883: 269).

There were some anomalies in this reworking. A Rajput state did not consist entirely of Rajputs and was perhaps no more than a moderated form of aristocratic despotism, for the rent-paying 'cultivating classes' which the Rajputs overcame had 'very few rights and privileges' and were often 'no more than rack-rented peasantry' (Lyall, 1899: 224–5). In some places, he also admitted, the original clan system had become 'superficially overlaid by feudal growth' and had long been rapidly sliding into the normal type of ordinary Oriental government, irresponsible personal despotism' (Lyall, 1899: 250–1). None the less, the pristine Rajput state did consist of the territories of a Rajput clan held for several centuries, and among the Rajputs of these states, at least, kinship acted as the unifying presence.

The discourse of Lyall, Maine, and Baden-Powell on Rajput states and sovereignty was of great importance in legitimating the rule of Britain in India.[6] It was vital, as Cohn (1983) has shown, in the constitution of the British Indian Empire as a sovereign state. Before that time, prior to the so-called Indian Mutiny, the British themselves had treated with the states of South Asia as though they were sovereign states (Keller, Lissitzyn, and Mann, 1938: 10–11).

One part of this reconstruction of the Hindu state as ancient or tribal and, hence, different in kind from the feudal or modern European state, still remained as a source of trouble. It was the idea that both were Aryan in origin. This permitted the possibility that India could change and become like its European cousins once again. The racialist ideology that envisioned empire as the outcome of conflict between higher and lower races (one might note how it explains why, in Maine's theory, certain tribes were more successful than others in extending their rule) came to prominence toward the end of the century, just in time to preclude this possibility. The idea that Indians and their institutions were primarily Dravidian (or aboriginal), and only modified by Aryan conquest, carried the tribalization of the Hindu state one step further and completed the process of making it into an institution different in kind from the European. Here is how our favourite proponent of this view, Baden-Powell, Dravidianized the Hindu kingship (1896: 192–200).[7]

Baden-Powell also took the 'clan monarchy' as the fundamentally Hindu state. He argued, however, not that it was a pristine Aryan institution, but that it was the result of conflict between the Aryans, with the stronger clan organization, and the Dravidians (and others) with the weaker, interacting in the Indian environment. To be sure, its personnel were, at least in the beginning, largely Aryan, but the form of rule itself, localized and clan-based, was essentially Indian.

The despotic state, the divine kingship of ancient Indian texts such as the Laws of Manu, what he refers to as the 'individual monarchy', was, in his eyes, a later and unstable outgrowth of the clan monarchy. He even went so far as to suggest that the large empires of ancient India were, in reality, fragile magnifications of the smaller clan states, in which the relation of emperor to vassal mostly replicated that of *raja* (usually taken to be the Indian term for

---

[6] The stripping away of sovereignty from the Indian states was not confined to the work of the Indologists. It was also taken up by Thomas H. Green (1886: II, 399–426), who seems to have been the English idealist philosopher most widely read by British students of moral and political philosophy in the last quarter of the nineteenth century (Passmore, 1966: 56–60). It also surfaced in the writing of imperial historians, the most famous of which was the textbook by Seeley (1971: 38, 41, 63, 163, 166–7, 179, 190, 193, 196). Finally, on the thinking that attempted to constitute the Raj as yet another of those transcendent European dream-states, consult Hutchins (1967).

[7] He relied heavily, as has so often been the case, on the work of a German Indologist, Heinrich Zimmer (1851–1910) (1879).

prince) to baron, and not centralized despotisms. The main difference between the imperial and the local in this image was that unity was more attenuated at the imperial level because the 'real' ties of blood have been replaced by 'fictive' ties, by those 'mythical' ancestors recorded in the *Purāṇas*.

To conclude, the essences that inhabited the scholarly discourse on India in the earlier part of the nineteenth century – utilitarian despotism and oriental feudalism – had been transmuted by the end of the century into the essences of force and kinship. The oriental despotism exemplified by the Marathas that Mill, among others, had represented as an abusive form of government, now came to have the exercise of force as its very essence. It ceased furthermore to be taken as the true Indian state. Many Indologists now considered it to be an aberration of another type, the clan monarchy. The feudal state of the Rajputs which Tod and others had opted for as representing the authentic Indian state has won out in the essentialist sweepstakes. But in order to hold this privilege it has had to abandon its life in the halfway house of Maine's ancient–modern typology and become representative of the earliest ancient polity above the level of the tribe itself, the diffuse clan monarchy. Its essence was now shared blood, and not that inchoate form of association and modernity, the feudal contract.

The 'true' Hindu state, based on kinship (clan) ties and necessarily small and weak, was just the sort of jungle plant (patients) the jungle officers could manage. Lyall drew this eloquent conclusion:

So it is; but if plants are to be hardy, we must give them time to grow. It is certain that these Rajput societies, held together by all the cumbrous bonds and stays of a primitive organism, present far more promising elements of future development, than powerful and well-ordered despotisms of the normal Asiatic type, where a mixed multitude are directly under the sway of one ruler, however able, who degrades or dignifies at his will. (Lyall, 1899: 260)

Many, if not most, Hindu states have been of the individual monarchy variety. But these, because they were severed from their roots, were inherently volatile, depending, as in any despotism, on the personal qualities of the monarchs. Which is to say that the actual Hindu states were for the most part deviations from their own 'normal' type, that of the clan monarchy!

The major point, though, was that neither of these new types of state possessed sovereignty. The earlier notions of despotism and feudalism had both presupposed sovereignty. They were assumed to differ only in degree from the European states of the time. Both of their awkward offspring differed in kind. So long as the idea that the past states of India were sovereign entities was allowed to persist, however, it would be flagrantly illogical for the British to claim that they had not violated the sovereignty of those states by superimposing their own imperial state. Once, however, the states of India had been theorized as 'ancient' in Maine's sense of the term, meaning that states were either 'tribal' (based on the principle of blood-relatedness) or the negation of that (based on conquest, the use of physical force, that is, 'despotic'), then one could wipe away the sovereignty 'mistakenly' attributed to Indian states in the past. Scholars and officials could look on the divine kingships of India as volatile, coercive organizations. Although such states tried to substitute the imagined divinity of the king for real blood as the principle of unity, they lacked genuine legitimacy not only in the modern world but in the ancient world of post-tribal India. The only rightful Indian kingships were the kin-based monarchies which Indian despots, masquerading as gods, had victimized.

The tribalization (and Dravidianization) of India set the scene retrospectively for the arrival of the British who, in their post-Mutiny view of India, had it as their destiny not simply to establish a trading venture in that subcontinent, but to build an Indian empire.

5.4 IMPERIAL MONARCHY, WESTERN ORDER IN THE EAST

5.4.1 Administrative Despotism

While scholars were busy emphasizing the difference between India's ancient, post-tribal polities and their own modern one in order to justify their replacement with the Indian Empire, they were also asking themselves what sort of government that should be in India. To some extent, of course, the answer depended on which party wielded power in Parliament. But for the most part, however, it depended on making arguments about what served British interests and what suited India. Clearly, they could not establish there the sort of representational polity they fancied themselves to have at home, especially if they believed their argument that Indian political institutions were fundamentally different in origin and essence from their own. But then that representational polity was itself changing. The latter half of the nineteenth century in Britain saw the 'negative' liberalism of the utilitarians begin to give way to a 'positive' liberalism, that of a Maine or Disraeli. The older position privileged the legislative branch of a government. It was the true instrument of the 'individual', the repository of 'sovereignty', for it was in the legislature that the interests of individuals, to which the state was reducible, were represented. The state as a subject was the most successful of individuals, the supreme legislator. The executive remained in the background as the enforcer of law and order, as the punitive disciplinarian patriarch, invoked only when the children misbehaved, when the selfishness constitutive of human nature got out of hand.

This image of the representational polity as an atomistic collection of competing individuals watched over by an aloof, authoritative magistrate came to be challenged by a more 'maternal' image. The worst features of capitalism, some argued, had to be ameliorated, and the best way to do this was for a state to whom individuals would give up some of their sovereignty to take a more active role. This entailed a shift to the executive, to the monarch or head of state as a 'symbol' of authority, justice, and unity, and to a more prominent civil service or bureaucracy which was supposed to take positive steps to ensure the welfare of the state's subjects. The 'administered polity', one in which an elite administrative corps became the effective sovereign instrument of the community, the organ of its 'general will', displaced the representational. Concurrently, the knowing subjects of this discourse began to use a new 'organic' metaphor, one that incorporated the determinism of the 'mechanical' metaphor, but which emphasized the welfare of the whole over the competition of the individual atoms. They saw the state as consisting of interdependent, yet hierarchically ordered parts, coordinated by a civil service.

The history of the state in India converged with this.[8] The end of the Mutiny was marked by the creation of a new polity there. The Mogul was despatched and the East India Company was seen off. By a proclamation in 1858, Queen Victoria created a new polity, the Indian Empire of which she was sovereign. An important ingredient in this new polity was the 'personal' relationship the princes and people of India were to have with their new sovereign. Before the Mutiny, states that apologist for the new imperium, W. W. Hunter, 'the problem for the Company was to divide and govern; the problem of the Queen's Government in India is to unite and rule' (1903: 41). The basis for this new unity was the contract implicit in the Queen's proclamation, in which promises were made. The most conspicuous of these was the promise to the princes that they would be given 'indefeasible hereditary title' to their states. This, in Hunter's analysis, not only removed a threat to British rule, one that had contributed to the Mutiny (along with 'religious fanaticism'). According to him, it also 'took a vast heterogeneous collection of powerful men, whose rights varied widely both in extent and in origin, and it united them into a body of firm supporters of the British rule (1903: 23–4).

The British thus appeared to be creating the very feudal confederation, which Burke had said, by way of the analogy he drew with the Holy Roman Empire, was there in India in the first place. This was, however, a pre-Raphaelite simulation of feudalism. Hunter makes it clear that these chiefs, who reigned over one-third of the country and one-fifth of the population of the subcontinent, were themselves administered, through the device of residency (Hunter, 1882: 6), and himself admits that the princes gradually took on the 'role of the stage-king in a Court pageant' and existed as '*tableaux vivants*' (1903: 45). The symbolic centralization of this new polity was accompanied, furthermore, by a gradual centralization of the 'administrative machine'. On the whole, Hunter considered this new empire a success: 'when one looks back on the race-hatreds of 1857, the most unexpected as well as the most beautiful of the new growths in India is the sentiment of personal loyalty to the Throne' (1903: 22).

The idea that contending princes, divided by race and subsisting in a post-tribal, Hobbesian state of war could be transformed, at a stroke, into an administered leviathan, an empire whose unity was symbolized by a monarch at the centre, permitted scholars to focus attention on the distinction between empires and individual monarchies in India. Philologists and historians, who were trying to come to terms with newly recovered texts (and with a wealth of inscriptional evidence), took up this new interest. They used much of this evidence to show that early India had imperial states and that they were administered polities. The ancient India that emerged from these characterizations began to look more and more like the mature ancient societies of

[8] The widely praised account of Thompson and Garratt distinguishes paternal from bureaucratic administration, claiming that the former type crested after the Mutiny (1962: 472–83), declining during a subsequent period of *laissez-faire*, from around 1870 to 1902 (483–98); the 'heyday' of bureaucracy none the less came during the period 1880–95 (527–40).

Alexandrian Greece and Rome than the post-tribal antiquity that preceding scholars had imposed on India. As we shall see, however, the imperial ancient India of this new image did not have the same origin or essence that scholars have attributed to late antiquity in Europe.

Among the texts scholars considered the most important in this respect was the *Indika* of Megasthenes, an envoy sent to the court of Chandragupta (Sandracottos) Maurya, around 302 BC, by Seleukos Nikator, the successor of Alexander in Asia. The collection (Schwanbeck, 1966) and translation (McCrindle: 1877) of the fragments of this text made available new and 'reliable' Western accounts (Lassen, 1858–74) of ancient India.

Vincent Smith, the hegemonic historian of ancient India, was a fish in the waters of the administered polity and parental monarchy. The state that appears in his *Early History* as fundamentally Indian was the absolute or individual monarchy normally engaged in hostile relations with its neighbours. Empires, however, appeared as an important exception to this rule of anarchy.

Such was the Mauryan state. According to Smith, Megasthenes had described it as an autocracy (1924: 126–40).[9] The Greek envoy (whose testimony on 'caste' was also used) describes an 'imperial court' that was, we are told, maintained 'with barbaric and luxurious ostentation', implying that it commanded vast resources. Being an autocracy, everything depended on the personality of the monarch: 'The strong hand which won the empire was needed to keep it, and the government was administered with stern severity.' The emperor maintained a standing army at 'enormous numerical strength', one that had attained 'a high degree of efficiency, as measured by an Oriental standard'. This was just the sort of instrument of force required for the maintenance of unity in a state based neither on rational compact nor on the emotional bond of blood. As one would expect, Smith infers from the Greek account that 'agricultural land' was 'crown property' and even rehearses the Marxian idea that irrigation was deeply implicated in this, as in any Asiatic despotism. But because this despotism had force as its essence, Smith reminds us that 'in the midst of all the gold and glitter, and in spite of the most elaborate precautions, uneasy lay the head that wore the crown.' None the less, Smith gives his condescending approval of this administrative despotism, telling us that Chandragupta is entitled 'to rank among the greatest and most successful kings known to history'.

The empire of Chandragupta Maurya was divided, according to Smith, into 'viceroyalties' that were normally entrusted to members of the royal family, that is, sovereignty (here denoting supreme power rather than a general will) was shared, as in a clan monarchy, among blood relations. Within each of these provinces, we learn, there was a 'civil administration' of 'inspectors' and 'magistrates'. The historian did not condemn this instrument of government as one of relentless oppression. He observed that although 'based upon the personal autocracy of the sovereign', it was 'something better than a merely arbitrary tyranny', implying that it was quasi-lawful.

[9] The earlier amateur history by James Talboys Wheeler (1824–97), civil servant in Madras and Burma from 1858 to 1891, also used Megasthenes to depict ancient Indian empires as despotisms (1874, III, 178–204).

The capital was administered by a 'municipal commission' divided into six boards or committees. Echoing the findings of the Census, Smith construed these boards as an upward elaboration of the caste council. As for the inspectors, Smith described them as 'special agents' or 'news-writers' in accord with the 'usual practice of Oriental monarchies', presumably because they were integral to the functioning of a state based on force rather than on sovereignty as an attribute of nationality and consisting of a general will. The people were generally honest and the criminal law efficiently administered, crime being 'repressed with terrible severity', including mutilation and capital punishment, when it did occur. The implication, once again, was that force was required to maintain order in an imperial Indian state.

The Mauryan state which Smith extracted from Megasthenes is clearly a modified oriental despotism. He has silently built the theory that Indian governments were based either on kinship or force and not on the European idea of sovereignty into his depiction, but he has selected the individual monarchy, the one based on the exercise of force in the form of an army and inspectors, as the true type of Indian state. He confirms this elsewhere when he asserts that the clan monarchies and other tribal forms of government, whether they were located in the Punjab of Alexander's time or in the Nepal and Bihar of the Buddha, were a Mongolian institution foreign to India and (hence?) 'gradually disappeared' (1924: 145–6). He has, however, conceded that family ties provided an element of unity in an empire.

The publication in 1905 of translated extracts from a major and ancient text on 'political economy', Kauṭilya's *Arthaśāstra*, followed by an edition of the work itself (1909) and then an English translation (1915), caused a stir in Indology.[10] Smith responded to this event in later editions of his account. The text was hailed, though not without the usual arguments and counter-arguments over its authorship and date, as one of great importance. Here, for the first time, we could gaze on ancient India through the eyes of an author – supposedly a Brahman courtier of the Mauryan emperor – that were not clouded by religion. According to Smith, 'Books like the so-called *Laws of Manu* and *Dharmasastras* set forth the Brahman ideal – the treatise of Chandragupta's minister openly discards ideals and presents a plain unvarnished statement of the immoral practice of kings and Brahman ministers' ... (1924: 152). At last, the cloak of divinity is removed to reveal – what? British Indologists took the *Arthaśātra* to 'endorse' and 'extend' what they had already squeezed from Megasthenes.[11] Smith, no exception, took the text as a warrant for his view that force overlaid with patriarchy was the essence of the Indian state (1924: 145–52).

The ancient Indian kingdoms and empires that Smith and his colleagues imagined was largely the product of the British theory of imperial government. Smith saw a successful ancient Indian monarch such as the Mauryan emperor as a sort of pre-modern hero of the administrative state, a civil servant's fantasy

[10] R. Shamasastri, curator of the Government Oriental Library in Mysore, was the scholar who did this.

[11] See the 1914 Preface of James Fleet, epigrapher and administrator-historian of the Deccan, where he spent thirty years, to the English translation.

come true. The language used by Lionel Barnett is even more revealing of the hegemony of the administered polity in contemporary discourse because, as an old-fashioned partisan of *laissez-faire*, he saw it as nightmarish. According to him, the *Arthaśāstra* describes a 'civil service' and a 'paternal administration;' it 'depicts a society choking in the deadly grip of a grinding bureaucracy' (1913: 104). That society was 'an infinitely elaborate organism' that required for its maintenance a 'vast machinery' which was 'centralised under the direction of the king, assisted by ministers, a large staff of officials, and an enormous host of secret agents working with more than Machiavellian methods in his service' (1913: 97–8).

Whether the British Indologists adhered to the older 'negative' liberalism or adopted the more conservative 'positive' liberalism so far as British politics was concerned, they tended to opt for the latter position when it came to British rule in India. As Smith said in a book of advice to India's constitutional reformers, 'No form of government except the autocratic was recognized as being suitable to Indian conditions' (1919: 19). Indians 'crave for government by a person to whom they can render loyal homage, which passes easily into worship'. The Indian 'ideal of government' that gratified this craving was 'that of the virtuous Raja, who works hard, is easily accessible, is sternly and impartially just, yet loves his people as a father loves his children, and is guided by the advice of wise ministers based upon immemorial tradition' (1919: 21–2).

The 'Indian conditions' of which Smith speaks were, of course, nothing more than the type of society over which a government in the subcontinent had to preside, a caste society, which meant for Smith a society of repellent molecules and centrigual forces. Despotism, the essence of which was force tinged with kinship and haloed by religious awe, was the form of government required for transforming the inherently disorderly caste society (jungle metaphor) into a hierarchic, ordered whole (organic mechanical body metaphor). Because he held Indian society to be in essence disorderly, the ordinary monarchies of the subcontinent could do no more than reflect or express that disorder. To the extent that Indian kingship succeeded in producing an organic, imperial unity it must, Smith assumed, have been due to the 'influence' of a world-ordering rationality injected into India from outside.

There were, thus, two sorts of divine kingship in India. In the transcendent, imperial sort, divinity embodied a non-Indian element, an absolute, unitary will. The pseudo-patrimonial or 'feudal' state the British had built in India, one which privileged a symbolically enriched imperial Crown presiding, through a Viceroy-Governor-General over an Indian Empire comprised of the British Territories and the Princes of the Native States and governed by the bureaucracy of civil service, was its very quintessence (1919: 83–4, 111–14). Contrasted with this was another divine kingship, an immanent sort, that in which the state was transcended by a divisive caste society and its Brahman priests. There divinity was merely a cover for the ineffectual exercise of force directed by the subjective imagination and dispersive passions of the Hindu mind, rather than a symbol of the exercise of lawful sovereignty by the objective reason and unitary will of the outsider.

The history of divine kingship, the political history of India above the 'level' of her changeless village communities, was, for Smith, a narrative of the rise and fall of transcendent, externally based empires against a background of ceaseless contests among immanent monarchies, divine kingships of the indigenous sort. Racial antagonisms inside India were responsible for the disorders that normally afflicted the body politic. Outside influences, on the other hand, were responsible for ancient India's two moments of imperial unity, under the Mauryas and the Guptas. Like so many other Indologists, Smith held that the world-ordering rationality which he assumed was needed to bring about this unity was the property of the Aryans and not of India's indigenes, the so-called Dravidians. But he differed from most in his belief that India's moments of imperial unity were precipitated by the Eastern, Iranian Aryans, bearers of the world-bearing force we know as oriental despotism, and not by the European Aryans, bearers of the reason and will that gave forth Europe's superior political and economic institutions (1924: 158–9, 289–90). The effect of this theory of Persian influence, of course, was to justify the transcendent despotism of the British Raj by showing that the polity that the British had erected in India was not only true to India's history, but even an improvement on it.

The subtext of this discourse may have been even more important than its main text from the standpoint of the Indian nationalisms that rose to prominence around the turn of the century. There is no question, in Smith's India, of returning to a glorious Aryan past that was Indian. That past, which in his scheme meant empire, was necessarily the product of an active male and Aryan rationality that was foreign. It arrived by conquest and imposed itself on a non-Aryan populace that was inherently divisive and not contingently divided. Indians, thus, needed outside rule in the remote past, as they did now, if they were to remain in a single, unitary state. Smith's history of ancient India was, thus, really a history of the present. As it had been in antiquity so it is in our own day.

5.4.2 From Ancient Unity to Medieval Anarchy

Smith and his successors have written the political histories of India down to the time of the Gupta Empire, the ancient India that ran parallel to ancient Greece and Rome, in the same triumphal mode that characterized histories of the West, for was not this early history one of the success of outside Reason in creating political unity? The history scholars have provided for India's divine kingships in the subsequent 'medieval' period, however, is a story of decline, one in which the real, underlying India, that selfish and quarrelsome *femme* of the *fin de siècle*, engulfs her male empire-builders and administrators. This image of a fragmented India was largely a fabrication. Chapter 6 will argue that the polities of the eighth to tenth centuries can be seen to have been organized into a single imperial formation in which the Rashtrakutas, whose headquarters were in the Deccan, exercised hegemony. First, however, let me show how Smith's dismal history was fashioned and why.

The denouement of Smith's history was the conquest of India by the Huns, one of those races every so often made to swarm by the Asian historian somewhere in Central Asia before fanning out to pillage and ravage the world. Noted for their 'strength', 'rapid motions', and 'cruelty', their invasions 'shook Indian society in Northern India to its foundations, severed the chain of tradition, and brought about a rearrangement of both castes and ruling families'. The descendents of these Huns, Hinduized, were the so-called Rajput dynasties of medieval India, the alleged ancestors of the very Rajputs whom Tod or Maine had taken as emblematic of a fractionating feudal or tribal kingship in India (1924: 340–1, 422–9). They emerged after the years of 'unrecorded anarchy' that followed Harsha's reign of unity. The clan monarchy which Smith marginalized in his account of early India thus came into prominence when he turned to his account of the 'medieval' period.

The Rajputs were themselves divided along racial lines. Those of north India, and intermittently in the Deccan, belonged to 'the Hun group of tribes or hordes' (1924: 427, 429). Mostly, however, the rulers of the Deccan were 'indigenous', apparently descended from 'the so-called aboriginal tribes, Gonds, Bhars, Kols, and the like' (1924: 429). One dynasty in south India was derived from 'criminal tribes', while others derived from one of the three local Dravidian dynasties.

Harsha had, according to Smith, established 'a strong paramount power able to control the conflicting interests of the various races, clans, and creeds subject to his temporary sway'. The Hunnish and indigenous kingships that followed, however, became the instruments of these conflicts:

The unceasing wars of the mediaeval period become a little more intelligible and interesting when they are regarded as being in large part a secular struggle between the foreign Rajputs of the north and the indigenous Rajputs of the south. Of course, this arrangement of the sides did not always hold good, and powers normally at feud sometimes made friends and contracted alliances with the other, or all parties momentarily combined against the Muhammadans. But I think it is true that, as a general rule, the Rājputs formed by the social promotion of 'aborigines' were inimical to the Rājputs descended from 'barbarian' immigrants. (1924: 430)

The idea of a general decline rests to a large extent on the need to see a Hindu India disintegrate politically, a need built into the hegemonic constructs of Indian civilization in their major variants. Teleologically, this provided an immediate 'cause' – the 'underlying' cause would, of course, prove to be caste as racial conflict – for 'the' Muslim 'conquest' of India that would be even more apocalyptic than the previous conquests. Certainly it cannot be denied that the notion of political fragmentation in the so-called early medieval period rests in part on (or is confirmed by) the observation that the number of 'independent' dynasties or kingdoms had increased in this period while the geographic extent of the largest empires had diminished. This evidence alone, however, did not permit Smith (and later historians) to depict medieval India as divided into smaller states. Two assumptions he made, one about political geography and another about population, assisted in this effort.

Smith assumed that nation-states and civilizations had their centres and peripheries. These were 'natural', that is, based on inherent considerations of strategy and resources, and were, therefore, unchanging. India was, for Smith, divided into three major geographic areas – the North, the Deccan, and the

South. These were themselves nothing but the territorial doubles of the racial groups Smith had constituted as the agents of India's history. He did not, however, treat these three agents as equals. The paramount power in India, when such existed, 'invariably had its seat in Northern India' (1924: 6) (a widely shared view that the British governors of the subcontinent realized, in red sandstone, when they shifted the capital of their Indian Empire from Calcutta to New Delhi in 1911). This Aryocentric geography was reflected in the organization of Smith's narrative. One major figure, a north Indian emperor and the empire over which he presided, was the focus of attention at each turn in Smith's narrative of the ancient period. When he related his account of the medieval period, however, he shifted from this unifocal principle to a three-part geographic one – the North, the Deccan, and the South – and gave his accounts of successive dynasties within these confines. This change in narrative strategies precluded the possibility of showing that the major centre of India shifted first to the Deccan and then farther to the South.

The second assumption made by Smith (and most other students of Indian history) was that the population of India reached its pre-modern peak, estimated at 100 million, during the time of the Mauryas. That is, he assumed that, when India developed into a full-fledged imperial state, it attained the teeming population that the discourses on oriental despotism and the Asiatic mode of production would seem to require. He also assumed either that India's population remained static from the time of the Mauryas until the Mughals (Davis, 1951: 24–5) or that it declined from its high point in Gupta India during the 'dark ages' of the Rajputs, just as it did in Western Europe.

Presupposing their Aryocentric geography and oriental demography, scholars have represented these states in their maps (Davies, 1959) and read the political history they fabricated from them. That history consisted of the narrative of a society that was made to be inherently dependent on the intervention of a Western political economy for its unity and prosperity.

The story of medieval India showed what happened when the barbaric Asian horde displaced the Aryan presence and the 'civilizations' of the Indian indigenes came to the surface: caste, the substantialized agent of Indian history, gained the upper hand. Just as the passions overcame the will in the Hindu mind of medieval India, so political anarchy, the concomitant of caste (itself the result of racial conflict), overcame the politically unifying influence of that double of the European, the Eastern Aryan. A transcendent, divine kingship, consisting of benevolent despotic empires strategically centred on a north India, gave way to an immanent form of divine kingship, that of the Huns and Dravidians, consisting of kingdoms that grew smaller and smaller in size and population and more and more antagonistic as a transcendent caste and its religion, Hinduism, took command.

To have represented the kingdoms of India as relatively autonomous agents, as complex, inter-related polities that could unite through pacts as well as 'force' within a single imperial formation and create new centres not deter-mined by a fixed military topography, would have undermined this whole orientalist project. So Smith despatched the cruel Huns to prepare the way for the still worse advent of Islam, which would, in turn, clear the way for the miraculous arrival by sea of the better Aryan, the Western or European. He would cut and clip in the Dravidian jungle and prevent the Russians setting fire to the whole green expanse. This history of medieval decline did not stop, however, by preparing for the modern. If Smith's history of ancient India was, in effect, a history of its present, his narrative of medieval India was really a parable of the future, of what would happen in India if the British withdrew.

5.5   IMPERIAL DEATH AND NATIONAL REBIRTH

5.5.1   One or Many, Contract or Dharma?

The administered polities that were in place throughout the Anglo-French imperial formation by the First World War were monist and absolutist in their view of sovereignty, and none more so than the new despotism the British had constructed in their Indian empire. Legitimate power, the general will, was to be exercised in the last instance by one agent, the central government. Early in this century, a range of views that have come to be called 'pluralist' began to be opposed to these statist ideas. Its advocates argued that sovereignty be denied the state in order to preserve personal liberty. Rather, power should be shared between the state and autonomous local governmental bodies and voluntary associations (Nicholls, 1975: 1–12). One strain of thought here, the European, retained an organic image of the community, but shifted the locus of activity from the centre to the periphery of the state. Of particular importance here was the protean writing of Harold J. Laski (1893–1950), Professor of Political Science at the London School of Economics from 1926. Another later strain, the American, retains an atomistic image of the community, viewing the state not only as mediator between conflicting 'interests' but also as active intervenor in the affairs of its citizenry (Nicholls, 1975: 113–19).

The nationalist and idealist attempts to rebut the prevailing despoticist view of India were formed against the background of these intellectual practices (American pluralism apart). The nationalists, of course, denied that a divine kingship based on force (or on post-tribal solidarity) and lacking sovereignty, the attribute of a 'true' nation-state, was the essence of Indian government. They pursued one (or both) of two strategies in mounting their counterattack. One was empirical and emphasized the parallels between Indian and European (British) thoughts and institutions. The other was more evaluative than empirical, allowing for differences to exist between the political ideas and practices of India and the West but placing a higher value upon those of the East than the orientalist construct did. I shall argue that while the national historians transformed the 'divine kingship' of that construct, they did not really abandon it. They turned Indian kingship into a constitutional monarchy and they transformed the divinity of the king into a sacred national unity, but they did not give up the ideas that some sort of social or cultural unity transcended the Indian state and that the Hindu kingships of medieval India were the symptom of the decline of a caste-divided society.

The most important of the early nationalist historians of ancient India was Kashi Prasad Jayaswal (1881–1937), a barrister educated at Oxford and at

Patna University. He argued that many of the 'tribes' Indologists had found in ancient India were artificially constituted 'republics' and not natural units. He also criticized Vincent Smith's theory that these republican tribes were of Mongolian rather than Aryan origin, and, hence, not really Indian (Jayaswal, 1924: I, 179–89). He concluded that 'democratic and republican states were experiments of the Hindus themselves' (1924: I, 189).

Jayaswal argued that Hindu monarchies in ancient India were similar to the British and not inherently despotic. They were based on the rule of law and had constitutional checks – executive authority was vested in a cabinet of ministers, legislative in a popular assembly, and so on. He denied that the theory of divine kingship advocated in Manu was ever really adopted. He took the coronation rites (*abhisheka*) of the Hindu king as a religious expression of the king's subservience to the law and to the public assemblies, those of the 'capital city' (*paura*) and of the 'realm' (*jānapada*), and of his participation in a contractual arrangement with the people. Correspondingly, he rejected the idea that the king was subservient to the Brahman priesthood (1924: II, 59).

Jayaswal concluded that Hindu kingship was a 'trust' given him 'for the prosperity of the People', which he meant in an 'immediate material' sense. The king was a 'servant of the people getting his wages' (1924: 188–9). This idea of a trust is, in retrospect, his most important idea, his version of a social contract. The people agreed to give up certain of their rights and wealth to a king in exchange for the protection that he would render them.

Scholars heavily criticized Jayaswal's interpretations of texts and his overall characterization, as one might expect, and few today would accept his views without considerable modification. The main problem, however, is that the state that he depicted appears to be simply another representational Anglo-Saxon state, transplanted to Indian soil and transported back in time to antiquity. He has thus traded one essence, the force that maintains a semblance of order, for the utilitarian's human nature. But has he? Not really, for he has simply postponed the arrival of the Indological basket of essences. They do not appear in the Indian branch of the Aryans until around 700, after the republics had disappeared and the 'classical' constitutional monarchies of ancient India had declined (II, 205). For Jayaswal, then, divine kingship remained what it was for most of the British despoticists, a force-based monarchy held in thrall by the imagination of Hinduism and largely ineffectual in uniting a caste-divided society. Where he differed was in denying that it was the essence of Indian government. Divine kingship was a medieval departure from that essence, constitutionality, and not fundamental to Hindu government from the very beginning.

Quite different was the somewhat later work of Beni Prasad, a conservative religious idealist (Prasad, 1927).[12] He hewed rather closely to the Romantic construct of India, one which depicts it as standing in a relationship of complementation to the West rather than portraying it as either an inherently defective version of it or, as in Jayaswal's case, a parallel one. According to Prasad, 'in India religion claimed the whole allegiance of man' (1927: 3), so he

[12] Professor of Politics at the University of Allahabad, his contributions to the second volume of the *History and Culture of the Indian People*, edited by R. C. Majumdar (1951–) were cut short by his death in 1945.

did not portray ancient India as a secular, modern polity. Unlike Jayaswal, he had no illusions 'with regard to the idea that India made notable contributions to the theory of politics, and that constitutional monarchy was early recognised' (1927: vi).

Prasad duly rehearsed the idea that Indian thought lacks the world-ordering rationality of the West. From the Indian mentality, characterized by the 'power of imagination' and always 'searching for unity' (1927: 2), he derived India's distinctive social institution: 'The Hindu tendency to push an idea to its logical extreme produced caste where Europe stopped at class' (1927: 6). Prasad held that political theory was very closely tied to ethics. 'Not only does it, as a rule, assume certain fundamental principles of morality but it always seeks to direct life' (1927: 4). The Indian state was, therefore, not the prophylactic agent constructed by the classical English philosophers. It was an institution with positive, albeit conservative goals. The 'ultimate object', that of salvation, was not, however, to be attained without first being a householder. Hence 'the worldly life has to be cared for if the excellence of souls is to be promoted' (1927: 348–9).

How, according to Beni Prasad, was the ancient Indian state constituted so as to accomplish these positive ethical goals? Sovereignty ultimately resided in Dharma itself. The king had to swear to uphold it at his coronation and he had to conduct his 'administration' lawfully. Effective sovereignty, however, resided in the monarch himself (1927: 358) and not in a ruling class (Maine) or in a balanced constitution (Mill, Jayaswal), a crown in parliament. Monarchy in India was 'despotic' (Smith), but the monarch was not supposed to be arbitrary. He was neither above the law nor himself the highest lawmaker. He was bound to consult with a council of ministers on a regular basis even though that council was an advisory body with no power of veto. The king was, thus, the administrator *par excellence*, responsible to no institution. More than that, however, he was an ethical leader and 'defender of the faith', that being nothing other than the reified, ecumenical Hinduism of modern Advaita Vedānta, monist, idealist, and pantheist.

He apparently followed the idealists who held that authority was in some sense inherently divine, arguing that because the king was the instrument of Dharma (1927: 347), he was treated as divine: 'In connection with the whole complex of institutions, Hindu theory views the governmental power as sustaining social life, and giving it security and completeness. So, the king who stands for the government and for the state, is extolled as divine and even more than divine' (1927: 345).

What Prasad meant by Dharma, of course, is our old friend, the idealist's version of caste: 'it is the scheme of life, as proposed in the sacred texts, which the Government must recognise and enforce. It is not the state which originates social organization' (1927: 343). The king was, therefore, no legislator. He was dependent on the Brahmans and the castes for knowledge of what the laws are: 'In Hindu theory the king is bound to ascertain social law or usage from those who know it, and to enforce it to the best of his capacity' (1927: 345). Comparing Hindu kingship with his rendering of Hegel's state, Prasad pronounced: 'There is one fundamental difference between Hegelianism and Hindu political thought. The latter will not subordinate the fundamental Law to the state or the government' (1927: 345).

Beni Prasad then noted what would seem to be a contradiction: 'But when after postulating this condition, the Hindus embark on the glorification of the sovereign power, they leave even Hegel far behind. The government claims all loyalty. It is the incarnation of the absolute, a super-personality which absorbs the real, living personality of men and women' (1927: 345). Beni Prasad 'explained' this with Jayaswal's theory that the king holds his power as a 'trust' from the society or people, for this acted as a device to displace agency from the state on to a transcendent, idealized society or, more precisely, the idea of Dharma: 'Theory found a check to misrule not in any constitutional checks but in the inculcation of the idea of Dharma' (1927: 346). The idea of Dharma, of an unchanging, organic, unified society, was, thus, the substantialized maker of India, the true agent of India's states in the wider sense of the term (see also 2.3.2). The king was not the agent of those states. He was their instrument, their servant. It was, apparently, because he was the idea of social hierarchy made flesh that he was so lavishly divinized.

The exemplary state for those who adhered to this position was not the more centralized and secular Maurya Empire, but the 'federal' and 'feudal' empire of the Guptas, supporters of a revived Brahmanism and classical Hinduism. One enthusiast said, *contra* the British despotical image, that 'judged by the modern test of what a nation is, Gupta India was a nation state.' He provides an excellent summary of this stance:

the Gupta monarchs in conformity with the monarchs of old looked upon Dharma as something sacerdotal and endeavoured according to their best to protect the people according to the *Rājadharma* prescribed. Viewed from every aspect it was Dharma that was responsible for the well-being of both state and society. In the words of the Upanishad (*Brihadaranyakopanishad*) 'Dharma is the king of kings' (1952: 284)[13]

The idea that sovereignty is ultimately vested not in the state, but in an organically constituted society, comes close to the view being advanced by the European pluralists. Both wanted to see the state as somehow subordinate to society. Prasad's view differs, however, in one major respect: the characteristics of society and the state have been transposed in his construct of the Indian state. Where in pluralist discourse society is conceived of as multiple and changing and real (groups have 'personalities'; they are not reducible to their individual members), for Prasad it is a single, hierarchic, and static whole. That is, *society* in India is given the attributes of transcendence and permanence

[13] This is the position of the south Indian scholar, V. R. Ramachandra Dikshitar (1932: 284; 1952: 97, 284). Consult also the work of Vishwanath Prasad Varma. He maintained a sharp boundary between the individualistic and freedom-loving West and Hegel's totalitarian but ineffectual East (1974: 81, 177–80, 270–1). His doctoral dissertation, completed in 1950 in the Department of Political Science at the University of Chicago under the tutelage of the ultra-conservative Leo Strauss, Professor of Philosophy (himself held captive in that empiricist department), provides irrefutable 'proof' of India's essential difference, for has not the Other (properly educated) said it himself?

normally assigned in discussing Europe to the *state*. On the other hand, the plurality and fluidity usually said to be characteristic of society in Europe is, in India, attributed to the state. By and large, it is the idealist position that predominates, for in the end the Indian state is deduced from the unitary *idea* of a society rather than being seen as responsible to or grounded in any concrete social institutions.

Implicit in Prasad's construct is the idealist fiction that somehow a political community can be established in which politics, construed as the very principle of disorder itself, will be extruded. The recipe for this state is provided not by its inhabitants but by a single, abstract, transcendent and unchanging Dharma, to the principle of which everyone is assumed to subscribe. The state, in the sense of a central government, is portrayed as having no commitments other than to the implementation of this abstract ideal.

Beni Prasad's depiction of ancient Indian polities was as monist or centralist as that of the Europeans, except that unity for him existed not in the form of an administered polity, but of an ideal ethical community united by his unchanging Dharma. For him divine kingship was as much the essence of the Indian state as it was for Hegel, the difference being that Prasad placed a much higher value on it as the embodiment of the organic society of caste committed to religious goals that he favoured.

Alongside Prasad's religious conservatism there appeared a more secular, modernist construct, advocated in the political arena by Jawaharlal Nehru (1951: 36–50, 522–37). Distinct from both of these, again, was a pluralist position that was, like the conservative monist, also religious and traditionalist in its orientation, but more innovative. This was, of course, to be found most prominently, among nationalist political leaders, in certain of the followers of M. K. Gandhi.[14] The state constructed for ancient India by scholars holding one or the other or both of these views came, in fact, to predominate over those of Jayaswal and Beni Prasad.

5.5.2   Bureaucracy Above, Democracy Below

Those scholars who, like Nehru, saw a more secular and modernist state as the instrument of a unitary ideal, were inclined to focus their attention on the 'administrations' of ancient Indian states, on their rural economies and revenue systems, and can be seen as the Indian heirs of the centralist position of the British despoticists. One of the earliest representatives of this position was Pramathanath Banerjea (1879–1960).[15] Assuming that ultimate sovereignty was to be found in some Indian spirit or character that was rooted in the soil rather than in a Dharma interpreted by Brahmans, he argued that effective sovereignty was in the hands of a ministerial system of government (which he

[14] For a good discussion of Gandhi's relation to the Fabians, anarchists (Kropotkin), and guild socialists, see B. N. Ganguli (1973: 162–79).
[15] His thesis for the D.Sc. in Economics at the University of London was later published as a book (1916); L. D. Barnett is the first to be thanked in his Preface. He was Professor of Economics and Political Science at various colleges in Calcutta.

called Sachivatantra) in ancient India, and accorded more importance to *artha*, worldly wealth, than to religious values.[16]

The secular centralists have tended to take the Maurya Empire (fourth to third centuries BC) rather than the later Gupta, favoured by the religious centralists, as the apotheosis of the indigenous Indian state. It expresses in its fullest form the very world-ordering rationality which the predominant view in Indology had long denied to the Indians. Banerjea portrayed the rise of the Mauryan empire as a sharp break with the state system that preceded it. That system, too, had its unity, but the king of kings in it exercised, as a result of his 'conquest of all the quarters', a sovereignty that consisted in 'nominal supremacy' over his erstwhile rivals, and a major object of this polity was 'to bring a large part of India together by binding the Kings in a sort of alliance for offensive and defensive purposes'. Chandragupta Maurya established a system of 'imperial rule'. He succeeded for the first time in bringing 'the entire country', under 'one direct authority'. The 'control' of this system, we are told, 'necessitated the use of a complex machinery of administration' (Banerjea, 1916: 47–9).

The state as a subject for these secular monists was, thus, a rational administrator rather than the upholder of religious values. Here divine kingship was either a residue left over from tribal times or even an intrusion from outside, the growth of which indexed the decline of the earlier administered polity into a smaller, feudal state expressive of an increasingly caste-divided society. Because it was hereditary and divine, Indian kingship might appear, in Weberian terms, to be a form of 'traditional' or even 'charismatic' authority, but it was really 'legal-rational'.

The attempt to show that the larger states of ancient India were held together not by armed force and espionage, but by a rationally organized central administration or bureaucracy, has a good deal to be said in its favour. Certainly it is much easier to read the *Arthaśāstra* as a discourse on 'political economy' than as a 'Machiavellian' work on statecraft confirming the depiction of Indian empires as despotisms.[17]

There are, however, problems with this formulation. First, there is the question of the extent to which the administrative system or political economy of the *Arthaśāstra* is to be found in later states than the Maurya. The argument that it is to be more or less confined to the latter hardly stands up, especially if one makes the weaker centralist argument, to wit, that systems of unitary administration were confined to the home territories of a king and did not

[16] Another early proponent of this perspective was Narayan Chandra Bandyopadhyaya (1891–1943), Lecturer in History and Anthropology at Calcutta University. His was the first extended attempt (1980) to trace a history of the pre-Islamic state in India. Among the more recent advocates of bureaucratic states in ancient India was the Bengali institutional historian, Upendra Nath Ghoshal (1886–1969), Professor of History at Presidency College. His studies of revenue and agrarian systems and of political ideas and public life in ancient India (1945–66; 1959), while carefully argued, detailed, and critical, are highly schematic and, in the end, fail to give the holistic account of ancient Indian polities that the much smaller work of Banerjea did. His articles also dot the early volumes of the *History and Culture of the Indian People* (Majumdar, 1951–) and *A Comprehensive History of India* (Nilakanta Sastri, 1956–).

[17] See here the neglected study of K. V. Rangasvami Aiyangar (1949). But he, too, could not escape from the clutches of India as a caste-divided society (1926–8: 180).

integrate imperial states. Finally, it has yet to be demonstrated that the discourse of the *Arthaśāstra* 'depoliticizes' the offices it constructs. Can one really speak of the officers or ministers in that text as bureaucrats who have, as a condition of their holding office, agreed to give up their own will and follow all 'legal' orders, whether politically prudent or not? This question cannot, I would argue, be satisfactorily addressed until we have elaborated the notions of 'mastery' and 'lordship', the constituents out of which a variety of discourses constructed the states of ancient and medieval India alike.[18] Finally, we confront an insoluble problem: the whole basis for a government in which bureaucracy is transcendent is the modernist assumption that there is a single right way to order the human world, to fulfil 'man's needs', and that social science can determine what those are. If, however, rationality is not an essence, if there are multiple, overlapping world-ordering rationalities deployable in a situation (which itself has to be known), then the question of alternatives and of both constitutive and distributive politics re-enters the picture, undermining the very rationale for the administered polity.

Many nationalists argued from a pluralist position against the idea of a unitary administered polity, but they did not, for the most part, criticize the logic of the rationality it was supposed to embody. One strategy they had pursued instead was to deny the validity of the monist or absolutist state for India. This was the very kind of state that the British had constructed on Indian soil after the Mutiny. At the same time, however, most wished not to opt for the individualist, *laissez-faire* state compared with which India had been found so wanting. Nor did most of those who aligned themselves with Gandhi, adherents of some form or the other of a reformed Hinduism (either romanticized and idealized or utilitarianized and scientized), desire to erect in India the collectivist state that had become a reality in Russia after 1917. One way to accomplish their objective while avoiding these 'extremes' was to align themselves in part with those in Western Europe, the pluralists of one stripe or another, who were also critical of the unitary state. Occupying this ground, they would not have to give up the idea of the nation-state or opt for the collectivist or individualist alternative.

Scholarship on the ancient Indian state that adhered, knowingly or not, to something of a pluralist position, appeared in these circumstances. It can be seen as the partial descendant of the view of the Hindu state as feudal or post-tribal, with the difference that Indian pluralists, like the monists, attributed the feature missing from the British construct, sovereignty, to an earth-dwelling spirit. One of the more atriculate of these was Radha Kumud Mookerji, a cultural and institutional historian from Bengal.

He referred, in his earlier work on local government, discussed above, to 'two contending schools of political thought' when it comes to administrative reform in India: 'One of these seeks to introduce self-government "from above" and the other "from below"' (Mookerji, 1929: 20). Mookerji came down on the side of the pluralist position. In a short essay on nationalism (1921) he drew a clear contrast between the organic and pluralist polity he saw in India and the

---

[18] See Inden (1985b), for an initial effort in this direction and 6.1, below.

individualist one of Western liberalism. After rehearsing the Mainean truism that in India, 'social and political composition is based on the group, and not the individual, as the unit', he argued that:

Such a principle of social construction minimises the friction and collision of atomic units and helps to harmonise the parts in and through the whole. Biologically speaking, such constructions correspond to the more developed forms of organic life which, in their nervous interconnections, show a greater power of integration than the looser and more incoherent organisms lower down in the evolutionary series. (1921: 99)

No anarchist, Mookerji argued for a pluralist form of nation-state in which effective sovereignty was shared by a central government and the groups that make up civil society:

The nationality formed on such principles is a composite nationality, and not one of the rigid, unitary type. The relation of the State to its constituent groups becomes, under this scheme, one of copartnership, each maintaining the others in their place. It is not the State that, by its sanction or charter, creates its own constituent bodies or corporations, but, on the other hand, the groups establish, and are established by, the State. (1921: 100)

Unfortunately, Mookerji does not seem to have developed this line of thought any further.[19] On the contrary, his position in later writing (Mookerji, 1960: 47–9, 124–9; compare 1919: 248–50) moved closer to the religious monist stance taken by Beni Prasad. He ended up taking the Hindu Gupta empire, compromise between the centralism of the Mauryas and the localism of the medieval period, as the fullest expression of an ancient Indian nationalism (1952: 129).

Mookerji's vacillation between monist and pluralist theories was not an isolated phenomenon. When India gained independence her leaders instituted a 'federal' constitution tilted in favour of a 'strong' centre while still claiming to adhere to a Gandhian pluralism. Both these variants of idealism were represented at the founding of the Indian Republic, the more secular (and monist) in the person of Jawaharlal Nehru, its first prime minister, and the more religious (and pluralist) in the person of Rajendra Prasad (1946: 1–77), its first president (1950–62). The two positions are also co-present in the flag of the Indian Republic. The wheel (*chakrā*) in the centre of that flag was, in its parent, the flag of the Indian National Congress, the spinning wheel (*charkhā*) which, in the words of Nehru himself, 'symbolized the masses of people, which symbolized their industry and which came to us from the message which Mahatma Gandhi delivered'. Because its spindle violated the rule calling for bilateral uniformity on a flag, however, it was removed and a new wheel, taken from the Sarnath Lion Capital of Asoka, was substituted. According to Nehru, this wheel was a symbol of India's ancient culture, a 'symbol of the many things that India has

[19] Some British scholars also challenged the despoticist construct, among them, Havell, the art historian (1915: xxv–xxvii, 129–30). For another early secular pluralist position, see another London dissertation involving Laski and L. D. Barnett, that of Har Narain Sinha (1938: 115, 134, 146, 154, 258, 273–5, 305, 328).

stood for', and he said he was happy it was associated with Asoka, 'one of the most magnificent names not only in India's history but in world history'. Although this wheel was well known as the symbol of the universal ruler (*chakravartin*), who sets the wheel of law in motion, Nehru denied that it was a flag of dominion.[20]

It is, thus, not surprising that the monist and pluralist positions merged in the work of the national historians done between 1940 and 1965. Their depiction of the state in ancient India, supposed ancestor of the Indian Republic, as centralized at the all-India 'level' but a pluralist, Panchayati Raj (ruled by village councils, see 4.3.2, 4.4.1) at the local had, by then, largely displaced the despoticist construct of imperial British scholarship.[21] A. S. Altekar can also be classed as a mixed pluralist in his textbook (1962: 55, 89–95, 98–102, 146–59, 381–7), as can K. A. Nilakanta Sastri (1892–1975), Professor of History at the University of Madras, in his writings on the Deccan and south India (1981: 730–47) and the Cholas (1955: 461–2), where his discourse, describing that government as distinguished from its rivals by 'the superior executive strength it was able to develop by bringing into existence a highly organised and thoroughly efficient bureaucracy', is self-contradictory. He attempts (following Smith?) to offload those features of the Mauryan empire which deviate from the essence of the Indian (Hindu) state on to the Persians (1951: 178, 189–90), permitting him to save Asoka's reputation as the great man in India's history (1951: 202–43).

The major vehicle for these pluralist views, apart from numerous monographs and textbooks and journals, was *The History and Culture of the Indian People*, edited by R. C. Majumdar (1951–).[22] This idealized image found qualified British spokesmen in the Indologist, A. L. Basham, and the political scientist, Hugh Tinker. The latter could write, as late as 1962, that 'parliamentary government' in India was not only threatened by divisive social and religious forces, but by the autocratic form of government India had traditionally required to maintain order in a society characterized not by the harmony and interdependence seen by the nationalists, but by competition and conflict: 'It is also sapped by the immemorial view of government itself as a dome of absolute authority, suspended high above ordinary folk; a power which they might supplicate, or might even, possibly, manipulate; but which they could never hope to draw into their own hands' (Tinker, 1962: 9). We can see here that

[20] See the speech given by Nehru on the occasion of the resolution to adopt the wheel-flag as the national flag, 22 July 1947 (Agrawala, 1964: 93–6).

[21] R. C. Majumdar, a founder of pluralist historiography, was a secularist (except when it comes to Islam) and hence more of an advocate of Asoka than some of the other pluralists, but he skated backwards when he compared ancient Indian government to Germany's before the Great War (1960: 156).

[22] Projected to consist of eleven volumes, of which no less than five have been devoted to India before 1300, it remains unfinished. It is also very uneven in quality and more than a little 'biased' in the direction of a Hindu nationalism. It has none the less become, for the history of the earlier period, the hegemonic text. It succeeds to the position never fully occupied by the incomplete *Cambridge History of India*. Not as widely used is the overlapping and rival *A Comprehensive History of India*, edited by K. A. Nilakanta Sastri (1956–), also incomplete.

Tinker has, in using the word 'authority', conceded sovereignty not only to the now independent India but also to the generic Indian state he projects on to the past. The images of the British and the Indians in the Commonwealth thus converge, although Tinker would still prefer to see a transcendent unifying principle for India in the form of a central government whose essence remained an Iranian despotic will (see 5.4.1) rather than in the form of an Indian Dharma or Spirit.[23] Despite recent criticism, it retains currency when scholars, especially Marxists, write about the Mauryas (Thapar, 1981).

So far as the later history of the Hindu state is concerned, the nationalists and post-imperial British scholars have challenged some of the more blatant features of the ideology that animated Smith's narrative, but virtually all of them have adhered to the geographic partitioning of an early medieval India that he began, and perpetuated his depiction of a politically fragmented country.[24] The divine kingship of this period supposedly became more important as Hindu states themselves became more impotent, permitting Basham to dismiss it with this remark: 'Despite the growth of royal pretensions through the centuries the claims of the king did not go unchallenged, and in practice his divinity often made little difference to the body politic. Divinity was cheap in ancient India' (Basham, 1954: 86). The British had erected their divine kingship of a British Raj and the nationalists had transformed that into a divine nation, yet both could wave aside the divine kingships that existed in India's earlier past.

The nationalist constructs all too easily collapse back into the positions of the predominant constructs they aim to criticize, namely, that India was ruled by a post-tribal caste system and an inherently imaginative and passionate mind. The very 'facts' which European scholars and rulers had revealed about India had the advantage of being easily appropriated by the nationalists and turned against their makers. Nationalists could replace the idea of a civilization divided by caste, that is racial, religious, and linguistic conflict, with the idea of a civilization united by 'social' harmony. The problem they faced was that these are not symmetrical ideas. Whereas the notion of a divided India is furthered by depicting it as including the largest number of heterogeneous groups, the notion of an India unified in accord with the exclusionist metaphysics of the nation-state could stand only by looking to some principle of unity that could miraculously overcome divisions (but could actually do that only by silently excluding or subsuming other groups).

This left India with a nation-state that remains ontologically and politically inaccessible to its own citizens. Its government continues to be, just like its immediate British Indian ancestor, merely a neutral enforcer of unity on a morselized society, continually in danger of being pulled apart by 'centrifugal' forces. It remains the instrument of an agent, a 'divinity' that stays beyond the

---

[23] For a Dutch rendering that converges with the religious conservative depiction of Prasad, see Jan Gonda's rambling study (1966).

[24] Seminal here is the work of H. C. Ray, who produced his highly atomistic account (1973: 1211–12) under the tutelage of L. D. Barnett at the University of London. See also Nilakanta Sastri (1966) and Yazdani (1960). The first of the two volumes (IV and V) of *The History and Culture of the Indian People* (Majumdar, 1951–) that deal with 'early medieval' India betrays Smith's Aryocentrism in its title, 'The Age of Imperial Kanauj'.

reach of its own people and institutions. That divinity no longer has an external home country as a platform from which to enforce its impartial unity. What the Indian nationalists substitute for the transcendent divine kingship of the British Raj is the equally transcendent *idea* of Indian unity. The more religious-minded found that idea in a non-sectarian transcendent Dharma (to which nobody had ever adhered). Secularist, modernist thinking claimed to discover an underlying unity in a neo-Bergsonian national 'vitality' or 'spirit'. This elusive entity, which everyone shared but none could now fully manifest, would somehow be transformed by a bureaucratic state grounded in a world-ordering reason that India had lost but could regain from the West. Either way, this is an essentialized ideal Oneness, dichotomously contrasted in the Indological construct with the immanent divisiveness of India's social and religious 'reality'. Since that Dharma or Spirit is the premise and guarantee of the Indian nation-state itself, specific here-and-now agents could not negotiate with it or construct it (whence a Pakistan; thence a Bangladesh). National historians could 'discover' it in India's ancient past, and nationalist politicians could invoke it and mobilize people in its name, but none of them could *make* it. Which is to say the nationalists have Indianized that old religious and scientistic dream of so many Europeans and Americans – a 'society' that would be free of politics because it hung from some immobile point in heaven or rested on an indisputable foundation.

5.6   INDEPENDENCE AND THE DISCOVERY OF THE THIRD WORLD

In short, the principal elements of the countrywide networks of India consist of familial and caste associations that persist through generations. These associations connect one set of villages with another or some of the families in one village with families corresponding in culture and social status in other villages. It is as if the characteristic social structure of the primitive self-contained community had been dissected and its components spread about a wide area. Rural India is a primitive or a tribal society rearranged to fit a civilization. (Redfield, 1956: 56–7)

5.6.1   From Administration Unity to Cultural Integration

The knowing subjects who have emerged in the US–USSR imperial formation that arose after the Second World War have begun to challenge this image of divine kingship in India as an administered polity, whether as the 'benevolent' despotism of the British imperialists or as the 'constitutional' monarchy of the Indian nationalists. We have by no means, however, rid ourselves of the orientalist construct of the Indian state. The scholars of the US–USSR imperial formation have, I shall argue, revived and modified the tribalist variant of Indian kingship in their effort to move away from the nationalist emphasis on ideal and administrative unity. Redfield's characterization can be taken as representative of this view of India as a post-tribal civilization.

The larger intellectual project to which post-Independence accounts from Europe and the US speak is the project of the social sciences that has taken shape since the Second World War, that concerned with the constitution and maintenance of a world order centred on the United States and its allies. The peoples of a newly discovered 'third world' are no longer to be appendages of European states; they are to be become independent, sovereign nation-states. Social scientists are to take up the question of how, in the absence of direct or even indirect 'administrative' subordination to European centres, these 'new nations' are to find their place in the world. The myriad of theoretical and practical discourses that arise on 'community development', 'modernization', 'cultural change', and the transition from tradition to 'modernity', backed up by 'area studies', are all concerned, though in various ways and various degrees of remove from the peoples taken as their object of study, with theorizing about this problem and implementing its solutions. They are, thus, the transformed descendants of those earlier discourses on 'oriental despotism', the 'primitive' and 'Asiatic' modes of production, and of the classification of societies as 'ancient' and 'modern'.

One of the themes that emerges in these discourses is of a great gap between the living standards of the traditional and modern types of society. Even so seemingly sophisticated a sociologist as Anthony Giddens sees no problem in rehearsing this point in a recent book. Rejecting the older Romantic view of the traditional society as a harmonious, secure community, he asserts that:

daily life was very often a much more tenuous, and potentially violent, affair in non-modern states than it is for most of the population in the Western countries today. The peasant subjects of traditional states have frequently lived in conditions of grinding poverty, whatever 'surplus' they produced being appropriated by tax-gathering officials; they have suffered famines, chronic disease and plagues. They have also been open to attack by bandits and armed marauders; and the level of casual violence in day-to-day life seems to have been high. (Giddens, 1985: 60)

Yet this increased gap between the traditional and the modern is not presented as the result of, or associated with, an inferior culture. If all the new nation-states are sovereign and, hence, formally equal, then their cultures must also be formally equivalent even though, as will be seen, the tradition of one society can be construed as biting into modernity in very different ways from others. Still, as Binder argues (1986), the more conservative brand of liberalism, which traces its ancestry to the German sociologist, Max Weber, has rejected the apocalyptic dichotomy between an inferior tradition and a superior modernity in which some of the earlier more evangelical American liberals and pragmatists (the US post-war descendants of the utilitarians) believed, but it has also opposed 'the idea that pragmatic change which holds nothing sacred is beneficial' (Binder, 1986: 15).

The more optimistic reader should not, however, conclude from this change of perspective that the metaphysics of dichotomy has been abandoned. Almost everywhere in the social scientific discourses that have sprouted after the US reluctantly assumed the onerous responsibilities of Number One, there is an opposition assumed to hold between a metaculture of the world as a whole (that is, of the 'first', 'developed', or 'free' world) on the one hand and the local or regional conditions, the institutional or infrastructural arrangements of the 'new nations' of the 'third' or 'underdeveloped' world on the other. Although the organizations of the world as a whole, its meta-institutions, formally and publicly the United Nations, the World Bank, the International Monetary Fund, and dozens of others, and *sotto voce* the multinational corporations and the governments of the Seven (US, France, West Germany, Japan, Italy, Britain, and Canada), are assumed to be ordered in accord with the principles of the metaculture (and heavily criticized, e.g. the International Court at the Hague, UNESCO, and even the UN, or simply ignored, if they are seen to deviate), the infrastructures of the nations in the third world are not so ordered. Whence their low levels of development.

The gap between the two worlds is, we are repeatedly told, to be bridged by an increasingly strengthened state in the third world countries, meaning a civil service or bureaucracy or, in some cases, the ruling political party or the military, or (usually) some mix of these three. Operated by a class of national leaders that is properly educated and trained, these states will be able to penetrate to the roots of the third-world countries and bring them the benefits of modernization. When administration from a European imperial centre was the major mode of integration for the imperial formation centred on Europe, efforts were made to weaken the claim of local leaders to act. Now that the major code of integration is to be the civic culture concocted after the Second World War, the focus on local leaders shifts from the question of how they can be immobilized (either by being converted into 'natural' leaders, the freeze-dried chiefs of colonial anthropology, or cut off from their own people by an alienating Westernization) to how they can be mobilized not only by the inducements of aid and trade but also, and perhaps most crucially from this perspective, by education. The way to do this is to identify those elements of the local tradition that have already been or could be activated in the modernization process, especially those that might be used to tease the local leadership in the direction of the metaculture.[25] At the very least, these leaders will be able to maintain stability, to keep the presumed beneficiaries, the ordinary people of these countries (with their atavistic tendencies), under 'control'.

The same metaphysics of dichotomy that we have seen at work in the Anglo-French imperial formation is also deployed here. Distinctions between two dubiously constituted levels are converted into an opposition. The local institutional arrangements are assumed to be immanent, multiple, and transitory while the metaculture is assumed to be transcendent, unitary, and constantly improving (or embodying timeless values). The one is the embodiment of disorder and low living standards, the other the embodiment of order and affluence. Ultimately, of course, real differences between the two will disappear. That is, the local will become subsumed in the global. The two will thus ultimately be reduced to the one. Yet because any number of differing traditions can be blended with modernity, there will continue to exist a wide variety of local (but increasingly penumbral) cultures.

The scholarly focus on 'the state' in the 'third' or 'underdeveloped' world has consequently shifted. Social scientists construe the newly 'independent' states

---

[25] For India, see Rudolph and Rudolph (1967); for an Indian political scientist taking much the same stance, see Kothari (1970).

as mediators between those who share the metaculture and the culturally variable (often rough and ready) 'locals'. That is, they are seen as instruments for adjusting the one to the other. Above all else in this age of supposedly universal suffrage and an omnipresent world economy, the state is depicted as an educator, as a socializer and acculturator, a producer of citizens and consumers and, less visibly, as Foucault would show, of docile, disciplined workers. It is an educator not just in the narrow formal sense, but in the wider, more diffuse sense of disseminating information, of licensing, regulating, and managing the popular media. All of this is to be done without, of course, giving up the complement of education, the maintenance of order, as policeman and judge. Just as scholars in the preceding Anglo-French imperial formation projected 'native' versions of the colonial states they had constructed in Asia and Africa on to the essentialist histories that they fashioned for them, so the scholars of the new US–USSR formation have more or less silently updated the pasts of the areas with which they are concerned. They fix their gaze on a tradition, culture, or ideology that historically is given the same role of integration that the civic culture of the world is now accorded, and try to see how the traditional states or kingships or tribal chieftains mediated between that tradition and particular local leaderships and their cultural, economic, and political interests.

Virtually all of the major work on ancient or Hindu states that has emerged from its situation in the post-war imperial formation takes this mediational view of the state, though its authors do not agree in their assumptions or conclusions. The first of the three post-Independence accounts of the ancient Hindu state I review here is that of the French sociologist Louis Dumont. I label it 'social structuralist' because Dumont makes the state into the fragmented and subordinated mediator between a hierarchic (caste) structure and an inherently divided political economy.

5.6.2 Where Caste is King: L. Dumont

Dumont argues that the relation which obtained between the Brahman and the king in ancient India was similar to the relation that he holds to obtain between the Brahmans and the dominant caste, that which enjoys the main rights in the soil (1980a). As he sees it, that caste reproduces the royal function at the village level (1980a: 291). He rightly criticizes those who have seen the superiority of the Brahman as 'contingent', rather than as a 'necessary institution' (292), the outcome of some supposed class conflict. The priest–king relation is, for Dumont, expressive of the hierarchic principle of India's caste society, as 'fundamental in itself and in its implications' (292). Dumont is talking here about an *opposition* between priest and king – 'the two aspects are absolutely separated' – he is not simply talking about a *distinction*. The two do not, however, exist as equals:

Further, the very word hierarchy, and its history, should recall that the gradation of status is rooted in religion: the first rank normally goes, not to power, but to religion, simply because for those societies religion represents what Hegel has called the Universal, i.e. absolute truth, in other words because hierarchy integrates the society in relation to its ultimate values. (1980a: 293)

Dumont thus reduces the two to the one. Power, construed as immanent, multiple, and transitory, becomes encompassed by purity or status, construed as transcendent, unitary, and unchanging. Here we have, in Dumont's scheme of things, the Indian equivalent of the Western and now universal metaculture.

This subsumption of power in religion found its embodiment in the social world. According to Dumont, 'in most of the societies in which kingship is found, it is a magico-religious as well as a political function' (1980a: 293). In India, however, the 'king depends on the priests for the religious functions, he cannot be his own sacrificer, instead he 'puts in front' of himself a priest, the *purohita*, and *then* he loses the hierarchical preeminence in favour of the priests, retaining for himself power only' (293). There is not too much I would quarrel with in this statement taken by itself. One could see the priest and king related in a hierarchic but complementary fashion, as together forming a complex agent. But there is a difficulty here. The king stands between the Brahman and the world of the Indian village. Dumont cannot, however, let the king stay there because he is committed to seeing the world through a metaphysics of mutual exclusion. Either the king is going to be classed with the Brahman in the realm of hierarchy, or he is going to be classed, along with the state, with the villagers. Dumont vacillates, but on the whole tends to class the king with the villager. The dichotomous thinking in which he is enmeshed thus leads him to this conclusion, that 'the function of the king has been *secularized* (293). The embarrassment of the Hindu king's divinity he explains away by attributing it to a 'popular mentality' that somehow lurks below the level of Brahminical thought (297–9).

Does Dumont's secularization (for primary evidence of which he turns to that vexing text on statecraft, the *Arthaśāstra* (1980a: 304) parallel that process in the West? Is Weberian economic and political rationality about to be liberated from the shackles of religion in India? Far from it. They are separated from the religious realm only to be more deeply hierarchized and devalued by it than before this secularization took place:

Being the negation of *dharma* in a society which continues to be ruled by *dharma*, the political sphere is severed from the realm of values. It is not in the political sphere that the society finds its unity, but in the social regime of castes.... The system of government has no universal value, it is not the State in the modern sense of the term and, we shall see, the state is identical with the king. Force and interest work only for strife and instability, but these conditions may thrive without anything essential being put in question; much to the contrary, social unity implies and entertains political division. (1980a: 304)

Which is to say that the caste society can exist only at the expense of its political fragmentation and economic underdevelopment.

Here is the conclusion that the French sociologist reaches, a classic piece of his explanatory rhetoric:

in the West, the political sphere, having become absolutely autonomous in relation to religion, has built itself up into an absolute: comparatively, the modern 'nation' embodies its own absolute values. This is what did not happen, I suppose, as long as the politico-economic realm was only relatively autonomous, and this in turn could not be otherwise while the individual remained, in essence, outside the social world. (1980a: 312)[26]

The theocratic despotism that Hegel concocted as India's essence Dumont has revived. The Indian state is necessarily fragile and disunited precisely because Indian civilization is characterized by social unity, by which is meant not the absence of social conflict in the ordinary sociological sense of the term – on the contrary, factionalism would seem the signature tune of Indian politics –, but in the sense that the principle of hierarchy, the religious absolute of Indian civilization, is itself never challenged from within. Divine kingship, for Dumont's extreme depiction, is thus a structural nonsense. Ancient Indians may have wished to pull their world of hierarchy and power together in one agent but they could not, for Dumont displaced their agency on to an organic social and ideological structure that seems unshakable. Caste, a substantialized agent, is the true maker of the Indians and not they of it.

Like many anthropologists, Dumont has been more concerned with the retrieval of the 'authentic' traditional Other than with the political and economic 'development' of the Other and his incorporation into the 'world system'. There are, none the less, implications in his construction of the Indian state for the present.

5.6.3   Transcendent Brahman, Social Disorder, Sacrificial King: J. C. Heesterman

The next image of the ancient Indian state I address is found in the essays of J. C. Heesterman (1985), Professor of Indology at Leiden and spokesman on India, especially on the issues formulated by the conservative liberal view of modernization, the one that attaches itself to Max Weber. I refer to it as 'individual idealist' because it depicts the ancient Indian state as the mediator between the transcendent personal value of renunciation and an inherently disorderly world.[27]

Like Dumont, Heesterman has a tendency to see the relation of the Brahman and king, or the secular and sacred, as one of opposition and not, at the same time, as one also of distinction. Only he disagrees with Dumont about what the ultimate value of Indian civilization is. He argues that it was not religious hierarchy, implying a social structure, but renunciation, implying the absence of a social structure. And hence it is the renouncer and not the priest who embodies this value. So the Indian world is, for Heesterman, divided up not as for Dumont into a stable, organic realm of hierarchic ritual caste relations on the one hand, and a constantly changing and inferior realm of the politico-economic on the other. It is instead divided into an individualized realm of ritual and renunciatory transcendence on the one hand, and a social realm,

---

[26] See also Dumont (1980c), where he argues that while in the West the individual and society coexist in a healthy tension, in India the individual can exist only outside of society, as the renouncer.

[27] For a more extensive critique, see Inden (1986c).

including caste, that is, like Dumont's realm of the politico-economic, one of self-interested immanence.

That being the case, Heesterman confronts the problem faced by Dumont and, for that matter, all who would see the state as mediator between ultimate values and empirical existence. The question regarding ancient India is: which of the realms is the king to be fitted into? For once the world is divided into two opposed realms he must be fitted *either* into the one or into the other. Since he cannot be accommodated in the higher, mental realm, he has to be placed in the lower, social one. Having reduced the social in his scheme to the same transitory, merely evidential status to which Dumont had reduced the politico-economic, Heesterman focuses not on caste or the village or the king as the centre of gravity in Indian society, but on the patrimonial 'man of substance'. Supposed to be the leader of a local, powerful lineage or 'brotherhood', such a figure is repeatedly referred to as the co-sharer in the realm with the king (Heesterman, 1985: 184). Here, then, we have India's equivalent of the local leader with which so much scholarship in the US–USSR imperial formation has been concerned. The result of the emphasis Heesterman places on these 'brotherhoods' is that he tends to reduce Indian states to temporary and unstable coalitions of big men and their lineages (a picture which Heesterman not only paints out of the Vedic ritual texts, but also manages to squeeze out of the *Arthaśāstra*). They become the 'real' actors of Indian politics, revealed once we peel away the appearances of unitary states. The very agents that the older British construct tried to reduce to the status of caste and village headmen or post-tribal clan chiefs suddenly re-emerge as the major actors of Indian society.

The intellectual shark circling this idea here seems to be that the anthropologist's favourite essence of the primitive society, 'kinship', is the essence of the social in India, too.[28] For Maine, a principle of kinship had been a principle of order, but in Heesterman's recension kinship seems to have become a principle of perennial disorder. Heesterman is surely right to reject the British attempt to displace their notion of order on to Indian tradition. Yet I think he goes too far in an equal-and-opposite direction. He ends up exchanging a unitary, static model of society for one that is in constant flux and virtually centreless. A part, the brotherhood, becomes the whole of the Indian polity. Caste as the true essence of Indian society is swapped for the even more visceral essence of kinship.

The image of a society that is integrated and reintegrated, but only in a purposeless, volatile, and ramshackle manner is, of course, not accidental, nor is it simply the result of empirical research; it is integral to Heesterman's dualist construct of Indian civilization. If kinship turns out to be the essence of the social and political in India, it is because it is the perfect emblem of an immanent social reality. We should not, however, make the mistake of seeing this as the single essence of Indian civilization. There is, we must remember, the other essence of Indian tradition, the one that is just the opposite of the outer, social, and objective essence of kinship. It is the inner, individual, and subjective essence of renunciation. He tells his reader, after a lengthy discussion of the

[28]On kinship and essence in Southeast Asia, see Hobart (1984).

brotherhood and the problem of unity, that when we touch the 'inner springs' of Indian civilization we find that 'its heart is not with society and its integrative pressures.' Supplying India with a unitary mind, he continues: 'It devalorizes society and disregards power. The ideal is not hierarchical interdependence but the individual break with society. The ultimate value is release from the world. And this cannot be realized in a hierarchical way, but only by the abrupt break of renunciation.' It is not just that renunciation and the social are distinct in India; they are irreconcilable opposites. India, furthermore, wants it that way:

Indian society and its ideal are separated by a chasm and cannot be united. Nor are they intended to be united. The chasm is intentional. Therefore all attempts, whether by the observer or the participant, at joining together the two orders in their different forms – king and brahmin, power and authority, jāti and varṇa, 'worship' and Veda, society and its rejection – are doomed to failure. Above the Indian world, rejecting and at the same time informing it, the renouncer stands out as the exemplar of ultimate value and authority. (1985: 182–3)

Tradition thus becomes two-tiered, consisting of a higher individualistic, universalistic, transcendent order of removal or renunciation and a lower social, particularistic, and immanent order. The one is the realm of the Brahman, the other that of the king and of the co-sharers in the real, the men of substance and the brotherhoods, the castes and villages. The one is the inner mental realm of Indian civilization, the other is, so to speak, its outer body. Each is as internally uniform and unchanging as it is fundamentally different from its would-be complement. And in the last analysis, it is the material or social in this binary opposition that is inferiorized and devalued.

The texts on which Heesterman relies talk of the king as being both the greatest of householders in the world and also as a god, as one partaking of the supposedly numinous realm inhabited by the Brahmans and the gods. But because Heesterman has committed himself to the dichotomous construction of the Indian world, he cannot accept at face value the statements made in those texts about the king. The king, in Heesterman's view, must either abandon society altogether (he cites examples of this from 'myths') or must, if he remains the king, become immersed in the chaos of the Indian secular world. Sovereignty remains with the Brahmanical value of renunciation while effective sovereignty is perpetually contested by kin-based faction leaders. The king tries to act as a mediator not only among those leaders and, even worse, between the opposed poles of Indian tradition, the renunciatory values of the Brahman and the aimless ambitions of post-tribal big men (1985: 113–14), but his acts do not accomplish anything, except perhaps for the moment; they are, rather, symptoms of the underlying double essence of Indian civilization in its classical form, namely, the civilization of spiritual and material extremes which remains fundamentally tribal because no attempts (such as those of Kauṭilya) are ever able to construct the kind of progressive order out of it that the West has. The king is, or we might say, the state is, ultimately the sacrificial victim of the dichotomous world that the Indians, that is, the Brahmans, have (mistakenly) made for themselves. India's divine kingship is, thus, not a case of oriental despotism but of a newly found 'oriental desperatism'.

5.6.4   Segmentary State, Ritual Sovereignty: Burton Stein

The third of these images of the ancient Indian state as an educative polity is that of Burton Stein, a historian of south India who has, more than the other scholars considered here, fixed his attention on the Hindu state. He has been highly critical of the national historians' image of the ancient Indian state as bureaucratically centralized (1980; 1985).

Stein wishes to distinguish a 'unitary' from a 'segmentary' state (1977; 1980: 264–85). The segments of the latter are its territorial units, each of which, from the largest – the kingdom – to the smallest – the village – resembles the other in its organization. The most important segments of the Hindu state are neither the kingdoms to which they are attached nor the villages of which they are composed, but the 'localities' (*nāḍu*) and 'supralocalities' (*periyanāḍus*). These are the most important because they are the largest political units, that is, the largest units in which administrative or political control is exercised. Now, the fact that the principles of the administered state are to be found *within* the locality or supralocality does not mean that even there administration was the principle of unity. No, the principle of unity within was kinship or shared ethnicity on the part of the dominant peasantry. The principle of unity without was that of complementary opposition (by which social anthropologists mean that neighbouring segments are in opposition to one another at the same level, but allied with one another along descent lines against the more distantly related). To the extent that these segments constituted a state, however, another principle, that of kingship, of ritual hegemony or supremacy, came into play in ordering them. This is the 'kingship' or 'overlordship' which the ruler of one of these localities claimed to wield over its neighbours. Stein calls it 'ritual sovereignty' (1985: 116) to distinguish it from the sovereignty exercised within the locality. As Stein puts it, the 'pragmatic competence' or 'chiefly sovereignty' of the localities 'sprang from being part of the dominant people, called *nattar*', through the 'idiom and fact' of kinship. Royal competence, on the other hand, arose from the 'homage' offered to an 'anointed king' through the 'idiom and fact' of 'service'. This ritual hegemony should not be confused with what is conventionally meant by a central government, for the ritual or royal centre here does not possess an administration capable of exercising control beyond its own locality boundaries. Revenue collection at the ritual centre was, lastly, not fiscal in nature, but tributary.

To some extent, Stein seems to be arguing that the south Indian state was not a modern nation-state, and especially what I have referred to as the administered polity. With this I have, of course, no quarrel. Certainly I agree with him that 'effective political control' and 'administration', as defined by the inhabitants and theorists of the nation-state, were not the unifying principles of ancient Indian polities. The 'model' of a polity as segmentary does not, however, avoid many of the troubling implications built into the typologizing of Indology and the social sciences. Stein claims to have borrowed his idea of a segmentary state from Aidan Southall, a social anthropologist who has worked on East Africa. Others, for example B. Cohn (1977), have already commented on one of the major difficulties that arise in using 'African models', to wit, that they are themselves derived in part from the British experience in establishing an administered state in India.

The shift in the imperial heyday to the idea of an administered polity as the model against which imperial Indian states should be described and the emphasis in nationalist, dynastic histories on administrative unity, to which Stein's model is a response, has induced a certain amnesia. The segmentary state seems like a new idea when it is compared with the administered state that dominated historiography earlier in the century, but it is not entirely new. The idea that the unifying essence of traditional polities in India (and in Africa, as well as the New World) was based on kinship and clanship or its penumbra, caste, rather than nationality or sovereignty, was the very idea used by the British to constitute an empire in India after the so-called Mutiny. Even the idea taken as the signature tune of the segmentary state, the principle of complementary opposition, is not as novel as it might at first seem. It has its ancestry in the agonism or the vendetta – dare I say, the feud – supposed to characterize early societies.

Like other post-imperial scholars Stein accords 'sovereignty' to south Indian states, but without rethinking the terms of the discourse whose purpose was to remove it. Hence, the assumptions that were part of the older despoticist and tribalist constructs carry on a robust existence in this new model. The village disappears into the *nāḍu*, but it is not clear that the *nāḍu*, the major unit in the segmentary state, is treated significantly differently than was the village republic of Indological discourse. Based on an ethnic or kin unity of the peasantry in it, the *nāḍu*, as an agent, is largely self-reliant and inward-looking. Its ruling society, the council, is the unproblematic product of a tribal structure and tradition just as the council or headmanship were. Because of the inner–outer dichotomy built into this atomistic construct, relations with institutions outside the *nāḍu* are always external to its own constitution.

Maine and Baden-Powell construed the Indian state as the earliest type of ancient (civilized) society. Stein did not intend to do this, yet this is often the effect of his presentation. Two features in particular of his segmentary type give this impression. One is his assumption, widely shared with other Indologists (including the author in aspects of his previous work (Inden and Nicholas, 1977)), that somehow 'kinship' must be the essence of south Indian society, and hence of the segmentary state. By this Stein means the organization of a society into lineages, not simply as one form among others, but in the sense that it has not yet departed from this form in its natural history (1985: 83–4). There are places where Stein seems about to break with the notion of kinship as the underlying principle of unity for the *nāḍu* (1980: 118), but these thoughts never quite take charge of the discourse.

Kinship is not just the glue for the ordinary peasants. All-purpose, it also holds together the upper reaches of the segmentary state, where 'ritual' becomes important as well. For example, when he attempts to clarify what he means by 'ritual' he says that one of its three components is kinship. It was the 'form of interconnection between king and chief', he says, 'in which the parity of ruling lineages – royal and chiefly – was expressed through a symmetrical exchange of women and the not uncommon giving of royal women as brides to chiefly families'. Here, and elsewhere in Stein's text, there is an inability to see the relations of kings and lords as also contractual. Maine's ghost haunts us. In India they have to have kinship ties as their 'real' basis (even though Stein himself tells us about a lineage of princes (*kumāravargam*) involving a '*mélange* of local chieftains of different places and subcaste affiliations in the Madurai region who became by royal enactment, members of a single lineage' (1985: 77)).

The second assumption Stein works with is that the exchange of gifts between kin-defined units is the essential institution of social integration in primitive or archaic societies. Whence his overemphasis on gift-giving. This is not to say that gift-giving was unimportant or that Stein has nothing of interest to tell us here. Certainly in his discussion of land grants to Brahmans Stein is correct to challenge the assumption that these gifts were motivated by an undifferentiated piety on the part of simply construed donors.

Finally, there are objections just to the terminology that is involved in articulating the idea of the segmentary state. The whole thing is built out of the functionalist tool-kit of the social anthropologist looking for the key to social unity and stability. And all the building materials – clans, lineages, chiefs, exchanges, predatory raids, segmental (as opposed to organic) unity and so on – partake of kinship as an essence. The notion of a 'peasant' society usually taken to stand, as a type, between the primitive and the industrial, only reinforces the conclusion, especially given the evocation of Marx's modes of production, that the segmentary peasant state of south India entails the Asiatic mode and is inferior to the 'later' ancient or feudal, never mind the modern or capitalist.

This is not to suggest that Stein has simply revived the older notion. The reinvented version has a major new twist, and that is the opposition drawn between the ritual or cultural and the political, and the idea of the state as the mediator between the two. Unfortunately, some of the most troublesome features of Stein's formulation of the south Indian state flow from this dichotomy, from his characterization of the 'dual sovereignty' in it. He refers to a higher level or royal sovereignty as ritual and to chiefly sovereignty as practical or political. The one is unitary or monarchic; the other is segmentary and, presumably, oligarchic (my word, not his). The fact that he chooses to use the term 'segmentary' to tag the type as a whole is an indication of the ontological status attributed to these two 'levels' of sovereignty. The higher level is not quite as real as the lower level. It is an ideological or (dare one say?) superstructural level. It is the plane of sacred actions, while the lower is that of pragmatic actions. This dichotomous thinking permits Stein to conclude, after a discussion of 'sacral kingship', that 'it is in being all of this that makes for difficulty in grasping the political system as something other than a stage for the enactment of a sacred drama' (1980: 282). Here we have in south India a distant cousin of the Balinese 'theatre-state'.[29]

The dichotomy to which Stein adheres sounds very similar to the opposition

---

[29] Geertz (1980), too, organizes his treatment of Bali around the conservative liberal dichotomy of culture and social arrangements.

Dumont wishes to sustain between caste and kingship. For Stein, the 'level' of the chiefdom is that of Dumont's 'power', while the 'level' of the state is that of 'sacred actions', royal *status*, of ritual, that is, of Dumont's hierarchy or purity. Stein has 'solved' the problem of 'sacred' kingship in which the king is 'secularized' and subordinated to a caste of priests by lifting the kingship to the transcendent realm of ritual and purity, that of caste values. There is, of course, a major difference between the two formulations. Where Dumont sees the political and economic realm embodied in an apparently divine but really secular kingship as demoralized and inferiorized by a transcendent religious and social realm, Stein sees a truly sacred kingship as epitomizing kinship and moral values rooted in the locality.

There are major problems with this unintended reformulation of Dumont's structure. Once more, a contingent distinction between aspects of actions and their association with certain jurisdictions has been turned into an essential contrast or opposition between 'levels'. It is as though there were gods worshipped and rites performed only at the royal capital and that these were all symbolically unifying, while political calculation and economic accumulation took place only at the local level, and that perceptions of self or communal interest brought about real coalitions there.

Equally serious is the dichotomy of the ritual and the political in classifying actions. Stein's construct assumes that because it was 'ritual' in nature and did not therefore entail the use of 'force', royal sovereignty did not involve the transfer of substantial resources or the mobilization of large numbers of men at a royal or imperial centre. Here Stein shares the assumption that the 'effective' unity of a state depended upon the use or the threat of use of military force, in the form of a 'physical' threat, with the very people he criticizes, the centralists. What is not taken seriously is that even works like the *Arthaśāstra* do not speak of states as depending for their existence primarily on the use of physical force. Here again I am afraid that we deal with the Utilitarian notion of the individual or the sovereign state as a creature that responds to the world 'outside' it through the receipt of painful and pleasurable sensations. Political actors will 'combine' together and obey other political actors only to the extent that it becomes painful not to do so. But why must we continue to work under the shadow of these assumptions? Could not those acts which Stein classes as ritual or symbolic acts also be political acts?

We might also want to know how a royal sovereignty defined as the opposite of chiefly sovereignty can be taken as expressive or 'symbolic' of it. Is it in its very oppositeness that its appeal to the locality chieftains lies? Or do they simply manipulate it for their own local purposes? Is there a *homo localis* lurking behind the skin of the chieftain who serves at the court of an anointed king? Or is he to be seen as bringing a valuable good or commodity, dharmic kingship, to the locality, otherwise deprived of it? The answer is perhaps to be found in another older dichotomy, that of the Aryan and Dravidian. The ritual is the Aryan (1980: 275); that 'explains' how it is so different from the locality system. Why do the south Indians adopt Aryan practices over the centuries? Is it because they recognize the Aryan as superior? Or is it because the Aryan is more effectively organized, perhaps into a patrimonial state?

The introduction of the Aryan here raises the question of how the segmentary state of south India compares with states in ancient north India.[30] Stein himself argues that the ideology of ritual sovereignty, of sacral kingship and its Dharma, are not southern but northern. It is, furthermore, assumed throughout his account to be opposed to the political arrangements of southern localities and to the form of sovereignty exercised by their peasant leaders. Is the north Indian state segmentary or feudal (that is, patrimonial in Weberese)?[31]

Finally, the depiction of a higher ritual and lower political level as differences of kind tends to vitiate Stein's own attempt to call attention to grades, to differences of degree among them. Stein is committed to the notion that one or the other terms of an opposition must, in the end, be reduced to the other. His sympathies clearly lie with the peasantry. So he repeatedly reduces the state to society when he, for example, asserts that 'the Chola state was the political embodiment of peasant agrarian and political relationships' (1985: 76).

But this dichotomy between a ritual or symbolic kingship and a local peasant society or political economy is not so easy to set aside. It seems necessary to the larger project in which Stein's own narrative of the gradual expansion and acculturation of a peasant society and its chieftains originated – the construction of the state in a post-colonial world as a mediator between a metaculture of free markets and citizenship and regional (and local) social arrangements in the 'third' world. Change is accepted as inevitable in the post-war conservative liberal view of the world, but it is considered highly desirable that it should be change of a gradual sort and that it should involve the slow but steady socialization of the regionally, and socially, disadvantaged. The dramatic and apocalyptic transformations of the kind favoured by either the radical economic liberal on the right or by the revolutionary Marxist on the left are to be shunned as leading to unpredictable and uncontrollable results. The story that Stein tells conforms rather well with the matrix from which it derives, although the outcome, the arrival in south India of 'sultanism', is not quite the triumphal history the liberal would like.[32]

One of the major achievements of Stein's work is to show his reader that when we look close up at peasants in the documents the Marxist preconception of a ground-down, morselized, and passive Asiatic peasantry is not confirmed, at least not when the story begins. On the contrary, far from being shown a peasantry construed as the mere instruments or patients of an overbearing unitary state, we are plunged into a veritable morass of the traces of peasants as agents, as constituting and reworking their own local ruling societies, which

---

[30] As Frank Perlin (1985: 115–16) points out, the historiographies of the two regions are largely isolated from one another (despite, I would add, the sweeping use of Aryan and Dravidian both make).

[31] The main difference to which Stein points is that north India was characterized by the 'tradition of a separated ruling stratum of kshatriyas' (1985: 85). It is not clear, however, whether the presence of such a stratum justifies us in considering the north Indian state as 'feudal' or whether it would constitute a subtype of the segmentary.

[32] Compare also the work, claiming to rely on Weber, of Hermann Kulke (1978a; 1978b) and his colleagues in Germany.

themselves turn out to be highly differentiated in their composition and quite complicated in the actions they undertook (1985: 84).

Yet Stein cannot reach his goal of reconstituting south Indian polities as agents because he remains ensnared in the metaphysics of typology. The acts of the transitory agents of medieval Tamilnad (now a state in south India) are themselves made into the expressions of that society's structure. This leads Stein (like others who displace agency on to a type of society) to presuppose as given the very groups and practices that are the product of the agents' acts. The *nāḍus*, the peasant communities, castes, and lineages, the Brahmans, the cultural-linguistic regions, the Aryan and Dravidian (indigenous) cultural and religious traditions may combine together in different ways and change their relative strengths, but somehow they end up falling outside of history itself.

This peasant essence seems, furthermore, to have had much the same consequence for the Indian state that Dumont's essence, caste or hierarchy, the opposition between the pure and the impure, had: 'Several important consequences stem from the coercive power and ruling ideology of dominant peasant lineages. These include: the relative instability of states in many parts of the subcontinent, the relative small scale of such states, and the vulnerability of most to predation and conquest' (1985: 84). So, although Stein has provided us with an excellent historical sociology, by which I mean an account of the changing distribution or deployment of resources by a certain type of society, what he has not done is provide us with an account of how 'medieval' Indians made their world.

5.6.5 Conclusion

To conclude, the post-Independence views of Dumont, Heesterman, and Stein all converge in their tendency to see the traditional Hindu state as the mediator between regional, factional, and tribal, caste, ethnic, or class interests on the one hand and a more or less static cultural plane of tradition on the other. They also agree in denying the existence of ancient and medieval India's imperial states as administered, unitary polities. All concur in depicting that state as successful in educating regional elites of India and transforming them into bearers of a high Indian culture. They also concur in portraying it as inherently the victim of what they see as the essence of that culture. For Dumont, that essence is caste ideology; for Heesterman, the value of renunciation; while for Stein, it is the parochial peasant mentality.

Because the concern for cultural unities is dominant in the US–USSR imperial formation, the scholarship on Indian political institutions does pay more attention to divine kingship than most of its ancestors did. Yet it continues to see in divine kingship a symptom of India's deficient political institutions, just as did its ancestors. Dumont treats it as a symptom of the systematic subordination of the political and economic to transcendent social and religious values on the one hand, and the refusal of the popular mind to accept this on the other, and, hence, a contradiction in terms. Heesterman looks at it as a symptom of India's foredoomed efforts to mediate between a transcendent value of renunciation and its opposite, a fragmented society of selfish local leaders. Finally, Stein sees it as the symptom of a transcendent cultural or ritual unity which is at odds with a segmented, local peasant society.

From a wider perspective, the divine kingship of all three can be taken as a transformed version of Frazer's divine king. He had (I paraphrase) argued that the king was the instrument and patient of his people in early societies rather than the other way round. When a king ceased to perform his magic-as-false-technology successfully and the crops failed or some other natural disaster overtook them, his subjects sacrificed him to the gods and found another (Frazer, 1911: 36). These scholars have given the king a Durkheimian transplant. His job is now to symbolize social unity and no longer to manage the weather. Over the centuries of a slow extension or simply the monotonous 'reproduction' of India's peculiar society, he is sacrificed to irresistible outsiders from the West in the name of a type of society – hierarchic caste, agonistic brotherhood, or ethnic peasant – and accompanying ideology – purity, renunciation, or localization – that could not cope with the world.

The historians of the high colonial period and their nationalist critics had transformed ancient India into a world of empires, international trade, and high culture followed by a medieval period of rapid decline. The commentators of the present imperial formation have to a large extent returned to the picture of India as an early ancient society, one that remains perennially post-tribal in its institutions and in which there is little difference between the ancient and the medieval. Yet the emphasis is different. Today's ancient India is a civilization not so much of overall *institutional* backwardness as it is of irreconcilable *values*. The intellectual dichotomies of America's Weber, that curious mix of economic empiricism and Kantian idealism, have become the cultural reality of twentieth-century India.

6

Reconstructions

Politics is still far from being a positive science, let alone an exact science. I have
no doubt that later generations will look back at many of our political systems with
the same feeling as a modern astronomer studies an astrological book or modern
chemist an alchemistic treatise. In politics we have not yet found firm and reliable
ground. Here there seems to be no clearly established cosmic order; we are always
threatened with a sudden relapse into the old chaos. We are building high and
proud edifices; but we forget to make their foundations secure. The belief that
man by the skilful use of magical formulae and rites can change the course of
nature has prevailed for hundreds and thousands of years in human history....
For there is, after all, a logic of the social world just as there is a logic of
the physical world. There are certain laws that cannot be violated with impunity.
Even in this sphere we have to follow Bacon's advice. We must learn how to obey
the laws of the social world before we can undertake to rule it. (Cassirer, 1946:
295)

6.1 FROM PATIENTS TO AGENTS

6.1.1 Eurasia's Four Imperial Formations

Europeans were not alone in constructing global schemes for ordering the
polities of the world. This is how Arab travellers, using a quadripartite model
that has a long history of its own in Buddhist India, China, and Tibet, described
the place of India in the 'medieval' world:[1]

The inhabitants of India and China agree that there are four great or principal kings in
the world. They place the king of the Arabs (Khalif of Baghdad) at the head of these, for
it is admitted without dispute that he is the greatest of kings. First in wealth, and in the
splendour of his Court; but above all, as chief of that sublime religion which nothing
excels. The king of China reckons himself next after the king of the Arabs. After him

[1] I plan to write about this elsewhere.

comes the king of the Greeks [Rum], and lastly the Balhara, prince of the men who have their ears pierced. (Sulayman, merchant, AD 851, completed by Abu Zayd Hasan around AD 916, in Elliot and Dowson, 1867: I, 3)[2]

Not saddled with the later European idea of a polity as an abstraction, as one of an indefinite number of formally equal, mutually exclusive sovereign nation-states, this account is able to talk about the sovereignty of humankind as both unitary and differentiated, ideal and empirical, and as embracing differences both of degree (wealth) and of kind (religion).

The Balhara, we are told next, is the paramount ruler of India:

The Balhara is the most eminent of the princes of India, and the Indians acknowledge his superiority. Every prince in India is master in his own state, but all pay homage to the supremacy of the Balhara. The representatives sent by the Balhara to other princes are received with most profound respect in order to show him honor. He gives regular pay to his troops, as the practice is among the Arabs. He has many horses and elephants, and immense wealth.... The kingdom of the Balhara commences on the sea side, at the country of Komkam [Konkan], on the tongue of land which stretches to China. The Balhara has around him several kings with whom he is at war, but whom he greatly excels. (Sulayman, merchant, in Elliot and Dowson, 1867: I, 3)

The account continues with brief descriptions of the major rivals of the Balhara, the most important of which were the kingdoms of the Gurjara, which was situated in western India between the territories of the Balhara in the Deccan and of the Arabs in Sind, and of Dharma, that is, Dharmapāla (770–810), in Bengal and Bihar, said to be at war with both the Balhara and the Gurjara.

The Arabs who travelled to India in the ninth and tenth centuries did not see her as a single imperial state under the central administrative control of an emperor; nor did they see India as a land of petty states, each warring against all. They had not convinced themselves that they were gazing on a society that was the eternal patient of caste and of foreign invaders. What they did see, using their idea of sovereignty, was, however, a single complex polity, what I call an imperial formation, a scale of kingships in which presumably contestable positions were continually displayed at royal courts. At the apex of this hierarchy in these two centuries was a king called Balhara whose capital was called Mankir.[3] Who was this 'king of kings' (as he is termed elsewhere by our Arab observers (Nainar, 1942: 155)), and what was his capital? The term Balhara was not, as the Arabs themselves say, a personal or dynastic name, but

[2] See also Sauvaget's annotated edition and translation (Sulayman, 1948: 11–12). For additional details on the Arab travellers' accounts of Balhara, consult S. Muhammad Husayn Nainar (1942: 155–65).

[3] Sauvaget explains away the paramount position given the Rashtrakutas in a note: the Arabs were led to exaggerate the prestige and power of their ally because they had amicable relations with the Rashtrakutas and were able to practise their religion in his domains (1948: 51). This despite the fact that the very next passage of the text surrounds the Balhara with rivals and goes on to praise the cavalry of one of these, the Gurjara king, an 'enemy of the Arabs', as the best in India and to describe the cloth from the kingdom of Dharmapāla as the finest in India.

an Arabic form of the title Vallabha-rāja, meaning 'the king who is the beloved', 'husband', or 'favourite', *vallabha*. The 'significant other' of whom the king was the beloved was *śrī*, 'fortune', or *prithivī*, 'the earth' (each of which was also the name of the two consorts of the Hindu god, Vishnu). This and similar titles were borne by the king of the Rashtrakuta dynasty, whose kingdom was not in the 'middle region' of India, the upper Gangetic plains, but in the western Deccan. Mankir, the capital, was none other than Mānyakheṭa (Malkhed). So our Islamic travellers of the ninth and tenth centuries saw a scale of kingships with its pinnacle in the Deccan occupied by the Rashtrakuta king. But they also saw more than simply this. They observed that this great lord went in procession to pay homage to a still greater lord visible in the form of an immense, jewel-encrusted image ('idol') of gold seated on a golden throne under a golden canopy and surrounded by thousands of lesser images:

The greatest of the buildings is the edifice at Mankir, which is a parasang in length. Mankir is the city in which there is the Balhara. It is forty parasangs long, [made] of teak, palm, and other sorts of wood. It is said that there are a thousand thousand [?] elephants there to transport the goods of the common people. At the king's stable there are sixty thousand elephants, and one hundred and twenty thousand elephants belong to the cloth bleachers there.

In the building of the idols, there are about twenty thousand idols made of a variety of materials, such as gold, silver iron, copper, brass, and ivory, as well as crushed stones adorned with precious jewels.

Every year the king goes to this building. He walks from his palace and then returns riding. In it there is an idol made of gold, the height of which is twelve cubits. It is on a throne of gold, under the center of a golden dome, all adorned with jewels – pearls and precious stones; red, yellow, blue and green. They slay sacrificial victims for this idol, and there is a certain day of the year, known to them, when they go furthest in making offerings of themselves as well. (Abu Dalaf, sent to India AD 942, in Ibn al-Nadim, 1970: II, 827–8)[4]

The 'edifice' that housed this image, the palace of this overlord, was the largest structure in Mānyakheṭa, leaving no one in doubt regarding his superiority. Quite possibly the principal idol at Mankir was the image of Vīra-Nārāyaṇa, a manifestation of Vishnu who descends in the form of a gigantic boar, Varāha, to rescue the Earth, and to whose consort, Mahālakshmī, the Rashtrakuta king Amoghavarsha I (814–*c*.878) once sacrificed his left little finger in order to avert some disaster (Bhandarkar, 1926).

Kings in India had their devotees too, men who were prepared to sacrifice themselves for their lords:

Among the kings of India, there are some who, when they accede to the throne, have some rice cooked and served to them in plantain leaves. The king has three or four hundred companions close to him who are willingly and without having been forced by him attached to his person. After he has partaken of the rice, he presents some of it to his companions. Each of them approaches in his turn and takes a small portion which he eats. All those who have eaten of this rice are obligated, when the king dies, or is killed,

---

[4] The length of a parasang in this context is, apparently, not known.

to be burned to the last man, on the same day that the king has died. It is a duty which does not permit delay and there must remain neither the body nor any other trace of them. (Abu Zayd Hasan, 1845: I, 120–2)[5]

The Rashtrakutas obtained the paramountcy of India between AD 753 and 760 and instituted the forms of image-worship called for by the theist discourses of the early medieval period in their kingdom. Thenceforth, a Rashtrakuta king, the Balhara of the Arabs, continued to preside over the more or less stable imperial formation that comprised all of India until around 975, when the ruling society of the Rashtrakuta imperium failed to defend and remake itself. The picture of the Balhara as one of the four great imperial rulers of the world and of temple Hinduism as a powerful, triumphant religion intimately connected with the imperial court and of soldiers committed to fighting for their king hardly squares with the portrait painted by the historians of an ancient India that was in irreversible decline.

Let me now turn to the question of reconstructing the ancient India the scholars of India have imagined. The major example I will draw on to counter this image is the Rashtrakuta imperial formation to which the Arabs have introduced us. This is not an idle choice, for the two centuries of their rule have been almost universally construed from the time of Vincent Smith's hegemonic *Early History*, as the nadir of India's inverted political history. The argument I wish to make is that if we shift our major assumptions and presuppositions, it is possible to 'show' that India was organized into an imperial formation in which a single state, the polity of the imperial Rashtrakutas, exercised hegemony. The political unity that the Rashtrakutas made and remade for a period of over two hundred years was, of course, not the unity that most Indologists and historians of India have wished to see absent or present in the subcontinent.

If we can construct a quite different picture of India during its medieval moment, when all of its essential features were supposed to have been most manifest, this will go some distance in challenging the depictions of India before this time, for the earlier chapters in this narrative of a civilization destined to decline but not disappear all depend on this outcome for their effect on their reader. It will not, of course, be possible here to do more, beyond filling in this major counterargument, to talk about the many ways in which a different picture of India could be constructed, beyond giving a few indications. That is a project in which I have been engaged for several years that will, I hope, see realization over the next several.

More generally, I undertake this partial reconstruction in order to challenge one of the most widely held assumptions of the human sciences, namely that a transcendent polity can be constructed and that 'scientific' knowledge of the human world will permit us to do this. The eminent philosopher who articulates this dream at the head of this chapter seems himself not to have considered that it might be the very suppression of human agency in the name of science or rationality that leads to the chaotic relapses he so abhors.

Here, then, are some suggestions about this history of a 'medieval' India by way of beginning the task of reading the Indian texts ('sources') from the angle of a theory of human agency. It would be presumptuous of me to present here

5 My translation. Consult also the rendering and note of Nainar (1942: 106–7).

in a full-blown form a new theory of Indian history, of the reading of Indian texts, or of Indian kingship. Recourse to the idea of a scale of forms would suggest that newer work done from its perspective should overlap with the previous work done. It would, for that reason, look askance at the announcement of some 'all new' theoretical apprehension of Others. At the same time it would also be counter to the approach I am advocating to stop only with the criticisms I have made of the historians of ancient and medieval India. The focus on human agency that I favour does indeed provide ways forward. It is not simply an exercise in epistemological analysis or 'post-modern' criticisms.

My strategy in what follows is first to take up 'caste' and then turn to the 'state', the institution that caste was designed to cripple. Throughout I will be trying to shift the focus from essence on to activities. Human agency is not, for reasons that will become clear, another essence that unifies and stabilizes our knowledge of Others.

Any attempt to reconstruct knowledge of India will inevitably have to tackle the problem of 'caste', for if we do not rework the substantialized agent of Indian civilization on to which scholarship has displaced the agency of Indians, talk of human agency will simply be perceived as so much noise around the periphery of the field. So the first task of this reconstruction is an attempt to represent caste as a form of subject-citizenry. My aim here its to show that 'castes' in 'medieval' India can be seen as agents. They do not have to be seen solely as the unproblematic (instruments or) patients of a post-tribal type of society. I will show that agency can be restored to the people of ancient India's village and towns without, however, turning them into anticipations of the modern 'individual' and his or her 'civil society'. Nor should we assume that because peasantries were agents that their rulers did not on occasion oppress them or that those peasantries did not oppress those over whom they ruled. Indeed, one aspect of agency I would hope to open up is the whole question of patiency which (as Foucault and Gramsci have taught us) is not as straightforward as repressive theories of domination have assumed.

There were certain activities, the performance of which had the effect of reiterating ('reproducing') or transforming (or destroying) the inter-relating polities that constituted an imperial formation. The argument I make is that the acts that did so for the polities of the countryside of a kingdom were those carried out by assemblies of villages or of unions of villages in connection with the activities of the agricultural year. Similarly, the activities carried out at meetings held in conjunction with the major marketing days were, I argue, the acts that had the effect of shaping and reshaping the mercantile and manufacturing polities of the towns.

I then take on the problem of the 'state', where I look into the holding of court and royal progresses, the activities which, in my view, reiterated and altered kingdoms as a whole and even entire imperial formations.

6.1.2 Castes as Subject-citizenries

Long ago, Hocart rejected both the occupational and racial theories of caste 'origin' and suggested that caste could be seen not only as a 'ritual' organization, but also as a form of political organization. However, he never elaborated on this latter point (1970: 114–18). I would like to make a few provocative comments here about how this might be done. Generally, discussions of 'citizenship' take place against a background which assumes that citizenship is opposed to 'subjecthood'. Studies of citizenship furthermore have assumed that citizenship itself in both ancient and modern Europe has been defined by an oppositional logic. The citizen is the man who is free; the non-citizen is not. The argument I would construct about Indian polities is that citizenship and subjecthood were both combined and that citizenship there – 'caste' – was defined not only by oppositions but also by distinctions and by differences of degree as well as of kind.

When ancient Indian texts such as the *Arthaśāstra* and the *Laws of Manu* talked about villagers, they did so within the framework of a classification system that construed villagers as one of the seven 'limbs' or 'constituents' (*aṅga*) of a 'rulership' or polity (*rājya*), which they considered a special form of 'lordship' or 'mastery'. They used the term *jānapada* to constitute them both as the subjects or people of a king and as 'residents of the countryside', the outermost of the limbs. They distinguish them from their superior complement, the *paura* or 'residents of the city', and especially of the more interior royal city. Both of these were distinguished from the higher class, consisting of those lords and masters who were at one and the same time royal servants and companions, the *amātya*, those who constituted the ruling society of a kingdom, the men entitled to attend the royal court on a daily basis. These were, in turn, distinguished from the king himself, the 'lord' (*svāmin*), the highest and spatially innermost of the limbs of a polity.

Virtually none of the Euro-American discourses on caste has attempted to relate the notion of *jānapada* (or of *paura*) to that of caste, *jāti* or *varṇa*. They have tried to unite within a single field, that of 'caste', phenomena which Indian discourses have treated otherwise. Those societies of rural India which, I would argue, can be seen as the *jānapada par excellence* are theorized in the anthropology of India not as the constituent of a polity but as the 'dominant' caste. The assumption with respect to a dominant caste is that a naturally and primordially closed group has retained or gained dominance over others less fortunate, whether by force of arms or hard work and population increase. Combined with arguments that the councils of villages were or are really the councils of these castes, such scholarship 'shows' that 'caste' is the unifying principle of social organization in Indian civilization.

The nationalist historian, Jayaswal (4.5.1), argued that the *jānapada* was a representative legislative body, a 'realm assembly' something like a House of Commons. Unfortunately he stretched the evidence and tried to impose an English legalist framework on it. Both he and his critics failed to see that *jānapadas* were political societies with the multiple assemblies and differing jurisdictions that they discussed under the heading of provincial or local 'administration'. As a result, they left the *jānapada* as an unorganized category of 'citizens' or 'the people', as in Altekar (1962: 146–57, 208–24).

One of the objections that would surely be raised against this idea of treating the *jānapada* as a citizen body is the fact that castes divide a community into numerous solidarity groups, while the idea of citizenship or nationality unites people into one. A closer scrutiny of this neat dichotomy, however, produces problems. Assuming that we have not been misled by scholarship on Europe, it would seem that citizenship or nationality there, even in ancient times was, as indicated above, defined in exclusivist terms. But why can one not speak of *inclusive* as well as *exclusive* forms of citizenship? If we look at 'caste' not as a system of groups given in nature but as a society of self-monitoring agents, the picture looks rather different.

The so-called dominant caste was in any demarcated territory, a village, union of villages, district, or province, the citizenry *par excellence*, the *jānapada*. The leading men of a locality, those referred to in the records as *mahattaras*, 'betters', were mostly the masters of households (*kuṭumbins*) making up that citizenry. But the other castes who were in the relationship of a dependency to it were not excluded from citizenship. The evidence collected on the strong councils of the lower castes suggests that they, too, were constituted in part as societies, and the evidence from the Punjab and elsewhere concerning the occasional plenary sessions of these caste councils under the leadership of that of the dominant caste would seem to be based on the assumption that the people of the lower castes may not have been full citizens, but were citizens none the less. If the idea that full citizenship rights were enjoyed only by the dominant caste itself precludes their 'caste' council from consideration as a government of the village, then we would have to do some serious rethinking about those organizations we have referred to as governments in the West's history until very recently, for universal suffrage is a relatively new practice (itself often vitiated by narrow and formalist ideas of what constitutes political participation as well as apathy on the part of the enfranchised).

Another objection, that caste society is, as Maine told us, based on kinship (status) rather than co-residence (contract) is both more serious and more trivial. Ideas of citizenship in virtually all of today's nation-states use tropes of family, blood, marriage, paternity, and kin to constitute themselves. It is difficult to see how caste as *jānapada* and *paura* is more determined by 'kinship' than is citizenship. Especially if one means by kinship, birth. The category of citizenship is no more (or less) territorial than is that of caste membership. Householders of the ruling society or dominant caste in one village did not possess any rights of mastery in another village, even within the same union (except possibly through marriage). If anything, the kin principle in the polis was more exclusivist than it was in the caste. Persons of other castes within the same village as the dominant caste were not reduced to the status of aliens or slaves (although the 'untouchable' notion comes pretty close).[6]

[6] Risley came close to the 'dangerous' idea of seeing caste as a form of citizenship. One of the seven 'types' of caste he distinguished was a residual one which he termed 'national'. Here is what Risley, hardly unaware of the difficulty he had landed himself in, says of this type: 'Where there is neither nation nor national sentiment it may seem paradoxical to talk about a national type of caste. There exist, however, certain groups, usually regarded as castes at the present day, which cherish traditions of bygone sovereignty and seem to preserve traces of an organization considerably more elaborate than that of an ordinary tribe' (*Census of India, 1901*: I (Pt. 1, Report), 525). Risley named, as two examples of this type, the Newars, the

Even a cursory glance at Indian discursive texts makes it clear that those classed as *jānapada* were considered to be subjects of a king or lord. The term *jānapada* and its synonyms, for example *prajā*, were used in those texts to constitute and designate a class of people which was at once territorial, economic, and political. It consisted of people who resided not in the capital city or the towns of a kingdom, but in the countryside. These were people, men, who were the masters of households (*kuṭumbin*) engaged for the most part in agriculture for their livelihood. They were supposed to be loyal to their king, making over to him the agreed-upon share of their agricultural produce. He in turn was supposed to protect them, not only in the prophylactic sense of preventing harm, but also in the positive sense of causing them to increase, to become more prosperous. These farmers, as masters of households (including their wives and children, fields and cattle, and plows), were, thus, subjects. They were ruled by kings and their ministers. Yet one must not assume that because they were subjects they were not also citizens. The Indian discursive texts on statecraft or polity and the charters issued by kings assumed that the countries or localities (*deśa*), families or clans (*kula*), 'castes' (*jāti*), and 'guilds' (*śreṇi*), and religious or political associations (*saṃgha*) comprising the urban and rural residents of a polity had an inherent, but limited and partial capacity (we might call it 'rights') to combine within and among themselves and order their own affairs. They also assumed, and often asserted, that the lordships or masteries exercised by the constituents of a polity or an entire imperial formation, which they saw as a scale of forms reaching from the lowliest of servants who did not possess mastery even over his own body to a paramount king of kings who was the overlord of the entire earth, could be successful or complete only when they were, by their varying activities, brought into the proper relationship to one another.

6.1.3 Assemblies of the Rural Citizenry

The examples I present here of both the *jānapada* and *paura* associations and of their place in the polities of the time comes from the charters of the Karnataka during the Rashtrakuta and Chola imperial formations (eighth to thirteenth centuries, 'early medieval' India).[7]

'predominant race' in Nepal, and the Marathas of Maharashtra, but he might as well have mentioned any number of others – the Jats and Gujars of noth and western India, the Rajputs of Rajasthan, the Patidars (Koonbees) of Gujarat, the Vakkaligas of Karnataka, the Vellalas of Tamilnad, the Nayars of Kerala, and the Reddis of Andhra, that is, those which more recent anthropologists might refer to as 'dominant' castes.

[7] The contents of these records were themselves first made available by the extensive labours of two colonialist scholars around the turn of the century. One was Benjamin Lewis Rice (1837–1927), educator in Mysore and Director of Archaeological Researches; he served as Secretary of the Education Commission headed by W.W. Hunter in 1882–3. The other was James Faithfull Fleet (1847–1917), who learned Sanskrit at University College, London, from Theodor Goldstücker (1821–72), before going to India in 1867, where he was a civil servant, in Bombay Presidency, for some thirty years. R. C. Majumdar first pointed to its significance (1918: 153–7). The later national historians, A. S. Altekar (1967: 188–211), and most recently, G. S. Dikshit (1964), have added to this knowledge.

The Okkalu or Vakkaliga, the 'farmers' or 'householders' (we might as well translate the terms as 'rural citizen') of the Karnata country, were certainly organized into villages, each of which had a headman called an *ur-gāvuṇḍa*.[8] But these headmen in turn appear to have met together under the headship of a locality or district lord, a *nāḍ-prabhu* or *nāl-gāvuṇḍa*; there were also, according to Dikshit (1964: 45), associations of at least as many as fourteen *nāḍus*, designated as *mahanāḍu*, or great districts. He makes only one reference, in a footnote (56), to the *paura* and *jānapada*. His account is, furthermore, highly idealist and voluntarist, concluding that 'There was no element of compulsion either in the formation of the *nāḍus* or in their integration into groups of *nāḍus*. It was a purely voluntary effort and was undertaken because the people themselves realized the value of cooperation', and retains the assumption of state and locality as opposites: 'the central government was not supposed to be interested in the internal affairs of the *nāḍus*. That government came into the picture only when there were disputes between the *nāḍus*. Otherwise it was no concern of the central government how these regional associations combined among themselves' (1964: 181). Kings who called themselves *rāshṭrakūṭas*, 'peaks of kingdoms', addressed the former in their Sanskrit charters as *grāmakūṭas* (village 'peaks'; from which, according to Dikshit, the term *gāvuṇḍa* is derived). The latter they addressed as *vishayapatis* (lords of districts). The largest sections ('subcastes') into which the Okkalu appear to have been divided were, not surprisingly, named after the still larger *nāḍs*, the medieval countries or provinces of the Deccan, viz., the Gangadikara (after Gangavadi) and the Nonaka (after Nolambavadi) whom Rice refers to as the 'subjects' of those places (1897: I, 228–31).

These territorial headships of the Okkalu were apparently conceived of more as small courts rather than as councils of shareholders, although the use of numerical figures to designate territories could be taken as evidence of the latter (see below). This organization into relatively unitary rulerships should not, however, be considered a timeless ethnic or customary form of governance. People within the same kingdom could be and were also organized into relatively plural rulerships. Organization in these forms was both a question of different purposes and of conscious strategies pursued on the part of ruler and ruled in differing situations. The organization into unitary rulerships made it possible for the lords of provinces, districts, and villages to combine on occasion with each other and the royal court to which they paid revenue. They could, in a

---

[8] Rice, who in his account of Mysore otherwise hews to the party line on village communities, adumbrates the notion of the *jānapada* and *paura* in ancient Karnataka when he says of the political organization of the medieval period in Mysore's history that: 'The chief men of *nāḍs* or rural circles were the *gāmuṇḍa*, a word which, after becoming *gauṇḍa*, now appears as *gauḍa*. Their head or chief was the *nāḍ-prabhu*, and they seem to have represented and been responsible for the agricultural classes, as the *paṭṭaṇa svāmi*, *paṭṭaṇa sheṭṭi* or town mayor was for the mercantile and industrial classes' (1897: I, 574). At another point in his account, Rice even analogizes local society with an idea of citizenship, albeit in exclusivist terms. He says of the hilly Malnad region that while Brahmanical influence is less there than in the plains, there is there a more marked difference between upper and lower classes, 'the whole population being as it were divided into two distinct grades, the Patrician and Plebeian; it might perhaps be said, the freemen and the slaves' (1897: I, 652–3).

word, constitute an army or armies. They could present themselves at the end of the rainy season, when the major act by which a kingdom reproduced itself, the annual holding of court, took place, and go with their overlord and perhaps his paramount overlord on the progress-cum-military campaign that followed it. Plural rulership, exemplified in the urban assemblies below, was the form deployed by political societies that, for a variety of reasons, remained apart from royal courts and progresses.

Now, it was unlikely that the heads of villages attended the imperial court of the Rashtrakuta emperor at his capital. Yet it would seem that they did meet under the leadership of district lords or governors of their own political society or caste who themselves did have occasion to assemble at the court of a provincial governor (viz. Nolambavadi), if not at the imperial court itself. So far in this account I have allowed the assumption that the Rashtrakuta was a distant figure in a remote capital to stand, but this too is largely a product of the dichotomous construct of the village and state. The imperial kings of Hindu India spent a good part of every year on progresses. When the emperor made a gift from the imperial camp, we may assume that those whom he addresses, informs, and commands in the grant assembled before him if he was in the vicinity of the land to be granted.[9] Some (probably the majority) of the lords of districts and the larger polities of which these were parts, the provinces or realms of an empire, were themselves also commanders of units in the imperial army.

The army (*daṇḍa*) was also a constituent of the Indian polity in its self-conception. It was the weapon with which a kingship, like a warrior lord, protected itself. Within a world where every man was potentially armed, weaponry was accorded a good deal of attention. The kind and quality of weapon a lord had was crucial both to his survival and to his success. It was also the outer sign of his inner power. I can hardly emphasize too strongly the importance of armies to a kingship in India, such as the Rashtrakuta, which claimed to exercise paramount overlordship. And in this connection the masters of the *janapada* were integral, for the army was also an agent that overlapped with the other agents that comprised a polity. A good number of the young men of the Okkalu caste undoubtedly spent the better part of their manhood as warriors, mostly foot-soldiers, on the march and in camp with the governor of a province or district and, on occasion, with the Rashtrakuta himself. The many *vīragals* or 'hero-stones' found in the Deccan bear witness to this participation and its importance to the polities that succeeded one another there.[10] One cannot but be convinced, even by a casual reading of these records, that battles were important events. They were not, as they are often seen to be, either exercises of physical force or decorative symbolic displays of a theatrical state. They were complex dialectical and eristical acts, determinative of relationships between the parts of polities and of polities to each other in an imperial

---

[9] When he was at a distance from it, they assembled before an emissary (*dūtaka*).

[10] Many of these, telling their story in strips of sculptures carved on the slab, with the text of grants acting as captions, were first edited and translated by Rice. For an account of the sculpture on one from the Rashtrakuta period, see Hayavadana Rao (1930: II.1, 158–9). One of the more well-worked is the Begur Inscription of Ereyappa; see Fleet (1900–01b) for a reading of both texts and sculpture.

formation. Success in battle, fighting for his overlord, was also the surest way for the master of an Okkalu or farmer household to persuade his lord of his devotion and win, as a result of his lord's 'grace' (*prasāda*), the lordship of a group of villages, a district *nāḍu*, or even a provincial *nāḍu*. From the standpoint of the slain and his followers, the same act was definitively eristical. As all the parties in this interaction also claimed to be the willing instruments of a god in his truest form, these acts could also be interpreted as signs of divine will (a vital point to be taken up in 6.2.2).

Here, in a multi-authored translation, is part of one of the two stone monuments which I give as examples. It records the grants of several provincial and district lordships that the Rashtrakuta emperor, Krishna III (939–68), made to Būtuga II, a prince of the Western Ganga dynasty and lord of Gangavāḍi (as well as his elder sister's husband) out of gratitude for the heroic deed he performed on the battlefield and contains the grant Būtuga II in turn bestowed on a warrior of his, Manalera. Note how Būtuga honours the latter's weapon, an act, called sword-washing (*bāl-gachchu*), parallel to the washing of the feet of Brahmans when a grant of the village or other revenues was made to them. Ereyappa, another Ganga prince, had earlier gained independence from his Rashtrakuta overlord.

Hail! While Būtuga (II), having fought and killed Rāchamalla, the son of the illustrious Erayappa, was governing the ninety-six thousand: –
At the time when Kannaradeva (Krishna III) was fighting against the Chola, Būtuga (II) stabbed Rājāditya with a dagger in the howdah, and thus fought and killed him; and Kannaradeva gave to Būtuga, in token of approbation, the Banavase twelve-thousand, the Belvola three-hundred, the Purigere three-hundred, the Kisukāḍ seventy, and the Bāgenāḍ seventy.
Being pleased with the manner in which Manalera stood out in front of him and pierced (his foes), Būtuga gave (to him), as a *bāl-gachchu*-grant, the Atukur twelve and the village of Kadiyur of (the) Belvola (district). May there be auspicious and great fortune![11]

The text of the second of these stones, translated by Rice, is dated to 911 AD. It is interesting in part because it shows that under certain circumstances a woman could hold a rural headship. The transaction recorded is a complex one. The gist of it is the grant of rice land made to a temple by Jakkiyabbe, the wife of a deceased district head, after the governor of Banavase 12,000, who held that lordship (of district size, as indicated by the number), along with the right to have five drums beat and the title of High King of the Periphery (*mahāsāmanta*) from his overlord, the Rashtrakuta emperor, Krishna II (*c*.878–914), appointed her to the position held by her husband:

Be it well. When Akālavarisha, favourite of earth and fortune, mahārājādhirāja parameśvara parama-bhaṭṭāraka, Kannara-Deva's kingdom was extending on all sides; – in the Saka year 834, the year Prajapati, &c, – When, entitled to the five big drums, the mahāsāmanta Kalivittarasa, of the Kālki-devaysar-anvaya, was ruling the Banavāsi Twelve Thousand, – on Sattarasa Nāgārjuna, who was holding the office of *nāl-gāvuṇḍa*

[11] The subsidiary record at the top of the stone containing the Ātukur inscription (Fleet, 1900–01b). Rice first edited and translated the text; the translation here incorporates marginal corrections made by L. D. Barnett, of Fleet's.

of the Nāgarakhaṇḍa Seventy, dying under the orders of Kalivittarasa, the king having given to his wife the grade of *nāl-gāvuṇḍa*, and Jakkiyabbe was holding the office of *nāl-gāvuṇḍa* – and Nanduvara Kaliga was holding the office of *perggaḍe* [administrator; revenue accountant], – and [?] the survivor of the Sundiga tribe was holding the office of *perggaḍe* to Koḍangeyur, – the Seventy and the Three Hundred granted Avutavūr to Jakkiyabbe as promised. And Jakkiyabbe, in giving away the dues of the *nāl-gāvuṇḍa* in Avutavūr on account of the Nāgarakhaṇḍa Seventy, granted 4 *mattal* of rice-land in Jakkili for the temple.

Skilled in ability for good government, faithful to the Jītendra śāsana, rejoicing in her beauty, Jakkiyabbe, when having received the Nāgarakhaṇḍa Seventy, she was protecting it well, though a woman, in the pride of her own heroic bravery, – at that time, bodily disease having made inroads deciding that worldly enjoyments were insipid, she sent for her daughter and making over to her her posterity, freed herself from the entanglement of the chain of desire ... came and in the *tīrtha* of Bandaṇike, O wonder, forsook (the body) of Jakkiyabbe ...

The writer was Nāgavarmmā ... The stone was set up by Mudda of the Sanduga tribe ... son of Beleyamma (Rice, 1902a)

The numerical figures attached to the territorial units in this and other grants are important. They have been taken as referring to the population, number of soldiers, number of villages or the amount of the revenue owed (Altekar, 1967: 139–49), but I concur with Stein (1980: 127–30) in seeing them as designating or signalling the capacity of subject-citizens to constitute headships (or assemblies) for villages (the tens), associations of villages (the hundreds), or even associations of a district (*nāḍu*, the thousands).

To sum up, what we see depicted in records like these, if we shift our major assumptions and presuppositions, is a polity comprised of overlapping societies that had political purposes as well as economic and ritual ones. We do not see a polity consisting of a distant, repressive state on the one hand and a natural 'society' of isolated, inwardly oriented villages organized into auto-reproductive castes on the other. (Nor do we see a polity that consisted of post-tribal, hierarchically ordered caste segments.) The rural society of Indian discourses, the *jānapada*, consisted of overlapping territorial societies. Higher local lords belonged to the *jānapada* associations of both the village and district, while the *jānapada* itself overlapped with the higher society of a royal court and with its army. At each turn in the constitution of these classes as agents we also see that subjecthood and citizenship were both present, which is to say that the same man was now a ruler and now among the ruled. Finally, we see that not only did the countryside and the royal and imperial courts as compound agents overlap, but the activities upon which their continued existence depended also overlapped. Especially crucial were their military activities. The old idea that these were confined to the armies of the oriental despots and had, at most, only a destructive effect on village life is certainly belied by the evidence from the charters, once we begin to take their discursive content seriously.

6.1.4   Assemblies of the Urban Citizenry

So far as the *paura* constituent of the polity is concerned it is hard to resist mentioning the evidence from the grants of the eleventh and twelfth centuries concerning the Masters or Svamis of Aihole 500, then apparently a major city in the Karnataka.[12] These identified themselves as protectors of the Vīra-Bananju-dharmma, which term itself seems to have been used to embrace both Jaina and Śaiva religious orders. These merchants held assemblies on market day. Records called the assemblies confined to the residents of the town in which they lived *nagara*, 'town', meaning (synecdochally) 'town assembly'. These merchants also called meetings that included masters not only of the town, but of the countryside of a district or province as well. They designated these as *mahānāḍu*, 'plenary district assembly'. The records refer to the participating units not only as 'castes' (*varṇa* or *jāti*), but as 'compacts' or 'societies' (*samaya*), or 'constituent props' (*prakṛti*), the latter of which usages suggest the associational and agentive aspect of these entities (Dikshit, 1964: 72–3).

Let us look at a portion of a charter that emerged from one of these assemblies.[13] After a genealogy and praise of the kings of the country, the voice of the charter turns to the narration of a royal servant of the king, a military commander (*daṇḍanāyaka*) to whom the king gives, as a favour, because of the valiant deeds he had performed on the battlefield, the province of Banavase-nāḍ (Shimoga District).

The charter then lists those who assembled for the purpose of making the grant. It begins with the 'great lord of a province' (*mahāmaṇḍaleśvara*) and his brother and brother-in-law; the two mayors (presumably of the two market streets) of the provincial capital (*paṭṭana-svāmin*), both merchants; the head priests (*ācārya*) of the three Śaiva orders, holders of tax-free land and recipients of other revenues and incomes assigned from the government accounts; and the other leading citizens; the administrator (*saudore herggaḍe*) for the town council and the religious orders, and his assistant; and, finally, the military men, depicted as heroes.

Next, the charter lists the merchants themselves – we have moved from those who belong to the minister class and their religious donees to the *paura* class. Note how the guild or association of these merchants, unlike those of the *jānapada* class, styles its members as being of 'different countries' (*nānādeśi*), as distributed over a variety of differing kinds of settlements and yet centred on Aihole. They formed a dispersed association. Here is Rice's translation of this passage:

And besides these, – firm, of great prudence, granters of their desires to dependents, of one word, devoted to the feet of Īśvara, followers of the policy which raises the prosperity of countries at the right seasons, of good character, of unshaken truth, of exalted merit, beloved by all, which is not flattery, members of the Bananju-dharmma; – thus entitled in many ways to honour, residents of Ayyāvole, Challunki and many other chief *grāmas* [villages], *nagaras* [towns], *kheḍas* [hamlets], *kharvvaḍas* [markets], *maḍambas* [village unions], *droṇamukhas* [garrisons], *puras* [fortified cities?], and *pattanas* [seaports], of Lāṭa, Gauḍa, Karṇṇāṭa, Baṅgāla, Kaśmīra, and other countries at the points of the compass;

[12] Note the use of the numerical figure, 500, to indicate an association or headship. See above, 6.1.3.
[13] Engraved in stone on one of the temples to which the gift is made, it is dated to AD ‡181 in the reign of Ahavamalla (1180–3) of the Kalachuri dynasty.

the two sects of Nānā Deśis, Manevarate and Jorūpa local men; the maṇigāra [manager] Māṇika-Seṭṭi and other seṭṭis (named), all of the merchants, – forming an immense (assembly) ... (Rice, 1902a)

The remainder of the text enumerates the items given. The Merchant 500 clearly formed a citizen body of considerable power. The voice that praises them goes so far as to depict them as sovereign with respect to trade in the same manner as a paramount king. Their assemblies and especially their plenary assemblies were no mere 'caste councils'. From those enumerated as donors in the charters of these Svāmis or masters – including grain-dealers, goldsmiths, flower-sellers, oilmen, cloth-dealers, potters, leather-workers, and basket-makers – it is clear that a number of castes or professions occupying different quarters of the towns were associated with and led by the long-distance Banajigas, the 'caste' said traditionally to be the head of the 'eighteen castes' or 'professions' of the Karnataka.

The relationship of the 500 to the royal court on the one hand and to the citizenries of town and country on the other is not simply represented or expressed in the assemblies which they orchestrated. It has rather to be seen as reiterated and transformed by those acts. Whence the language used. The words of praise delivered in assembly on their behalf are not to be dismissed as yet another example of the charter's subject, here the merchants, 'blowing their own trumpets with the note of fantastic and ludicrous exaggeration which they occasionally affected' (Barnett, 1927–8). They are better seen as integral to the stream of acts by which the merchants renewed their position in the polity and, given their far-flung network, the imperial formation of the day. They were meant to persuade both the royal court and the other citizens of different castes that previous agreements reached on all sides should be renewed (or perhaps even 'improved' upon). At the same time, however, they have also a potentially coercive or eristical aspect. Their clear implication, with all their overtones of universal sway, is that a regional king or local guildsmen who would oppose the 500 would find themselves in difficulty.

Once again we can see the merchants as the citizenry *par excellence* not only among the residents of the cities and towns, but also in relation to the rural citizenry within an Indian polity. Their powers were not just different in kind (long-distance) from their inferiors (local), they were also different in degree (both could participate in decisions affecting their communities and both could make donations to its religious institutions but the powers of the merchants were greater). Their assemblies were not, furthermore, simply confined to *complementing* those of the villagers of a district or group of districts. Their plenary assemblies could, on occasion, also *include* those assemblies of the countryside within a given district or province.[14]

The guild of merchants was, however, organized not as a unitary lordship, as were many of the *jānapada* associations, but, as the repeated use of the term 'Svamis 500' announced, as a plural lordship or rulership. They were not the

---

[14] The associations of the Right-hand and Left-hand 'castes' in the Chola and post-Chola imperial formations of Hindu India could well be seen as variants of the *paura* and *jānapada*. See Stein (1980: 173–215).

only communities organized in this way. The charters do not supply the privileged settlements of Brahmans (donated to them by kings), whether they resided in the countryside (*agrahāra* villages), or in the cities (Brahmapuris), with a headman or lord. On the other hand, they do refer to them, as they do the merchants, by a number, viz., the 420, the 220, the 40, the 10, and the honorific term 'distinguished men' (*mahājana*). It would thus seem that they, too, were organized as plural rulerships. The reason for this difference in organization was closely connected with the different modes of participation in the polity. The peripatetic merchants and the settled Brahmans attained their respective mercantile and religious ends by remaining, *as societies*, apart from royal courts. Some of them undoubtedly participated personally in royal courts and as a body when the royal court or its emissary appeared in their vicinity to transact business involving them; but they did not march off to participate as a single body in a royal court.

The image of India as essentially rural, the picture of an Indian countryside divided into 'castes' organically related to one another within tens of thousands of villages and agonistically related outside of them, could not be more at odds with the picture I have sketched here. Those 'castes' can be retheorized as subject-citizenries. The mercantile 'castes' of cities, towns, and markets, those classified as *paura*, were dispersed associations governed by urban assemblies. The agricultural 'castes' of the countryside *jānapada* were territorial associations governed in 'early medieval' Karnataka by local lords. Both were complex agents, overlapping with one another and with royal courts. Far from being opposed in their thoughts and actions to an 'external' state, they were continuous with them. Rather than being excluded from the life of Indian polities, they actively participated in it. Indeed, by so doing they partly constituted it.

The periodic assemblies of these rural and urban citizenries with imperial and royal courts, whether through emissaries when they were at their permanent capitals or face to face when those courts were on progresses and camped in or near the localities concerned, were the acts that made and remade Indian polities. They were not merely expressions of underlying structures or symbolic representations of a social order. Nor can they be reduced to a premodern form of administrative 'control', a word whose use often implies that people can be manipulated at will, as if they were objects with no minds of their own. Rather, these acts are better seen as dialectical and eristical interactions between and among complex and shifting agents. The displays of weaponry, regalia, the mustering of armed men, horses, elephants, and the speeches delivered on these occasions in the form of petitions, praises, and commands, the placing of people in positions relative to one another, were meant on the part of both imperial and royal courts and of the citizenries of city and countryside to persuade those involved to come to or renew agreements. It would be a grave error, often committed by those of an idealistic turn of mind, to replace the objectifying, world-ordering administrative model with an intersubjective model of friendly communication and 'dialoguing' and harmonious political participation freely entered into. The very same significations had also an eristical aspect. Those on whatever side who had taken positions of disagreement could take these words and deeds, and the visual displays of which these assemblies consisted, as implicit threats or potential insults. Or they could, conversely, engage in these acts with the intent of showing would-be opponents that they could be defeated or crushed or caused a great deal of anguish if they did not at least keep still.

6.2   THE IMPERIAL FORMATION OF THE RASHTRAKUTAS

6.2.1   Holding Court and Issuing Orders

The idea that the essence of government in India was some sort of divine kingship has formed a major pillar in the constructs of India, complementing the idea of India as a caste society. This combined the notion of a type of government – traditional monarchy – with a type of mentality – that of the Hindu, which was dominated by a faculty, the imagination, differing from (and considered lower than) that of reason.

The despoticists tended to see divine kingship as the instrument of India's caste society. Feudalists, on the other hand, tended to view divine kingship as its patient (or victim). Either way, the excessive divinity or sacrality of Indian kingship has been taken as a symptom of its peculiarity. To the extent that divine kingship was a conscious policy of the rulers, it was seen as an attempt to manipulate the superstitious, caste-ridden masses. To the extent that it was actually a belief of the rulers, it was seen as symptomatic of the imagination – a lower form of female reason – that prevailed in the Indian mind, of its inability to focus on the world in a consistent and moderate manner. Indian rulers were either caught up in dreams of glory and salvation or plunder-happy, bloodthirsty manipulators whose Machiavellian policies were simply self-seeking and not directed toward any higher social good. During those brief moments when India approached political unity, it was because an outside conqueror – Aryan, Persian, Greek, Mogul, or British – had inserted a degree of masculine rationality into her body politic. Virtually everyone saw the increasing divinity of the king over time as an index of the state's weakness, its growing 'medievality'.

The only depiction that departed considerably from this construct was, once again, that of A. M. Hocart, not surprising given his views on caste. I have just shown, following Hocart's lead, that caste can be theorized as a form of political organization. If the notion of caste as a lingering post-tribal form of society that constitutes the very antithesis of a unified polity collapses, then the divine kingship that was supposed to be its instrument or patient will also want revision. His arguments (1927; 1970), long and diffuse, and not without problems, deserve a detailed discussion which I cannot enter into here. Because he rejected the psychology of imagination and symbol that others had imposed on the peoples with 'divine' kings, Hocart was able to argue that the world of which the ancients or primitives conceived was a whole. Within it, the kingship equated with the sun, its officialdom with the lesser gods of the sky, the queen with the earth, were, together with the commoners, all parts. Each and every one of these constituents was divine in some degree and respect. Their divinity was, however, not simply given. The divinity of the king was, therefore, not to be seen either as the product of a popular psychology or as an elitist ploy to sway an ignorant populace. The divinity at issue was the result of particular rites which bring all of the constituents of a kingdom into contact with the powers of the gods, as necessitated by the cosmology and theology of the particular people involved.[15]

My own views are a critical extension of Hocart's. I argue that a world-ordering rationality can be seen as integral to Hindu kingship, that the divinity of that kingship can be seen as an issue of 'reason' and 'will' in the formation and re-formation of political societies in ancient India. This may not have been the world-ordering rationality that discourses on India have repeatedly assumed to be absent from divine kingship, but it can be seen there. As in my discussion of caste, my emphasis will be on activities rather than on essences.

The annual holding of court, preceded by a 'ceremonial bath' (*abhisheka*) and followed by a royal progress (which might turn into a extended military campaign) was the act that reconstituted or reproduced the ruling class of a polity as a self-ruling society. The agent of this activity for a simple kingdom, a kingdom consisting of one 'country' (*deśa*), was the lord of that kingdom and his entourage. The agent for an imperial kingdom, a realm compounded of several countries, was a man called by the term *rājarāja*, 'king of kings', or by some variation upon it, and his associates. The agent that remade all of India, the 'entire earth', as an imperial formation was the king of kings who, together with his court, succeeded, in the eyes of those who constituted the polities of an imperial formation, in exercising his supremacy over other would-be claimants. He was the king called a Chakravartin, a 'universal monarch' or 'lord of the entire earth' (*sārvabhauma*). What I am referring to here as an 'imperial formation' is almost exactly what texts on statecraft, beginning with the *Arthaśāstra*, theorize as the 'circle of kings' (*maṇḍala, rājamaṇḍala*).[16]

The idea of the Chakravartin, of a universal monarch, and with it the idea that 'sovereignty' or, rather, overlordship over the earth, was a whole to be embodied in one polity (and not a particular to be instantiated in independent, sovereign nation-states) appeared before the time of the Mauryas. Buddhists, Smārta Brahmans, Śaivas and Vaishnavas, as well as the Jainas dialectically shaped and reshaped political theologies of the Chakravartin from that time on. That is, all of the major religious orders incorporated into their soteriologies the idea of a universal monarch or paramount king of India, a 'great man' (*mahāpurusha*) who, endowed with special powers, was able to complete a 'conquest of the quarters' of India in the name of a still greater agent, the one taken as overlord of the cosmos. The names given to this compound activity, the 'conquest of the quarters' (*dig-vijaya*) and 'conquest in accord with cosmomoral order' (*dharma-vijaya*), referred to a royal progress that was supposed to display the performer of it as the overlord of each of the four directional regions,

---

[15] One should mention in this regard the very important work of Frankfort, who argued (1948) that the civilizations of Egypt and Mesopotamia were quite different from one another and not reducible in some evolutionary scheme to a common 'stage'.

[16] That text devotes nine of its fifteen books to this topic. Glossed usually as 'diplomacy', 'foreign policy', or 'international relations', it begs for an extensive analysis from the viewpoint of human agency.

together with a middle region, taken to comprise the whole of the earth. Kings who recognized him as universal king offered submission or worked out some sort of accommodation in the form of an 'agreement' (*sandhi*). For a variety of reasons, mostly having to do with imperial ideology, British scholars like Vincent Smith (and many of the Indian national historians, too) have brushed this idea of the Chakravartin aside as one more example of the Indian imagination's incapacity to connect with reality. This, despite Europe's periodic fascinations with an Alexander the Great, Roman imperial cults, French Sun-Kings, Elizabethan Astreas, returning Fredericks, and, more recently, a Führer, il Duce, Lenin's or Stalin's personality cult, the US presidency, and a soap-operatic monarchy in Britain.[17] If, however, we shift the perspective from which we view Indian polities – and this involves changing the content of every one of the major terms used to 'translate' the terms in Indian discourses – it becomes evident that notions of universal kingship were embedded in the day-to-day practices of India's polities.

The Rashtrakuta kings were the kings of kings who for about two centuries successfully claimed not only the 'paramountcy' of the Deccan, but also succeeded (against their major rivals, the Pratihāras of north India and the Pālas of eastern India) in exercising 'paramount kingship' over the 'entire earth'. Every year, at the end of the rainy season, on one or the other festival days, the lords who had participated in the imperial court of the Balhara and who expected to do so again were supposed to arrive with revenue or tribute and a retinue of elephants, cavalry, and foot soldiers for his durbar. Included were not only the lords of the imperial domains themselves but also of the domains peripheral or adjacent to the imperial domains. From time to time the Rashtrakutas even caused one of their major rivals (who attempted to displace the kingship of the Rashtrakutas with their own) to participate in their court (Altekar, 1967; in Majumdar, 1955: IV, 1–18; in Yazdani, 1960: 253–314; Nilakanta Sastri, 1981).

This annual event, one in a continuing series of daily, annual, and sporadic acts, was part of an ongoing dialectical process in which, if successful, princes not in agreement reached agreement. It was also an eristical process, in which lords at odds with each other attempted to gain victory over one another. One should not think of this process as confined to or consisting primarily of speech. The very activities themselves, consciously performed so as to convey messages, were constituted in a dialectical-eristical manner. To assume a dichotomy between the activities of 'peace' and 'war' in the representations of these states has been very misleading. The building of a temple was, for example, as much an act of war as it was an act of peace, as much a political as it was a religious act. The result of this complex of activities, if successes (from a particular imperial perspective) were obtained, was the ongoing constitution of a polity as a sort of chain of being. If a court failed to sustain and reshape itself as circumstances changed, its more powerful lords would begin the making of other courts that would eventually displace one imperial court with another.

[17] Two excellent studies are Price (1984) and Yates (1975); see also Lane (1981: 204–20).

These acts were not isolated or separated political acts (as Hocart indicated). They were assumed to be acts continuous with the acts by which a postulated overlord of the cosmos created or, better, refashioned, the universe, with its life of a cosmic eon at one end of a vast chain of being and with the acts by which humans and lower beings sustained and changed themselves from one day or moment to the next. The acts performed by these greater and lesser agents were assumed to be scaled in accord with the lordships or masteries that they constituted. So the first time a Rashtrakuta monarch held court after his ceremonial bath of installation was more important than its subsequent annual version. Similarly, the texts accorded still more import to the sequence of acts by which the Rashtrakutas transformed themselves into the overlords of an empire and into Chakravartins, the paramount overlords of India.

The 'texts' I use for the purpose of reconstructing these central activities of the Rashtrakutas are the same 'charters' from which the historians of ancient India have themselves provided India with her downward spiral of a history. These documents were themselves the products of the daily holding of court. They are the traces of the central agents and their activities in fashioning, refashioning, and maintaining an imperial formation. More often than not, those records that survive were the products of the court meeting on special days when the court or kingdom was renewed or even reconstituted. We have already had a glimpse of the contents of certain of these grants in our reconstruction of village, local, and urban and countryside councils.

Those charters of India's ancient kingdoms that have survived are engraved on permanent materials and are of two major kinds. The first consists of portable documents engraved on one or more copper plates (held together by a ring through holes in the plates). They mostly contain grants to Brahmans whom the donor deemed to be especially qualified in their knowledge and practices. The second major class consists of records engraved in stone and built into a temple, monastery or other shrine, or erected in the form of a memorial stone to a dead warrior. These consist largely of grants to the images in temples, to monks in monasteries.

The grants of the Rashtrakutas begin with an invocation (*maṅgala*) of the deities, followed by several dozen verses in Sanskrit or old Kannada narrating the exploits of the donor, and sometimes of his overlord, and of his ancestors. The actual order (*śāsana*) comes next, including a statement of those to whom it is addressed; the name of the place from which the command is issued; the names and qualifications of the donees; a detailed description of the gift; the purpose of it; and the date on which it was made. It concludes with one or more verses on the merits of giving land and the demerits of confiscating donated land and the name of the engraver or others involved in the order's execution (Sircar, 1965: 103–60). The voice that delivers the 'eulogy' (*praśasti*) of the 'acts of fame' (*kīrti*) of kings, in order of their succession, is not that of the kings themselves, but the court eulogist. The perspective this voice takes is of a master who has privileged knowledge, of someone situated between the realm of the gods and the realm of men. When we get to the part of the charter that follows the eulogy, to the command or order announcing the grant itself, the voice changes. The words we now hear are those of the king of kings himself.

Who comprised the 'audience' of the charters? First and foremost, it consisted of those making up the society of princes who ruled an imperial formation, i.e., the 'ruling class', a continually transforming court with a fluctuating membership. Included also were the officials of these princes and those who formed the ruling societies of the subject-citizenries of the cities and countryside. Finally, the donees, Brahmans selected for their high qualifications, and the images installed in temples and their attendants, are to be mentioned among those who would have heard or read the contents of these charters. The style in which the eulogies were composed is an elaborate form of Sanskrit verse known as *kāvya*. A variety of metres are used and several verses resort to *ślesha*, paranomasia or punning (to which Sanskrit and Latin lend themselves more gracefully perhaps than English or French). Even if these verses were translated into Kannada or other 'vernaculars', it must be assumed that the audience for these eulogies was, by any standard, highly sophisticated.

The composers of the charters used a number of metaphors (*lakshaṇā*), among which the most important for our purposes is that of light, that of the sun, of the moon, and of fire as power or more accurately, as will, exercised in complex, ambiguous modes. Earlier historians, holding to the representational theory of knowledge, saw language as descriptive or expressive of an external reality rather than partly constitutive and transformative of it and they dismissed most of the language in these records as exaggerated or hyperbolic, as distorted representations of reality. They treated these texts as sources and took their main task to be the extraction of simply isolable historical facts from them, using the criteria of a positivist history. I assume that language partly constructs reality and take an 'interdiscursive' approach to these texts: hence, I assume that metaphors and other figures of speech are integral aspects of these charters (as they are of my text) and that these texts have to be understood as discourses and narratives.

The 'intertextuality' of these grants should be emphasized. The details specified in many of the grants about what is being given away presuppose the existence of an elaborate inventory or assessment of those movable and immovable forms of wealth that constituted the domains of the variety of lords and masters knit together in a polity. The grant portions of the charters were themselves thus documents or duplicates of documents in record offices. Furthermore, the surviving documents of this archive are virtually all of just one class. That is, these grants should be seen as generated by way of a classification of the entire range of these enunciatory documents. For example, grants in perpetuity should be seen in comparison with grants made, iconically, on impermanent bark, on condition of continued service.[18]

In order to approximate a reading of these texts closer to that which a contemporary of the Rashtrakutas might have given them, it should also be pointed out that the eulogistic portions of the documents were taken as extensions or amplifications of the knowledge contained in that vast corpus of narrative texts, the so-called *Epics* (*itihāsa*) and the *Purāṇas*, 'accounts of the

---

[18] For a discussion of intertextuality from a deconstructionist angle, see Leitch (1983: 55–163).

ancient past'. These texts were themselves not read simply as disorderly collections of legends, myths, and folktales, but from the highly selective and ordering angle of one or the other of the *Purāṇas* (such as the *Vishnudharmottara*) and the particular soteriology it advocated. Listeners took one of these, in a recent recension, as a body of knowledge suitable for the times and circumstances in which he or she lived and as offering the 'truest' account of the cosmological and terrestrial events described in the other older texts.

6.2.2   Ceremonial Baths and Luminous Wills

The inscriptions describe the king, in their genealogical portions, as an emanation of one of the high gods, and depict him either as holding court in the outer assembly hall of his palace after his coronation (and sometimes as enjoying himself in the inner apartments of it) or as engaged in the even more constitutive complex of activities, the conquest of the quarters. Given the great efficacy of such acts, it is hardly surprising that we should have come into possession of more Rashtrakuta records concerned with them than with lesser, more routine acts, and that no record-making direct mention of an annual Rashtrakuta holding of court should have yet come to light so far as I know. If we want a description of the holding of court, we shall have, therefore, to look at one of the better accounts of a coronation assembly, that of Krishna III (*c*.939–67).

The records of the Rashtrakutas use several terms to name this event. One, *rājyābhisheka*, 'affusion into kingship', refers to the ceremonial bath administered to the king by the pouring of water and other substances over the king's head. A synonym, *paṭṭabandha*, the 'tying of the fillet', denotes the enthronement and coronation that followed the bath. References to an *utsava* or 'festival' as accompanying the *abhisheka* of an imperial ruler of that dynasty state that this act was also considered a public celebration involving a 'procession' (*yātrā*).

After describing his feats in battle as a prince, the eulogist of the Karhad charter declares Krishna III the lord of all India but for his submission to his own father. It then says that his father, satisfied that his son, successful as a general, was an emanation of Vishnu, the most excellent of men (*purushottama*, i.e., a Chakravartin), with the capacity to exercise overlordship, decided to die. We then come to a brief description of Krishna's coronation.

When the festival of the coronation [*rājyābhishekotsava*] of this beloved of prosperity [lover of Śrī, consort of Vishṇu], who had greatly propitiated [pleased] Hari (Vishnu), at which celestial nymphs danced and heavenly Rishis [sages] pronounced benedictions, had taken place amidst joy, the quarters which began to tremble and be submissive [loyal] on account of this preparation to exact tribute [collect revenue], as girls would have manifested tremor and affection at his preparation to take their hand, became pleasing to him in consequence of their observing the proper time for paying it of their own accord, as the others would have been dear to him in consequence of their keeping to the auspicious juncture for giving themselves away. (R. G. Bhandarkar, 1896–7)

Several things are assumed in this description. What are they?

To begin with, the coronation was the moment when the king of kings, tested in the field as a general by his father, came to realize his potential as a king of kings and as a royal emanation of Vishnu. The eulogist also presented it as causing the quarters of the earth, in which are subsumed both the other lesser kings and the territorial lords and subject-citizens of the towns and country-sides, to recognize the Rashtrakuta as a universal monarch to whom they are, therefore, willing to pay revenues. Assumed in this depiction is a notion of lordship in which the king of kings is the lord while the earth and its properly husbanded resources, its 'prosperity' or 'fortune', likened to young brides, are his domains. The representation of the Rashtrakuta as a Chakravartin and emanation of Vishnu is homologous with this terrestrial 'marriage', for Vishnu was considered to have the goddesses Śrī or Lakshmī, the divine mistress of properly husbanded resources in the form of movable wealth, and Bhū or Pṛithivī, the earth, properly cared for, as his two consorts. The Rashtrakutas followed the practice (taken up from their predecessors, the Chalukyas) of calling themselves the 'beloved' or 'husband' of these two consorts of Vishnu in their court.

The relationship between lord and domain is hardly represented as egalita-rian in these practices, but nor is it represented as the relation between an owner and an inanimate, mute thing, disposable of at will. Those people constituting the domains of the overlord of the earth are represented through the man–bride metaphor as differing in both kind and degree from their lord. They are his instruments and patients, but they are also themselves agents, capable, like disaffected wives, of a thousand acts of resistance, vengeance, and sabotage, the most devastating of which would be to select another king as their true lover and master. The ceremonial bath and the holding of court that followed it was thus the act that established an association between the king of kings as ruler and the people and lands that made up his domains.

The daily, annual, or regnal holding of court was invariably preceded by a ceremonial bath (*abhisheka*). Indeed, virtually all of the rites having to do with the making or remaking of a Hindu kingdom during the period of the Hindu kingdom's glory, the eighth to twelfth century, consisted of a more or less elaborate bathing ceremony either of the king or of an image of a god. This was followed by a sequence of offerings to images and other articles, enthrone-ments, installations, processions on horse- and elephant-back, distribution of gifts and other honours, feasts, or, as will be seen below, the building of a temple. Virtually all of these baths were performed at critical moments, as determined by the movements and conjunctions of heavenly bodies, globes of light, whose activities indexed the will of the gods.

These ceremonial baths (on which I again follow the *Vishnudharmottara*) were very important because they were, as I see it, intimately involved in the metaphysics of the contending religions or soteriologies of the period, and not because I have a predilection for seeing in 'ritual' the essence of primitive or traditional societies. And it is these overlapping, dialectically and eristically formed systems of metaphysics that are recursively presupposed by, and altered in response to, the actions of agents in the Rashtrakuta imperial formation. Indeed, the ontologies, cosmologies, theologies and anthropologies of these metaphysics, here consciously elaborated, there unconsciously presupposed, are themselves the products of, and the plans for, the actions that made and remade the agents of that imperial formation.

The ceremonial baths of kings and images are of particular interest from the standpoint of agency, for they were (like the 'initiation' rites long studied by anthropologists, though not from this perspective) construed by those involved in their performance as modifying the capacity of agents to act. Those baths were also intimately involved in the divinization of kings and, hence, must figure in even a preliminary re-evaluation of the idea of 'divine kingship' in India. The overlord of the cosmos, Vishnu or Siva, had created the world out of his divine body. The extent of the cosmos in time and space was, accordingly, considered to be a lifetime of the overlord of the cosmos. The smaller periods of time and correspondingly smaller areas of the cosmos were in turn considered the lives of lesser lords. The whole universe was, in other words, thought of as successions, as in a genealogy, of the lives of higher and lower lords and their domains. Everything in the universe consisted of three components, the three *guṇas* or 'strands' about which so much has been said in Indian religious and philosophical discourses. These were *sattva*, 'quiescent goodness', *rajas*, 'restless activity', and *tamas*, 'lethargic darkness'. The shifting proportions of these components, themselves the result of the actions of the lords of the cosmos, determined its qualities (Inden, 1985a).

Now, the entity that gave everything and everyone in the world its/his/her power to realize the destiny with which it was assumed to be provided was its *tejas*, the symptom of which was brightness or light. *Tejas* itself consisted of a preponderance of quiescent goodness over restless activity such that the two together were able to predominate over the component of lethargic dullness. When they did, knowledge and order prevailed and people were able to prosper and attain to their lives' goals and, ultimately, to a permanent and direct union or 'participation', *bhakti*, in the life of Vishnu or Siva.[19] When, on the other hand, the opposite of *tejas*, lethargic dullness with restless activity, whose symptom was darkness (*timira*), held sway, ignorance, disorder, dissolution, and death overtook the world. We are not dealing here, however, with dichotomized and absolutized forces of light and dark, knowledge and ignorance, good and evil. The lives at issue in this cosmos themselves consisted of the alternation between periods of life and death, spoken of metaphorically as days and nights. What mattered more than where one was classed for the moment was what one did as an agent (and what was done to one as a patient), for one's condition was always the result of some agent's action. The question of how to act was very much a matter of timing and placement, of knowing when and where and how to act.[20]

Rituals, which I take here to be interactions between those whom their performers class as 'humans' and 'gods', according to laid-down procedures,

[19] Scholars usually translate this term as 'devotion', but I prefer the term 'participation' because it connotes the sharing in the life of a lord by a person which could involve a number of activities and attitudes. The exact nature of this participation and the kind of devotion that was appropriate as its expression were, of course, matters of dispute among theologians of different orders.

[20] On the problem of knowing and reading signs, see Inden (1986a).

came into the picture for the following reason, among others. The luminous, goal-directed energy (*tejas*) in everything connected with the human world was, claimed the Vaishnavas, highly entropic. Unless people interacted repeatedly and correctly with the overlord of the cosmos with the purpose of acquiring new infusions of his *tejas*, the human world would quickly disintegrate, for people would be unable to complete themselves and eventually obtain the goal of union with the absolute godhead. There was, however, no firmly grounded knowledge on which people could automatically act. The quest for and decisions about what knowledges to follow were themselves part of the process of interacting with the gods Vishnu or Siva. It was only when knowledgeable action seemed to produce decisive manifestations, among which the most important was the 'universal monarch', the king of kings who succeeded in conquering the quarters, that people would know and feel that they were on the right path.

The rites of bathing, in their many forms, were of particular importance in this regard, for they were the rites by which people, in conjunction with the appropriate gods, not only purified themselves of the darknesses that impeded action; they also imbued themselves with the 'luminous energy' of Vishnu (*vaishṇava-tejas*) using as its medium the water into which the royal priests had invited it. Anthropologists have long been concerned, in their analyses of 'ritual', with notions of power that may be compared with the idea of *tejas*. Here there is nothing new. The difficulty that has arisen is that they have usually compared these (even Hocart did this) with the notion of electricity; that is, they have viewed it as an objective, physical force. This is, of course, consistent with the effort to 'explain' ritual as a form of false technology. The performance of rites on these occasions is, we are accordingly told, connected with 'nature'. They are attempts to 'control' the movements of the sun and moon and bring fertility through rites of sympathetic magic. Again, there is some basis for such an answer. Notions of resemblance and participation do indeed underlie these rituals. The assumption, however, that the king, through his priest, was attempting to control the cosmos is part of the construction of the Vedic and Hindu Indian as irrational, as a person trying to do something he obviously cannot do. It is not part of the Hindu metaphysics of which these rituals were an enactment. Nor is it sufficient to say that these baths purified. There is nothing wrong with this answer except that it is so general as to be of little use. Almost every rite in Hinduism can be said to purify somebody or something. Or, to put it another way, purification is itself one of the parts of the ritual that requires explanation. Merely to invoke it does not address the wide variety of forms, enactments, and articles used in these ceremonies. Nor does it address the question of the historicity of these rites, of the centrality of *bathing* in the rites of 'early medieval' Hinduism.

My approach to these rituals, which I can only indicate here, partially incorporates these earlier views but goes, one hopes, beyond them. The ceremonial bath was a rite that not only purified, it also imbued the king with the divine power or energy, or, as I prefer to put it, with divine will. It augmented the entropic will in him. Now the reason for seeming to revert to an old-fashioned notion of 'will' here is precisely because the power involved, though physical and objective in the eyes of the rite's performers, was *also* mental and subjective, social and political. Considered an attribute of both the 'mind' (*manas*), the faculty of desire, and of the higher 'intellect' (*buddhi*), this was none other than a world-ordering rationality. It was the power to accomplish certain agreed-upon acts, namely, those enjoined in the theology or soteriology of those who had fashioned the ritual procedure. That is, it was not some commodity-like power to do with as one pleased. To be ceremonially bathed in a Vaishnava milieu was different from being bathed in a Śaiva or Buddhist milieu. Thus, the will of Vishnu enabled a king of kings to act and to be successful in those actions which would bring about a Vaishnava kingdom, a polity in which the goals and values of the Vaishnavas (as presently constituted in some particular order) were accorded precedence. On the other hand, the will at issue here is not to be confused with the unitary will attributed by Smith and others to the despot and denied to his people. The will embedded in the practices of the Vaishnavas was both transcendent *and* immanent and not simply transcendent, an attribute of the 'state', but not of 'civil society', as in so many 'modern' theories where will is taken as a prerequisite and guarantee of political order. The Vaishnavas rather saw will as both the starting point and the outcome of repeated interactions on the part of overlapping and often contending agents. That is perhaps why they not only bathed their kings with the will of Vishnu, but with the will of his rival, Siva, and a host of other divinities, and anti-gods as well, who acted as lords of domains in the world. It is probably also the reason why representatives of the estates and ministers also bathed the king with waters indicating the commitment of their wills to him before Vishnu poured down his luminous will.

Nor was the king of kings the only one to be bathed with the will of the gods. That was also the purpose of the daily bath supposed to be taken by every Hindu and of a large variety of other baths for different kinds and degrees of persons ranging from the images of gods in temples down to animals and weapons and tools. In other words, an Indian polity was constituted as a scale of divine and human wills and not as a dichotomy between a divine and absolute ruler on the one hand and a secular and powerless officialdom or populace on the other. We would, thus, do better if we talked of theophanic polities rather than of a divine kingship when we turn to ancient Hindu states.

This metaphysics and the agents and actions in which it is entailed have wide-ranging implications for our understanding of Indian polities that will require several monographs to explore. For one thing, there is implicit in this theory of divine affusion an ideology of modal rulership or, if one wishes, sovereignty. Sovereignty in its lower mode consisted of what we might call the capacity that people had for ordering their affairs that was inherent or immanent in themselves and the world from the time of 'creation' or 'emission' and, in more immediate terms, from their last affusion, direct or indirect, with the luminous will of Vishnu at the beginning of a dynastic period or even a year. As construed by the political theology of the Vaishnavas, sovereignty in this lesser mode was hardly a source of order and unity. It was, rather, given the entropic nature of the luminous energy in the world, divisive, dispersive, lethargic, indecisive, confused, disaffected, ignorant. In it, as in the Kali age, that of dissension, 'darkness', *tamas* combined with activity, *rajas*, to predominate over goodness, *sattva*.[21] Sovereignty in its higher mode, let us call it 'divine sovereignty', was a different matter. In it, *sattva* and *rajas* combined to predominate over *tamas*. Transcendent, but with an inexhaustible capacity for immanence, it was, as described by the Vaishnava theologians, the very source of order and fulfilment. Two lower repositories of that luminous energy were the sun and the moon, from the divine lords of which many of the kings of India claimed descent. But the luminous will of Vishnu was itself not everlasting in its immanent, manifest form. It also needed constantly to be renewed by correct action and interaction with the lords who possessed it.

For those prepared tacitly to concede at least the correctness of this cosmology, in one or the other soteriological formulations, participation in the lives of those human and divine lords and overlords who themselves had continuing access to the divine will, through the device of the *abhisheka*, would have been considered a necessity for success in both their present and their future lives, and not a luxury or a matter simply of personal piety. So, far from constructing polities that were turned inward toward some given essence, political agents were encouraged to look outward and consider their relations with higher and lower lords.

Perhaps the most interesting point about this political theology is that it eschews the attempt to build the sorts of transcendent, scientifically grounded polities with which political theorists (including even critical philosophers, as at the head of the chapter) have been so taken in the European world. Consistent with the idea of persons or lives as fluctuations between periods of order and disorder, the Rashtrakutas and their contemporaries thought of polities not as permanent 'states' or as imperfect realizations of a perfect state, but as continually reconstructed and reconstructing agents with both dispersed and unitary moments. Instead of assuming that periods of disorder threatened the ideal unity of a state, the Hindu theorists assumed that oscillation between periods of order and disorder were inevitable and normal.[22] They were built into the very notions of persons, polities, and time with which they populated their world. There was, from this perspective, never a question of eliminating forces of darkness, evil, or destruction, but rather of domesticating and placing them. Nor was the doing of this a job that could be done once and for all. It had to be done over and over again. Battles between gods and anti-gods, between contenders for the position of cosmic overlord and their terrestrial supporters, had to be fought anew not in order to return India to some primordial *status ante quo*, but because circumstances themselves, including human knowledge of divinity, continued to change. It is ironic, what with all the talk about Indian or Hindu 'concepts' of *karma* and *samsāra* – the magic ingredients for 'understanding India' – that nobody seems to have seen in the specific discursive

---

[21] The last and worst of a cycle of four ages, the age of 'strife' (*kali*), in which people now reside. It is better seen as a highly agentive notion, which theologians used to explain one's present world and also to imply a course of action, rather than as a sign of Hindu pessimism or fatalism.

[22] Tambiah (1976, 102–32) comes close to this position with his idea of 'galactic polity', despite the naturalism that still lingers. Had he made explicit use of a scale of forms, his analysis would have been much more powerful.

formulations of the theologies in which such terms were used the actionist implications for political institutions.

6.2.3 Kings, Lords, and Officials

The composition of the ruling society constituted by an imperial court was complex, as I have indicated elsewhere (Inden, 1981). The holding of court in general brought the king into association with the land and people of which he was supposed to be the lord. The point on which I wish to focus here, however, is this: what distinguished an *imperial* court politically, and especially one whose king successfully claimed to be the universal king of India, was that it was primarily a society of *kings*. Belonging to this society were kings of two complementary, but historically shifting types, the ally or friend (*mitra*), whose territory was discontiguous with the conquering king's own, and the kings on his periphery who had submitted. Kings in between were one's foes. The Arabs of Sind were among those whom the Rashtrakutas took as allies. One record of the Rashtrakutas which speaks of a Tājika (Persian, used to designate Arabs coming from outside Arabia) named Madhumati (=Muhammed) as a king and provincial lord of the northern Konkana 'by the grace of Krishna' II (878–915), and has him approve of the grant to a Hindu temple and monastery, confirms the Arab traveller's account of an alliance between Arab and Rashtrakuta (Sircar, 1967). This need not be taken either as an act of unknowing betrayal of a 'Hindu' cause or as an indication that religion did not count in early medieval Indian politics. Rather, we could see this alliance as an attempt by the Rashtrakutas to include, by metonymy, the imperial formation of the Arabs in their own, while at the same time squeezing their major rivals in the north, the Gurjaras.[23]

While allies did, on occasion, attend one another's courts and engage in joint undertakings, it was those who surrounded his own domains that were expected to visit regular attendance on their overlord at court. The terms used to refer to these kings are *maṇḍalin* or *maṇḍaleśvara* (denoting the lord of a circumscribed domain rather than of the entire earth) and *sāmanta*, *mahāsāmanta*, etc. (denoting a king who is on the periphery of one's own domains). These are the terms that are variously translated as 'vassal', 'feudatory', or, as below, 'subordinate chief' (Gopal, 1963). Some of the lords tributary to the Rashtrakutas were the collateral Rashtrakutas of Lāṭa, the Śilāhāras of the Konkana, the Gangas and others of Gangavadi 96,000, the Pallavas of Tondaimaṇḍala, the Chalukyas of Vengi, and the Paramāras of Mālava. The presence of such tributary kings in the court of a Chakravartin, their participation in a complex, ordered kingship of which the Chakravartin was the prime agent, was constitutive of that kingship. They were not mere appanages of a polity. This becomes clear when we read, in the next passage, about the holding of court that followed the ceremonial bath of installation, the first time when he presented himself as a Chakravartin fully imbued with the divine will to the other kings of India:

He, a powerful master of the science of politics, desirous of obtaining a lofty position, deprived some of his subordinate chiefs *maṇḍalin* of their places and established others

[23] One of the few more recent histories to take this idea seriously is Devahuti (1970: 135–41).

who were deserving, separated some from each other by producing disunion and united others, and thus arranged them in a high or low position; as a proficient master of the science of words (i.e. grammar), desirous of making up a long form, drops some letters from their position and introduces others in their *guṇa* form, separates some on account of their dissimilarity and unites others, and places them in order, above or below. (Karhad Plates in R. G. Bhandarkar, 1896–7)

The court is assumed here to be more of an enunciative assembly than it was a deliberative one. It was the site where decisions or agreements reached beforehand were announced rather than a place where issues were openly debated. The idiom in which the court ordered itself was, consistent with its enunciative quality, hierarchical. It was supposed to be an ordered assembly and not simply a mêlée. Persons became aware of what part they were to obtain in the state in relation to others – signalled by where they would stand and sit – and of what tasks they would be given to perform and of what lands they would be given to enjoy as their 'livelihoods'. This arrangement of the court displayed the king of kings as an overlord of the earth, a universal monarch seated on an elaborate lion-throne and receiving obeisances from lesser lords who had recognized his characteristics as a universal ruler and become his servants. We should not, however, be misled by this emphasis on display into thinking that 'real power' lay elsewhere, either in a fundamentally different 'organ' of government, a cabinet or administrative staff (as in the bureaucratic empire) or at a fundamentally different 'level' of 'society', in the hands of localized clan monarchs, a landlord or peasant class (as in a tributary system, feudalism or the segmentary state). The display at court was taken precisely as a manifestation of divine and human wills relative to one another in a complex agent, the compound kingship that ruled all of India.

Certain metaphors are indeed used to emphasize the power of the king of kings relative to that of the tributary lords that made up his court. One that is frequently used is that of the king of kings as a cultivator who is able to treat other powerful kings as though they were plants. The one used above is that of the king of kings as a grammarian. As the comparison of grammar with the science of statecraft already implies, the ordering of a court entailed the following of rules. The evocation here is quite specific. Vital, in the discourses on Indian statecraft, was the capacity of a king of kings, one who would succeed as a Chakravartin, to bring about agreements (*sandhi*) between himself and among other kings whom he had won over to his position, and to bring about dissension or separation (*vigraha*) among those who remained hostile. Both of these terms were also used in grammatical discourse, so there can be little doubt that what was being talked about here was the making of a royal court in the sense of a society of kings. We must also keep in mind that the sometime reduction of tributary lords to the status of mere patients (plants, letters) in the charters was aimed eristically at those wavering or would-be tributary lords, or downright foes of the king of kings. Yet it should be emphasized that the point here was not to do away with other kings as such and produce a single, absolute kingship, blessed by a monotheist deity, for all India. We should not be misled by the metaphors used to represent the relation of a Rashtrakuta Chakravartin to his tributary lords into inferring that we have here the exercise of the private, arbitrary will of the absolute monarch, bolstered by the razzle-dazzle of 'divine right' (Mill's and Smith's despoticism).

Still, the hearer of these eulogies is clearly left with the idea that the capacity of the king of kings far exceeded that of other kings. Certainly the paramount king claimed to have the capacity to change the order of precedence of the kings in attendance (without apparently any more formal consultation than a modern prime minister or president who wishes to shuffle cabinets). Thus, while a forth-coming coronation was the occasion for renegotiating the terms for belonging to this society, the agents involved were not thought of as abstract individuals, as persons formally and legally equal in their capacities. Those involved used, on the contrary, a very concrete notion of persons, one that placed a primacy on knowing what the differences among persons were and testing for them.

The notion of agreement (and non- or disagreement) is built into the very idea of the Chakravartin. The Chakravartin was supposed to be the willing instrument of divine will, yet persons of the ruling society had also to *know* who was a Chakravartin, to be able to test for his presence. That is, the recognition, making, and sustenance of a universal monarch was an ongoing dialectic process. Succession to the throne in the Rashtrakuta 'dynasty' was by no means automatic. The greater personages of a court, starting with the tributary kings, allies, and lords of the imperial domains (including the reigning monarch) had to recognize the presence in a prince of the signs of a universal monarch. He had to present himself to them as one such; together they had to persuade the gods that they had made the right decision; and the gods had to signal that this was so by imbuing him with divine will, the proof of which was the success of the royal recipient of it in his subsequent acts. This in turn persuaded those kings (and ministers) who had had their doubts to commit themselves, to combine their wills with his. This combining of wills was, by the way, repre-sented in the coronation when the king of kings bathed lesser kings into their kingships or when ministers bathed the king with graded waters indexing their relative wills. Acts such as these, once again, persuaded the king of kings that he really was divinely favoured.

Whatever the relative power of a Chakravartin and his tributary lords, there should be no mistaking the accession rite and the holding of court which followed it as simply a 'symbolic' or representational rite. It was a major moment, entailing a rational and complex political theology, in the reproduction and transformation of imperial kingship and in determining whether a particu-lar king of kings would become the universal monarch of India. The court that met on this occasion was supposed to be a moment of unity in the 'life' of an imperial polity, but it could, under circumstances where agreement was not forthcoming, also be agentive of rebellion, as the records of the Rashtrakutas themselves admit (Sanjan Plates in D. R. Bhandarkar, 1926).

The emphasis I have placed so far on the primacy of kings in an imperial court should not be taken as an endorsement of the idea that 'administration' was absent outside the confines of the locality in ancient or medieval India. Closer to the king of kings than anyone except his chief queen and heir apparent, if not politically as important as the tributary kings, were his 'ministerial companions' (*amātya*) or counsellors (*mantrī*). Some of these men, who were supposed to be aged and wise, had been territorial and military lords, royal officers, or even tributary kings when younger men. The complement of these within the imperial domains, next in political importance to the kings that sat in an imperial court and continuous with them, were those whom I refer to as territorial (and military) lords, the persons usually called the officers of provincial government in the histories. The persons whom the Rashtrakuta emperor addressed certainly projects the image of a polity that consists, within the imperial domains but outside the royal capital, first of a hierarchy of territorial lords and only second of appointed functionaries. Those first named, in Sanskrit, are the *rāshṭrapati*, the *vishayapati*, and the *grāmakūṭa*. The latter is, no doubt, the *ur-gāmuṇḍa* or *gāvuṇḍa*, the village headman, of the Kannada records. The *vishayapati* would seem to be either the lord of a smaller territory ('district') granted to a lord by the emperor or the *nāḍprabhu* or *nālgāvuṇḍa*, the lord of a *nāḍu* or *vishaya* who was also a village headman, that is, a man of both the *jānapada* class and the *amātya* class. That is, there is good reason for seeing these lords as persons who belonged *both* to the higher echelons of the subject-citizens of the countryside *and* to the imperial army and court.

Next in importance to these lords were those whom I refer to as 'functionaries', those who had been appointed (*yukta*) to take charge of a discrete set of activities (*adhikārika*), some of which were carried out in offices (*adhikaraṇa*), such as justice (*dharma*), agreements and disputes (*sandhi-vigraha*), revenue-records (*akṣhapaṭala*), and those appointed (*upayukta*) in turn by them.

The class of *mahattaras*, the better or greater or richer ones, are listed either before the officials (Karhad Plates in R. G. Bhandarkar, 1896–7) or after them (Cambay Plates in D. R. Bhandarkar, 1902–3). They were the men of the urban or rural locality *par excellence*, those who constituted the city, 'village', or 'caste' council or, where there was none in a formal sense, the informal advisers of the city mayor and village or district headman. The tax-paying masters who constituted the ruling societies of the subject-citizenries of the towns and countryside, they were the complex agents whose consent was required for the execution of an imperial or lordly order.

As indicated above, the holding of court after an accession or some other event in the 'life' of the kingship was not only an occasion for the sharing out of livelihoods from within the imperial domains (the extent of which periodically changed), it was also the occasion for making gifts, for distributing livelihoods to particularly qualified Brahmans and to the images of the gods for the support of their liturgy. As if to signal the strength of the compound and fluctuating will of their polity, the Rashtrakutas seem to have liked making gifts of villages in their domains that were quite distant from the royal capital or encampment in which they were residing at the time. Indra III (915–27), for example, performed the weighing of the Man on the Scale (Tulāpurusha) on the occasion of his coronation at Kurundaka (probably Kurundvad, Kolhapur District, on a tributary of the Krishna), on which account he gave away a village in Lāṭa, some 400 miles or 35 days' march distant. After descending from the balance, he gave away thirty lakhs (1 lakh = 100,000) of *drammas* (silver coins), together with Kurundaka and other villages, to the total of four hundred, said by him to have been confiscated (*vilupta*) by previous kings (Bagumra Plates in D. R. Bhandarkar, 1907–8).

Now, the area over which the Rashtrakutas made these gifts consisted not simply of the district or *nāḍu* in which they built their capital, Mānyakheḍa 6,000, but of a much larger area, that which the Rashtrakuta emperors took as their own domains. This consisted of the Karnata or Kuntala, what they took to be the country drained by the river Krishna and its tributaries, the larger country of which the Rashtrakuta capital was the centre. It also included Aśmaka-Mūlaka, or Maharashtra, and Vidarbha (Berar), the countries watered by the river Godavari and its tributaries and, from time to time, one or more countries along the Kaveri river to the south, and the Tapti and Narmada to the northwest (Lāṭa).

Bañkeśa or Bañkeyarāja, born in a distinguished subject-citizen line, was a 'cherished servant' (*ishṭa-bhṛtya*) of Amoghavarsha I and the commander of a division of hereditary forces (*maula-bala-prabhu*), one of those devotees of the king to whom the Arab travellers had referred. Himself described as 'knowledgeable in conflict and agreement' (*samara-samaye*), he had rescued the kingship of his overlord from rebellion, vowing to enter fire if he did not succeed, and come by royal favour to be the provincial lord (*rāshṭrapati*) of Banavāsi and other domains. Since we are clearly told in the Konnur grant (Kielhorn, 1900–1a; D. R. Bhandarkar, 1926: 236–7) that he wished to make a grant to a Jaina establishment, we must not assume that charters which represent the grants of villages as the gifts of the Rashtrakuta emperors themselves were 'in reality' the gifts of unnamed local donors. It would thus seem that the Rashtrakuta had the capacity to make grants within a very large territory (the extent of which no doubt compensated for its relative lack of fertility).

Just what precise means were used to collect revenue over this large 'middle region' of the Rashtrakuta empire is not known. We are, I think, justified in inferring that records of gifts to Brahmans, temples, and Jainas were kept at the capital (as well as in the village or district headquarters) in the Office of Justice and Gifts and perhaps also in a separate revenue record office. It does not seem outlandish to assume that the masters or supervisors of these offices were also in communication with one another, though they did not constitute a discrete chain of command apart from the territorial lords to whom they were attached.[24] We may also assume that on the occasion of the annual holding of court agreed-upon amounts of revenue were made over to the Rashtrakuta treasury by the lords who had marched to the capital or encampment in order to participate in the court.

I hope this is enough to indicate that just because the Rashtrakuta imperial formation was not an administered polity, we need not conclude that there were no administrative activities carried out at the centre beyond the compass of a

---

[24] Line 57 of Konnur (Kielhorn, 1900–1a): 'This is recorded (*likhita*) by the Head Accountant (*bhogika*; should be *senabhogika*), Vatsarāja, in the Office of Justice and Gifts (*dharmādhikaraṇastha*), son of Śrīharsha, born in the Vālabha Kāyastha lineage, (and by/ through the?) servant (*bhṛtya*) of Nāgavarman Prithvīrāma, keeper of village charters and war-elephant among scribes (*grāma-pa[tta]lādhikṛta-lekhakaraṇahasti*). The agent (*mukhya*) of Bankeyarāja is the wise Mahattara, Gaṇapati by name. This all has been executed by him in the presence of the king.'

naturally or ethnically given locality of the imperial king himself. On the contrary, I would contend that one of the major activities in which the Rashtrakuta imperial court engaged was the constitution and remaking of extensive imperial and tributary domains which provided the livelihoods for the imperial court, and that these activities entailed a substantial redistribution of people and resources. We need not at this point let the notion of 'bureaucracy' creep back into this account either in a positive or in a negative sense. Just because the Rashtrakutas were able to exercise *a* world-ordering rationality in the shape of Vishnu's 'luminous will' this does not have to be taken to mean that this rationality was an anticipation of *the* world-ordering rationality of Weber's rational-legal bureaucracy. There is, thus, no reason to believe that territorial lords (or even the functionaries attached to them) were constituted as depoliticized instruments of their lords and overlord. Neither do we have to accept the other Weberian option. The use of terms like lord and lordship, terms which are used in discourses on feudalism or the traditional state, inevitably evokes, you might say, notions of rule or administration that are arbitrary, personal, and decentralized. I am quite aware of this. I use these terms none the less because I wish to show that there is or was nothing *inherent* about lordship practices that made them so. On the contrary, the ruling society of the Rashtrakuta imperial formation assumed that lordships were the *sine qua non* of order and unity, the best basis for a polity.

The strongest evidence one could present of the centrality of the court and of the importance of the lords in it comes from what we know about the 'rise' of the Rashtrakutas themselves. The term from which the dynasty takes its name, *rāshtrakūṭa*, 'preeminent in the country', could itself be taken to mean 'provincial lord'. It is clear from the charters that the Rashtrakutas had themselves been tributary lords of the Chalukyas. Dantidurga, first of the imperial Rashtrakutas, designated himself a *mahāsāmantādhipati*, 'high lord among tributaries'. He and his entourage were able to constitute themselves as the central figures in a new ruling society because the Chalukyas had lost the capacity dialectically to reconstitute the ruling society of their own. Because the premier ruling society or polity of an imperial formation and its lesser rivals were dialectically and eristically mutually constituted, the collapse of the premier ruling society was the signal for the reshaping of the other ruling societies of the subcontinent, that is, for the making of a new imperial formation.

6.3   CONQUERING THE QUARTERS

6.3.1   From Tributary Lord to Overlord of the Earth

The holding of court after the accession of a king of kings was itself preparation for that procession known as the conquest of the quarters or regions. The king of kings who claimed to be a Chakravartin, the paramount overlord of India, displayed his character as a true Chakravartin by his conquest of the quarters, for it was the successful completion of that act which distinguished the king who was most truly a Chakravartin from those who were only partial or incomplete – note that I avoid the term 'false' – Chakravartins. Let me now turn to the accounts given in the Rashtrakuta charters of their conquests and see if we can answer the question of whether they were claiming to construct a single polity out of India's diverse polities or whether they were, as earlier historians have assumed, merely acting as the instruments of a perennial racial and regional conflict, that between North and South, Aryan and Dravidian (or, in the nationalist version, expressing the unity of a pre-given cultural-linguistic region, Maharashtra or, according to some, the Karnataka).

The eulogists of the first imperial ruler of the dynasty, Dantidurga, described him in terms that make it clear that they considered Dantidurga a Chakravartin and an emanation of Vishnu. One of them proclaims that 'his spotless deeds, like those of Hari (Vishnu), are not to be equalled by the kings of the past, present, or future' (Indraji, 1883). Another charter's poet plays upon the metaphysics of 'luminous will' when he declaims: 'The one famed as Dantidur-garāja, sun to the lotus of his own family, the flood of whose majesty (abundance of whose troops), the luminous will of which was clear, subdued the quarters of the atmosphere (regions of foes).'[25] Yet another eulogist declares Dantidurga to be, 'like Him of the Hundred Sacrifices (Indra, king of the gods), the 'enjoyer (husband) of the Earth girdled by a sash (the waves) of the four oceans' (Paithan Plates in Kielhorn, 1894–5). The eulogy continues its praise. He is the king

who with a mere few footsoldiers unexpectedly overwhelmed the countless forces, invincible to others, of the Karṇāṭaka, themselves practiced in accomplishing the scattering of the lord of Kāñchī, the king of Kerala, the Chola, and the Pāṇḍya and Srīharsha and Vajraṭa. (Paithan Plates in Kielhorn, 1894–5)

The first four of these were the rulers of the countries – Toṇḍai, Chola, Pāṇḍya, and Kerala – making up the coastal parts of present-day Tamilnadu and lying clearly outside the empire of the Chalukyas and its tributary kings. That is, the Chalukya is assumed to be the emperor of the entire Dakshiṇāpatha (peninsular India) except for those four countries on its southern periphery. Srīharsha, of course, had been the paramount king of the geopolitical comple-ment of the Deccan, northern India, the Uttarāpatha. The name Vajraṭa probably designates the Maitraka king, Sīlāditya III (662–84), who had (like his predecessor, Dharasena IV) declared himself a ruler of imperial rank in Gujarat, the region northwest of Maharashtra, after the death of Harsha and the break-up of his imperium.[26] So the Chalukya emperor is himself made out by the Rashtrakutas to have been the Chakravartin or paramount king of India. One grant (Bhandak Plates in Sukthankar, 1917–18) in the verse previous to these states that the mother of Dantidurga, the queen Bhavagaṇā, a Chalukya princess, made gifts in every one of 400,000 villages. This seems to be a reference to that part of the Chalukya kingdom (the valley of the river Godavari and its tributaries, Maharashtra) which Dantidurga had constituted as the

[25] My translation, v. 13 of Bhandak Plates in Sukthankar (1917–18).
[26] But see, for other suggestions, Altekar (1981).

domains under his command before his defeat of the Vallabha. It was seen as the 'middle region' of the newly constituted Rashtrakuta state.

Dantidurga is then described as he 'who overcame, in an instant with the mere wave of his sceptre, the Vallabha, who, though he had knit his brows did not draw his sword, and who, though he seemed not tired and his power to command appeared unhindered, had lost his determination (*yatna*).'[27] The implication in this description is that divine grace had been withdrawn from the Chalukya, the previous Chakravartin. Hence he and his seemingly superior army were unable to act and so retreated or fled from the field of battle.

His eulogist in another inscription says that after Dantidurga conquered the 'overlord of all kings', he led the lord of Kāñchi (the Pallava, chief rival of the Chalukyas), the lords of Kaliṅga and Kosala, and of Śrīśailadeśa (Telugu-Choḍas, presumably) to the east of his domains in the Deccan), and the kings of Mālava, Lāṭa, and Tamka (The Gurjaras or Pratihāras, successors of Vajraṭa in western India) into submission (Indraji, 1883).

By now the geopolitical scope of the narrative in these Rashtrakuta charters is clear. The Rashtrakutas considered the Chalukya king of kings to be the paramount overlord not just of the Deccan, but of the whole of India. By his defeat of that king, Dantidurga was signalling to the other kings of the earth that he was to be considered by them the true successor of the Vallabha as the Chakravartin, the paramount overlord of the entire earth. Lest any of India's kings doubt his intentions, the account of his deeds continues with the explicit statement that, after his defeat of Vallabha, Dantidurga obtained the 'kingship over kings' (*rājādhirāja-*) and 'paramount overlordship' (*parameśvaratā*), and that,

> Through the power of his valour he brought under one (royal) umbrella this earth from the Setu, where the coast-mountain has tossing waves flashing along the line of its large rocks, up to the Snowy Mountain (Himalaya), where the masses of spotless rocks are strained by the snow, as far as the boundary line beautified by stretches of the sandy shores of the eastern and western oceans. (Bhandak Plates in Sukthankar, 1917–18)

This is not the only evidence of the Rashtrakuta claim to be Chakravartins that we could point to in their records. We could look at more. But there is more to this eulogistic discourse of the Rashtrakutas than some claim to exercise 'control' over the physical space of the subcontinent and the populations and resources in those territories. To begin with, the Rashtrakutas were not only trying to take command of space, a point on which historians traditionally focus

---

[27] D. R. Bhandarkar translates this (v. 6 of Alas Plates) as 'Without knitting his brow, without using any sharp weapon, without (anybody's) knowledge, without giving orders, without effort, he suddenly conquered Vallabha by the (mere) force of (his) royal sceptre (i.e. majesty) and attained to the state of "king of kings" and "supreme lord"' (1900–1); in a footnote (3) he sides with Bühler (Kāvi Plates), against Fleet (Samangad Plates), in taking the phrases, e.g. *abhruvibhangam*, as adverbs instead of adjectives. Alas and Paithan Plates both read *daṇḍa-balena* instead of *daṇḍalakena*, but the editors conclude that the meaning of *d-balena* is not clear). Altekar (1933–4), corrects reading of lines 21–3 of Paithan (=Bhor 18–19). Verse 15 is the same as in Paithan. The next verse reads *Karṇāṭakaṃ balam acintyam-ajeyam* instead of *balam anantam*; and *abhrūvibhangam*.

a great deal of attention: they were also attempting to take command of time, a point to which, ironically, historians have paid little attention. Second, the Rashtrakutas were trying to demonstrate that they were in the process of taking command of both the time and the space of India, not in some objective, physical sense, but as these were constituted in contemporaneous Indian soteriological discourses. Finally, the rising Rashtrakutas were attempting to display their command of these times and spaces not simply in the weaker sense of being able to protect the crucial times of the year and places of the landscape from presumed wrongdoers, but in the much stronger sense of being able to renew and rework time and space and the institutions situated in them. Foremost among these were the universal kingship of India and, from a Hindu perspective, the main shrine in which the image or sign of the divine overlord of the cosmos was worshipped. Another way of stating the matter is to say that the Rashtrakutas were not just trying to seize power in a pre-given world. They were striving, with every political act, to give a better account of the world than had their predecessors. What this involved for the Rashtrakutas was that they had dialectically to address the Chalukyas, those who had exercised the universal kingship of India, and the religious order to which they had given their primary support. The persuasive remaking and deployment of rituals was vital to this process.

Dantidurga describes himself as having marked his military triumphs on the periphery of the Chalukya empire by the performance of a 'great gift' (*mahādāna*) ceremony. A successor of Dantidurga, Amoghavarsha I (814–c. 878), describes his ancestor as the king 'by whom the lesser kings beginning with the Gurjara lord were made into gatekeepers (*pratihāra*) when the [Great Gift called the Golden Embryo was celebrated at Ujjayinī by princes'.[28] The term *pratihāra*, 'gatekeeper', was the name taken by one of the two dynasties that become the major rivals or 'Others' of the Rashtrakutas in northern India. Ujjayinī was the earlier capital of the Pratihāras, in Malwa. Quite clearly this account of the rite makes the Gurjara (Nāgabhaṭa I. c. 730–56) into a peripheral or tributary king of the Rashtrakuta. An inscription engraved in a cave shrine excavated at the command of Dantidurga says that the Golden Embryo consisted of 'gold in great quantity, dazzling in splendour', and that 'it was strung with pearls and studded with rubies.' The ceremony itself was performed 'after thinking of a marvellous rule', and included 'unprecedented entertainments (*krīḍā*) unobtainable by other kings even in their dreams'. The euology continues, declaring that 'when Brahmā saw his distinguished suitability for supporting the burden of the entire earth ('possessor of riches')', he 'bestowed the overlordship of the continent … on that lion among kings who had caused the Kali Age to be plundered of his joy' (Indraji, 1883). It is highly likely that the 'rule' (*vidhāna*) for the ceremony performed by Dantidurga was itself an elaboration of an earlier ceremony, one that earlier imperial kings had performed as a complement to, and partial displacement of, the much older

[28] My translation of v. 9: *hiraṇyagarbhaṃ rājanyairujjayanyāṃ yadāsitaṃ/pratihārkritam yena gurjareśādirājakam//* (Sanjan Plates, in D. R. Bhandarkar (1925–6). R. G. Bhandarkar (1928: 63) ignored the Hiranyagarbha and simply said: 'At Ujjayinī he gave large quantities of gold and jewels in charity.'

Horse Sacrifice.[29] What appears to have distinguished this reworking of the ceremony was that it stood alone and replaced the Horse Sacrifice.

The place of these 'great gifts' in the making and remaking of Indian time and space and of the religious orders and the imperial kingdoms situated in them has, like so much else here that has been essentialized and, hence, dehistoricized, a long and intricate history which, given their importance, should not be surprising. Let me just say here that the purpose of this rite was to bring about a rebirth of the king who had completed a conquest of the quarters, to endow him with a 'divine body', but not just in the same degree as did the imperial-style ceremonial bath into kingship (*rājyābhisheka*). That rebirth, that infusion of a king of kings with the luminous will of Vishnu, provided the king and his subjects with the will to begin a regnal year. Another 'great gift' ceremony, the Man on the Balance (Tulāpurusha), the weighing of a king against gold and silver (given away, as in the Golden Embryo rite), was performed by a king of kings to mark the beginning of a reign (or, as on the occasion of a solar eclipse, to mark his participation in the renewal of calendrical time). The execution of the Golden Embryo, performed less often, but more important, brought about the beginning of a new royal era which was tantamount, in the instance where it was performed by a king claiming the paramount overlordship of the entire earth, to the inauguration of a new period of time, invariably depicted as the end of an Age of Strife (Kaliyuga), as above, and the beginning of a new Golden Age (Kṛtayuga). The performance of this rite by Dantidurga may, therefore, be taken as an attempt on his part dialectically (and eristically) to transform in a witnessed deed the whole of India into a new polity, what I refer to as an imperial formation. When word of this reached the Chalukya king we may presume that he knew very well what the intentions of his erstwhile tributary lord were. The moment of triumphal unity of a newly fashioned polity was a moment of humiliation and dispersal for the old.

Closely connected with the performance of this rite was the carving of the cave itself in which the representation of the rite is inscribed. This was the so-called Dasavatara cave at Ellora (Elapura), in the hills above a tributary of the Godavari river. The Rashtrakutas made this the soteriological centre of their kingdom, complemented later by the political capital they built at Mānyakheṭa, on a tributary of the Krishna river.[30] Major temples were not built by just anyone or at a miscellaneous 'auspicious' time. The building of a temple was undertaken, in this period, as part of the conquest of the quarters itself, what we might call its grand finale. Dantidurga topped off his conquest of the quarters with the cave shrine at Dasavatara. He thereby attempted to complete himself as the new king of kings and paramount overlord of the entire earth. More importantly, by participation ('devotion', *bhakti*) in *his* overlord, the god he and his preceptor and the major devotees of the religious order ('sect') took to be the true cosmic overlord in and for the dynastic era he had inaugurated, he would transform his very being, moving closer and closer to union with that god.

---

[29] For some preliminary comments on the great gift, see Inden (1979).
[30] The earlier kings of the dynasty appear to have had a shifting political capital.

These acts of participation he would, of course, perform both directly, by appearing on major occasions before the image or sign of that overlord and, on a periodic basis, through the ministrations of a college of priests. The god to whose worship this cave was dedicated was Siva, but it also exhibits a strong Vaishnava presence as well. The Chalukyas had been, until the reign of Vikramāditya I (654–81), who was initiated into a Śaiva religious order in 660, worshippers of Vishnu while their *alter egos*, the Pallavas of Toṇḍaimaṇḍalam (in Tamilnad) had been devotees of Siva. Neither of their versions of Vaishnavism and Saivism gave much of a part to the worship of the other's high god.[31] Whereas the Chalukyas represented themselves as terrestrial emanations of Vishṇu, the imperial Pallavas depicted themselves as royal devotees of Siva, as manifestations of Skanda, son of Siva and youthful general of the gods, and, on occasion, as Siva himself. The Chalukya conversion to Saivism was also an attempt to reform that religious order. In it, the worship of Vishnu and his emanations, who are left in charge of the world of householders, was accorded almost as much space as the worship of the ascetic Siva. The Rashtrakutas, like their predecessors, committed themselves to the reformed worship of Siva in which they acted as the earthly manifestations of Vishnu. Unfortunately, Dantidurga seems to have died before at least the dedicatory inscription above the cave's entrance was finished.

The heir of Dantidurga, who apparently was sonless, was his father's brother, Krishnarāja (*c.* 758–72/5). He is described as he 'Who overcame in battle Rāhappa, the pride/arrogance of whose strength arose from his own arms, with the blows of a sharp sword-blade and quickly displayed/manifested/attained (*tatāna*) the supreme lordship of the great king of kings, radiant (*śubha*) with the row of Pālidhavajas'.[32] This foe was probably none other than Kīrti-varman II, the last of the early Chalukya imperial monarchs, the one from whom the Rashtrakutas took 'sovereignty' (Nilakanta Sastri, 1981: III.1, 446). A eulogist in a later charter portrays the event thus:

Then in battle field which turned into the courtyard where a maiden chooses her husband, Śubhatunga-Vallabha, without having to heed the circumstances, forcibly took away the (maiden) Fortune of the Chalukya family, wearing the garland of the fluttering banners in rows.[33]

6.3.2 Displaying a New Overlordship

As part of their effort to show that they were now the true Chakravartins, the early Rashtrakuta rulers appropriated the era that the Chalukyas had used, the

[31] Harihara in the Great Cave (III) at Badami (Burgess, 1877), early capital of the Chalukyas, and Narasiṃha in the Kailasanatha temple of the Pallavas (Rea, 1909: 18–42).
[32] Paithan Plates in Kielhorn (1894–5), lines 21–3: *Rāhappam-ātma-cu(bhu)ja-jāta-va(ba)lāca(va)lepam-ājau vijitya nithi(śi)t-āsilatā-prahāraih/pāli[dhva]j-āvali-[śu]bhām-acir[e]ṇa yo hi rājādhirājaparameśvaratām tatāna//.*
[33] My translation, v. 10 (Sanjan Plates in D.R. Bhandarkar 1925–6). His translation: 'Then in the battle field which proved a [place] of choice marriage, Śubhatunga-Vallabha listlessly and forcibly wrested away the Fortune of the Chalukya family, bearing the garland, namely, the waving Pālidhvajas.'

so-called Śāka Era, which begins in AD 78–9 (Sircar: 1965: 258–67; Mirashi: 1961a, 1961b). They also appropriated two other signs of the paramount rulership of the Chalukyas, their titles and their banner. One should add that the poesy of the Chalukyas, which they in turn had taken from Harsha, was also appropriated by them (Kielhorn, 1900–1b).

Having taken the kingship of kings and the paramount overlordship of the Chalukyas, they accordingly took the long-used 'titles' (*biruda*) that proclaimed this, those of Mahārājādhirāja, 'great king of kings', Parameśvara, 'paramount overlord', and, in addition, Paramabhaṭṭāraka, 'grand master' (designating the king of kings as pre-eminent in knowledge, a consequence of the divine will with which he was endowed). Another title taken by the Rashtrakutas had been peculiar to the Chalukyas. It was the title Śrī-pṛthivī-vallabha, 'beloved,' 'favourite,' or 'husband' of the wives of Vishnu, Śrī, goddess of Fortune, and Pṛthivī, goddess of the Earth. The appropriation of this title (combined with the later declaration of their descent from the moon and from Yadu, ancestor of Vishnu as Krishna) made the Rashtrakuta (and no longer the Chalukya) appear as the truest earthly manifestation of Vishnu that a Chakravartin was, according to the Vaishnavas and Śaivas, supposed to be. The assumption of epithets indicating they were particular emanations emphasized the point. Govinda III, for example, was called Kīrtinārāyaṇa (the Vishnu of famous deeds, a reference to him as the avatar of Vishnu, Vikrama, who encompassed the earth in three strides, dispossessing the demons) and also Nṛpati-Trinetra (Siva among kings).[34] The Rashtrakutas, beginning with Krishna I, also gave themselves titles peculiar to their dynasty, the most prominent of which ended with -*tuṅga* ('pre-eminent among', evoking the term -*kūṭa* ('most prominent in', of their dynastic name) and -*varsha* ('rainer down of gifts'). The titles of Kirshna I (and all subsequent Krishnas) were Śubhatuṅga, 'pre-eminent among the handsome', and Akālavarsha, 'constant rainer down of gifts' (Fleet, 1900–1a, 167–92).

The second of the signs taken by the Rashtrakutas, their banner, called Pālidhvaja, was, if anything, more important. Every lord had his weapon and his own distinct banner or standard, used to identify him on the battlefield and in procession. The weapon of a king was his army. That of a king who claimed not only to be a king of kings, but to be paramount king of India was supposed to be the foremost army on earth, comprised of units from everywhere. The standard which signalled the presence of the Chakravartin and his 'weapon' was, not surprisingly, supposed to be invested with the divine will of Vishnu and capable of showing that investment.

From references in the charters and elsewhere it is possible to reconstruct this Pālidhvaja. It appears to have consisted of a higher central standard or flagstaff, on top of which was mounted an image of Garuḍa, the eagle, Vishnu's vehicle.[35] Since the paramountcy (*parameśvaratva*) of the Rashtrakuta emperor

---

[34] Amoghavarsha I was called Vīra-Nārāyaṇa, (heroic Vishnu, a reference to him as Varāha, the cosmic boar, who rescued the Earth from the flood waters at the end of a cosmic cycle), and Govinda IV was named Vikrānta-Nārāyaṇa (Vikrama again).

[35] Govinda IV is described as 'lofty with a flagstaff surmounted by the king of birds' (Barnett, 1915–16).

is said to be 'adorned with (the emblems) of Pālidhvajas glittering in the east, north, west, and south',[36] we may infer that it consisted of shorter standards, apparently attached to the main standard by ropes, and arranged in rows stretching out from the central Garuḍa standard in each of the cardinal directions. These bore the emblems of the dynasties which the Rashtrakuta had defeated in battle. One charter expressly states that:

Jagattuṅga ['pre-eminent in the world', title of the Rashtrakuta, Govinda III, *c.* 793–814], whose sign was Garuḍa, the eagle, took these – the fish from the lord of the Pāṇḍya country, the bull from the Pallava lord, the tiger from the Chola, the elephant from the Gaṅga, the bow from the Kerala, the boar from the Āndhra, Chālukya, and Maurya, the board bearing the doorkeeper, Lakshmaṇa from the Gurjara lord . . ., the names from the lords of Kosala and Avanti, as well as Simhala, and the renowned goddess Tārā from Dharma, lord of Vaṅgāla – and the other insignia of the lords of the earth. Śrīvallabha arranged it on earth so that his very own Garuḍa eagle, with a face of beauty [śrī], was supported by those, namely, the insignia of the kings of the south . . . (My translation, Nesarika Grant in Gupta, 1961; Sircar, 1961)

It was apparently this arrangement which gave rise to the term *pālidhvaja* itself, 'flags in rows'. The ensemble as a whole, with the icon of the Rashtrakuta in the middle and the emblems of other kings placed in the lesser supporting positions of regional kings, was, thus, an active visual icon not of just one of India's armies, but of the troops of an entire imperial formation, that over which the Rashtrakuta emperor claimed to preside. At the same time, it was also an indexical sign of the Rashtrakuta's power relative to that of the lesser imperial and regional or peripheral kings as well as a symptom of the grace or favour of the god whom the Rashtrakuta took as overlord of the cosmos, Vishnu. This use of the eagle was, it will be noted, also consistent with the titular claim, also taken from the Chalukyas, to be emanations of Vishnu and, as such, the beloved or husband of the goddesses Fortune and the Earth.

The use of this banner was also important historically. It was not uncommon for kings to take the banners of the princes they defeated and display them as banners of victory (Chidanandamurthy, 1973). The Chalukyas, whom the Rashtrakutas claimed to succeed as overlords of the earth, had been perhaps the first imperial rulers of India, or at least the first paramount kings, to incorporate the banners of defeated kings into a single compound flagstaff, the 'flag in rows', after they had vanquished the king of kings of the Uttarāpatha, the event which validated their claim. When the Rashtrakutas claimed to take for themselves the supreme overlordship of the earth from the Chalukyas, they thus also laid claim to the use of the 'flag in rows'.[37] They did not, however, simply 'borrow' the flag of their predecessors; they transformed it. The standard of the Chalukyas had apparently been surmounted by an image of one of the descents of Vishnu, that of Varāha. The Rashtrakutas took as their standard's emblem a different animal, the eagle, the vehicle of Vishnu himself,

[36] Paithan Plates in Kielhorn (1894–5), lines 33–4, v. 21, as corrected in Bhor Plates by Altekar (1933–4).
[37] Fleet (1896: 338), as usual, says nothing of the political significance of the Chalukyas' *pālidhvaja*.

and the emblem that the Guptas had used in their imperial formation of the fourth to the sixth centuries.

The Jainas, probably more numerous and wealthy in the Karnataka than elsewhere (and unaware that a later Indology would consign them to the place of an inherently minority religion), were also implicated in the practice of using this banner. They seem to have advanced a claim to be placed by the Rashtrakuta emperor, Amoghavarsha I (814–*c.* 878), whom they claimed as a devotee of their founder, the Jina, in the position of India's highest, truest religious order. Consistent with this claim, a text of theirs from the period gives to the Jina a 'flag in rows'. The universal king was conventionally spoken of as the overlord of the earth. Indexical of the even greater overlordship of the Jina which, like that of Vishnu or Siva, was said to consist of the overlordship of the three cosmic realms (*tribhuvaneśitvam*), namely, of the sky and the atmosphere, as well as of the earth, his flagstaff was described as a much grander, more complex affair than that of a lesser overlord of the earth alone. The other flagstaff that presumably outshone the Garuḍa flagstaff of the overlord of the earth was the flagstaff of the other, more successful contender for overlord of the cosmos, Siva. Two of these, carved in stone and surmounted by his weapon, the trident (and not by his vehicle, the bull, for that had been used by the Pallavas on their standard) survive at the temple which Krishna I built.

Having put an end to the last Chalukya emperor, Krishna, described by his encomiast as a descent of Vishnu, 'By which Giant Boar of the Dissolution, the Earth, agitated (*vyākulā*), sunk as she was in the ocean of strife, which had transgressed its bounds, was rescued' (my translation, Bhandak Plates, v. 23, in Sukthankar, 1917–18) set about to complete his overlordship of the earth. The cave excavated by Dantidurga was a relatively modest affair. The temple Krishna built as the grand finale to his conquest of the earth was probably the largest structure of permanent materials built in India up to that time.[38] One record describes it, in the course of eulogizing Kirshna I, not as a reduced imitation of some original, but as an innovation that causes even the gods to do a doubletake. He is said to be:

the king who indeed had a temple constructed on the hill at Elapura, an astounding edifice, on seeing which the best of the immortals who move in celestial cars, astonished, repeatedly say to themselves: "This is a temple of Śiva come into existence on its own (*svayambhū*); such beauty is not seen in a thing constructed," a temple, the master builder of which, because his energy for another such work was used up, was himself suddenly struck with astonishment, saying, "Oh, how was it that I built it?" (Baroda Plates of Karka II, Ś734 in Fleet, 1883 and R. G. Bhandarkar, 1883)[39]

Mount Kailāsa in the Himalayas was the place where the Gaṅgā, India's main river, descended from its heavenly stream-bed (the Milky Way) to earth. Siva,

---

[38] Its only rivals were those of their political Others, the Buddhist temple built at Somapurī in eastern India by the Pālas, and possibly a temple or temple complex built by the Pratihāras at Kanauj.

[39] My translation, based on Fleet (1883) as corrected by R. G. Bhandarkar (1883). The central cella presumably had not an anthropomorphic image installed therein but, as now, a lingam.

whose ashram or retreat was at that site, broke the fall of the Gaṅgā by causing it to land on his matted locks. The complex agent that built the Kailāsa temple at Ellora depicted the scene of this cosmogonic act on the structure of the main temple itself. Alluding to this scene, among others, the encomiast speaks next of an anthropomorphic image worshipped in its central shrine, probably in the pillared 'assembly pavilion' attached to the central cella, praising Krishna I as the king,

by whom Sambhu (Siva), who resides in it, even though adorned with those very amazing ornaments – the stream of the river Gaṅgā (which broke its descent from heaven to earth by falling first on his head), the cool rays of the Moon (whose crest he wears in his matted locks), and the poison (that had turned his neck blue at the churning of the ocean) – was further adorned with every sort of thing beginning with rubies and gold. (My translation, Baroda Plates in Fleet, 1883, and R. G. Bhandarkar, 1883)

Another inscription refers to Krishna I as 'he who constructed temples of Īśvara (Siva), white as clouds in autumn, by which the earth shines for ever as if decorated by many Kailāsa mountains' (Karhad Plates in R. G. Bhandarkar, 1896–7). The temple in question, called, by convention, the Krishneśvara (the Siva of Krishna), was, of course, the one that Smith referred to as an 'architectural freak', the so-called Kailāsa temple carved out of solid rock at Ellora. The other shrines at this site are cave sanctuaries, but the Kailāsa gives the appearance of being a giant structural temple that has sprung up where one would have expected yet another cave temple. It stands over 100 feet high, 100 feet wide, and 200 feet long, in a huge excavated courtyard nearly 300 feet in length and 175 in breadth. Made in the Dravidian style, like its Chalukya and Pallava predecessors, it surpassed them in both size and complexity of feature.

But there was more to the building of this temple than some attempt by a 'successful individual' to outdo rivals and predecessors in his 'patronage' of the arts and religion, as if the amount of money expended were the major criterion of success. I have already spoken of the building of a temple as the act that was considered to bring about the completion of a king of kings's overlordship. Yet even this does not tell the whole of the story.

6.3.3 Commanding and Remaking Time

The activities culminating in the construction of a temple were all in aid of achieving the purpose of the complex act referred to as the 'conquest of the quarters'. What was this purpose? It was not, as historians have often casually assumed, either materially the acquisition of wealth and territory, or symbolically of glory and prestige. It was an attempt on the part of a complex agent – the imperial court and the advocates of differing soteriologies – both to determine a truth greater than that of his predecessors and would-be rivals, the truth most suitable for the times, and to make that manifest in the world so that people would recognize its validity and strive to attain the goal of participation in the god who represented that truth.

The construction of this temple was, in other words, not only a sign of the emperor's commitment to, and participation in, a Vaishnavized Saivism, but also, at the same time, an attempt to make manifest at the soteriological centre of the kingdom that was now the centre of the earth, the religion of the truest form of the overlord of the cosmos, the Rashtrakutan Siva. The completion of a temple was itself also simultaneously to be seen as a symptom of the grace of the god taken as overlord of the universe by the universal monarch: that god, in the particular form designated by this emperor, had chosen to manifest himself in his devotee's temple. In order that a temple be viewed in this way, its builders had, dialectically, to persuade the lords who had joined the ruling society and those who had not but might, that this temple and its theology and liturgy gave a better account of a divine presence than did its contenders. The overlord of the cosmos, in his manifested form, and his devotee, the self-proclaimed overlord of the earth, would have to demonstrate not just that they were in command of both the time and the space that constituted their joint domains, but that they were capable, by virtue of the exercise of their divine will, of renewing and reworking time and space and the institutions situated in them. When those domains comprised the 'entire earth', that is, all of India, the order was a tall one.

The activities by which the religious institution embodied in this temple (and in others as well) was sustained on a yearly basis were parallel to those by which the imperial kingdoms of the Rashtrakutas and of their rivals were renewed, namely the annual holding of an audience by an image of the god, which had previously been ceremonially bathed, and the carrying out of a procession. It is quite likely that this took place on Kārttikī (full-moon day of Kārttika, October–November). This was a major turning-point in the year, as constructed by the Vaishnavas and Śaivas of this period (and also, earlier, the Buddhists). Like all other major units of time, the year was assumed to be a life or period of life. As such, it was divided into moieties; the one, equivalent to a day in the life of the gods, included the cold and hot seasons. The other, a night of the gods, consisted of the four-month rainy season (June–July to October–November). The day portion was a time for consciously ordered activity, for accomplishing the tasks people set for themselves. It was the period when the bright and the good component of the world had the upper hand. The night, on the other hand, was a period of rest and withdrawal, a time for rebirth, but also a time when ordered existence became messy. As the dark, ignorant, and lethargic component of the world predominated then, what acts that were performed had to be undertaken with great caution. The images of the gods were, for the duration of this period, put to 'sleep', a metaphor for the process of death and regeneration. The last several days of the bright half of Kārttika (October–November), ending with the full-moon day, Kārttikī, the worshippers of the gods awakened them. After elaborate celebrations in which they enacted their knowing participation in the life of the gods, their devotees resumed those activities they had suspended for the length of the rainy season.

Now, it was just at this time of the year that both the liturgy of the god who was the overlord of the cosmos and the overlord of the earth resumed the holding of court and royal touring. That is, the two major activities of the year, those that sustained the major religious orders and those that sustained the polities of an imperial formation, were coordinated. The king and his court, along with a variety of preceptors, chronologers, and priests, were agents in and of both these ceremonial events. It is most likely that the Rashtrakutas carried out the annual holding of court on or about this date. This is why. The Vaishnavas (those of a Bhāgavata order) to whom the predecessors of the Rashtrakutas, the Chalukyas, had been committed, had, with royal permission and support, gone into the hills of the Deccan and excavated caves dedicated to the worship of Vishnu. They apparently had succeeded by the sixth century, in the Deccan, in wresting command of this turning-point of the year from the Buddhists.[40] An inscription of Mangaleśa, son of the king who transformed the Chalukya polity into an imperial kingdom, declares that he made the 'great gift' of a village to 16 Brahmans for the performance of the worship of Nārāyaṇa (Vishnu) in one of these caves above the capital at Badami on Mahākārttikī, the 'high' full-moon day of Kārttika, and another record of that dynasty refers to the day of Vishnu's awakening, the twelfth lunar day of that month, as the 'most honourable' or 'worshipful' day in the entire year (Badami Pilaster Inscription of Mangaleśa in Burgess, 1877: VI, 363–4; Nerur Plate of Mangaleśa in Fleet, 1878).

It is clear from a statement in one of the Rashtrakuta inscriptions recording the grant of a village to one Gagana-śiva, a Śaiva-siddhāntin, and abbot (*sthānapati*) of a monastery, for the purpose of distributing seats and clothes to the ascetics there on Kārttikī (Karhad Plates), that the Śaiva-siddhāntas in the Rashtrakuta domains had, with Rashtrakuta support, in turn attempted to take this crucial day in the calendar from the Bhāgavata Vaishnavas.[41] We may assume that Kārttikī was also the major festival celebrated at the Kailāsa temple, for that temple at Ellora was itself built as a mountain hermitage or ashram for the highest of ascetics, Siva. May we go one step further and suggest that this day was also the day in the year on which the annual holding of court took place?[42] If so, then the conjoint performance of these annual acts at this crucial time would have not only shown that the Rashtrakuta and his Siva were co-agents; it would have demonstrated that they together were able to order the renewal of the human world of which they were jointly the overlords. It was undoubtedly to this annual awakening of the image that one of the Arab

[40] The Buddhists had been the first to divide the year into moieties of activity and retreat and to make this time of year the point at which the Buddhist monastic community and its royal supporters came together at the hill caves to renew their world through, among other activities, the making of a 'great gift' (the Kaṭhina) to the monks (Bareau, 1966: III, 66–76, 126–40). Doing so, they displaced the cycle of still earlier Vedic rites known as the Four-Monthly (*cāturmāsya*) Sacrifices.

[41] The observant reader will note how this mountain retreat differs from the third ashram or life-stage, that of the forest-dweller, of Manu, who is supposed to render hospitality but accept no gifts; like the Buddhist monastery, the Śaiva retreat and its ascetic adepts may receive donations of the requisites for their ritual practices.

[42] It would seem that several centuries later, the two days focused on the putting to sleep and awakening of the gods are yet again displaced as the major days in the calendar by the theological and liturgical reforms of the last Hindu empire (Vijayanagar, if we may discount here the Maratha revival). It is from their acts that the Daśaharā (following Navarātrī, with its Durgā-pūjā) in the previous month of Āśvina (September–October) comes to be the day for the annual holding of court.

travellers referred, though he was apparently giving an account of that ceremony as performed not at Ellora, but at the political capital of Mānyakheṭa, which was built later. The records of the Rashtrakutas report the building there of temples, one of which in a given reign, considered a lesser version of the remote Kailāsa, was probably used for the performance of the Kārttikī when the court was in residence in the capital (Mirashi, 1963).

There was, however, more to this ritual renewal of time when it came to the building of a monumental temple by the founder of a dynasty claiming the universal kingship of the earth. The establishment of an ashram for Siva (and his devotee worshippers) in the form of Mount Kailāsa at Ellora in the first place was, of course, the act that began not just the year; it was an act that began the time or period of the Rashtrakutas and of their version of the Śaiva liturgy as a whole, a 'day' that was supposed to be one which surpassed the 'night' of Chalukya decline.

I have written as though the Kailāsa temple were the product of Krishna I and his court, but this was not strictly so. The evidence suggests that successive rulers made their distinctive additions to the temple complex (Goetz, 1974: 91–107). They treated it as a scale of forms. That is, each succeeding emperor saw the temple and its liturgy, as modified by his polity, as a new whole, a more complete, truer version of the divine presence than those of his predecessors, which, encompassed in his own work, had become parts of that work.

6.3.4   Recentring the Indian World

If taking command of time, if having the moment when the premier soteriology of the world, by imperial denomination, and the premier imperial kingdom of the 'entire earth' by the grace of the high god so denominated, in its charge, was vital to the initial making and ongoing sustenance of an imperial formation, so was taking command of the crucial places of the landscape. Here the construction of a temple supposed to resemble or surpass a mountain named Kailāsa was vital.

Smith was not totally wrong when he asserted that the centre of India was always in the north. The ruling societies of early India also held that their Bhāratavarsha or more narrowly, Sāgaradvīpa, 'Ocean Island' (by which they meant the entire earth inhabited by mortals and not just the contemporary geographer's 'South Asia') was surrounded on four sides by oceans. This was not, however, symmetrically constituted, as it might at first seem. Itself the southern realm of a large circular continent, its premier mountains were those to its north, the Snowy Mountains (Himalaya), themselves the source of India's major rivers. Most important among these mountains was the mountain named Kailāsa. Near it, the premier river of the world, the Gaṅgā, is said to have first descended from its heavenly source and form (the Milky Way). Those mountains were held to constitute India's northern boundary while the Bridge (Setu, also called the Bridge of Rama, Ramasetu), which separated India from Lanka (today's Sri Lanka) formed her southern limit.

The texts that describe this geography also divided it into two parts, an Uttarāpatha or northern India in the largest sense and a Dakshiṇāpatha or southern India, also in the largest sense. They also held, in addition, that Bhāratavarsha was divided into a set of five 'directions', the east, south, west, north, and middle. Just as Bhāratavarsha as a whole was considered a rain basin for the Gaṅgā and its tributaries, so, too was each of the parts or regions construed as a rain basin bounded by mountains and drained by its distinct river or rivers. The major streams of northern India were the Gaṅgā (Bhāgīrathī) and the Sindhu. The major rivers of the middle region, those which distinguished it from the other directional regions, were again the Gaṅgā and, this time, the Yamunā, its tributary.

Like most schemes of political or sacred geography, this one was constructed by using the tools of metonymy. Agentive notions of which region was better, and better suited, therefore, as the domain of a higher, more pre-eminent king, were built into it. The king and people associated with the better region were, in other words, considered better. This might even be converted into synecdoche. The king of a better part might be taken not simply as the higher, more powerful king, but as the king of the whole. At the same time, however, the scheme also relied on homology. The Gaṅgā was taken to be the ultimate source of all rivers in India and each region was constituted of features held to resemble those that constituted the others. The Vindhyas, the mountains that divided the Uttarāpatha from the Dakshiṇāpatha, were, for example, considered homologous with the Himalayas, and several rivers of the later region were taken as equivalent to the Gaṅgā.

Now, there can be little doubt that the 'authors' of this scale of topographic forms were the royal or imperial courts of the Gangetic basin, the 'middle region'. A king from any other region who wished to assert his overlordship over the 'entire earth' from a capital in that other region would have to contend with this particular scale of forms and with the practices implied in it. He would have to take advantage of the ambiguities that are inherent in any of these schemes and attempt to rework it, not just in the medium of words, but in the activities that caused this scale as a scale of realms to be sustained through time.

This is just what the Rashtrakutas did. Mount Kailāsa was the chief mountain among the Himalayas, in the sense that it was the place where India was fashioned at the beginning of a cosmic cycle, and the place where creatures took refuge at the end of one. The foremost pilgrimage places of the Vaishnavas and Śaivas, Badarikāśrama and Kedāra, were both situated there. At these sites, the highest forms of these contending high gods were to be found, both in the form of great masters of knowledge. Kailāsa and the Gaṅgā were, thus, both the epistemological and ontological centre of India, that is, of the earth as inhabited by mortals. So when Krishna I and his successors built and extended the Kailāsa temple at Ellora they were not simply doing obeisance to some distant and awe-inspiring model of a sacred place; they were claiming to make that place, as constituted by them, appear in the Sahyadris or Vindhyas, in the mountains of the Deccan homologous with the Himalayas. If, as seems likely, the original *point d'appui* of Bhāratavarsha (which I take to have been Chowkhamba or Badrinath and not the Kailas of today in Tibet, another topic that needs to be opened up) had been occupied by Tibetans; if the lord of the

Uttarāpatha had failed to protect the site, that would have made the Rashtrakuta claim all the more credible.

The complement of the place of knowledge and point of origin of a country, situated above it in the mountains where its major river originated, was the plains below, the area drained by that river or rivers. There the political centre of a country was to be situated. Consistent with the attempt to make the true Kailāsa appear in the mountains to the north of their domains was the work the Rashtrakutas did to convince the kings of India that their domains, the country defined by the Godavari and Krishna rivers, had displaced the country that was the complement of the Himalayan Kailāsa. That country was, of course, the middle region of India, the region defined by the Gaṅgā and its tributary, the Yamunā, the political centre of which was the city of Kānyakubja (Kanauj). The Rashtrakutas installed carved images of the Gaṅgā and Yamunā, as river goddesses, on either side of the entrances to the Kailāsa temple and central shrine. The Chalukyas, their predecessors, had appropriated this practice of northern temple-builders after they claimed to have defeated the lord of the Uttarāpatha around the end of the seventh century. Once again, we see that the strategy which the Rashtrakutas used has a history. They could do this not only because they had appropriated the universal kingship of the Chalukyas, but because they had humiliated one of their major rivals, the Pratihāra, when they performed the Golden Embryo in his capital, on the soil of northern India. But the Rashtrakutas did not stop there.

The successor of Krishna I was Govinda II (772/5–9). His short reign was taken up by a struggle for the throne with his younger brother, Dhruva (*c.*780–93), who, upon his accession, took the titles Dhārāvarsha ('rainer down of gifts in streams'), Nirupama ('unequalled'), and Kalivallabha ('favourite of warriors/ of the Age of Strife'). He was the first of the Rashtrakutas to lead a military campaign into the 'middle region' itself, the land defined by the Gaṅgā and Yamunā Rivers. One charter praises Dhruva as he 'Who seized the white umbrellas [of state], the lotuses of the sport of Royal Fortune [Lakshmī, supposed consort of the Rashtrakuta] from the Gauḍa king as he fled from between the Gaṅgā and Yamunā' (Sanjan Plates, v. 14, in D. R. Bhandarkar, 1925–6). Another, that of his son, asserts that 'By his matchless armies having quickly driven into the trackless desert Vatsarāja who boasted of having with ease appropriated the fortune of royalty of the Gauḍa, he in a moment took away from him, not merely the Gauḍa's two umbrellas of state, white like the rays of the autumn moon, but his own fame also that had spread to the confines of the regions' (Radhanpur Plates, v. 8, Kielhorn, 1900–1b).

The major rivals of the Rashtrakutas, the only ones to challenge their claims to universal sovereignty, themselves rivals for the overlordship of the Uttarāpatha, were the Gurjaras or Pratihāras, of Malwa, kings over kings in the western region, and the Pālas, of Bengal, emperors of the eastern region. Vatsarāja was the Pratihāra ruler, while the Gauḍa was the Pāla king, Dharmapāla (*c.*770–810). What the Rashtrakuta charter claims to record is Dhruva's defeat of Vatsarāja, who had earlier defeated Dharmapāla in his attempt to take command of the middle country. Dhruva was not, however, content simply to prevent either of these rivals from setting up as a paramount king of northern

India. He did something else which had the effect of displaying Dhruva and his country as the true middle region. Karka II, Mahāsāmantādhipati, the Rashtrakuta lord of Lāṭa, speaks of his 'overlord' (*svāmin*), Dhruva, as he who, 'taking from his enemies the Gaṅgā and the Yamunā, charming with their waves, acquired at the same time that supreme position of lordship [which was indicated] by [those rivers in] the form of a visible sign'.[43] This is an important statement. What was its significance? Fleet had speculated that these allusions to the Gaṅgā and Yamunā were to be read as saying that the Rashtrakutas, like the Chalukyas before them, had brought statues of the two river goddesses back with them to their capital (Fleet, 1896: 338, note 7). It is more likely that they brought the waters of those two streams back with them in large jars. That is what the Cholas, the successors to the universal kingship of the Rashtrakutas, did. There is at Ellora, in the form of an addition to the Kailāsa temple, a shrine of the three river goddesses, Gaṅgā, Yamunā, and Sarasvatī (supposed to run underground to the confluence of the other two). It is likely that Dhruva built this shrine to celebrate this victory over the middle region and her would-be kings, outdoing, by adding Sarasvatī, his predecessors. So it seems clear that the Rashtrakutas, who had made Mount Kailāsa appear in the mountain range north of their domains, also caused the rivers that had originated there, the rivers that defined the middle region of India, to appear in their empire in the Deccan. This is not so improbable as it might seem. When we consider that all rivers were said ultimately to originate from the Gaṅgā, when we take into account the fact that some of the *Purāṇas* refer to the Godavari and the Krishna, the rivers constituting the imperial domains of the Rashtrakutas, as Gaṅgās of the south, when we remember that the Rashtrakutas were talking about these topographical features not simply as physical places, but as the domains of purposive agents interacting with time, country, universal king and cosmic overlord to make and remake a divinized polity, it all makes good sense.[44] The Kailāsa temple at Ellora, above the Godavari, would be the new Kedāra. Later, when the Rashtrakutas built their political capital at Mānyakheṭa, on the Krishna, they would have the city that would surpass Kānyakubja.[45]

Dhruva's successors continued the process of decentring any attempt to establish a unified Uttarāpatha at Kanauj. Govinda III (*c.*793–814) claims to have played an even greater role than his father, Dhruva, in the politics of northern India. His encomiast claims that he defeated Nāgabhaṭa II (*c.*800–*c.*830), the Pratihāra successor of Vatsarāja, whom his father had defeated, and then proceeded to the middle region. There, earlier (*c.*790–800), the emperor of Gauḍa and Vaṅga (Bengal), Dharmapāla, recovering from his earlier humiliation, had constituted himself the paramount king of the Uttarāpatha by

[43] /yo Gaṅgā-Yamunā taranga-subhage grhnan-parebhyah samam//sākshāt-cihna-nibhena cottama-padaṃ tat-prāptavān-aiśvaraṃ// (Baroda Plates in Fleet, 1883. Also in the Cambay/Sangli/Andura Plates).
[44] For a Pallava antecedent in the form of Siva Gaṅgādhara sculpted in a cave temple at Tiruchirapalli, above another Gaṅgā, the Kāverī, by Mahendravarman I (*c.*610–30), see Lockwood and Bhat, 1977.
[45] Compare Richard Krautheimer (1983: 41–67) on the building of Constantinople as a 'second Rome' and an explicitly Christian capital.

his conquest of the quarters, during the course of which he visited Kedāra, at Kailāsa. He held a court in the city of Kānyakubja, where he installed, by way of a ceremonial bath, the king of Pañchāla, the smaller country of which it was the capital, as a tributary king after himself defeating Nāgabhaṭa II:

Signalling with a furl of his dancing eyebrows, he offered the illustrious king of Kānyakubja his own golden water-jar for his ceremonial bath of installation, taken up by the excited elders of Pañchāla, and agreed to by the Bhoja, Matsya, Madra, Kuru, Yadu, Yavana, Avanti, Gandhāra, and Kīra kings who were paying homage with the bending down of their quavering diadems.[46]

Dharmapāla's imperium was disturbed by Tibetan invasions from the north and by the return of Nāgabhaṭa II from the west. Govinda's kingship seems to have decided to display its hegemony by intervening. Here is how Govinda's expedition, which apparently included at least the sending of a small force to the Himalayas, is described, in terms that clearly presuppose the political theology of luminous will:

The sun whose treasure of luminous will (*tejonidhi*) was difficult to sustain, himself gone to Northern India (into the northern part of the elliptic), whose feet of wise policy (well-guided rays) extended in every direction over the heads of kings (peaks of the mountains), whose occurrence of merit (auspicious rise) by its majesty (radiant energy, *tejas*) traversed all other countries (the whole of the atmosphere), whose heat (glory, *pratāpa*) increased at every bound, who is, moreover, possessed of a loyal circle of tributary kings (reddened disc) and delighted by the hand of the Goddess of Royal Fortune (delighting the clumps of lotuses), stole away the unstealable fortitude (*dhairya*) consisting of the fame of the kings Nāgabhaṭa and Chandragupta and, intent on the acquisition of fame, uprooted deficient kings from their lands like so many (defective) rice plants (from their fields) and reinstated (transplanted) still others. To him, the great one, the waters of the springs of the Snowy Mountains were drunk by whose horses and the sound made by the plunging trumpeting into the heavenly waters (*gāṅga*) of whose elephants was redoubled in its gorges, Dharma and Chākrayudha submitted (*upanam*) on their own; because of his similarity to the glory (*kīrtti*) of the Snowy Mountains, he is Kīrttinārāyaṇa.[47]

With the defeat of Nāgabhaṭa and the submission of Dharmapāla, the paramount king of northern India, and his protégé at Kanauj, Govinda III validated his claim to be the paramount king not just of the Deccan, but of the entire earth. This moment of unity which the court of Govinda III created did not last for very long. Throughout most of the ninth century and during the long reign of his son, Śarva, best known by his title, Amoghavarsha I (c.814–78), the Pala kingship, under Devapāla (c.810–50) and the Pratihāra kingship, under Bhoja (c.836–c.885), who succeeded in establishing his capital at Kanauj, contested the overlordship of the Uttarāpatha. Only once, however, during this period of relative Rashtrakuta torpor, did Devapāla claim (on the basis, apparently, of a campaign down the east coast around the margins of the

---

[46] My translation, Khalimpur Plate in Kielhorn (1896–7), based on D.R. Bhandarkar's correction (1902–3: VII, 31).
[47] My reworking of D.R. Bhandarkar's translation (1925–6).

Rashtrakuta domains and against the 'Dravidas') to hold the overlordship of all of India (Majumdar, 1981). The only other candidate for universal kingship, Bhoja, could claim no more than to have invaded the domains of the tributary lords of the Rashtrakutas (which their own records concede). Mostly these rivals remained content with the claim to overlordship only over the Uttarāpatha (also called Āryāvarta).

In the first quarter of the tenth century, the Rashtrakutas, led by Indrarāja III (914–28), once again were able to adopt a more assertive policy toward northern India. He went on an expedition to Kānyakubja and gained victory over the Pratihāra ruler of it, Mahīpāla I (913–43) Here is how Indra's son's eulogy, rhetorically ruining and belittling the major royal city of northern India, celebrates this victory:

His steeds crossed the unfathomable Yamunā which rivals the sea. He completely devastated that hostile city of Mahodaya (also, the highly prosperous city of the enemy), which is even to-day greatly renowned among men by the name of Kuśasthala (also a spot of mere kuśa grass) (Cambay Plates, v. 19, tr. D. R. Bhandarkar, 1902–3).[48]

The conquest of the quarters was the act by which a universal monarch dialectically and eristically constituted and reconstituted the Indian 'circle of kings', what I refer to as an imperial formation, as a single polity. The Rashtrakutas used this conquest of the quarters or regions as part of their long-term strategy not to establish themselves as paramount overlords of India in its middle region, but to displace the middle region from the Gaṅgā–Yamunā region on to their own imperial domains. This enabled the eulogist of his son, Govinda IV (930–4/5), by which time the Rashtrakutas were in considerable difficulty, to say of the Gaṅgā and Yamunā: 'As he cannot tolerate the idea that his rivals would have an army the equal of his, possessed of extraordinary qualities, so the Gaṅgā and the Yamunā, who cannot tolerate the idea that his enemies would have rivers the equal of themselves, resort to his irreproachable palace' (my translation, Cambay, v. 28, D. R. Bhandarkar, 1902–3).[49] The implication here is that the palace of the Rashtrakutas at Mānyakheṭa, with the two rivers of the middle region standing outside it, had indeed surpassed and displaced the palace of the Pratihāras at Kānyakubja.

In 972, Harsha or Śīyaka II (*c.*945–73), one of the Paramāras, who had established a tributary kingdom in Malwa in the interstices of the Rashtrakuta and Pratihāra domains, defeated the last imperial Rashtrakuta, Khoṭṭigadeva (967–72), and sacked his capital, seriously damaging the idea that the country

---

[48] The Cambay, Sangli, and Andura Plates of Govinda IV contain virtually the same text for their eulogies.

[49] The verse: *sahate samavāhinīmayam na pareshāṃ saviśeshaśālinīm/ yad-anindita-rājamandiraṃnanu gaṅgā yamunā ca sevate//*. D. R. Bhandarkar's translation: 'Surely [thinking that] he cannot bear the army of [his] foes, which is equal (to his own and) which is possessed (of men) of excellent qualities, the Gaṅgā and the Yamunā resort to his flawless royal abode [because they themselves are *samavāhinī*, i.e., flowing in a level and possessed of excellences].' Fleet's, Sangli Plate : 'Verily it is because he bears not with any equal army, possessed of distinguishing qualities, of [his] enemies, (as they themselves do not bear with any equal river), – that the Gaṅgā and the Yamunā do service to his palace.' (1883)

which it dominated was the middle region of India. His assumption of the Rashtrakuta titles, those of the Chakravartin, makes it clear that the Paramāra kingship was laying claim to that position. The kings who can be said to have succeeded in this, however, were those of another southern kingdom, the Cholas, of Tamilnad. They had replaced the Rashtrakutas as the dominant power in peninsular India, and taken up an altered version of their strategy for making themselves into the paramount overlords of the entire earth. The most powerful king of that dynasty, Rājendra (1012–44), in alliance with most successful of the Paramāras, Bhoja (1011–55), and of the Kalachuris of Dāhala, near Jabalpur in Madhya Pradesh, Gangeyadeva (*c.*1015–34), was able to carry out a conquest of the regions which took one of his armies to the banks of the Gaṅgā (which the last of the Pratihāras had failed to protect against a devastating attack by Mahmud of Ghazni in 1019), and caused her waters to be brought back and placed in a Gaṅgā tank at his new capital (Nilakanta Sastri, 1955: 194–228; Bhatia, 1970: 37–50, 74–96). I would argue that by this act and an expedition by sea to 'Indianized' states in south-east Asia, his court transformed the Chola country, on the Kaveri, into the middle region of a new imperial formation, but this is another story that awaits telling elsewhere.

Concluding Remarks

Studies of India have employed the presuppositions and assumptions of empiricism and its supposed opposite, idealism, to constitute their object. Whichever of these positions they have favoured, they can almost always be seen as trying to know and control a human world ordered in systems that consist of mutually exclusive or dichotomously defined but interdependent parts. Those parts and the systems to which they belong are all assumed to be reducible to essences, to stable, objective, and determinate features or natures presumed to underlie the surface phenomena of observation. Such thinking runs counter to a social science that wishes to study people and institutions as agents because it consistently devalues the actions of transient, historical agents.

Indologists and the other commentators on India, to the extent that they have done their research and writing in accord with the canons of this discursive formation, have treated the transitory agents of the Indian past as though they were simply the accidents of a substantialized agent, 'caste' or its Hindu 'mind'. In their more empiricist and materialist moments those discourses have treated the actions of Indian agents as departures from a utilitarian, individualist human nature or, more positively, as the expressions of underlying structures such as the 'caste society' (and an even deeper structure said by some to underlie *that*, racial conflict or an isolated post-tribal system of 'kinship' and networks) and its institutional manifestation, the self-sufficient village of communal actors (the Asiatic mode of production *in extremis*).

In their more idealist moments, discourses on India have wanted to represent the actions of Indians as expressions of a spirit or mind, of an Indian (Hindu) culture, tradition, or mentality differing from a Western one. The Indian mind, they tell us, is inherently imaginational rather than rational: it thinks in mythic, symbolic (that is, iconic), and ritualist rather than in historical, semiotic, and practical terms. That mind is also governed by passions rather than will, pulled this way and that by its desire for glory, opulence, and erotic pleasures or total renunciation rather than prompted to build a prosperous economy and orderly state. The Indian mind is, in other words, devoid of 'higher', that is, scientific rationality.

Throughout this book I have argued that the problem with orientalism is not just one of bias or of bad motives and, hence, confined to itself. The problem lies in my view, with the way in which the human sciences have displaced human agency on to essences in the first place. Taking up some leads of Collingwood, I have tried to show how an alternative approach that focuses on human agency might be constructed, and how it might be used, as a vantage-point from which both to criticize previous scholarship and to reconstruct our knowledges of the human world. There are, doubtless, other ways of moving from the essentialism that still holds sway in the social sciences to an emphasis on human agency (indeed my approach would insist on this possibility of alternatives). Let me summarize the suggestions I have made.

My overall proposition calls for the replacement of classical notions of system and essence, premised on the existence of a determinate, objective reality and a representational theory of knowledge, with another notion of system. I refer to that, following Collingwood, as a *scale of forms*. This is built out of *overlapping classes* rather than mutually exclusive or even opposed ones. Agency is integral to a system in this sense, for it is assumed that systems of this sort are made and not simply found and that they are continually being completed, contested and remade.

The social sciences have, of course, not been devoid of their own theories of human agency. One family of these, the individualist, attributes human action to a human nature. Another, the socialist, attributes it to some sort of structure. A third, the hermeneuticist, develops a richer theory of agency than these two, but confines it to a study of the intentions and meanings of natural persons. In order to deal with the difficulties posed by these three perspectives I have, again taking up suggestions made by Collingwood, argued that distinctions have to be made between relatively simple and complex agents and that the cover term of 'society' should be replaced with the more problematic notion of *polity*.

Throughout, it is necessary to assume that an external reality is not to be grasped and represented as it is. This presupposes that reality is determinate. The position I prefer to take is that knowledge of something represents it *as* something else *in* a particular situation. Another way I have put this is to say that knowledge is underdetermined by reality.

The shift from a quest for essences to a focus on agency, the shift from the positing of a substantialized agent to the description of actual, transitory agents entails a heightened focus on the actions of those agents and the constitution of those agents themselves. For we are now assuming that those agents are the makers of the imperial formation to which they belong and no longer the instruments or accidents of an underlying and unchanging substance. And we are also assuming that their acts were not the expressions of eternal inherent essences but were themselves the changing or repeated contents of that history. The implications of these shifts are far-reaching not only for the study of the Indian subcontinent but for the practice of the social sciences themselves. Let me conclude with some comments on 'the state'. I do this because the efforts to displace the agency of Others onto Selves has had a great deal to do with theorizing about society and the state in the human sciences.

Virtually all of the views of the Indian state, looking through their Euro-American spectacles, have denied to it the static, eternal unity and transcendence which they have often attributed to polities of the West under that all-purpose label of 'society' or of 'the modern nation-state'. The state as the embodiment of political and civic values, we are told, never existed in India. They have, accordingly, construed the Indian (which almost always turns out to be the Hindu) state as a relatively simple, unitary and neutral instrument of an agency that lies beyond it, that of a Hindu society, or caste, which is endowed with the same permanence and transcendence with which they endow the state in the West. Haloed by the eternal Dharma it was supposed to serve, the divine kingship of the Hindus somehow stood outside of the actual societies it was supposed to safeguard, while standing below the eternal ideal caste society it was supposed to perpetuate.

Yet there is a problem here, for the Western state imagined by most Euro-American commentators seems, with its constitutions (Pocock, 1973: 202–32), autocrats, sovereignties (Stankiewicz, 1969: 67–85, 160–96, 275–88), two-bodied kings (Kantorowicz, 1957: 193–272), abstract individuals (Lukes, 1973: 73–93), rational-legal bureaucracies, civic cultures and civil religions, to be constituted as an ideal or mystical entity. The thread that runs through most of these ideas is the attempt to find a basis on which a state that is above politics can stand. Needless to say, there have been many disagreements over the content of this ideal and over which actual polities have best exemplified it. Advocates of the represented state have created abstract 'individuals' and a 'constitution' to guarantee them protection and harked back to nineteenth-century Britain and the United States as their embodiments. Proponents of the administered polity, on the other hand, have fabricated state sovereignty and an omniscient civil service or party and looked variously to twentieth-century France, Germany, or Russia as their models. Both, however, have tended to couch their histories and political studies in terms of a dichotomy between a higher ideal polity where the political has been reduced to a minimum, if not eliminated, and a lower mundane arena of political contention, strife, evil, and disorder. In other words, Western scholars of the state, whatever its provenance, have had a strong predisposition to see the state, or society (among those Anglo-Americans who find the term 'the state' distasteful), as a self-centred, unitary, homogeneous and permanent entity (the state as stasis) only imperfectly realized at the actual 'level'.

Oriental discourses make this major distinction: in the West actual states have been made the instrument and embodiment of an ideal, modern polity and economy, the essence of the West, while in India, the state has been made the fragile (or overbearing) instrument of a perpetually traditional or even economically backward caste society. Seldom have scholars viewed a polity in either parts of the world as a complex agent situated in specific circumstances and attempting to construct a world order in accord with those knowledges and practices which it judged suitable and itself constructed or appropriated for its purposes.[1] We are, then, not dealing with a problem of scholarship that is

[1] Even a materialist like Perry Anderson falls into this trap (1979) according to Paul Q. Hirst (1985).

confined only to the study of others in a land far away. It is only that, in the case of India, scholars have precluded even the ideal polity from having more than a tenuous existence by focusing single-mindedly on the fiction of Hindu society that they have concocted.

So, when it comes to India, instead of seeing royal courts and village and caste councils as continuous with one another and engaged in continuing interaction with one another over the terms of participation in, and the very constitution of, the polity (and themselves) which they all make and remake, the knowing subjects of Indology have, almost to the last, viewed that Indian state as the upholder of a caste system whose constitution and interrelations, they assume, are and were unproblematic. Their depictions do not see South Asian states as attempting to construct single scales of forms which try to reconcile diverse religious orders by making them aspects of the one supported by a paramount kingship. They do not see their actions as dialectical and eristical attempts to encompass past constructs in the buildings and sculptures which it erects. Rather they have persisted in representing the Indian state as (at best) the neutral and impartial 'patron' of religion and the arts which they have considered to be unchanging in their essence or as evolving (or, more usually, degenerating) according to natural or ideal principles lying beyond the agency of any particular Indian kingship.

The agents for whom the state was supposed to be the instrument in this construct are assumed to be the Indian equivalent of the Western 'individual', the household, lineage, or caste, and the religious sect. The hegemonic texts of Indology and its allies have not represented these and other agents as constituted in accord with the principles of 'lordships' and 'masteries'. Instead, they have, for the most part, assumed what they take to be the 'fundamental' units (a move already reductionist in its direction) to be constituted according to the same principles as the abstract individual of classical economics, Utilitarianism, and Lockean political philosophy. Like that individual (which appears in families, corporations, and nation-states) the constituents of the Indian world are assumed to be in competition with one another for the maximization of the same goods, but with this difference: the inherently uniform needs and desires ascribed to the individuals in this metaphysics, and the acts by which they fulfil them, have been grossly distorted by the social holism of the caste system (itself reducible in many Indological accounts to racial or ethnic conflict).

There are a couple of major variants on this theme. The classical Marxist or neo-Marxist constructs would see castes as classes in conflict rather than individuals in competition as the fundamental agents of Indian history, and make the state the unproblematic instrument of a landlord class. Certain idealists, conservatives, Hindu nationalists, and Durkheimians, with differing evaluations, would see the castes as genuinely different and as inherently cooperative, as hierarchically complementing one another in their duties. They would make an organic whole, caste either as caste system or the idea of a hierarchic Dharma (or its negation, individual renunciation), the true agent of India's civilization. The state, in these views, is mediator between transcendent cultural ideal and a peasant or tribal populace requiring education (including disciplining). While points of intersection and overlap can certainly be found in

Indian discourse with these Euro-American discourses, I would claim that they have failed to confront the fact that most Indian discourses assume, and even theorize, quite different notions of agents and agency than those built into Indological constructs.

The point of chapter 6 has been to give some indications of how different the history of India could look from the perspective of a metaphysics that focuses on human agency. Instead of seeing the eighth to tenth centuries as a period in which a determinate world-ordering rationality carried by the Aryan race (or, more politely, culture) was diminishing, it is possible to see that rationalities were indeed at work. They were not identical with the unitary rationality favoured by so many scholars, nor were they carried by any 'race' or 'culture'. They were exercised by complex human agents. I have identified these agents as the *councils*, *assemblies* or *courts* that convened on regular and special occasions. If these were as important as I have claimed, then we will want to know a great deal more about them, about their composition – which seems not to have been fixed, as we are led to believe corporate entities have been in European polities, but protean – and about the occasions on which they met and what procedures they folowed. This is a desideratum not because we want to see these agents as expressions, or anticipations, or the contractual, voluntarist world assumed to be universal, fixed in human nature, by the followers of Locke or Adam Smith. It is precisely because they exhibit different assumptions about human agents and deploy differing rationalities that I want to know more about them.

The polity that I have reconstructed in outline was what I have called an *imperial formation*, what Indian discourses theorized as the 'circle of kings'. Today it would be unwise to think of the world as constituting more than one imperial formation, that of the US and USSR and represented in the cosmology of the 'three worlds'. During the eighth to twelfth centuries, however, it makes more sense to speak of Eurasia and North Africa as constituting four imperial formations, much as the Arab travellers did. These themselves overlapped and their agents did contest with one another what they considered to be (from differing perspectives) the 'sovereignty' of the world. None the less, I do not believe that any of the polities that dominated these four formations was able to validate its claims to universal rulership in its interactions with the others.

India was constituted as one of these four imperial formations. It was neither a unitary administered polity, an empire or nation-state, nor a system of atomistically conceived, formally equal sovereign states. As an imperial formation, it consisted (as did the other imperial formations of the time) of one (or more) empires and a number of other kingdoms. It was a scale of polities, of rulerships that overlapped one another. It was, however, not a static hierarchy. The imperial states in it contested each other's claims at opportune moments, attempting as they did so to constitute themselves as the highest polity in the scale. Which is to say that these states were constituted and sustained by their ongoing dialectical and eristical relations with one another. The foremost of the acts in which councils and courts conducted these inter-relations were *processions*. These were of a wide variety, ranging from merchants' caravans and the cattle raids of farmer-citizens in one locality against those in another to pilgrimages, journeys with a lord to the capital, royal progresses through and around the capital or imperial domains, through processions of images, to military campaigns.

The total population of this imperial formation was probably something around 70 million in AD 900, compared with a population of some 50 million in the Gupta imperial formation (and perhaps 30 million in the Maurya). Accompanying this population increase and the extension of settlement implied in that, was an increase in the number of polities active in the subcontinent. The polity that dominated this imperial formation was not one centred in north India at Kanauj, but the polity with its centre in the Deccan, that of the Rashtrakutas. I have tried to show here that the institution of universal kingship, that of the Chakravartin or overlord of the earth, was no mere fantasy or ideal hovering unchanged over a progressively morcellizing polity. Nor is it to be equated with the 'great man' or 'hero' around whom the nineteenth-century national historians constructed their political narratives. It was a specific institution, shifting in its content as it was remoulded by differing kings and dynasties, in different regions.

The political activity in these states was not what I have referred to as simply distributive, a question of who gets what within a polity whose constitution is assumed as given. The politics of these states was also constitutive. The debate about how a polity or an entire imperial formation should be constituted was largely conducted in the language of the major religious orders. But since these were all cosmological, and not merely confined to matters of personal morality and salvation, there is no reason to see these debates as displacements from a political reality any more than one would want to see the ideological debates that go on today between various lefts and rights in the name of a science of human needs in the same way. These differences between Vaishnava and Śaiva religious orders, overlooked by Indological discourse's quest for a unitary, perennial Hinduism underlying the 'sects', are another area that needs exploration. One difference that would repay scrutiny has to do with the contrast between the more dispassionate, gradualist practices of the Vaishnavas with their emphasis on the moral householder, and the more intensely emotional, irruptive practices, including the sacrifice of oneself for one's lord, of the Śaivas. I strongly suspect that these mobilized different parts of a polity's population, viz., merchants and soldiers, in different ways for different purposes.

Probably the most interesting and ironic aspect of these Indian states derives from their political theologies, their discourses on divine will and its production and deployment in rituals, rites closely tied to the meetings of courts and councils and the processions these organized. Holding to a metaphysics that is much closer to the idea of a scale of forms with overlapping classes than to the metaphysics of taxonomy which has dominated social science discourses for over two hundred years, the makers of India's polities were anti-utopian. They did not think of their polities as transcendent. But this should not lead us to conclude (with Hegel and Dumont) that Indians devalued the political. On the contrary, they have treated the political aspects of life as integral. Unlike those

European theorists who have wished to create states that would be free of politics or those who would 'educate' the unlettered into a transcendent civic culture, embodied in their elite selves, the Indian theorists assumed that political activity would always have to be engaged in, because the circumstances in which humans lived were continually changing. Evil and ignorance could never be excluded from a polity; they could only, at best, be placed in positions of subjection within a polity, whether that was a village or an entire imperial formation. When conditions altered, this work would have to be done anew. Just as there were alternations between periods of light and dark, so there were moments of political unity and moments or periods of dispersal and disunity. The more skilful could make the moments of unity grander and longer, but not forever, for these people recognized that moments of dispersal and even of destruction were themselves part of the processes by which unity was made. It is, I would argue, precisely because of what I will call their 'theological realism' that Indian discourses could make their royal houses be descended from either the Sun or the Moon and could talk about either Vishnu or Siva as the cosmic overlord (depending on which of the two made the best case for himself). It is why they included discussions of dissent (*vigraha*) along with discussions of agreement (*sandhi*), why they included the rival of a king of kings in a discussion about the Chakravartin, why they allowed lesser gods to be gods and lesser kings to be kings instead of absolutizing a Will and placing it in one God or People and one State.

The moments of unity were, according to Indian discourses on religion, the result of a conjoint will that had been built up by a Chakravartin and his court interacting not only with the gods but also with numerous other courts and councils. Indological discourse has long opposed the 'will' of an autocrat or despot to that of a passive rural populace. They have assumed that this autocratic will was the personal and exclusive property of the person who possessed it, the despot, reinforced with some propaganda about divine right. Everyone from Mill through Baden-Powell to Smith assumed that, in so far as there was a strong state in India (including the British), it was because those individuals who had strong wills had somehow, through the operation of some invisible hand, won out over others with weaker wills. The interdiscursive approach I have used here has shown just how misleading this theme and its variations have been in the construction of Indian polities and their histories. We have begun to learn that the Indians and their Vaishnava and Śaiva theologians knew better. They knew that the will of a Chakravartin or 'divine kingship' was a composite entity and that its composition was problematic. That is why they worried so much about it and devoted so much time to the production and display of it in different settings.

I have, thus, talked about substituting the notion of a theophanic polity for that of divine kingship, but I would not want to impose this notion on a polity whose king took the Buddha as the cosmic overlord, for the gods in Buddhism were hardly accorded the same ontological status that they are in Vaishnava or Śaiva religious orders. There is even difficulty in talking about the Buddha as a cosmic overlord in the same way that the Vaishnavas or Śaivas do.

One last thought. Some will no doubt consider what I have done here a retreat from 'social' history, a turning away from the study of the oppressed to the study of the oppressor, the ruling class of ancient India. To a certain extent I must plead guilty. But I will beg the indulgence of the social historian on two grounds. First, it is precisely where the ideas and practices of the Indian ruling classes are concerned that orientalist discourse differs from the discourses of the social sciences about its own European and American worlds. Those discourses may have (and still often do) systematically displaced the agency of internal others, working classes, women, children, the insane, the dissenting, the racially distinct minority, or even, more broadly, the masses or the people, on to some essences and, ultimately, on to themselves. When, however, it comes to polities or entire imperial formations that are, or could be, on a par with its own, it is not just the ordinary people of those places from whom the power to know and act has been taken; it is from the rulers of those polities as well. Which is to say that the political and intellectual histories that made the writing of an intelligible social history possible in the first place in Europe simply do not exist as such for South Asia. Second, the very opposition between levels that is implied in the dichotomy between political history and social history is an opposition that I have criticized and rejected. If rulers and ruled were overlapping classes that were mutually, if not symmetrically, defining, a point Gramsci made again and again, we cannot do the history of the one without also doing the history of the other.

Bibliography

Abu Zayd Hasan (1845), *Silsilat al-Tawarikh*, published as *Relation des voyages faits par les Arabes et les Persans dans l'Inde et à la Chine*, tr. M. Reinaud, Paris: L'Imprimerie Royale, 2 vols.

Agrawala, Vasudeva S. (1964), *The Wheel Flag of India, Chakradhvaja: Being a History and Exposition of the Meaning of the Dharma-Chakra and the Sarnath Lion-Capital*, Varanasi: Prithivi Prakashan.

Altekar, Anant Sadashiv (1927), *A History of Village Communities in Western India*, Bombay: Oxford University Press.

—— (1933–4), 'Two Bhor State Museum Copper Plates', *Epigraphia Indica*: XXII, 176–91.

—— (1962), *State and Government in Ancient India*, Delhi: M. Banarsidass; 1st pub. 1949.

—— (1967), *Rastrakutas and Their Times*, Poona: Oriental Book Agency; 1st pub. 1934.

—— (1981), 'The Chalukyas of Badami', *A Comprehensive History of India*, III.1 (AD 300–985), 410–39.

Anderson, Perry (1979), *Lineages of the Absolutist State*, London: Verso; 1st pub. 1974.

Appadurai, Arjun (1986), 'Is Homo Hierarchicus?', *American Ethnologist*: XIII.4, 745–61.

Asad, Talal (1973), 'Two European Images of Non-European Rule', in *Anthropology and the Colonial Encounter*, ed. Asad, London: Ithaca Press.

Ayer, A.J. (1968), *The Concept of a Person and Other Essays*, London: Macmillan.

Baden-Powell, B. H. (1892), *The Land Systems of British India*, Oxford: Clarendon Press, 3 vols.

—— (1896), *The Indian Village Community*, London: Longmans, Green.

—— (1899), *The Origin and Growth of Village Communities in India*, London: Swan Sonnenschein.

Bagehot, Walter (1976), *The English Constitution*, Glasgow: Fontana; 1st pub. 1867.

Bandyopadhyaya, Narayan Chandra (1980), *Development of Hindu Polity and Political Theories*, ed. and intro. Narendra Nath Bhattacharya, New Delhi: Munshiram Manoharlal; 1st pub. 1927.

Banerjea, Pramathanath (1916), *Public Administration in Ancient India*, London: Macmillan.

Bareau, André (1966), 'Le Bouddhisme indien', *Les Religions de l'Inde*, Paris: Payot, III, 7–246.

Barnett, Lionel D. (1913), *Antiquities of India*, London: Philip Lee Warner.

—— (1915–16), 'Kalas Inscription of the Rashtrakuta Govinda IV: Saka 851', *Epigraphia Indica*: XIII, 326–38.

—— (1927–8), 'Two Inscriptions from Kolhapur and Miraj: Saka 1058 and 1066', *Epigraphia Indica*: XIX, 30–41.

Barth, Auguste (1963), *The Religions of India*, tr. fr. French by Rev. J. Wood, Varanasi: Chowkhamba; 1st pub. 1879.

Basham, A. L. (1954), *The Wonder That Was India*, New York: Grove.

——— (1961a), 'James Mill, Mountstuart Elphinstone and the History of India', in *Historians of India, Pakistan and Ceylon*, ed. C. H. Philips, London: Oxford University Press, pp. 217–29.

——— (1961b), 'Modern Historians of Ancient India', in *Historians of India, Pakistan and Ceylon*, ed. C. H. Philips, London: Oxford University Press, pp. 226–74.

——— (1974), 'Hinduism, History of', *Encyclopaedia Britannica*, VIII, 908–20.

Beidelman, Thomas O. (1959), *A Comparative Analysis of the Jajmani System*, Locust Valley, NY: J.J. Augustin, for the Association for Asian Studies.

Bendix, Reinhard (1969), *Nation-Building and Citizenship*, New York: Anchor, Doubleday; 1st pub. 1964.

Bernal, Martin (1987), *Black Athena: The Afroasiatic Roots of Classical Civilization*, I (The Fabrication of Ancient Greece 1785–1985), London: Free Association Books.

Bertalanffy, Ludwig von (1968), *General System Theory: Foundations, Development, Applications*. New York: Braziller.

Bhandarkar, D. R. (1900–1), 'Alas Plates of the Yuvaraja Govinda II: Saka-Samvat 692', *Epigraphia Indica*, VI, 208–13.

——— (1902–3), 'Cambay Plates of Govinda IV: Saka-Samvat 852', *Epigraphia Indica*: VII, 26–47.

——— (1907–8), 'Two Grants of Indraraja III: Saka-Samvat 836', *Epigraphia Indica*: IX, 24–41.

——— (1925–6), 'Sanjan Plates of Amoghavarsha I: Saka-Samvat 793', *Epigraphia Indica*: XVIII, 235–57.

Bhandarkar, R. G. (1883), 'The Rashtrakuta King Krishnaraja I and Elapura', *Indian Antiquary*: XII, 228–30.

——— (1896–7), 'Karhad Plates of Krishna III: Saka-Samvat 880', *Epigraphia Indica*: IV, 278–90.

——— (1913), *Vaisnavism, Saivism and Minor Religious Systems*, Strasbourg: Trübner.

——— (1928), *Early History of the Dekkan, Down to the Mahomedan Conquest*, Calcutta: Chuckervertty, Chatterjee; 1st pub. 1884; also in 1896 *Gazetteer of the Bombay Presidency*: I.2, 1–143.

Bhaskar, Roy (1979), *The Possibility of Naturalism: A Philosophical Critique of the Contemporary Human Sciences*, Brighton: Harvester Press.

Bhatia, Pratipal (1970), *The Paramaras*, New Delhi: Munshiram Manoharlal.

Bhattacharya, Jogendra Nath (1896), *Hindu Castes and Sects*, Calcutta: Thacker, Spink.

Biardeau, Madeleine (1981a), *L'Hindouisme: Anthropologie d'une civilisation*, Paris: Flammarion.

——— (1986), *Le Mahabharata*, extraits tr. Jean-Michel Péterfalvi, Paris: Flammarion.

——— ed. (1981b), *Autour de la Déesse hindoue*, Paris: Éditions de l'École des Hautes Études en Sciences Sociales.

Biès, Jean (1973), *Littérature française et pensée hindoue dès origines à 1950*, Strasbourg: Librairie C. Klincksieck.

Binder, Leonard (1986), 'The Natural History of Development Theory', *Comparative Studies in Society and History*: XXVIII.1, 3–33.

Black, Max (1962), *Models and Metaphors*, Ithaca, NY: Cornell University Press.

Bloomfield, Maurice (1908), *The Religion of the Veda*, New York: G. P. Putnam's.

Bongard-Levin, G., and A. Vigasin (1984), *The Image of India: The Study of Ancient Indian Civilization in the USSR*, Moscow: Progress Publishers.

Bose, Nirmal Kumar (1947), *Studies in Gandhism*, Calcutta: Indian Associated Publishing.

Brody, Baruch A. (1980), *Identity and Essence*, Princeton: Princeton University Press.

Brome, Vincent (1980), *Jung: Man and Myth*, London: Granada.

Brown, W. Norman (1953), *The United States and India and Pakistan*, Cambridge, Mass.: Harvard University Press.

Bryant, Christopher G. A. (1985), *Positivism in Social Theory and Research*, London: Macmillan.

Burgess, James (1871), *The Rock Temples of Elephanta or Gharapuri*, London: Sykes.

—— (1877), 'Badami Pilaster Inscription of Mangalesa', *Indian Antiquary*: VI, 363–4.

Burke, Edmund (1784), *Mr. Burke's Speech on the 1st December 1783, upon the Question for the Speaker's leaving the Chair, in order for the House to resolve itself into a Committee on Mr. Fox's East India Bill*, London: J. Dodsley.

Burrow, J. W. (1970), *Evolution and Society*, Cambridge: Cambridge University Press.

Byres, T. J. and Harbans Mukhia, eds (1985), 'Feudalism and Non-European Societies', *Journal of Peasant Studies*: XII.2–3.

Caldwell, Robert (1874/1913), *A Comparative Grammar of the Dravidian or South-Indian Family of Languages*, London: Kegan Paul, Trench, Trübner; 1st pub. 1856.

Cambridge History of India, Cambridge: Cambridge University Press, 1922—.

Campbell, George (1852), *Modern India: A Sketch of the System of Civil Government, to which is Prefixed some Account of the Natives and Native Institutions*, London: John Murray.

Campbell, Joseph (1962), *Oriental Mythology (The Masks of God)*, New York: Viking.

Carchedi, G. (1983), 'A Critical Note on Bhaskar and Systems Theory', *Radical Philosophy*: 33, 27–30.

Cassirer, Ernst (1946), *The Myth of the State*, New Haven: Yale University Press.

Census of India, 1901 (1903), Calcutta: Superintendent, Government Printing.

Census of India, 1911 (1913), Calcutta: Superintendent, Government Printing.

Chalmers, A. F. (1976), *What is This Thing Called Science?*, Milton Keynes: Open University Press.

Chidanandamurthy, M. (1973), 'The Meaning of "Palidhvaja": A Reinterpretation', *Srikanthika, Dr. Srikantha Sastri Felicitation Volume*, Mysore: Geetha Book House, pp. 85–8.

'China, History of' (1974), *Encyclopaedia Britannica*, 15th edn, IV, 297–358.

Chirol, Valentine (1926), *India*, London: E. Benn.

Clark, Grahame and Stuart Piggott (1970), *Prehistoric Societies*, Harmondsworth: Penguin.

Cohn, Bernard S. (1960), 'The Initial British Impact on India: A Case Study of the Benares Region', *Journal of Asian Studies*: XIX, 418–31.

—— (1977), 'African Models and Indian Histories', *Realm and Region in Traditional India*, ed. Richard G. Fox, Durham, NC: Duke University, pp. 90–113.

—— (1983), 'Representing Authority in Victorian India', *The Invention of Tradition*, ed. Eric Hobsbawm and Terence Ranger, Cambridge: Cambridge University Press: pp. 165–209.

Colebrooke, Henry Thomas (1873), *Miscellaneous Essays*, with a life of the author by his son, T. E. Colebrooke, London: Trübner; 1st pub. 1837; repr. 1977 as *Essays on History Literature and Religions of Ancient India*, New Delhi: Cosmo.

Collingwood, R. G. (1933), *An Essay on Philosophical Method*, Oxford: Clarendon Press.

—— (1939), *Autobiography*, London: Oxford University Press.

—— (1956), *The Idea of History*, New York: Oxford Galaxy; 1st pub. 1946.

—— (1971), *The New Leviathan or Man, Society, Civilization and Barbarism*, New York: Thomas Y. Crowell; 1st pub. 1942.

—— (1972), *Essay on Metaphysics*, Chicago: Henry Regnery, Gateway; 1st pub. 1939.

Coomaraswamy, Ananda K. (1956), *The Transformation of Nature in Art*, New York: Dover; 1st pub. 1934.

—— (1977), 'The Philosophy of Mediaeval and Oriental Art', in Roger Lipsey, *Coomaraswamy*, Princeton: Princeton University Press, I, 43–70.

Cottingham, John (1984), *Rationalism*, London: Granada.

Coward, Rosalind (1983), *Patriarchal Precedents: Sexuality and Social Relations*, London: Routledge and Kegan Paul.

Creuzer, Friedrich (1810/1819–23/1825–41), *Symbolik und Mythologie der alten Völker*, Leipzig and Darmstadt; tr. into French by J. D. Guigniaut as *Religions de l'antiquité, considerées principalement dans leurs formes symboliques et mythologiques*, Paris: Treuttel et Würtz.

Crick, Bernard (1982), *In Defence of Politics*, Harmondsworth: Penguin, 2nd edn.

274   *Bibliography*

Crooke, William (1896), *The Tribes and Castes of the North-Western Provinces and Oudh*, Calcutta: Superintendent, Government Printing, 4 vols.
Dale, Roger (1984), 'Nation state and international system: The world-system perspective', *The Idea of the Modern State*, ed. Gregor McLennan, David Held, and Stuart Hall, Milton Keynes: Open University Press.
Dandekar, R. N. (1979), *Insights into Hinduism*, Delhi: Ajanta Publications.
Das, Veena (1977), *Structure and Cognition: Aspects of Hindu Caste and Ritual*, Delhi: Oxford University Press.
Dasgupta, Surendranath (1922–55), *A History of Indian Philosophy*, Cambridge: Cambridge University Press, 5 vols.
Davies, C. Collin (1959), *An Historical Atlas of the Indian Peninsula*, Oxford: Oxford University Press; 1st pub. 1949.
Davis, Kingsley (1951), *The Population of India and Pakistan*, Princeton: Princeton University Press.
Day, Lal Behari (1906), *Bengal Peasant Life*, London: Macmillan, 1st pub. 1874.
Deppert, Joachim, ed. (1983), *India and the West: Proceedings of a Seminar Dedicated to the Memory of Hermann Goetz*, New Delhi: Manohar.
Derrett, J. D. M. (1977), 'Sir Henry Maine and Law in India: 1858–1958', in his *Essays in Classical and Modern Hindu Law*, Leiden: E. J. Brill, II, 40–55.
Deussen, Paul (1966), *The Philosophy of the Upanishads*, New York: Dover; 1st pub. 1921.
Devahuti, D. (1970), *Harsha: A Political Study*, Oxford: Clarendon Press.
Dewey, Clive (1972), 'Images of the Village Community: A Study in Anglo-Indian Ideology', *Modern Asian Studies*: VI.3, 291–328.
Dijkstra, Bram (1986), *Idols of Perversity–Fantasies of Feminine Evil in Fin-de-Siècle Culture*, New York: Oxford University Press.
Dikshit, G. S. (1964), *Local Self-Government in Medieval Karnataka*, Dharwar: Karnatak University.
Dikshitar. See Ramachandra Dikshitar.
Dubois, J. A., Abbé (1906), *Hindu Manners, Customs and Ceremonies*, tr. H. K. Beauchamp, Oxford: Clarendon Press.
Dudley, Guilford, III (1977), *Religion on Trial: Mircea Eliade and his Critics*, Philadelphia: Temple University Press.
Dumont, Louis (1966), 'The Village Community' from Munro to Maine,' *Contributions to Indian Sociology*: IX, 67–89.
—— (1970), 'A Structural Definition of a Folk Deity of Tamil Nad: Aiyanar, the Lord', *Religion/Politics and History in India*, Paris: Mouton; 1st pub. in French in *Journal Asiatique*: XLI, 1953.
—— (1980a), 'The Conception of Kingship in Ancient India', Appendix C, *Homo Hierarchicus*, rev. edn, tr. Mark Sainsbury, L. Dumont, and Basia Gulati, Chicago: University of Chicago Press, pp. 287–313; 1st pub. 1962 in *Contributions to Indian Sociology*: VI.
—— (1980b), *Homo Hierarchicus: Le systéme des castes et ses implications*, rev. English tr., Chicago: University of Chicago Press.
—— (1980c), 'World Renunciation in Indian Religions', in *Homo Hierarchicus*: pp. 267–86.
—— and David Pocock (1958), 'A. M. Hocart on Caste', *Contributions to Indian Sociology*: II, 45–63.
Dutt, Nalinaksha (1954), 'Buddhism', *The History and Culture of the Indian People*, ed. R. C. Majumdar, Bombay: Bharatiya Vidya Bhavan: III, 373–408.
Eisenstadt, S. N. (1969), *The Political Systems of Empires*, New York: Free Press; 1st pub. 1963.
Eliade, Mircea (1969), *Yoga: Immortality and Freedom*, tr. Willard R. Trask, Princeton: Princeton University Press, 1st edn, 1958, from the French edn. 1954, *Le Yoga. Immortalité et Liberté*, Paris: Payot.
—— (1963), *Patterns in Comparative Religion: A Study of the Element of the Sacred in the History of Religious Phenomena by a Distinguished Catholic Scholar*, tr. Rosemary Sheed, Cleveland: Meridian; 1st pub. 1953, from *Traité d'histoire des religions*, Paris: Payot.

Eliot, Charles (1954), *Hinduism and Buddhism: An Historical Sketch*, New York: Barnes and Noble, 3 vols; 1st pub. 1921.

Elliot, Henry M. and John Dowson (1867–77), *The History of India as Told by its own Historians*, London: Trübner, 8 vols.

Elphinstone, Mountstuart (1887), *The Rise of the British Power in the East*, ed. and completed by Edward Colebrooke, London: J. Murray.

——— (1905), *The History of India: The Hindu and Mahometan Periods*, with notes and additions by E. B. Cowell, London: J. Murray, 9th edn; 1st pub. 1841.

Eschmann, A. H. Kulke, and G. C. Tripathi, eds (1978), *The Cult of Jagannath and the Regional Tradition of Orissa*, New Delhi: Manohar.

Fabian, Johannes (1983), *Time and the Other – How Anthropology Makes Its Object*, New York: Columbia University Press.

Fay, Brian (1975), *Social Theory and Political Practice*, London: Allen and Unwin.

Femia, Joseph V. (1987), *Gramsci's Political Thought: Hegemony, Consciousness, and the Revolutionary Process*, Oxford: Clarendon Press.

Fergusson, James (1899), *History of Indian and Eastern Architecture*, New York: Dodd, Mead; 1st pub. 1876.

Feyerabend, Paul (1978), *Against Method: Outline of an Anarchistic Theory of Knowledge*, London: Verso; 1st pub. 1975.

Fisch, Jörg (1985), 'A Pamphlet War on Christian Missions in India 1807–1809', *Journal of Asian History*: XIX, 22–70.

Fleet, J. F. (1878), 'Sanskrit and Old Canarese Inscriptions', *Indian Antiquary*: VII, 161–2.

——— (1883), 'Sanskrit and Old Canarese Inscriptions', *Indian Antiquary*: XII, 156–65.

——— (1896), *The Dynasties of the Kanarese Districts of the Bombay Presidency from the Earliest Historical Times to the Musalman Conquest of A.D. 1318*, in *Gazetteer of the Bombay Presidency*: I.2, 227–584; 1st pub. 1895 Bombay: Government Central Press.

——— (1900–1a), 'The Appellations of the Rashtrakutas of Malkhed', *Epigraphia Indica*: VI, 167–92.

——— (1900–1b), 'Three Western Ganga Records in the Mysore Government Museum at Bangalore', *Epigraphia Indica*: VI, 45–57.

Forbes, Alexander Kinloch (1924), *Ras Mala, Hindoo Annals of the Province of Goozerat in Western India*, ed. H. G. Rawlinson, London: Oxford University Press, 2 vols; 1st pub. 1856.

Fordham, Frieda (1983), *Introduction to Jung's Psychology*, Harmondsworth: Penguin; 1st pub. 1953.

Foucault, Michel (1973), *The Order of Things*, New York: Vintage.

——— (1976), *The Archaeology of Knowledge*, New York: Harper and Row.

——— (1977), *Discipline and Punish: The Birth of the Prison*, tr. Alan Sheridan, New York: Pantheon Books.

——— (1980), *Power/Knowledge: Selected Interviews and Other Writings, 1972–1977*, ed. Colin Gordon, New York: Pantheon Books.

Frankfort, Henri (1948), *Kingship and the Gods: A Study of Ancient Near Eastern Religion as the Integration of Society and Nature*, Chicago: University of Chicago Press.

Frazer, James George (1911–36), *The Golden Bough: A Study in Magic and Religion*, London: Macmillan, 3rd edn, 13 vols.

Freud, Sigmund (1952), *On Dreams*, tr. James Strachey, New York: Norton.

——— (1965), *The Interpretation of Dreams*, tr. J. Strachey, New York: Avon.

Fuller, C. J. (1989), 'Misconceiving the Grain Heap: A Critique of the Concept of the Indian Jajmani System', in J. P. Parry and M. Bloch, eds, *Money and the Morality of Exchange*, Cambridge: Cambridge University Press, pp. 33–63.

Galey, Jean-Claude (1973), 'Les conceptions relatives à la tenure foncière dans l'Inde avant l'independence', Nanterre: Université de Paris, Ph.D. thesis.

——— (1986), 'Les Angles de l'Inde', *Annales ESC*: V, 969–98.

Gandhi, M. K. (1957), *Socialism of My Conception*, ed. Anand T. Hingorani, Bombay: Bharatiya Vidya Bhavan.

Ganguli, B. N. (1973), *Gandhi's Social Philosophy*, Delhi: Vikas.

Geertz, Clifford (1963), 'The Integrative Revolution: Primordial Sentiments and Civil Politics in the New States', *Old Societies and New States: The Quest for Modernity in Asia and Africa*, ed. C. Geertz, Glencoe, Ill: Free Press: 105–57.

—— (1980), *Negara: The Theatre State in Nineteenth-Century Bali*, Princeton: Princeton University Press.

Ghoshal, Upendra Nath (1945–66), *A History of Indian Public Life*, Oxford: Oxford University Press.

—— (1959), *A History of Indian Political Ideas: The Ancient Period and the Period of Transition to the Middle Ages*, Oxford: Oxford University Press; 1st pub. 1923 as *A History of Hindu Political Theories*.

Giddens, Anthony (1976), *New Rules of Sociological Method: A Positive Critique of Interpretative Sociologies*, London: Hutchinson.

—— (1977), *Studies in Social and Political Theory*, New York: Basic Books.

—— (1979), *Central Problems in Social Theory: Action, Structure and Contradiction in Social Analysis*, Berkeley: University of California Press.

—— (1981–5), *A Contemporary Critique of Historical Materialism*, Berkeley: University of California Press, 2 vols.

—— (1984), *The Constitution of Society: Outline of the Theory of Structuration*, Cambridge: Polity Press.

—— (1985), *The Nation-State and Violence*, Berkeley: University of California Press.

Glasenapp, Helmuth von (1960), *Das Indienbild deutscher Denker*, Stuttgart: K. F. Koehler.

Goetz, Hermann (1974), 'The Kailasa of Ellora and the Chronology of Rashtrakuta Art', *Studies in the History, Religion and Art of Classical and Mediaeval India*, ed. Hermann Kulke, Wiesbaden: F. Steiner Verlag, pp. 91–107; 1st pub. 1952 in *Artibus Asiae*: 1–2.

Gonda, J. (1966), *Ancient Indian Kingship from the Religious Point of View*, Leiden: E.J. Brill.

Gopal, Lallanji (1963), 'Samanta – Its Varying Significance in Ancient India', *Journal of the Royal Asiatic Society*: 21–37.

Goodman, Nelson (1976), *Languages of Art: An Approach to a Theory of Symbols*, Indianapolis: Hackett.

—— (1984), *Of Mind and Other Matters*, Cambridge: Harvard University Press.

Gough, Kathleen (1981), *Rural Society in Southeast India*, Cambridge: Cambridge University Press.

Gramsci, Antonio (1971), *Selections from the Prison Notebooks*, ed. and tr. Quinton Hoare and Geoffrey Nowell Smith, New York: International Publishers.

Green, T. H. (1886), *Works*, ed. R. L. Nettleship, London: Longmans, Green.

Gupta, Parmeshwari Lal (1961–2), 'Nesarika Grant of Govinda II: Saka 727', *Epigraphia Indica*: XXXIV, 123–34.

Habermas, Jürgen (1971), *Knowledge and Human Interests*, tr. Jeremy J. Shapiro, Boston: Beacon Press.

Hacking, Ian (1983), *Representing and Intervening: Introductory Topics in the Philosophy of Natural Science*, Cambridge: Cambridge University Press.

Halbfass, Wilhelm (1981), *Indien und Europa: Perspektiven ihrer geistigen Begegnung*, Basel: Schwabe.

Halevy, Elie (1928), *The Growth of Philosophic Radicalism*, tr. Mary Morris, London: Faber and Gwyer.

Hall, John A. (1986), *Powers and Liberties: The Causes and Consequences of the Rise of the West*, Harmondsworth: Penguin.

Harland, Richard (1987), *Superstructuralism: The Philosophy of Structuralism and Post-structuralism*, London: Methuen.

Havell, E. B. (1915), *The Ancient and Medieval Architecture of India: A Study of Indo-Aryan Civilisation*, London: J. Murray.

—— (1918), *The History of Aryan Rule in India, from the Earliest Times to the Death of Akbar*, London: Harrap.

—— (1924), *A Short History of India, from the Earliest Times to the Present Day*, London: Macmillan.

Hayavadana Rao, C., ed. (1930), *Mysore Gazetteer*, Bangalore: Government Press, 5 vols.
Hedderly, Frances (1970), *Phrenology: A Study of Mind*, London: L. N. Fowler.
Heesterman, J. C. (1985), *The Inner Conflict of Tradition: Essays in Indian Ritual, Kingship, and Society*, Chicago: University of Chicago Press.
Hegel, G. W. F. (1895), *Lectures on the Philosophy of Religion*, tr. E. B. Speirs and J. B. Sanderson, London: Routledge and Kegan Paul.
—— (1956), *The Philosophy of History*, tr. J. Sibree, New York: Dover; 1st pub. 1899.
—— (1971), *The Philosophy of Mind*, tr. William Wallace and A. V. Miller, foreword by J. N. Findlay, Oxford: Clarendon Press.
—— (1975), *Lectures on the Philosophy of World History*, tr. H. B. Nisbet, Cambridge: Cambridge University Press.
Henriques, Julian, Wendy Hollway, Cathy Urwin, Couze Venn, and Valerie Walkerdine (1984), *Changing the Subject: Psychology, Social Regulation and Subjectivity*, London: Methuen.
Hesse, Mary (1983), 'The Cognitive Claims of Metaphor', in *Metaphor and Religion*, ed. J. P. van Noppen, Brussel: Vrije Universiteti; Theolinguistics, II, 27–45.
Hindess, Barry (1977), *Philosophy and Methodology in the Social Sciences*, Brighton: Harvester Press.
—— (1987), 'Rationality and the Characterization of Modern Society', *Max Weber, Rationality and Modernity*, ed. Sam Whimster and Scott Lash, London: Allen and Unwin.
—— and Paul Q. Hirst (1975), *Pre-capitalist Modes of Production*, London: Routledge and Kegan Paul.
'Hinduism' (1974), *Encyclopaedia Britannica*, VIII, 889–908.
Hiriyanna, M. (1932), *Outlines of Indian Philosophy*, London: Allen and Unwin.
Hirsch, Fred (1977), *Social Limits to Growth*, London: Routledge and Kegan Paul.
Hirst, Paul Q. (1976), *Social Evolution and Sociological Categories*, London: Allen and Unwin.
—— (1985), 'The Uniqueness of the West – Perry Anderson's Analysis of Absolutism and Its Problems', in his *Marxism and Historical Writings*, London: Routledge and Kegan Paul, pp. 91–125.
—— and Penny Woolley (1982), *Social Relations and Human Attributes*, London: Tavistock.
Hobart, Mark (1984), 'The Art of Measuring Mirages, or Is There Kinship in Bali?', in *Cognation and Social Organization in Southeast Asia*, ed. F. Huesken and J. Kemp, The Hague: Nijhoff.
—— (1985), 'Is God Evil?', in *The Anthropology of Evil*, ed. David Parkin, Oxford: Basil Blackwell, pp. 165–93.
Hobbes, Thomas (1946), *Leviathan*, ed. and intro. Michael Oakeshott, Oxford: Basil Blackwell.
Hocart, A. M. (1927), *Kingship*, Oxford: Oxford University Press; reprinted 1969.
—— (1950), *Caste: A Comparative Study*, London: Methuen.
—— (1970), *Kings and Councillors: An Essay in the Comparative Anatomy of Human Society*, intro. Rodney Needham, Chicago: University of Chicago Press.
Hollis, Martin and Steven Lukes, eds (1982), *Rationality and Relativism*, Oxford: Basil Blackwell.
Howard, Michael (1982), 'Empire, Race and War in pre-1914 Britain', *History and Imagination*, ed. H. Lloyd-Jones, Valerie Pearl and Blair Worden, New York: Holmes and Meier: 340–55.
Hubert, Henri and Marcel Mauss (1898), 'Essai sur la Nature et la Function du Sacrifice', *L'Année sociologique*, Paris, tr. into English 1964 as *Sacrifice: Its Nature and Function* by W. D. Halls, foreword by E. E. Evans-Pritchard, Chicago: University of Chicago Press.
Hughes, H. Stuart (1958), *Consciousness and Society: The Reorientation of European Social Thought, 1890–1930*, New York: Knopf.
Hunter, William Wilson (1903), *The India of the Queen and Other Essays*, ed. Lady Hunter, London: Longmans, Green.
—— (1882), *The Indian Empire: Its History, People, and Products*, London: Trübner.
Hutchins, Francis (1967), *The Illusion of Permanence*, Princeton: Princeton University Press.

Hutton, J. H. (1963), *Caste in India: Its Nature, Function and Origins*, London: Indian Branch, Oxford University Press, 4th edn.

Huyler, Stephen (1985), *Village India*, New York: H. N. Abrams.

Ibn al-Nadim (1970), *Kitab al-Fihrist*, ed. and tr. Bayard Dodge, New York: Columbia University Press, 2 vols.

Imperial Gazetteer of India (1907–9), published under the authority of HM Secretary of State for India in Council, Oxford: Clarendon Press.

Inden, Ronald (1976), *Marriage and Rank in Bengali Culture: A History of Caste and Clan in Middle Period Bengal*, Berkeley: University of California Press.

—— (1979), 'The Ceremony of the Great Gift (Mahadana): Structure and Historical Context in Indian Ritual and Society', *Asie du Sud, Traditions et changements*, Paris, pp. 131–6.

—— (1981), 'Hierarchies of Kings in Early Medieval India', *Contributions to Indian Sociology*: New Series, XV, 99–125; also in 1982, *Way of Life: King, Householder, Renouncer: Essays in Honour of Louis Dumont*, ed. T. N. Madan, New Delhi: Vikas.

—— (1985a), 'Hindu Evil as Unconquered Lower Self', in *The Anthropology of Evil*, ed. David Parkin, Oxford: Basil Blackwell, pp. 142–64.

—— (1985b), 'Lordship and Caste in Hindu Discourse', in *Indian Religion*, ed. Audrey Cantlie and Richard Burghart, London: Curzon Press/New York: St Martin's Press, pp. 159–79.

—— (1986a), 'Kings and Omens', in *Purity and Auspiciousness in Indian Society*, ed. John Carman and Frédérique Marglin, *Journal of Developing Societies*: II, 30–40.

—— (1986b), 'Orientalist Constructions of India', *Modern Asian Studies*: XX.3, 401–46.

—— (1986c), 'Tradition Against Itself', *American Ethnologist*: XIII.4, 762–75.

—— and R. W. Nicholas (1977), *Kinship in Bengali Culture*, Chicago: University of Chicago Press.

Indraji, Bhagwanlal (1883), 'Dasavatara Stone Inscription of Dantidurga at Ellora', *Archaeological Survey of India*: V, 87–9.

Irwin, Robert (1981), 'Writing about Islam and the Arabs', *Ideology and Consciousness*: IX (Winter), 103–12.

Iyer, Raghavan (1983), *Utilitarianism and All That: The Political Theory of British Imperialism*, London: Concord Grove Press.

Jacobi, Jolande (1973), *The Psychology of C. G. Jung: An Introduction with Illustrations*, foreword by C. G. Jung, New Haven: Yale University Press.

Jayaswal, Kashi Prasad (1924), *Hindu Polity: A Constitutional History of India in Hindu Times*, Calcutta: Butterworth; reprinted 1967, Bangalore; based on work begun and published in 1911–12.

Jha, Dwijendra Narayan (1979), Presidential Address to Section I at the Fortieth Session of the Indian History Congress, *Indian History Congress Proceedings*, pp. 15–45.

Jones, Sir William, *Works* (1807), ed. Anna Maria Jones, with life of the author by Lord Teignmouth, London: J. Stockdale and J. Walker, 13 vols.

Kakar, Sudhir (1978), *The Inner World: A Psychoanalytic Study of Childhood and Society in India*, Delhi: Oxford University Press.

Kantorowicz, Ernst H. (1957), *The King's Two Bodies: A Study in Medieval Political Theology*, Princeton: University Press.

Kantowsky, Detlef (1982), 'Max Weber on India and Indian Interpretations of Weber', *Contributions to Indian Sociology*: New Series, XVI, 141–74.

Kautilya (1909), *Arthasastra*, ed. R. Shamasastri, Mysore: Mysore Government Oriental Series.

—— (1915), *Arthasastra*, tr. R. Shamasastri, Mysore: Mysore Printing and Publishing House.

Keith, A. B. (1925), *The Religion and Philosophy of the Veda and Upanishads*, Cambridge, Mass.: Harvard University Press; Harvard Oriental Series, 31–2.

Keller, Arthur S., Oliver J. Lissitzyn, and Frederick J. Mann (1938), *Creation of Rights of Sovereignty through Symbolic Acts, 1400–1800*, New York: Columbia University Press.

Kielhorn, F., ed. (1894–5), 'Paithan Plates of Govinda III: Saka 716 (AD 794)', *Epigraphia Indica*: III, 103–10.

——— (1896–7), 'Khalimpur Plate of Dharmapaladeva', *Epigraphia Indica*: IV, 243–54.

——— (1900–1a), 'Konnur Spurious Inscription of Amoghavarsha I: Saka-Samvat 782', *Epigraphia Indica*: VI, 25–38.

——— (1900–1b), 'Radhanpur Plates of Govinda III: Saka-Samvat 730', *Epigraphia Indica*: VI, 239–51.

Klass, Morton (1980), *Caste: The Emergence of the South Asian Social System*, Philadelphia: Institute for the Study of Human Issues.

Kosambi, Damodar Dharmanand (1956), *An Introduction to the Study of Indian History*, Bombay: Popular Book Depot.

Kothari, Rajni (1970), *Politics in India*, Boston: Little, Brown.

Kramer, Fritz (1977), *Verkehrte Welten. Zur imaginären Ethnographie des 19. Jahrhunderts*, Frankfurt: Syndikat.

Krausz, Michael, ed. (1972), *Critical Essays on the Philosophy of R. G. Collingwood*, Oxford: Clarendon Press.

Krautheimer, Richard (1983), *Three Christian Capitals: Topography and Poltics*, Berkeley: University of California Press.

Krishnaswami Aiyangar, Sakkottai (1931), *Evolution of Hindu Administrative Institutions in South India*, Madras: University of Madras.

Kuhn, Thomas (1970), *The Structure of Scientific Revolutions*, Chicago: University of Chicago Press.

Kulke, Hermann (1978a), 'Jagannatha as the State Deity Under Gajapatis of Orissa', in *The Cult of Jagannath and the Regional Tradition of Orissa*, ed. A. Eschmann, H. Kulke and G. C. Tripathi, New Delhi: Manohar, pp. 199–208.

——— (1978b), 'Royal Temple Policy and the Structure of Medieval Hindu Kingdoms', in *The Cult of Jagannath and the Regional Tradition of Orissa*, ed. A. Eschmann, H. Kulke and G. C. Tripathi, New Delhi: Manohar, pp. 125–37.

Laclau, Ernesto and Chantal Mouffe (1985), *Hegemony and Socialist Strategy*, London: Verso.

Lambert, Richard D. (1973), *Language and Area Studies Review*, Philadelphia: American Academy of Political and Social Science.

Lane, Christel (1981), *The Rites of Rulers: Ritual in an Industrial Society – the Soviet Case*, Cambridge: Cambridge University Press.

Lanman, Charles (1920), 'India and the West with a Plea for Team-work Among Scholars', *Journal of the American Oriental Society*: XL, 225–47.

Lassen, Christian (1858–74), *Indische Althertumskunde*, Leipzig: L. A. Kittler, 2nd edn, 5 vols. in 4.

Le Bon, Gustave (1887), *Les civilisations de l'Inde*, Paris: Libraire de Firmin-Didot.

Le Goff, Jacques (1980), 'The Medieval West and the Indian Ocean: an Oneiric Horizon', in his *Time, Work, and Culture in the Middle Ages*, tr. A. Goldhammer, Chicago: University of Chicago Press.

Leitch, Vincent B. (1983), *Deconstructive Criticism: An Advanced Introduction*, London: Hutchinson.

Lévi, Sylvain (1898), *La Doctrine du Sacrifice dans les Brahmanas*, Paris: Ernest Leroux.

Lévi-Strauss, Claude (1966), *The Savage Mind*, Chicago: University of Chicago Press.

Lipsey, Roger (1977), *Coomaraswamy*, Princeton: Princeton University Press, 3 vols.

Lively, Jack and John Rees (1978). See Mill, James (1978).

Lloyd, Genevieve (1984), *The Man of Reason: 'Male' and 'Female' in Western Philosophy*, London: Methuen.

Lockwood, Michael, and A. Vishnu Bhat (1977), 'The Philosophy of Mahendravarman's Tiruchirapalli Epigraph', *Studies in Indian Epigraphy*: III, 91–102.

Lohuizen de Leeuw, J. E. van (1970), 'India and Its Cultural Empire', in *Orientalism and History*, ed. D. Sinor, Bloomington: Indiana University Press, pp. 35–67.

Lorenzen, D. (1976), 'The Life of Sankaracarya', in *The Biographical Process*, ed. Frank E. Reynolds and Donald Capps, The Hague: Mouton.

—— (1982), 'Imperialism and the Historiography of Ancient India', in *India: History and Thought – Essays in Honour of A. L. Basham*, ed. S. N. Mukherjee, Calcutta: Subarnarekha.

Lukes, Steven (1973), *Individualism*, Oxford: Basil Blackwell.

Lyall, Alfred C. (1899), *Asiatic Studies, Religious and Social*, London: John Murray, 1st pub. 1882.

McCrindle, John Watson (1877), 'The Fragments of the Indika of Megasthenes; collected by Dr. E. A. Schwanbeck, 1846', *Indian Antiquary*: VI, 113–35, 236–50, 333–49; and pub. 1877 as *Ancient India as Described by Megasthenes and Arrian*, London; reprinted 1901, 1975.

Mackenzie, John M., ed. (1986), *Imperialism and Popular Culture*, Manchester: Manchester University Press.

Macpherson, C. B. (1962), *The Political Theory of Possessive Individualism*, Oxford: Oxford University Press.

Maine, Henry Sumner (1888), *Ancient Law, Its Connection with the Early History of Society, and Its Relation to Modern Ideas*, New York: Holt; 1st pub. 1861.

—— (1907), *Village-Communities in the East and West*, London: J. Murray; 1st pub. 1871.

—— (1883), *Dissertations on Early Law and Custom*, New York: H. Holt.

Majumdar, R. C. (1918), *Corporate Life in Ancient India*, Calcutta: S. N. Sen.

——, ed. (1951—), *The History and Culture of the Indian People*, Bombay: Bharatiya Vidya Bhavan.

—— (1960), *Ancient India*, Delhi: M. Banarsidass.

—— (1981), 'The Palas', *Comprehensive History*, III.1, 650–80.

——, H. C. Raychaudhuri, and K. K. Datta (1961), *An Advanced History of India*, London: Macmillan.

Mandelbaum, David G. (1970), *Society in India*, Berkeley: University of California Press, 2 vols.

Mandelbaum, Maurice (1971), *History, Man, and Reason: A Study in Nineteenth Century Thought*, Baltimore: Johns Hopkins.

Marriott, McKim, ed. (1955), *Village India*, Chicago: University Press.

—— and Ronald Inden (1974), 'Caste Systems', *Encyclopaedia Britannica*, 15th edn, III, 982–91.

Marshall, Sir John, et al. (1931), *Mohenjo Daro and the Indus Civilization*, London: A. Probsthain, 3 vols.

Marshall, Peter (1970), *The British Discovery of Hinduism in the Eighteenth Century*, Cambridge: Cambridge University Press.

Marx, Karl (1973), *Grundrisse: Foundations of the Critique of Political Economy (Rough Draft)*, tr. and intro. Martin Nicolaus, Harmondsworth: Penguin; written in 1857–8.

—— (1964), *Pre-Capitalist Economic Formations*, tr. Jack Cohen, ed. and intro. E. J. Hobsbawm, London: Lawrence and Wishart.

—— (1968), *Karl Marx on Colonialism and Modernization*, ed. Shlomo Avineri, New York: Doubleday.

Masson, J. Moussaief (1980), *The Oceanic Feeling: The Origins of Religious Sentiment in Ancient India*, Dordrecht, Holland: D. Reidel.

Mathieu, Pierre-Louis (1976), *Gustave Moreau, sa vie, son oeuvre; catalogue raisonné de l'oeuvre achevé*, Paris: Bibliothèque des Arts.

—— (1984), *L'Assembleur de Rêves. Écrits complets de Gustave Moreau*, Paris: A. Fontfroide.

Mayer, Adrian C. (1960), *Caste and Kinship in Central India*, Berkeley and Los Angeles: University of California Press.

Megasthenes. See Schwanbeck (1966); McCrindle (1877).

Mélanges d'Indianisme à la Mémoire de Louis Renou (1968), Paris: Éditions E. de Boccard.

Meszaros, Istvan (1986), *Philosophy, Ideology and Social Science: Essays in Negation and Affirmation*, Brighton: Harvester/Wheatsheaf.

Mill, James (1858), *The History of British India*, ed. Horace Hayman Wilson, London: J. Madden; Piper, Stephenson and Spence.

_____ (1978), 'Essay on Government', *Utilitarian Logic and Politics*, ed. Jack Lively and John Rees, Oxford: Clarendon Press, pp. 53–95.

Miller, Barbara Stoler (1983), *Exploring India's Sacred Art: Selected Writings of Stella Kramrisch*, Philadelphia: Pennsylvania University Press.

Mirashi, V. V. (1961a), 'A Further Note on the Spread of the Saka Era in South India', in his *Studies in Indology*, Sholapur: S. V. Mirashi, II, 104–9.

_____ (1961b), 'The Spread of the Saka Era in South India', in his *Studies in Indology*, Sholapur: S. V. Mirashi, II, 95–103.

_____ (1963), 'Andura Plates', *Epigraphia Indica*: XXXVI, 257–72.

Mitter, Partha (1977), *Much Maligned Monsters: History of European Reactions to Indian Art*, Oxford: Clarendon Press.

Monier-Williams, Monier (1891), *Brahmanism and Hinduism or, Religious Thought and Life in India, as Based on the Veda and other Sacred Books of the Hindus*, London: John Murray, 4th edn; 1st pub. 1883 as *Religious Thought and Life In India*.

_____ (1894/1951), *Hinduism*, London: Society for Promoting Christian Knowledge/ Calcutta: Susil Gupta; 1st pub. 1877.

Montesquieu (1949), *Esprit des Lois*, tr. Thomas Nugent as *The Spirit of the Laws*, New York: Haffner; 1st pub. 1748.

Mookerji, Radha Kumud (1919), *Local Government in Ancient India*, Oxford: Clarendon Press.

_____ (1921), *Nationalism in Hindu Culture*, London: Theosophical Publishing House.

_____ (1960), *Chandragupta Maurya and His Times*, Delhi: M. Banarsidass; 1st pub. 1943.

_____ (1952), *The Gupta Empire*, Bombay: Hind Kitabs; 2nd edn.

Moore, Barrington, Jr. (1967), *Social Origins of Dictatorship and Democracy: Lord and Peasant in the Making of the Modern World*, Boston: Beacon.

Mouffe, Chantal (1979), 'Hegemony and Ideology in Gramsci', in *Gramsci and Marxist Theory*, ed. C. Mouffe, London: Routledge and Kegan Paul.

Müller, Friedrich Max (1849–74), *Rig-Veda Sanhita, the Sacred Hymns of the Brahmans, together with the Commentary of Sayanacharya*, London: Trübner; Published under the Patronage of the Honourable East India Company.

_____ (1864), *Lectures on the Science of Language*, London: Longman, Green; 1st delivered 1861.

_____ (1869–), *Rig-Veda Sanhita, the Sacred Hymns of the Brahmans, tr. and explained*, London: Trübner.

_____ (1877), *The Hymns of the Rig-Veda in the Sanhita and Pada Texts*, London: Trübner; 2nd edn.

_____ (1880), *Lectures on the Origin and Growth of Religion, as Illustrated by the Religions of India (Delivered in the Chapter House, Westminster Abbey, in April, May, and June, 1878)*, London: Longmans, Green.

_____ (1882), *Introduction to the Science of Religion: Four Lectures Delivered at the Royal Institution in February and May, 1870*, London: Longmans, Green.

_____ (1898a), 'Letter to Mr. Risley on the Ethnological Survey of India, Oxford, 20 July, 1886', in his *Chips from a German Workshop*, London: Longmans, Green, I, 255–63.

_____ (1898b), 'On the Classification of Mankind by Language or Blood', in his *Chips from a German Workshop*, London: Longmans, Green; presidential address to the Anthropological Section of the British Association, Cardiff, 1891, I, 217–55.

_____ (1973), *The Six Systems of Indian Philosophy*, New Delhi: Associated Publishing; 1st pub. 1899.

Mukherjee, S. N. (1968), *Sir William Jones: A Study in Eighteenth-Century British Attitudes to India*, Cambridge: Cambridge University Press; 2nd edn 1987, London: Sangam.

Mukhia, Harbans (1980), 'Was There Feudalism in Indian History?', *Journal of Peasant Studies*: VIII.3, 273–310.

Murr, Sylvia (1977), 'N. J. Desvaulx (1745–1825), véritable auteur des Moeurs, institutions et cérémonies des peuples de l'Inde' de l'Abbé Dubois', *Collection Purusartha*: III, 245–58.

_____ (1983), 'Les conditions d'emergence du discours sur l'Inde au Siècle des Lumiéres', *Collection Purusartha*: VII, ed. Marie-Claude Porcher, 233–84.

Musée Gustave Moreau, Paris (1983), *Catalogue des Peintures, Dessins, Cartons, Aquarelles*, Paris: Éditions de la Réunion des musées nationaux, 3rd edn.

Nainar, S. Muhammad Husayn (1942), *Arab Geographers' Knowledge of Southern India*, Madras: University of Madras.

Neale, Walter C. (1957), 'Reciprocity and Redistribution in The Indian Village: Sequel to Some Notable Discussions', in *Trade and Market in the Early Empires: Economies in History and Theory*, ed. Karl Polanyi, Conrad M. Arensberg, and Harry W. Pearson, New York: Free Press, pp. 218–36.

Nehru, Jawaharlal (1951), *The Discovery of India*, London: Meridian Books; 1st pub. 1946.

Nicholls, David (1975), *The Pluralist State*, New York: St Martin's Press.

Nilakanta Sastri, K. A., ed. (1951), *Age of the Nandas and Mauryas*, Delhi: M. Banarsidass.

—— (1955), *The Colas*, Madras: University of Madras.

—— (1963), *Development of Religion in South India*, Bombay: Orient Longmans.

—— (1966), *A History of South India from Prehistoric Times to the Fall of Vijayanagar*, Bombay: Oxford University Press; 1st pub. 1955.

—— (1967), *Cultural Contacts Between Aryans and Dravidians*, Bombay: Manaktalas.

—— (1981a), 'The Rashtrakutas', *A Comprehensive History of India*, III.1 (AD 300–985), ed. K. A. Nilakanta Sastri et al., Calcutta and New Delhi: Indian History Congress, 440–84.

—— (1981b), 'Political Organisation', *A Comprehensive History of India*, III.1 (AD 300–985), ed. K. A. Nilakanta Sastri et al., Calcutta and New Delhi: Indian History Congress, 730–47.

—— et al., eds (1956—), *A Comprehensive History of India*, Calcutta and New Delhi: Indian History Congress.

Nisbet, Robert A. (1969), *Social Change and History*, London: Oxford University Press.

O'Flaherty, Wendy Doniger (1984), *Dreams, Illusions, and Other Realities*, Chicago: University of Chicago Press.

Oldenberg, H. (1898), *Ancient India, Its Language and Religions*, Chicago: Open Court.

O'Malley, L. S. S. (1932), *Indian Caste Customs*, Cambridge: Cambridge University Press.

—— (1934), *India's Social Heritage*, Oxford: Clarendon Press.

Oppert, Gustav (1893), *On the Original Inhabitants of Bharatavarsa*, Westminster: A. Constable.

Ortony, Andrew, ed. (1979), *Metaphor and Thought*, Cambridge: Cambridge University Press.

Overing, Joanna (1985), *Rationality and Rationales*, London: Tavistock.

Parsons, Talcott (1951), *The Social System*, New York: Free Press.

Passmore, John (1966), *A Hundred Years of Philosophy*, Harmondsworth: Penguin.

Perlin, Frank (1985), 'Concepts of Order and Comparison, with a Diversion on Counter Ideologies and Corporate Institutions in Late Pre-Colonial India', *Journal of Peasant Studies*: XII.2–3, 87–165.

Pletsch, Carl (1981), 'The Three Worlds, or the Division of Social Scientific Labor, circa 1950–1975', *Comparative Studies in Society and History*: XXIII.4, 565–90.

Pocock, J. G. A. (1973), 'Burke and the Ancient Constitution', *Politics, Language and Time*, New York: Atheneum pp. 202–32.

Potter, Karl H. (1981), *Encyclopedia of Indian Philosophies*, III (Advaita Vedanta up to Samkara and His Pupils), Delhi: M. Banarsidass.

Powers, Jonathan (1982), *Philosophy and the New Physics*, London: Methuen.

Prasad, Beni (1927), *Theory of Government in Ancient India (post-Vedic)*, Allahabad: Indian Press; University of London Ph.D. thesis, 1926, with a foreword by the Sanskritist, A. B. Keith, reprinted, Allahabad: Central Book Depot, 1968, with an introduction by Amba Datt Pant.

Prasad, Rajendra (1946), *India Divided*, Bombay: Hind Kitabs.

Pratt, Vernon (1978), *The Philosophy of the Social Sciences*, London, Methuen.

Price, S. R. F. (1984), *Rituals and Power: The Roman Imperial Cult in Asia Minor*, Cambridge: Cambridge University Press.

Pulleybank, Edwin G. (1970), 'China', in *Orientalism and History*, ed. D. Sinor, Bloomington: Indiana University Press pp. 68–92; 1st edn 1954.

Quine, W. V. O. (1964), *Word and Object*, Cambridge, Mass.: MIT Press.

—— (1978), 'A Postscript on Metaphor', in *On Metaphor*, ed. Sheldon Sacks, Chicago: University of Chicago Press, pp. 159–60.

Radcliffe-Brown, A. R. (1957), *A Natural Science of Society*, Glencoe, Ill.: Free Press.

Radhakrishnan, S. (1928), *The Vedanta According to Samkara and Ramanuja*, London: George Allen and Unwin.

—— (1959), *Eastern Religions and Western Thought*, New York: Oxford University Press; 1st pub. 1939.

Ramachandra Dikshitar, V. R. (1932), *Mauryan Polity*, Madras: University of Madras.

—— (1952), *The Gupta Polity*, Madras: University of Madras.

Rangaswami Aiyangar, K. V. (1926–8), 'The Evolution of Ancient Indian Polities', *Sir Asutosh Memorial Volume*, Patna 'Pataliputra': J. N. Samaddar; 2 parts in 1 vol.

—— (1949), *Indian Cameralism: A Survey of Some Aspects of Arthasastra*, Madras: Adyar Library; delivered at the University of Calcutta, 1934.

Rau, Heimo (1983), 'The Image of India in European Antiquity and the Middle Ages', *India and the West: Proceedings of a Seminar Dedicated to the Memory of Hermann Goetz*, ed. Joachim Deppert, New Delhi: Manohar, pp. 197–208.

Ray, H. C. (1973), *The Dynastic History of Northern India*, Delhi: Munshiram Manoharlal; 1st pub. 1931–6. University of Calcutta, 2 vols.

Rea, Alexander (1909), *Pallava Architecture*, Madras: Archaeological Survey of India, New Imperial Series, XLII.

Redfield, Robert (1955), *The Little Community: Viewpoints for the Study of a Human Whole*, Chicago: University of Chicago Press.

—— (1956), *Peasant Society and Culture: An Anthropological Approach to Civilization*, Chicago: University of Chicago Press.

Renou, Louis (1968), *Religions of Ancient India*, New York: Schocken Books.

Rice, B. Lewis (1897), *Mysore*, Westminster: A. Constable, 2 vols.

—— (1920a), 'Shikarpur', *Epigraphia Carnatica*: VII, 119.

—— (1920b), 'Shikarpur', *Epigraphia Carnatica*: VII, 219.

Richards, I. A. (1936), *The Philosophy of Rhetoric*, London: Oxford University Press.

Riepe, Dale (1970), *The Philosophy of India and Its Impact on American Thought*, Springfield, Ill.: Charles C. Thomas.

Risley, Herbert H. (1891a), 'The Study of Ethnology in India', *Journal of the Royal Anthropological Institute*: XX, 235–63.

—— (1891b), *The Tribes and Castes of Bengal*, Calcutta: Bengal Secretariat Press, 4 vols.

—— (1915), *The People of India*, ed. and intro. William Crooke, Calcutta: Thacker, Spink; 1st edn. 1908.

Robertson Smith, W. (1972), *The Religion of the Semites: The Fundamental Institutions*, New York: Schocken.

Rorty, Richard (1979), *Philosophy and the Mirror of Nature*, Princeton: Princeton University Press.

Rudolph, Lloyd and Susanne Rudolph (1967), *The Modernity of Tradition: Political Development in India*, Chicago: University of Chicago Press.

Ryan, Michael (1982), *Marxism and Deconstruction: A Critical Articulation*, Baltimore: Johns Hopkins University Press.

Said, Edward (1978), *Orientalism*, New York: Pantheon.

Sarkar, Sir Jadunath (nd), *A History of Dasnami Naga Sanyasis*, Daraganj, Allahabad: Sri Panchayati Akhara Mahanirvani.

Schlegel, Friedrich von (1890), *Philosophie der Geschichte*, tr. as *Philosophy of History*, by James Burton Robertson, London: George Bell.

Schutz, Alfred (1967), *The Phenomenology of the Social World*, Evanston, Ill.: Northwestern University Press.

Schwab, Raymond (1984), *The Oriental Renaissance: Europe's Rediscovery of India and the East, 1680–1880*, tr. Gene Patterson-Black and Victor Reinking, New York: Columbia University Press; 1st pub. in French 1950.

Schwanbeck, Eugen Alexis (1966), *Indica; fragmenta collegit*, Amsterdam: A. M. Hakkert; 1st pub. 1846.

Seeley, John Robert (1971), *The Expansion of England*, ed. and intro. John Gross, Chicago: University of Chicago Press; 1st pub. 1883.

Senart, Émile (1930), *Caste in India: The Facts and the System*, tr. E. Denison Ross, London: Methuen.

Shanin, Teodor (1971), *Peasants and Peasant Societies*, Harmondsworth, Penguin.

Sharma, Ram Sharan (1965), *Indian Feudalism: c.300–1200*, Calcutta: University of Calcutta.

Shils, Edward (1961), *The Intellectual Between Tradition and Modernity: The Indian Situation*, The Hague: Mouton.

Singer, Milton (1972), *When a Great Tradition Modernizes: An Anthropological Approach to Indian Civilization*, New York; Praeger.

Sinha, Har Narain (1938), *Ancient Indian Polity: A Study in the Evolution of Early Indian State*, London: Luzac.

Sinor, Denis, ed. (1970), *Orientalism and History*, Bloomington: Indian University Press; 1st edn. 1954.

Sircar, D. C. (1954), 'Vaishnavism', in *The History and Culture of the Indian People*, ed. R. C. Majumdar, Bombay: Bharatiya Vidya Bhavan, III, 373–408.

—— (1961), 'Note on Nesarika Grant of Govinda III: Saka 727', *Epigraphia Indica*: XXXIV, 135–40.

—— (1965), *Indian Epigraphy*, Delhi: M. Banarsidass.

—— (1967), 'A Chinchani Inscription', in his *Studies in the Society and Administration of Ancient and Medieval India*, Calcutta: Firma KLM, pp. 74–85.

—— (1969), *Landlordism and Tenancy in Ancient and Medieval India as Revealed by Epigraphical Records*, Lucknow: University of Lucknow.

Skorupski, John (1976), *Symbol and Theory: A Philosophical Study of Theories of Religion in Social Anthropology*, Cambridge: Cambridge University Press.

Smith, Richard Saumarez (1985), *Contributions to Indian Sociology*: New Series, XIX.1, 153–76.

Smith, Vincent A. (1924), *Early History of India, from 600 B.C. to the Muhammadan Conquest, Including the Invasion of Alexander the Great*, Oxford: Oxford University Press; 4th edn, rev. S. M. Edwardes, Clarendon Press.

—— (1919), *Indian Constitutional Reform*, Oxford: Oxford University Press.

—— (1919), *Oxford History of India*, Oxford: Oxford University Press; 3rd edn 1958, rev. Mortimer Wheeler, A. L. Basham, and T. G. Percival Spear.

Spear, T. G. Percival (1958), *India, Pakistan and the West*, Oxford: Oxford University Press.

Srinivas, Mysore N. (1952), *Religion and Society Among the Coorgs*, Oxford, Oxford University Press.

Staal, Frits (1975), *Exploring Mysticism*, Harmondsworth: Penguin.

Stankiewicz, W. J. (1969), *In Defense of Sovereignty*, New York: Oxford University Press.

Stein, Burton (1977), 'The Segmentary State in South Indian History', *Realm and Region in Traditional India*, ed. Richard G. Fox, Durham, NC: Duke University, Program in Comparative Studies on Southern Asia, pp. 3–51.

—— (1980), *Peasant State and Society in Medieval South India*, Delhi: Oxford University Press.

—— (1985), 'Politics, Peasants and the Deconstruction of Feudalism in Medieval India', *Journal of Peasant Studies*: XII.2–3, 54–86.

Stevens, Richard (1983), *Freud and Psychoanalysis*, Milton Keynes: Open University Press.

Stokes, Eric (1959), *The English Utilitarians and India*, Oxford: Clarendon Press.

Sukthankar, V. S. (1917–18), 'Bhandak Plates of Krishnaraja I: Saka 694', *Epigraphia Indica*: XIV, 121–30.

Sulayman (1867), *Akhbar al-Sin*, in Henry M. Elliot and John Dowson, *The History of India as Told by its Own Historians*, London: Trübner.
—— (1948), *Akhbar al-Sin*, ed. and tr. Jean Sauvaget, Paris: Societé d'edition 'Les belles Lettres'.
Tambiah, S. J. (1976), *World Conqueror and World Renouncer: A Study of Buddhism and Polity in Thailand against a Historical Background*, Cambridge: Cambridge University Press.
Taylor, Charles (1975), *Hegel*, Cambridge: Cambridge University Press.
—— (1985), *Human Agency and Language: Philosophical Papers, 1* Cambridge: Cambridge University Press.
Thapar, Romila (1981), 'The State as Empire', in *The Study of the State*, ed. Henri J. M. Claessen and Peter Skalník, The Hague: Mouton, pp. 409–26.
Thapar, Romila and Percival Spear (1966), *A History of India*, Harmondsworth: Penguin.
Therborn, Göran (1980), *Science, Class and Society*, London: Verso.
Thompson, Edward and G. T. Garratt (1962), *Rise and Fulfilment of British Rule in India*, Allahabad: Central Book Depot.
Thompson, Grahame (1982), 'The Firm as a "Dispersed" Social Agency', *Economy and Society*: XI.3, 233–50.
Thomson, Robert (1959), *The Psychology of Thinking*, Harmondsworth: Penguin.
Thorner, Daniel (1966), 'Marx on India and the Asiatic Mode of Production', *Contributions to Indian Sociology*: IX (Dec.), 33–66.
Tinker, Hugh (1962), *India and Pakistan: A Political Analysis*, New York: Praeger.
Tod, James (1920), *Annals and Antiquities of Rajasthan or the Central and Western Rajput States of India*, ed. William Crooke, London: Oxford University Press; 1st pub. 1829–32, London: Smith Elder.
Todorov, Tzvetan (1977), *Theories of the Symbol*, tr. C. Porter, Oxford: Basil Blackwell.
Tucci, Giuseppe (1970), *The Theory and the Practice of the Mandala*, New York: Samuel Weiser.
Turner, Bryan S. (1978), *Marx and the End of Orientalism*, London: Allen and Unwin.
Varma, Vishwanath Prasad (1974), *Studies in Hindu Political Thought and Its Metaphysical Foundations*, Delhi: M. Banarsidass; 1st pub. 1954.
Vishnudharmottara Purana (1912), ed. Indian pandits, Bombay: Srivenkatesvara Steam Press.
Wallerstein, Immanuel (1974), *The Modern World-System: Capitalist Agriculture and the Origins of the European World-Economy in the Sixteenth Century*, New York: Academic Press.
—— (1979), *The Capitalist World-Economy*, Cambridge: Cambridge University Press.
Weber, Max (1958), *The Religion of India*, tr. H. H. Gerth and D. Martindale, Glencoe, Ill.: Free Press; 1st pub. in Weber's *Gesammelte Aufsätze zur Soziologie und Sozialpolitik*, Tübingen: J. C. B. Mohr.
—— (1959), *The Methodology of the Social Sciences*, New York: Free Press.
Wheeler, James Talboys (1867–81), *The History of India from the Earliest Ages*, London: Trübner, 1867–81, 4 vols. in 5.
Williams, Raymond (1976), *Keywords*, London: Fontana.
Wilson, Horace Hayman (1846), *Sketch of the Religious Sects of the Hindus*, Calcutta: Bishop's College Press; 1st pub. in *Asiatic Researches*: XVI (1828) and XVII (1832); republished in Wilson's *Essays and Lectures*, ed. E. R. Rost, London: Trübner, 1862.
Wilson, Bryan R., ed. (1977), *Rationality*, Oxford: Basil Blackwell.
Winch, Peter (1958), *The Idea of a Social Science*, London: Routledge and Kegan Paul.
Wiser, William Henricks (1958), *The Hindu Jajmani System: A Socio-Economic System Interrelating Members of a Hindu Village Community in Services*, intro. Oscar Lewis, Lucknow: Lucknow Publishing House; 1st pub. 1936.
Yates, Frances (1975), *Astraea: The Imperial Theme in the Sixteenth Century*, London: Routledge and Kegan Paul.

Yazdani, G. ed. (1960), *Early History of the Deccan*, London: Oxford University Press, under the authority of the Government of Andhra Pradesh, 2 vols.

Zimmer, Heinrich (1879), *Altindisches Leben: Die Cultur der vedischen Arier nach den Samhita* ..., Berlin: Weidmann.

Zimmer, Heinrich (1956), *Philosophies of India*, New York: Meridian Books.

Index

Okkalu 221–3
Oldenberg, H. 119
O'Malley, L. S. S. 131, 147
Oppert, G. 119–20
oppositions 34, 76
order 203–4, 238
organism, homeostatic 18, 26, 88
orientalism 36, 198, 264, 270
orientalists 20, 37, 45, 50, 67
Orients 37, 50; caste and 51; evolutionism and
    52; Hegel and 50; images of 49; India and
    51; irrationality of 52; Other and 49
Ortony, A. 10
overdetermination 41
Overing, J. 20
overlapping classes 22, 160, 224, 264, 267–8,
    270
Oxford 13, 45, 99, 104, 138, 188

Pakistan 50, 198
Palas 230, 252, 258; Devapala 260;
    Dharmapala 258–60
Pallavas 239, 246, 249, 251–2, 259;
    Mahendravarman I 259; religion of 249;
    temples of 253
Panchala 173, 260
Pandyas 245, 251
Panjab 99, 140, 147, 183, 219
pantheism 67, 87, 93–5, 190
Paramaras 239; Bhoja 262; Siyaka II 261
Parsons, T. 12
Passmore, J. 178
patients 23
Patna University 189
patronage 208
peasants, religion of 115
Perlin, F. 156, 210
Persia 50, 53, 54, 68, 169, 185, 196–7, 239;
    Aryan 50
Persian 37, 44
Peshwa 170
Phantasie 94
philology 37, 59; comparative 13; race and 60
philosophy: German 50, 67, 96; Indian 67, 94,
    97, 101, 103–5
phrenology 61
Piggott, S. 120
pilgrimage 118
Plato 25, 101, 103, 124
Platonism 15
Pletsch, C. 32, 76
pluralism 188, 191–2, 194–6
Pocock, D. 74
Pocock, J. G. A. 265
political economy 51
polity 28; administered 163, 180, 182, 184,
    188, 192–4, 198, 206–7, 211, 243, 265;

agency and 162–3, 191, 204, 210, 222; army
    and 182–3, 193, 206, 209, 216, 222–4, 230;
    atomism and 180; bureaucracy and 180–1,
    194, 206; caste and 164, 171, 187, 197, 202,
    217–19, 266; centralization and 163, 181,
    192; centre and periphery 188, 209, 217,
    242; civil service and 180; depoliticized
    163–4, 169–72, 186, 244; despotism and
    164, 178; as educator 201, 206, 211, 266,
    269; essence of 163–4, 175, 180, 182–4,
    188–9, 191–2, 196–8, 203–4, 207, 211, 214,
    228, 265; European 164, 167, 170;
    feudalism and 164, 169, 172–6, 177, 181,
    193, 240; hegemony and 29; Hinduism and
    187, 190; historical narratives and 164;
    individual and 203, 205; individualism and
    163; kinship and 177, 183; legislature and
    180; as mediator 201, 203–4, 208, 210–11,
    266; monarchy and 190; monist, 192;
    nation-states and 176–7, 186, 191, 195, 197,
    199, 206, 265; order and 199–201;
    paternalistic 180–1, 184; peasantry and 210;
    post-tribal 164; race and 185;
    representational 163, 166, 168, 170, 180,
    189, 265; revenue collection in 168, 171,
    189, 192, 206, 230, 233, 242–3; as a scale of
    forms 28, 220, 224, 230, 237; secular 192,
    202; segmentary 208, 210, 240; socialism
    and 163; society and 192; sovereignty and
    181, 183–4, 188, 190–2, 194–5, 197, 199,
    205, 207; as theatre-state 208, 222; theology
    and 166–7, 172, 203, 216, 229, 237–8, 241,
    254, 260, 268–9; theophanic 269; tribal
    177–80; utilitarianism and 168–9; Vaishnava
    237; villages and 185, 202, 206, 222
polytheism 97
Popper, K. 47
Porus, king 56
positivism 10, 18, 35; logical 33
post-structuralism 21
Powers, J. 21
pragmatists 199
Prasad, B. 189–92, 195, 197
Prasad, R. 195
prasada 223
prasasti 231
prasthana 114
Pratiharas (Gurjaras) 214, 230, 239, 246, 252,
    258, 262; Bhoja 8, 260; Mahipala I 261;
    Nagabhata I 247; Nagabhata II 259–60;
    Vatsaraja 258–9
Pratt, V. 2
Presidency College, Calcutta 149, 193; Madras
    119
Prester John 48
presuppositions 11
Price, S. 230

Saivism 114, 117, 225, 229, 249, 254, 257, 268, 269; Saiva-siddhanta 255; Trika (Kashmiri) 117; Vaishnavized 253
Saka Era 250
Samanta, Govinda 151
Samhitas (Vaishnava) 117
samsara 101
Sanchi 55, 60
Sankara 102, 114, 117; illusionism and 108, 114
Sankaracharyas 107
Sankhya 103; dualism of 103, 110
Sanskrit 37, 44, 51, 232
Sanskritists 55, 69, 90, 175, 220
Sarkar, J. N. 107
Satavahanas 156
sattva 235, 238
Sauvaget, J. 214
scale of forms 20, 22, 25, 33–5, 214, 217, 220, 226, 256, 264, 266, 268; geographic 257
Schlegel, A. W. 67
Schlegel, F. 49, 67–9, 94–5, 102
School of Oriental and African Studies 46
Schopenhauer, A. 103
Schutz, A. 19
Schwab, R. 67
Schwanbeck, E. 182
Schweitzer, A. 105
science: classical 25; metaphysics of 20, 21, 40; social 22, 27, 163, 198–200, 206, 216, 263–4, 268, 270
Scythians 54, 172
secondary revision 41–2, 53
secularization 202, 209
Seeley, J. 178
Seleukos Nikator 182
self-regulation 13
Selves and Others 2–3, 48, 54–5, 83, 99, 120–1, 129
semiotics 11
Semites 119
Senart, E. 57, 62, 137
Shamasastri, R. 183
Shanin, T. 152
Sharma, R. 155
Shils, E. 78
Shudra (servant) 57
Sibree, J. 47
Sind 214, 239
Sindia 177
Singer, M. 78
Sinha, H. N. 195
Sinology 37, 54, 71
Sinor, D. 20
Sircar, D. C. 114, 156, 231, 239, 250–1
Siva 27, 107, 109, 115–16, 125, 235–7, 249, 252–5, 259, 269

Skanda 249
Skorupski, J. 91
slavery 156, 177, 219
Smith, A. 267
Smith, R. S. 58
Smith, Sydney 49, 56, 65
Smith, V. A. 7–12, 16–18, 21, 31, 45–6, 65, 72, 86, 182–7, 189–90, 197, 216, 230, 237, 241, 253, 256, 269
Smith, W. Robertson 99
Social Darwinism 59, 64
social formation 30
society 27; ancient *v* modern 139; civil 163; communal *v* individual 139; mechanism and 27; non-social community and 28; social formation as 30; types and stages of 16; voluntarism and 27
sociology 66; critical 21; developmental 52; historical 211
Somapuri 252
South Asian studies 44
Southall, A. 206
sovereignty 265; in British India 188; bureaucracy and 194; divine 238; dual 208; essence of 175–6, 179, 183, 192; Indian 176–80; individual and 180; Mauryan 182; monarchy and 209, 237; nation-states and 229; plural 221; polity and 188, 191, 194–5, 197, 205, 207; in post-Independence India 199; ritual 206, 208, 210; as a scale of forms 214
Soviet Union 50; *see also* Russia; imperial formations, US–USSR
Spain 176
Spear, P. 46, 85
Spencer, H. 59, 129
spinning wheel (charkha) 195
Sri 215, 233, 250–1, 260
Sri Lanka 256
Sriharsha 245
Sringeri 107
Srinivas, M. 151, 153
Srisailadesa 246
Staal, F. 105
Stankiewicz, W. J. 265
Stein, B. 155, 206–11, 224, 226
Stokes, E. 45, 169
structuralism 19–20, 33, 78; Hinduism and 96; social 201
structuration 21
structure, social 19, 73
subjectivity 19, 20, 38, 95, 96
Sukthankar, V. S. 245–6, 252
Sulayman 214
sultanism 210
Sung dynasty 54
suttee 92